VIETNAM

A History and Anthology

D0064321

VIETNAM

A History and Anthology

Edited by

James W. Mooney   Thomas R. West

BRANDYWINE PRESS • St. James, New York

Cover Photo: Vietnam Veterans Memorial, Washington, D.C., photos by Mark Buckley.

ISBN: 1-881089-28-2

1st Printing 1994

Telephone Orders: 1-800-345-1776

Printed in the United States of America

TABLE OF CONTENTS

INTRODUCTION

A great historical mistake is to think of the brief American involvement in Vietnam as central to the country's story. Vietnam and the surrounding region have a long history of coping with external forces, both resisting and borrowing from them. China has been a traditional danger. Yet Vietnam took from her huge northern neighbor both farming techniques and elements of culture. Then in the mid-nineteenth century came the French, an occupation far longer than the American and surely more culturally important. There was, of course, also the Japanese occupation, ending with the defeat of Japan in 1945. In time, and except for its terrible destructiveness, the American war that as a full scale conflict went from 1965 to 1973 will be an incident in Southeast Asia's history. In the end, mundane matters of trade, technology, and cultural exchange with the United States may leave their deeper mark on a nation that like any other country borrows, absorbs, adapts.

In the second half of the nineteenth century, France had established control over what has been known as Indochina, consisting of present-day Vietnam, Laos, and Cambodia. Even before the French seizure of Vietnam, Roman Catholicism made converts there, and eventually the country became patterned of Buddhists and a minority of Catholics, of peasants holding to traditional ways and intellectuals acquainted with the West.

Among these last was Ho Chi Minh, one of several names this impassioned nationalist would assume: in Vietnamese, it suggests the enlightenment of his leadership. A member of the Parisian literary community in the years after World War I, Ho under the name Nguyen Ai Quoc or Nguyen the Patriot was a Vietnamese nationalist attracted to the Communist movement as a vehicle of anticolonialism. An indication of the complexity of Vietnam's relations with the outside world is that the young opponent of French imperialism was also a Francophile, enamored of the humanity of French civilization and capable of denouncing, in a published article, the introduction of English words into the great language.

Ho years later formed under Communist leadership a nationalist organization known as the Vietminh, intended to fight against the Japanese occupiers and French collaborators. Briefly upon the expulsion of the Japanese in 1945, Ho was *de facto* head of Vietnam, looking for American support. The United States at the end of World War II hoped that the European colonial nations would grant independence or self-government to their former possessions, but Washington did not press the issue. The French at their postwar return to power in Vietnam set up a rickety and supposedly independent government with as its occasional titular sovereign the emperor Bao Dai. When in 1954 Ho's military commander Vo Nguyen Giap took the French and Vietnamese garrison at Dien Bien Phu, a remote fort besieged by artillery Ho's forces had dragged through the nearly impenetrable jungle, the French war was effectively over. During the conflict, the United States under President Harry Truman had contributed massive funding to the French military effort. In 1954 a conference in Geneva representing a number of countries with an interest in Vietnam temporarily divided it into North and South, the intention being to have unifying elections under international supervision in two years. The United States was not a signatory to the agreement. North Vietnam was Communist; South Vietnam came under the control of Ngo Dinh Diem, a Catholic and one of many nationalists who had liked neither French rule nor the Communists.

After the establishment of a separate South Vietnam, Diem resolved not to allow the elections that as like as not would have made for Communist rule of the whole country. Two regimes, then, were to divide Vietnam into the indefinite future. That in the North with Hanoi as its capital was austere, highly disciplined, and totalitarian, allowing no opposition to Communist ideology and party control. It redistributed land, but did so by a savage if brief period of terror. The southern regime, its capital in Saigon, was defensive in its determination to keep separate. It opposed land reform, kept order by widespread imprisonment, torture, and killing, and ruled a nation in which a few enjoyed great wealth in the midst of Third World wretchedness. Affluence amidst poverty was not rare among countries that the West supported during the Cold War. In Vietnam it would continue after the Communist victory of 1975, numbers of Communist families enjoying both privilege and the cheaply bought valuables of the defeated bourgeoisie. The population of South Vietnam included Catholic and other refugees from the more repressive North. Against the Saigon regime arose a revolutionary movement that later began receiving extensive aid from Hanoi. Eventually the insurrectionists became the National Liberation Front, which came to be called the Vietcong, or Vietnamese Communists.

The Eisenhower administration, spanning the years from 1953 to

1961, supported Diem. The administration's grim Secretary of State was John Foster Dulles, whose brand of anticommunism—scarcely different from that of many liberal Democrats—made him suspicious of nationalist and left movements throughout the Third World. The reasons for Washington's belligerence, continued in the administration of John Kennedy when our commitment to South Vietnam could still have been ended, may preoccupy historians for a long time.

One theory of the Cold War holds that the western confrontation of the Soviet Union and the various Communist and leftist movements throughout the world was essentially for the sake of capitalist economic interests. The narrowest rendering of this notion would claim that wherever throughout the world American military and diplomatic involvement appears, the reason lies in the needs of some American business interest. That would be the crudest kind of economic determinism. It requires at the least the discovery of some large corporate investment or a desirable natural resource in whatever region is in question, either of them so extensive as to command the efforts of the American government and armed services. A somewhat more plausible interpretation as it specifically applies to Vietnam will see the American commitment there as a byproduct of a more general effort to enrich capitalism and business profits worldwide. Yet even this ignores the real complexity of human motive and assumes that, among the myriad concerns that occupy most people, cold warriors were driven only by economic calculation.

Nations hunger for economic gain. They also hunger, probably more strongly, for power: economic success is but one form of power, desired more for that than for the lesser comforts that the prosperous enjoy. And power is inextricably connected with ideas and creeds: ideas that justify power, ideas that depend on it to extend their reach, ideas that are themselves power over those who believe them and empower their believers to act, sometimes to their material detriment.

A convincing explanation, then, of why the United States allowed itself to be drawn into Vietnam is that compounded considerations of power, interest, and belief had set the nation years before to confronting Communism wherever it appeared. More precisely among the convictions was the knowledge that state Communism in its many varieties over the globe was the death of freedom. As an internal strife produced by traditional quarrels, ideological differences, and competition for control, the war in Vietnam between Hanoi, the insurgents, and Saigon was in no way vital to the United States. But prevalent in American thinking during the 1950s was what is known as the domino theory, the fear that the fall to Communism of one regime in that region would lead to the fall of another, and another, and another, dominoes collapsing one upon the next. The United States was propelled on its Vietnam journey by the whole force of its cold-war anticommunist mentality, so often articulated and so intimately connected with global policies that by 1954, or 1963, or 1965 it could not think its way out of a defense of Saigon.

The American war in Vietnam was the logical extension of liberal foreign policy. The logic is traceable to the beginnings of the Cold War.

It was liberals rather than conservatives who established the basic institutions of that long, bleak and for stretches of time bloodless war between the West and the Communist powers. The liberal Democratic President Harry Truman gave American aid to Greece and Turkey to bolster their resistance to Communism, sending American troops to Greece to support anticommunist forces during a civil war. In 1948 he set up the Marshall Plan, a great program of economic aid to western Europe, torn to economic shreds by World War II. A purpose of the Marshall Plan was to keep that portion of the world from falling under Communism. In the same year Truman directed the airlifting of supplies to West Berlin when the USSR cut off access by land. In 1949 the United States entered into the North Atlantic Treaty Organization, or NATO, as a military defense against a possible invasion by the Soviet Union. Under authority of the United Nations, Truman sent troops to South Korea in 1950 to halt the North Korean Communist invasion of that country. The Truman presidency set for the United States the terms of the Cold War. Under the Eisenhower administration, representing the mildly liberal internationalist wing of the Republican Party, an armed, restless, hostile peace prevailed between the Communist and the western world. Circumstances brought to much of Kennedy's presidency new foreign engagements dictated by the Cold War.

Yet liberals, perhaps for being more willing than conservatives to maintain widespread military and diplomatic engagements abroad, were increasingly prepared to find distinctions among insurgencies throughout the world, complications of motive in Soviet foreign policy, and reasons for mixing aggressiveness with restraint. Besides, it suited the liberal temperament to resist the excited emotions that conservatives brought to any discussion of Communism foreign or domestic. Liberals preferred a drier language and mentality, closer to the hard dispassionate virtues of the modern science and instruments of production that they trusted to remake society for the better.

The fine fusion of determination and restraint was difficult to maintain politically: conservatives promised the public quicker emotional gratifications. In Vietnam the liberal formula could not hold.

The American intervention in Vietnam expressed the assumptions on which the liberals had waged the Cold War: that Communism was an abomination, and that its success in any major part of the world threatened its neighbors. But intervention, which liberals effected in Korea in

1950 and in the Dominican Republic fifteen years later against a leftist movement there, went contrary to the liberal attempt to understand the full complexity of the world. The North Vietnamese and the Vietcong, as Communists, were the enemy that the Cold War defined. But as Third World nationalists whose lives were a witness against the poverty and social injustice of the region, they were the kinds of forces that liberals had been more willing than conservatives and right-wingers to understand and attempt to accommodate. The pressure of events and alliances and institutions that liberals had created sent a Democratic administration into full-scale engagement in 1965. Thereupon, cold-war liberals could not explain satisfactorily even to themselves why we were there.

Two programs under President John F. Kennedy, who in January 1961 brought the Democratic Party back to the White House after eight Republican years, were especially revealing of the components of the liberal mind.

The Peace Corps was designed to send volunteers to remote parts of the world, rotted with poverty and therefore vulnerable to Communist insurgency. There they might teach villagers to improve their crop yield or learn simple principles of health care. As though in anticipation of the Peace Corps, William J. Lederer and Eugene Burdick had made the homely hero of their 1958 novel *The Ugly American* a retired engineer. He and his wife bring to an Asian village honest American skills and an unassuming simple concern, while their pampered compatriots lead luxurious existences in the capital of the fictional third-world nation. The Special Forces, better known as the Green Berets, complemented the Peace Corps. They were to be soldiers trained at once for guerrilla warfare and for organizing anticommunist resistance within the kinds of communities in which the Peace Corps would do its life-giving work: they seemed exactly fitted for Vietnam. Both programs were appropriate in spirit to what the Kennedy presidency represented: combining cold-war militancy with a commitment to a measure of political and economic democracy, the cool virtues of advanced technique with the warmer sentiments of Democratic liberalism.

In April 1961, Kennedy acted with the aggressiveness that had characterized his Democratic predecessor Truman, and in so doing suffered his greatest defeat, the failed landing at Cuba's Bay of Pigs of exiles trained by the United States. That and the subsequent preoccupation with removing Fidel Castro expressed the cold warrior side of the Democratic administration. Yet the President showed enough restraint not to give the invasion air cover when it was clearly beyond saving. Kennedy's design of the Alliance for Progress for Latin America, an economic aid program to be accompanied with efforts to get recipient regimes to initiate social reform, expressed the accompanying concern for issues of poverty and inequity. That it was also supposed to fight Communism by offering a progressive alternative makes it a representative liberal scheme. The program never fulfilled its initial promise.

Much of the foreign policy of the Kennedy administration was oriented not to Vietnam and the rest of Asia but to encounters with the USSR in Europe and the Western Hemisphere. In June 1961 a summit meeting in Vienna between Kennedy and Khrushchev failed to settle the difficult question of the future of Berlin. When it became clear that Moscow wanted to alter the situation there, Kennedy in July responded in the spirit of the Cold War, calling for an increase in military spending and announcing that he was doubling draft calls and mobilizing reserves. Soon afterwards the Communists—supposedly at the initiation of the East Germans, who wished to claim East Berlin as part of their sovereign nation—began building the wall that was to keep in Germans who had been flooding to the West, taking with them skills and knowledge vital to the East German economy. Kennedy sent troops to West Berlin, and during weeks of confrontation Washington acted as though the freedom of the western part of the city were endangered. In October of the following year came Kennedy's naval blockade of Cuba to cut off Soviet construction of missiles, ending with arrangements whereby Moscow agreed to withdraw the weapons.

During their time of greatest hostility, Moscow and the United States had resumed nuclear testing. But after the Cuban missile crisis, something like friendship developed between Khrushchev and Kennedy, and late in 1963 the two negotiated a treaty banning nuclear testing above ground. Once more, Kennedy the cold warrior was revealing the other pole within the liberal mentality: in this case, a willingness to enter into an agreement of a sort to horrify ideologues of the political right. After Kennedy's death the Senate ratified the treaty.

In Kennedy's tenure, when so much of the flow of energy was between Moscow and the capitals of the West, only one crisis of sorts involved Indochina. When it looked as though factional fighting in Laos might pull in the United States on the side of an anticommunist leader, the major powers agreed instead to honor the neutrality of the country. But the President would not consider a neutral South Vietnam: it had to be anticommunist. Unclear as to what he wanted to do in Vietnam, recognizing the danger of an increased entanglement, yet perhaps thinking of Vietnam as a problem that could be put off, he ended by sending a total of 16,000 American advisers to Diem's military, along with much combat hardware.

Even as the administration was deepening its involvement, an event in Vietnam signaled the moral morass that the war was going to be for the United States. In June 1963, the Buddhist monk Thich Quang Duc set himself afire in Saigon, offering his death in protest against the repressiveness of Diem's regime. As the war widened, the act would be repeated in Vietnam and the United States.

By his last days, Diem was facing widespread hostility. Some members of Kennedy's administration wanted him removed as a hindrance to Saigon's successful prosecution of the war, and became complicit in a military coup that early in November 1963 ousted him from office. Washington, however, was not a party to the subsequent assassination of Diem and Ngo Dinh Nhu, his brother who had also been a powerful and controversial member of his government. It happened just shortly before Kennedy's own assassination and the coming to office in this country of Lyndon Johnson, whose political fortunes were to be bound inextricably to Vietnam.

Johnson seems to have had at first no clearer idea than his predecessors of the size and nature of the Vietnam problem. In keeping with a reflexive anticommunism, in July 1964 he increased the American auxiliary military presence there. Then on August 4, in response to skirmishes in the Gulf of Tonkin off the coast of North Vietnam that are unclear in nature, Johnson ordered air strikes that damaged or destroyed some vessels and a nearby oil storage site. Quickly afterwards Johnson got through the Senate by a vote of eighty-eight to two and the House with no negative votes the Gulf of Tonkin Resolution, as it is called, in essence giving him unrestricted authority to act in Vietnam. A strong spokesman for it was J. William Fulbright, chairman of the Senate Foreign Relations Committee and a leading foreign policy liberal. In the Senate only Wayne Morse of Oregon and Ernest Gruening of Alaska opposed the resolution. Fulbright would later turn against the war. Yet at the time, liberals and conservatives together had given Johnson legal cover for the escalated American presence in Vietnam.

The politics of the presidential campaign, which pitted Johnson against the Republican conservative Barry Goldwater, were typical of the Cold War in one respect: the liberals had designed a foreign policy tough in action; conservatives were tough in rhetoric. Johnson presented himself as the peace candidate, and the Republicans spoke in a way that made them seem a danger to the peace. Johnson's overwhelming win appeared to be a triumph for a sensibly moderate foreign policy. But in March 1965 he initiated a radically new program of bombing North Vietnam that went by the title of Rolling Thunder, and soon he sent 50,000 additional troops. That marked the time of full American engagement in Vietnam, to continue until the war was won, lost, or negotiated. There was no talk now of confining the American military to advising the South Vietnamese. Americans were committed to combat on their own.

Draft calls reflected the new reality. Even in the years of uncertain American peace between the Korean War and Vietnam, students though protected by educational deferments had lived with the draft as a possibility and a nuisance, or a patriotic duty. Now the chances of getting called were far greater, and conscription might mean not spending time in a drab army post but being sent to a war for which the government was presenting no convincing justification. On campuses as well as among less favored young Americans, the draft became a preoccupation.

As the years of American fighting lengthened, conscription came under heavy attack. Until late in the conflict, when the Nixon administration substituted a draft lottery for student deferments, young men clung to that temporary protection. Some sought the status of conscientious objector, which if granted ensured that while the government might require of the holder some kind of hospital or other humanitarian service, he would not go into combat unless possibly as a noncombatant paramedic.

It would be a mistake, however, to think that the protest quickly erupting on college campuses against the American involvement had as its central motive the fear of being drafted. All women students were ineligible for conscription. So were those of their male classmates who for any reason—and there were many—failed to meet the physical or psychological standards for the military. Among students who might in time face the draft, deferments to last during college were available until the later years of the war and offered the possibility of keeping out until some other escape from the military offered itself. Black and white working-class youth who did not go to college were most likely to be called to military service. The Vietnam draft represented for opponents not so much the personal danger of conscription as more generally the war's evil presence within American society. Resisters publicly burned their selective service cards, for which they willingly received prison sentences. Others returned their cards to their local service offices, thereby inviting their draft boards to attempt to induct them and then opening themselves to criminal prosecution when they refused induction.

The complexities of the draft and the moral questions that came with it would reveal themselves as the war progressed. In the early days of American escalation, most of the public supported the conflict. Simple patriotism accounts for much of this. But the conflict also had behind it the whole logic of the West's waging of the Cold War, a logic to which the Communists, including the Vietnamese variety, contributed by the brutal repressiveness with which they wielded any power they could seize. Liberals, more given to doubts and questionings than conservatives, might have been expected to generate reservations about the Vietnam venture. But the Cold War was of their own designing, the rescue of South Vietnam was widely thought to be integral to the waging of the Cold War, and it was a liberal President who was conducting that rescue. Secretary of State Dean Rusk, Secretary of Defense Robert McNamara, presidential advisers McGeorge Bundy and Walt Rostow: such members of the Kennedy and Johnson administrations gave to the prosecution of the war an appearance of reasoned resolve.

In those early days of American escalation, South Vietnam was under the dual leadership of General Nguyen Van Thieu and Nguyen Cao Ky, a vice air marshal known for his uniform and scarf, his pistol, and his swagger. To support him Washington by the end of 1965 was committing close to 200,000 troops; and by the middle of 1966 the war had claimed some 2,600 American combat deaths. The United States was also pounding North and South Vietnam with bombs. Among the objectives of the bombing was to stop the flow of troops and material from North Vietnam to the fighting in the south. Especially identifiable with this stream was what became known as the Ho Chi Minh Trail, not a single jungle trail but an elaborate transportation network that moved southward in part through Laos. The failure to stop the movement was one of the signal American frustrations of the war. And the continuance of the bombing in later years was the most devastating of American assaults on Vietnam, and possibly the most discreditable to the thinking of opponents of the war. Cluster bombs that burst in mid-air and flung out maiming shrapnel, explosives designed to cling to skin and scorch it, poisonous defoliants intended to clear areas where the enemy might lurk turned the war into a futuristic horror. A marine veteran who praises the tenacity of both the Americans and the enemy in the ground fighting recalls his anger at the unseen bombers that destroyed, without being near it, the country beneath them.

Later in the war prominence would be given to a controversial policy, planned by the Central Intelligence Agency, known as the Phoenix program. It coordinated the activities of South Vietnamese agents who would go into villages, spot leaders of the Vietcong, and have them arrested or killed. Antiwar activists perceived it as murder, and reports tell of inefficiency, corruption, killings motivated by personal rivalry. It also appears that the program did much damage to the Vietcong infrastructure.

In March 1965 occurred the first of the significant public protests against the war. At the University of Michigan, the nationwide campus organization Students for a Democratic Society (SDS) held what was called a teach-in, a name recalling the sit-ins of the civil rights movement. It began on the evening of March 24 and did not end until the following morning. The method was for people knowledgeable about the issue to meet in a long session with whoever wanted to attend, refuting the administration's positions and generating further resistance to the war. Defenders of Johnson's policy were also invited, but the weight was on the side of the opposition. Teach-ins followed at Columbia and the University of Wisconsin, and in May at Berkeley a session lasted for a day and a half and drew 20,000. In April SDS sponsored an antiwar demonstration that attracted 20,000 people in Washington, D.C.

The teach-in reveals much about the nature of student radicalism at the time. It reflected both respect for learning and a will to discard the formalities of the university; it hinted at the vision of a campus as a place for a continuing discussion no more than lightly structured. In all this, the teach-ins are suggestive of what SDS was calling participatory democracy. Its adherents looked to a future society made up of individuals engaging widely in decision making processes, gathering into small democratic bodies for argument and agreement according to the issue to be settled. Noteworthy of the teach-ins was civility. Absent as yet was the sullen anger that in time became virtually a radical style.

Also absent, at least from much of the antiwar movement, was the mood characteristic of some later radicals of complete disaffection from the American government and society, along with veneration of Hanoi and the National Liberation Front. Early opponents conducted themselves as though they assumed that if they continued questioning the war, the American government and society would listen to them. Among the first prominent foreign-policy liberals to dispute Johnson's course was Senator Fulbright, earlier a chief supporter of the Gulf of Tonkin Resolution and in no way a ranter. The poet Robert Lowell turned down an invitation to a White House Festival of the Arts in the spring of 1965, and some of those who did attend took the opportunity to attack the President's war policy. On other occasions that would be a breach of manners, and perhaps it was on this one; but these were artists and writers, accustomed to presentation of ideas, and the seriousness of the issue gave them a certain warrant to speak their mind in an event intended to celebrate their craft of speaking it.

Students gave the antiwar movement much of its distinctive character. It is often forgotten, however, that the movement drew broadly on the middle classes. A remarkable number of parents and children could be seen in the marches for peace.

Johnson's government attempted nothing like the campaign of harassment that Woodrow Wilson's administration had unleashed against opponents of the country's participation in the First World War. The memory of the red-baiting of the 1950s, of which liberals generally had been the opponents, may have been a reason for the government's declining to label antiwar people collaborators with the foe. As could have been expected, much popular hostility to the antiwar movement did erupt. But the liberal administration's defense of the war stayed largely within bounds of discussion.

Still, by the end of 1965 the attack on the war had become steady and dramatic. In August demonstrations marked the twentieth anniversaries of the two American atomic bombings of Japan: Hiroshima and Nagasaki. About 350 protesters were arrested. There were burnings of draft cards. Late in November 30,000 demonstrators were at the White House. These actions and that of three opponents of the war who like Vietnamese Buddhist monks burned themselves to death, one at the United Nations, one at the Pentagon, and another in Detroit, signified that the opposition to the war was now entrenched, impassioned, and prepared to pass beyond the conventions of American politics. In time it also gained, in Martin Luther King, Jr., a powerful moral voice.

By late 1966 Vietnam was an issue not only in the streets but in electoral politics. As protests continued and the Senate liberals George McGovern of South Dakota, Eugene McCarthy of Minnesota, Robert Kennedy of New York, and Frank Church of Idaho raised their doubts, some peace candidates entered the autumn elections.

In 1967 appeared the National Coordinating Committee to End the War in Vietnam as an umbrella organization for antiwar activities. On April 15 of that year the Mobilization to End the War in Vietnam, formed in 1966 and led by the seasoned peace advocate David Dellinger, staged demonstrations. The Mobe gathered between 100,000 and 200,000 protesters in New York City, taunted by supporters of the war as they marched to the United Nations Building, where Martin Luther King spoke to the rally. In San Francisco the stadium in Golden Gate Park with a capacity of 65,000 could not contain all those in attendance. Other big cities added their numbers to this largest nationwide demonstration up to its time in American history. Another large protest that year, 100,000 strong, was held in late October in Washington, D.C., bringing together the political left and elements of the more celebrative counterculture. Some 35,000 of the demonstrators marched on the Pentagon. Along with the Mobe, a leader of that action was Jerry Rubin, a spokesman for the hippies of a political turn who were calling themselves Yippies. Rubin, conformably to the countercultural search for the mysterious healing forces of earth and sky, promised that the Pentagon was going to levitate. He exaggerated. But demonstrators occupied Pentagon property in defiance of soldiers and marshals who had been called to keep order, and some occupiers were beaten or arrested. The government also used tear gas. Some protesters spat at the federal forces or otherwise provoked them.

Publicly destroying a draft card or returning it to the selective service system was an especially dedicated form of protest. In 1967 acts in open resistance to the draft were a prominent means of opposition to the war. On April 15 in Sheep Meadow in New York City's Central Park, between 150 and two hundred draft cards were consigned to flame. In mid-October the Resistance, an antiwar group that centered on the draft, was one of a number of agents of a week's action that included returns of selective service cards and other protests against conscription. At Oakland, California, that week activists carried out street tactics, shutting off one and another access to the induction center, pulling parked cars into the streets, ducking the police. The Oakland resistance was in essence an enactment of the participatory democracy preached earlier by SDS, combining spontaneity with cooperation. It looked as though, for a moment, the centralized structures of government and industry, which had made possible the American war in Vietnam, had given way to the free but combined activities of citizens, inventing as they went along. That suggests a point of union between the political left and the counterculture, those hippies and communards distinguished for their distancing themselves from ideology and political action, their turn to agriculture and handicrafts, their immersion in drugs and music and sexuality. The counterculture too had, in fact, a largely unspoken politics, an antipolitics of secession from those larger institutions that the left intended to overthrow or transform.

Meanwhile, a similar consciousness in resistance to the war had been growing within the religious left.

On May 17, 1968, nine war resisters entered the selective service offices at Catonsville, Maryland. Prominent among them was the Jesuit priest Daniel Berrigan and his Josephite priest brother Phillip, one of four who had already violated the law by pouring animal blood on draft records in Baltimore. The intruders proceeded to destroy records, afterwards waiting for the police to arrive and arrest them. In the wake of their trial, they became known as the Catonsville Nine. They fled for a time, sheltered by fellow activists and hoping that as fugitives they could bring others to work against the war. Other war resisters conducted similar raids on draft offices.

Southern black evangelical ministers and congregations had been central to the civil rights movement, to be joined in time by northern Jewish and white Christian religious figures. In the spirit of Mahatma Gandhi, the great opponent of British rule and caste injustice in India, they had adopted in resisting segregation the methods of nonviolence and civil disobedience, both of them requiring a difficult composure in the face of mobs, angry store owners and patrons, or police. Transferred to action against the war in Vietnam, nonviolence presented itself as a fitting witness to peace. Draft resistance, when it took the form of peaceably burning a draft card or refusing induction and then accepting the consequences, was an instance of nonviolence. Many liberals, belligerently anticommunist though they might be, had their own preference for reasoned self-constraint in policy and conduct, a repudiation of chauvinistic and other violent emotions on the right. Prowar liberals might therefore see in the controlled calm that attended antiwar acts of nonviolence a distant likeness to their own beliefs.

While radicals in Catonsville and elsewhere were attacking American policy from outside conventional politics, the nation as a whole was reassessing the war. This was largely the result of an offensive that the enemy under Ho's general Vo Nguyen Giap had begun at the end of January 1968. It took place in the midst of a truce that Vietnamese were supposed to be observing during their New Year season of Tet.

At that moment North Vietnamese and southern guerrilla forces struck throughout South Vietnam, overrunning government posts and taking the ground war to the cities. And in Saigon, supposedly well out of the range of any major attack, guerrillas seized part of the United States embassy compound. For over three weeks thereafter in the city of Hue, Communists hung on stubbornly and brutally, slaughtering people they defined as opponents. In the end, the Tet offensive was crushed, at great loss to the attackers. But the discovery that an enemy supposedly coming under the control of the South Vietnamese and American forces could wage so extensive a campaign turned Americans to doubting both the effectiveness and the purpose of the war.

Beginning before Tet and lasting for two months, the Communists besieged marines and South Vietnamese troops holding the outpost at Khe Sanh, in the northwest of South Vietnam, the Communists sustaining terrible losses from American air power. They had to end the siege. But in June General William Westmoreland, then the commander of American forces in Vietnam, withdrew the Americans from the post. Thus was demonstrated the folly of the Communist attack on Khe Sanh, the pointlessness of the American defense of a base that could later be so casually abandoned, or the mindlessness of the events of war.

Yet at Khe Sanh, in the lines of defense during Tet, and throughout South Vietnam, the American army held. Even as Americans at home were devising the tactics of resistance and, at moments, the participatory future it envisioned, the American military and the individual troops had been reinventing themselves on the field.

They had to do so. An army trained for conventional warfare found itself fighting a guerrilla foe, amidst a people it was supposed to be serving even as any unknown part of that population might be secretly working for the other side. So those Americans in Vietnam who were in serious combat had to learn the stealth and craft of guerrillas, operating in small units far from large military bases. This they trained themselves to do in skilled coordination with American air and other heavy weaponry. Patrols came to recognize that the ground on which they walked, the ground a walker can ordinarily trust as surely as gravity or air or sunlight, might at any moment be the enemy in the form of a mined booby trap; they had to find how to work with this treacherous earth.

Americans were also attempting, for reasons both of principle and of strategy, to effect social reform in South Vietnam. Their aim was in the liberal mode combining mild redistribution of wealth with modernization. The Americans urged on Saigon a policy of land reform and economic development that would win the countryside politically while weapons defended it. Integral to the plan was the setting up of strategic hamlets, protected by military means and improved economically and socially. The South Vietnamese government liked the strategic hamlets, but used them to enable officials to tighten their control over the peasantry. The American concept made no adequate headway.

After Tet Americans continued to conduct search-and-destroy missions, and in May 1969, early in the presidency of Richard Nixon, troops now under the command of General Creighton Abrams won a peak near the Laotian border grimly known as Hamburger Hill. Yet as skepticism about American involvement increased at home, morale suffered. Some of the reasons are simple enough: awareness that domestic support had waned, growing doubt that the war had point or justification. As policy in Washington changed, now implying the logic of withdrawal of troops from aggressive combat, the whole business of killing and risking death came to seem meaningless. Racial clashes also plagued the army. After the increase in hostility toward whites in sections of the formerly integrationist civil rights movement, there was disaffection among black troops and, when they were not in the field of combat, antagonism between the races. The American army had fought with a measure of restraint within a population in which anyone might be an enemy. It is the fate of that army to be remembered for an atrocity: the massacre at My Lai, in March 1968, of Vietnamese including women and children. It was one of a number of wanton acts by American troops, in a war fought in the midst of a civilian population and therefore inviting atrocities on both sides.

Back at home, the political mood in the year of Tet was responding to the turn the war had taken.

As the New Hampshire Democratic presidential primary of March 12 approached, an army of college and graduate students invaded the state to aid a challenger to President Johnson. Introspective, dry and understated, Senator Eugene McCarthy of Minnesota was a bit aloof from the political process. That, in time, would give him a special appeal in the universities and within a sector of the electorate, as though he embodied cool detached sanity in opposition to the hot madness of the

Vietnam venture. To win over voters whom more scruffy student antiwar activists would alienate, McCarthy's young workers in New Hampshire made a point of neatness and, among the males, short hair. March 12 was a surprise. President Johnson's write-in total did exceed the popular vote for McCarthy; early figures indicated forty-nine percent to forty-two. But for an incumbent President to do no better in one of his own party's primaries amounted to a political defeat for him. Whatever the New Hampshire Democrats were trying to say—a poll of McCarthy supporters suggested that over half of them thought that the war effort should actually be increased—the count indicated deep dissatisfaction with the government's handling of the conflict.

McCarthy's showing had pried open Johnson's grip on the Democratic nomination. But was he the best antiwar candidate? Doubting that the urbanely distant McCarthy could wage the kind of campaign that would capture the voters, the ambitious Senator Robert Kennedy of New York announced his own candidacy.

Seeing that he had lost control of events, Johnson on March 31 made a national speech. Inviting Hanoi to join in negotiations, he announced that he was limiting the bombing of North Vietnam. Though he did not say so, his shift in strategy was in line with the recommendations of his new Secretary of Defense Clark Clifford, who soon after replacing McNamara in that office was suggesting that the administration put limits on an American war effort that now had over a half million troops in Vietnam. Johnson's address then made a startling announcement. To lessen the partisanship that had infected politics, he was withdrawing from that year's presidential race. Johnson, the nation discovered in an instant, would be President for only a few more months, and the political process was now wide open.

At the beginning of that tormented spring and summer, on April 12 Martin Luther King was assassinated in Memphis. Civil rights and the antiwar movement had lost their most powerful voice. Riots that followed the killing tore up cities and the civil peace. McCarthy and Kennedy ran against each other for the nomination, Kennedy the candidate of a vigorous popular politics appealing to minorities, McCarthy appearing at moments disengaged from the whole business. Kennedy lost in Oregon's Democratic primary; McCarthy lost in Indiana. In California, where in black and Mexican neighborhoods Kennedy was joyously greeted, he narrowly won. But on June 4, the night of his victory there, he was assassinated by a Jordanian Palestinian who identified him with support for Israel.

In Chicago that August, the Democratic National Convention held its proceedings. The party's own occupant of the White House was not a candidate. The killing of Robert Kennedy had deprived the Democrats of an energetic leader, capable of appealing to a variety of interests. McCarthy, the remaining contender who had fought in primaries, was reclusive and nearly severed mentally from the popular politics in which a nominee would have to be immersed. Edward Kennedy did not choose to run that year. The Convention settled on Lyndon Johnson's Vice President Hubert Humphrey. Humphrey had strong credentials in domestic liberalism. He was also a Johnson loyalist, then defending the American involvement in Vietnam and therefore acceptable to Democrats who for reason of nationalism, anticommunism, or partisan faithfulness to Johnson supported the prosecution of the war. That also meant, of course, that the Democratic candidate was going to be carrying around with him the political burden of the war. But more sensational than the deliberations within the Convention hall were the events outside.

For some time radical elements within the antiwar movement, the Mobe and Jerry Rubin among them, had been planning to hold demonstrations in Chicago at the time of the Convention. Only an estimated 2,000 protesters came, fewer than expected, but they were enough to enrage local authorities. Before long the police were clubbing indiscriminately. In the Convention Senator Abraham Ribicoff of Connecticut denounced the tactics of the police, and in one of the best remembered of the Convention's televised incidents Chicago's mayor Richard Daley, who was leading a shouting assault to drown out the Senator, yelled at him an easily detectable obscenity. The later trial of the Chicago Eight—reduced to Seven when the black militant Bobby Seale insisted on being tried separately—for conspiracy to bring on the riot was among the most public events of the radicalism of the times.

The divisiveness reflected in the violence without and the brawling within the Democratic Convention hall defined the political terms with which the Democratic candidate was forced to live. Humphrey had the disdain of radicalized liberals who might otherwise have been a vigorous part of his candidacy. Nor was it useful to him to have to be hostage to whatever might at any moment be the fortunes of the war. Hanoi, having become interested in discussion even before Johnson's overtures, had been engaged since May 10 in peace talks with the United States in Paris. Saigon would later join the negotiations. As November approached, Humphrey increasingly presented himself as being in quest of peace, and as he did so he rose in the polls. But the breakthrough in negotiations that might have saved him was not forthcoming. Singly or in combination the war, the public's turn against Democratic domestic policy, and the claim of the Republican candidate Richard Nixon to have a plan to end the fighting made for the narrow November victory of Nixon. George Wallace of Alabama, the right-wing candidate, finished third.

In its later years the antiwar movement even as it gained energy was beginning to unravel. Such collective insurrectionist acts as the blocking of the Oakland induction center were sane, quite orderly, and inventive even as they took possession of the streets. Sane as well was the draft resistance movement as a whole: in the burning or sending back of a selective service card, conscience and courage expressed themselves in an act of elegant simplicity. But as this rebel impulse gained among opponents of the war, some elements were dabbling in lunacy.

From an early day, combatants in other causes, among them civil rights workers and insurgents against the university establishment, had found shared ground between the issue of peace abroad and that of justice at home. They discovered a common enemy in massive institutions of power that could work social oppression, put the universities to their service, pulverize Vietnam. There was SDS, initially reflective and sophisticated in its concept of a future of power dismantled, turned into the hands of free individuals and small democratic communities. But as anger grew, thoughtful ideas of personal and social reconstruction gave way in some sections of the movement to revenge-maddened visions of a radical vanguard wielding power against American society as a whole. Black revolutionaries such as the Black Panthers, so some white radicals were convinced, would be in the vanguard. So would a handful of whites, properly alienated from their American surroundings and properly instructed in Marxist or Maoist doctrine.

The year 1968 brought not only antiwar demonstrations but campus disorders at Columbia, San Francisco State, and elsewhere throughout the country. In its Chicago convention in June 1969, what was left of SDS tore itself to pieces. In what had begun as an organization of young intellectuals who in the following years thought their way through the dilemmas of power, freedom, and community, two factions captivated by impassioned abstractions now fought to inherit the wreckage. The Progressive Labor contingent espoused Maoism along with conventional clothing and morals, thinking other leftists to be self-indulgent. The Revolutionary Youth Movement, or RYM, under Bernardine Dohrn favored free form in style, sex, and drugs, and a revolution with youth as leaders. RYM won and had PL expelled from whatever might be conceived as the remains of SDS.

Ms. Dohrn, along with Mark Rudd and others of a newer generation of leadership, thereupon took a phrase from a song by Bob Dylan and formed a group they called the Weathermen (or sometimes the collective singular Weatherman), an imaginative title later changed to the cumbersome Weather Underground. The Weathermen, or Underground, practiced a nihilism of self-gratifying violence. In October 1969 the Weather people spent four Days of Rage rampaging through Chicago. It was supposed to start a revolution or something. In early March of the following year three members of the group were killed by an accidental explosion in a New York City townhouse that they and their companions had been using as a bomb factory.

Yet the antiwar movement had an integrity that could outlast not only its conservative opponents but the ideological fevers that ravaged the minds of some of its members. The Moratorium of mid-November 1969 has been estimated to be the largest of all gatherings in Washington against the war. Even more important for the movement was the increasing participation of Vietnam veterans, who could offer an unchallengeably authentic opposition to American policy.

The presidency of Nixon nonetheless defined a social chasm, on the one side the middle and working classes, on the other the antiwar movement and all the cultural forces it represented. It is not that the new President unleashed against dissenters a patriotic mob. Simply in representing their presidency as the agency of solid hard-working Americans, the Republicans managed to marginalize much of the opposition to the war, some of which helped by making a point of being unlikable.

Nixon continued, especially with the aid of his adviser and later Secretary of State Henry Kissinger, the Paris peace talks that had begun under Johnson. At the beginning of the Paris negotiations, Ho Chi Minh had been head of the Hanoi government; his death in 1969 did not change North Vietnamese policy. Yet as Nixon sought peace and a policy, again begun under Johnson, of having the South Vietnamese take over the whole war, he continued the conflict along with increasingly heavy bombings. In late April 1970, he sent American forces into Vietnam's neighbor Cambodia, itself torn by civil war. Shortly before, some South Vietnamese troops had also made incursions into that country. Until then Vietnamese Communists had used Cambodian territory as a protected base of supplies and troops. Nixon's invasion of Cambodia, which at the moment widened the war that he was claiming to contract, brought wide protest in the United States, and on May 4 bullets fired by national guardsmen sent to keep order at Kent State University in Ohio killed four students. A few days later in an unrelated but equally numbing event on a college campus, police took the lives of three students at Jackson State University, a black institution in Mississippi.

A subject especially important to the administration was the fate of American airmen shot down over North Vietnam and held as prisoners of war. Relatives were pressuring the administration to work for their release, and their freedom was becoming a passionate issue with the public at large. Opposing tactics presented themselves: military strikes against North Vietnam that might pressure Hanoi to release the POWs, or concessions that would encourage the Communists to do so. In late November 1970, Washington attempted the most direct of means, a commando raid on a supposed prisoner of war camp. The raid was smoothly conducted, but no POWs were found.

In the final days of American engagement, Nixon launched massive air attacks over North Vietnam. In the end, it was in the interest of the United States to withdraw from the war, and in the interest of the Communists to accept an agreement short of Hanoi's largest aims. On January 27, 1973, Hanoi, Saigon, the South Vietnamese Communists, and the United States signed a peace accord, in effect leaving the South Vietnamese government and the Communist opposition each in possession of whatever territory it was then holding. Soon all but a few American troops had left Vietnam, and the American prisoners of war had been released. So ended a war that had cost 58,000 American and by one estimate 1,600,000 Vietnamese lives. Two years later the Saigon regime crumbled, the Communists took over, and the two Vietnams became a single nation under Hanoi. Saigon was renamed Ho Chi Minh City. Laos and Cambodia too came under Communist control, and after years of unspeakably brutal rule of Cambodia by the Khmer Rouge Vietnam invaded that country and installed a milder regime.

In the literature that followed the First World War, one fact gives background to the boredom, the horror, the meaningless succession of incidents, even the moments of clarity and understated good conduct: the war was about nothing. It cannot be said that Vietnam was about nothing. The cause of national liberation confronted the cause of anti-communism, each having a reasoned moral basis. But no grain of logic gives a common texture to French colonial policy, Vietnamese national politics, liberalism in its arrogance and decencies and delusions, the fury of the antiwar forces, and the incommunicable experience of the warrior. In the last analysis, the American war in Vietnam was about a number of things, but not any one coherent thing—unless it was the tragic contradictions that unfolded within a way of thought that at its origins had possessed much humane rationality.

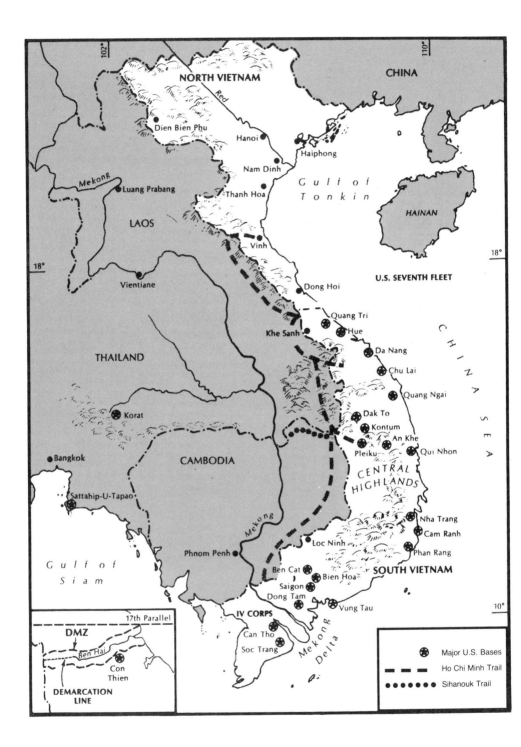

CHINA

NORTH VIETNAM

Red

Dien Bien Phu

Hanoi

Haiphong

Nam Dinh

Mekong

Thanh Hoa

Gulf of Tonkin

Luang Prabang

HAINAN

LAOS

Vinh

18°   18°

Vientiane

Dong Hoi

U.S. SEVENTH FLEET

Quang Tri

Khe Sanh   Hue

THAILAND   Da Nang

Chu Lai

Quang Ngai

Korat   Dak To

Kontum

An Khe

Bangkok   Pleiku   Qui Nhon

CAMBODIA   CENTRAL
                                                    HIGHLANDS

Sattahip-U-Tapao

Nha Trang

Cam Ranh

Mekong

Phnom Penh   Loc Ninh   Phan Rang

Gulf of
Siam   Ben Cat   SOUTH VIETNAM

                        Saigon   Bien Hoa

                        Dong Tam

                                                    Vung Tau   10°

IV CORPS   Mekong
                        Can Tho   Delta

                        Soc Trang

17th Parallel

DMZ

Ben Hai

Con
Thien

DEMARCATION
LINE

Major U.S. Bases

Ho Chi Minh Trail

Sihanouk Trail

CHRONOLOGY

	In Vietnam	**In the World**
1858	France invades Danang.	Napolean III rules the Second Empire (1852–1870).
1859	France occupies Saigon.	Work begins on Suez Canal.
1867	France annexes Cochinchina.	U.S. buys Alaska.
1884	France imposes its rule throughout Vietnam.	Third Republic in France since 1870.
1914		World War I begins in Europe.
1919	Nguyen Ai Quoc (Ho Chi Minh) petitions for Vietnamese independence at Versailles.	Clemenceau represents France at Versailles. First commercial radio broadcast.
1930	Indochinese Communist party is set up.	Economic depression worldwide.
1936	Unrest throughout Vietnam.	France: Popular front government under Léon Blum. Spanish Civil War begins.
1939		World War II begins.
1940	Japanese troops in Vietnam. French arrive at an understanding with them.	Germany defeats France.
1941	Vietminh is founded. Fights Japanese and French.	Japanese attack Pearl Harbor.
1944	Giap sets up the Liberation Army.	D-Day invasion of France. Paris is liberated.
1945 Mar	Japanese coup removes French from power in Vietnam. Bao Dai cooperates with Japanese.	
Apr		President Roosevelt dies. Truman takes over. UN meets.
May–Jun		War in Europe ends.

Jul		Potsdam Conference meets to discuss postwar plans.
Aug	Vietminh seize power from Japanese. Bao Dai abdicates.	Atom bombs dropped on Japan.
Sep	Ho announces Declaration of Independence. British and Chinese forces accept Japanese surrender.	Japan surrenders.
1946	Negotiations and conferences on the status of Vietnam satisfy neither side. War breaks out by end of the year between Ho's forces and the returned French.	Republicans gain in the fall elections in the U.S. Cease fire in the Chinese civil war is signed and falls apart.
1947		Truman Doctrine.
1948		Marshall Plan. Berlin airlift.
1949	Elysée Agreement is signed. Bao Dai becomes chief of state in French-controlled Vietnam.	Truman inaugurated for second term in office. NATO established. Mao takes control of China. U.S.S.R. tests nuclear weapon.
1950	Mao and Stalin recognize Ho's government. U.S. recognizes Bao Dai's government; sends increased aid and a military assistance advisory group.	U.S.: Alger Hiss found guilty of perjury. Rise of Joseph McCarthy. Korean war begins.
1951	Ho Chi Minh establishes Lao Dong party. General Giap's offensive fails.	Truman relieves MacArthur of command in Korea.
1953	Navarre becomes commander of French forces in Vietnam.	Eisenhower becomes president. Stalin dies. Armistice in Korea.
1954 Jan		Nautilus, first atomic submarine.
May	Fall of Dien Bien Phu to Vietminh.	Brown vs Board of Education decision rules segregation illegal.
Jun	Diem returns to South Vietnam.	Army–McCarthy hearings end in the U.S.
Jul	Geneva Conference Accords reached. Vietnam is temporarily divided at the 17th parallel.	British surrender Suez Canal.
Sep		Southeast Asia Treaty Organization (SEATO) established.

Nov		French commit forces to Algeria.
1955 Jan		U.S. Congress passes Formosa Resolution.
Apr		Bandung conference of Asian and African Peoples.
May		Warsaw Pact signed.
Jul	Diem refuses to plan for 1956 elections with North.	Geneva summit with Russia.
Oct	Diem defeats Bao Dai in referendum. Republic of Vietnam established.	
1956 Feb		Khrushchev denounces Stalin.
Apr	Military Assistance Advisory Group (MAAG) set up by U.S.	
Oct		U.S.S.R. intervenes in Polish and Hungarian uprisings. Suez Crisis.
Nov		Eisenhower reelected.
1957 Mar		Eisenhower Doctrine for Middle East declared. Ghana becomes independent of Great Britain.
May	Diem makes successful U.S. tour.	
Oct		John F. Kennedy wins Pulitzer Prize for *Profiles in Courage*. Sputnik I launched by U.S.S.R.
1958 Feb		United Arab Republic established.
Oct		Jets used by U.S. on overseas flights. Pope John XXIII elected.
Dec		Fifth French Republic proclaimed.
1959 Jan		Castro comes to power in Cuba.
May	Repressive Law 10/59 goes into effect.	
Jun		Vice President Nixon goes to Moscow.
Sep		Khrushchev tours U.S.
1960 Apr	Manifesto of the 18 protests Diem's policies.	
May		U.S. U-2 spy plane shot down by U.S.S.R. Paris summit fails.

Jun		Civil war in Congo.
Nov	Coup attempt against Diem fails.	John F. Kennedy elected President.
Dec	National Liberation Front emerges.	
1961 Mar		Peace Corps established.
Apr		Bay of Pigs Invasion of Cuba fails.
		U.S.S.R. launches first man in space.
May	Vice President Johnson visits.	
Jun		Vienna summit with U.S.S.R. fails to ease relations.
Aug		Berlin Wall separates city.
Sep		UN Secretary General Dag Hammarskjold dies in plane crash.
Oct	General Maxwell Taylor and W. W. Rostow visit.	
Dec	Diem and Kennedy exchange letters. U.S. aid increases.	State Department White Paper concludes North Vietnam is invading South.
1962 Feb	Assistance Command, Vietnam (MACV). MAAG becomes Military.	John Glenn orbits the earth for U.S.
Jun	Strategic Hamlet Program in full operation.	Students for a Democratic Society (SDS) formulate Port Huron Statement.
Jul		Telstar communications satellite launched by U.S. Algeria wins independence from France.
Sep		James M. Meredith enrolls at University of Mississippi.
Oct		Cuban Missile Crisis. India–China Border War.
Nov		U Thant becomes Secretary General of United Nations.
1963 Jan	South Vietnamese Army with U.S. advisers defeated at Ap Bac. 3 Americans killed.	
Apr		U.S. sees civil rights demonstrations in Birmingham.
May	Buddhist protests begin.	Organization of African Unity formed.
Jun	Thich Quang Duc burns himself to death.	

Aug	Nhu's Special Forces raid Buddhist pagodas.	Martin Luther King Jr. leads march on Washington. U.S. and U.S.S.R. negotiate Nuclear Test Ban Treaty.
Sep		U.S. network television news goes to half-hour format.
Nov	Coup overthrows Diem. Diem and Nhu killed. General Minh takes over.	President Kennedy assassinated.
1964 Jan	Nguyen Khanh's coup overthrows Big Minh.	France recognizes People's Republic of China. Unrest in Panama has anti-American flavor.
Feb		Cassius Clay (later Mohammed Ali) wins heavyweight crown in U.S.
May		Nehru dies in India. Palestine Liberation Organization established.
Jun	General William C. Westmoreland takes command of MACV. Maxwell Taylor becomes new U.S. ambassador.	Three civil rights workers murdered in Mississippi. De Gaulle calls for an end to all foreign intervention in Vietnam.
Jul		Civil Rights Act becomes law in U.S. Riots in Harlem and other U.S. ghettoes.
Aug	Gulf of Tonkin incident. U.S. bombs North Vietnam. Khanh gives new constitution. Musical chairs in Saigon government.	Tonkin Gulf Resolution passed.
Sep	Governmental instability in Saigon.	Warren Commission Report accepted in U.S. Free speech movement begins at Berkeley.
Oct		Martin Luther King wins Nobel Peace Prize. Brezhnev and Kosygin replace Khrushchev. China explodes atomic bomb.
Nov		Johnson defeats Goldwater.
Dec	Buddhists and students demonstrate in Saigon.	
1965	Operation Rolling Thunder. U.S. troops in ground combat. Kosygin visits North Vietnam.	Cambodia breaks relations with U.S.

Mar	First American combat troops at Danang.	Prime Minister Ky and President Johnson meet in Hawaii.
Dec	U.S. combat strength reaches almost 200,000.	
1966	Vietnamese Communists set up bases in Cambodia.	
Jan	37-day bombing pause ends on January 31.	
Mar	Demonstrations against Ky in Hue and Danang.	
Apr	B-52s attack North Vietnam for first time.	
Jun	U.S. bombs outskirts of Hanoi and Haiphong.	
Sep		De Gaulle urges U.S. to withdraw and then negotiate.
Oct		McNamara discouraged by slow U.S. progress. Johnson meets with Asian leaders in Manila.
Dec		Harrison Salisbury reports that U.S. had hit civilian targets in Hanoi.
1967 Jan	Operation Cedar Falls—major U.S. search and destroy mission.	Treaty between U.S., U.S.S.R., and Britain bans nuclear weapons in outer space.
Mar		Ellsworth Bunker becomes U.S. ambassador to Saigon.
Apr		Antiwar protests in New York and San Francisco.
May	Operation Junction City—another major search and destroy mission.	
Jun	Ky withdraws from presidential election campaign.	Haight-Ashbury Summer begins in U.S. Six-Day War between Israel and Arab states.
Jul		Race riots in many U.S. cities
Sep	Thieu-Ky ticket receives 35% of the vote and wins.	LBJ announces San Antonio formula for peace.
Oct		Antiwar demonstrators march on the Pentagon. Ché Guevara killed leading rebels in Bolivia.
1968 Jan	North Vietnam surrounds Khe Sanh. Tet Offensive begins.	Students riot in Warsaw. North Korea seizes USN Pueblo.

Feb	ARVN recaptures Hue.	U.S. Senate questions McNamara about Gulf of Tonkin.
Mar	LBJ announces bombing halt. My Lai massacre takes place.	Eugene McCarthy gets 42% of the New Hampshire primary vote. Robert Kennedy seeks Democratic nomination. LBJ announces he will not run for re-election.
Apr	U.S. Marines survive in Khe Sanh. North Vietnam agrees to talks.	Martin Luther King assassinated. Unrest at Columbia University.
May	Peace talks begin in Paris.	Students riot in Paris.
Jun	U.S. troops leave Khe Sanh. Abrams replaces Westmoreland as Commander of MACV.	Robert Kennedy assassinated.
Aug		Violence in Chicago during Democratic Convention. Russian troops crack down on Czechoslovakia.
Oct	LBJ announces total halt of North Vietnam bombing.	Black Power demonstrations at Mexico City Olympics.
Nov		Nixon wins presidency, defeating Vice President Humphrey.
1969 Jan		Lodge replaces Harriman at Paris Peace Talks.
Mar	U.S. begins bombing of North Vietnamese bases in Cambodia.	
Apr		Unrest at Harvard and other campuses. De Gaulle resigns from office in France.
May		Nixon Administration begins wiretapping of suspected information leaks.
Jun	Provisional Revolutionary Government (PRG) is formed by NLF. Nixon and Thieu meet on Midway Island.	First U.S. troop withdrawal is announced.
Aug		Woodstock music festival.
Sep	Ho Chi Minh dies.	Second U.S. troop withdrawal announced.
Oct		Vietnam moratorium in U.S. Nationwide peace demonstrations.

Nov		Another moratorium attracts record numbers.
		U.S. Army begins to investigate My Lai massacre.
Dec		Harris Poll shows 46% in favor of the aims of the November moratorium.
1970 Mar	ARVN troops first attack Vietnamese bases in Cambodia.	Sihanouk deposed in Cambodia. Lon Nol takes over.
Apr	U.S. forces join ARVN in Cambodian incursion.	
May	U.S. bombs North Vietnam for first time since 1968.	Four demonstrators killed at Kent State. Two hundred colleges close in protest. Demonstrations in Washington.
Jun	U.S. troops leave Cambodia.	Cooper-Church Amendment limits U.S. role in Cambodia. Senate repeals Gulf of Tonkin Resolution.
Aug		White House sets up "plumbers" to end information leaks.
Sep		Allende elected President of Chile.
		First U.S. ambassador to Cambodia since 1965 arrives.
Nov		De Gaulle dies in France.
1971 Jan		Idi Amin takes over in Uganda. MEDTC set up by U.S. in Cambodia.
Feb	ARVN troops invade Laos with U.S. air support.	
Mar	ARVN forced out of Laos.	
Apr		500,000 protest in Washington. U.S. table tennis team visits China.
May		Disorderly May Day demonstrations in Washington.
Jun		*New York Times* begins publication of the Pentagon Papers.
Aug	Big Minh withdraws from election.	
Oct	Thieu reelected with 80% of the vote.	Lon Nol cancels democratic government on grounds of "emergency" in Cambodia.
Dec	U.S. bombs North Vietnam as protective reaction strikes.	

1972 Jan		Nixon announces secret talks in Paris.
Feb		Nixon visits China.
Mar	First major North Vietnamese ground offensive since 1968.	
Apr	Easter Offensive continues. U.S. bombs North Vietnam.	U.S. antiwar demonstrations protest bombings.
May	ARVN retreats from Quang Tri. U.S. mines North Vietnamese ports. Bombing continues.	Nixon visits Russia.
Jun		Break-in at the Democratic National Committee headquarters at the Watergate Hotel.
Aug	Last U.S. ground troops leave.	
Oct	Preliminary peace agreement.	Kissinger says peace is at hand.
Nov	Thieu rejects the treaty.	Nixon reelected.
Dec	U.S. bombs Hanoi and Haiphong. Bombing halt over the North announced on December 30.	
1973 Jan	Peace Agreement signed in Paris.	Lyndon Johnson dies.
Feb	Return of POWs begins.	
Mar	Last U.S. troops leave South Vietnam.	
Apr		Watergate investigation implicates president.
May		U.S. Congress votes to block money for Cambodia bombing.
Jun	Kissinger and Le Duc Tho meet again in Paris.	
Aug	U.S. bombing in Southeast Asia ends.	
Sep		Kissinger becomes Secretary of State. Allende is overthrown in Chile.
Oct		Agnew resigns as vice president. Yom Kippur War in Middle East.
Nov		Energy crisis begins worldwide.
Dec		Gerald Ford becomes vice president.
1974 Jan	Thieu declares war has begun again.	

Jun   Nixon visits Soviet Union again.

Aug   Communists make military   Nixon resigns. Ford takes over
gains.   as president.

Sep   Ford pardons Nixon.

Oct   Politburo of North Vietnam
plans military strategy.

Nov   Democrats make big election
gains in U.S.

1975 Mar North Vietnamese take Ban
Me Thuot.
ARVN retreats from Pleiku.
North Vietnamese take
Danang.

Apr   Thieu resigns.   Khmer Rouge wins in
Saigon surrenders.   Cambodia. Lon Nol flees to
Hawaii.
U.S. Embassy staff leaves
Phnom Penh.

Dec   President Ford visits China.
King of Laos abdicates.
People's Democratic Republic
set up.

Part 1

BEGINNINGS

Any choice of where to begin a history is, of course, arbitrary. Ho Chi Minh's declaration of Vietnamese independence in 1945 followed the surrender of Japan at the end of World War II. That in turn followed the Japanese dissolution of the shadow French administration of Vietnam. When the Japanese invaded Indochina, they had allowed for a time the continuance of the French administrative bureaucracy there under Japanese control, as an extension of the French Vichy regime under the mastership of Japan's ally Germany. And before the Japanese period lay the years of French occupation of Indochina; and before that the long centuries of Vietnam's encounters with its huge and occasionally expansive northern neighbor China.

A reason for starting the story with the year 1945 and Vietnam's apparent achievement of independence is that it was a moment at which the history of Vietnam, France, and the United States could have taken a vastly different form. Ho, for his own nationalist reasons, wanted American support. In Washington, there was much discomfort at France's desire to return to Indochina. Had the Americans sided with Ho and persuaded the French to stay out of the region, Vietnam would probably have been an independent state, and neither the French war ending in 1954 nor the American war that is the subject of this reader would have happened.

Ho Chi Minh, Communist leader of Vietnam from 1945 through the Vietnam War, wrote that the Communists "swam like fishes in the peasant sea." *(Courtesy, AP/Wide World Photos)*

1

"Our Goal Must Be . . . Independence"

Charles Taussig, one of President Franklin D. Roosevelt's advisers, in a memorandum refers in passing to FDR's thoughts on peoples who had been under the colonial rule of British nations. Speaking in very general terms, Roosevelt is sketching out a wish for the independence of formerly colonized countries. The American government at the end of the war desired independence for such countries, but never kept clearly to that goal or worked out an effective policy for getting France to accept it. The memorandum carries the date March 15, 1945.

. . . The President said he was concerned about the brown people in the East. He said that there are 1,100,000,000 brown people. In many Eastern countries, they are ruled by a handful of whites and they resent it. Our goal must be to help them achieve independence—1,100,000,000 potential enemies are dangerous. He said he included the 450,000,000 Chinese in that. He then added, Churchill doesn't understand this.

The President said he thought we might have some difficulties with France in the matter of colonies. I said that I thought that was quite probable and it was also probable the British would use France as a "stalking horse."

I asked the President if he had changed his ideas on French Indo-China as he had expressed them to us at the luncheon with Stanley. He said no he had not changed his ideas; that French Indo-China and New Caledonia should be taken from France and put under a trusteeship. The President hesitated a moment and then said—well if we can get the proper pledge from France to assume for herself the obligations of a trustee, then I would agree to France retaining these colonies with the proviso that independence was the ultimate goal. I asked the President

Source: U.S. Department of State, *Foreign Relations of the United States: Diplomatic Papers, 1945*, I, General: The United Nations (Washington, D.C.: United States Government Printing Office, 1967), 124.

3

if he would settle for self-government. He said no. I asked him if he would settle for dominion status. He said no—it must be independence. He said that is to be the policy and you can quote me in the State Department. . . .

2

How to Achieve Independence

This policy paper of June 22, 1945, prepared in the Department of State, represents reflections within the government in the early days of President Harry Truman, Roosevelt's Vice President who had become President on the death of FDR on April 12. The paper expresses the same sympathy as Roosevelt's comments toward the idea of independence. Yet it insists on the necessity for keeping unity within the United Nations and speaks of the gradual as opposed to the immediate attainment of self-government. That indicates that there would be no concerted will within Washington to act aggressively and consistently to keep European nations out of their former colonies.

When V day comes in the Far East and the Pacific it will be the result in largest measure of the military might and the sacrifices of the United States. In return the American people ask for a reasonable assurance of peace and security in this great area and economic welfare. Peace and security, and economic welfare, however, depend on a number of conditions.

One of these conditions is the right of all peoples to choose the form of Government under which they will live. The United States, therefore, has a definite interest that there should be a progressive enlargement of the political responsibilities, both as individuals and as groups of all the peoples of this region in order that they may be prepared and able to assume the responsibilities of natural freedom as well as to enjoy its rights. To this end we would wish to see in China and in other inde-

Source: U.S. Department of State, *Foreign Relations of the United States: Diplomatic Papers, 1945,* VI, The British Commonwealth: The Far East (Washington, D.C.: United States Government Printing Office, 1969), 556–58.

pendent countries governments established on a broader basis of the population, and the elimination, so far as international security conditions and arrangements permit, of those conditions favoring foreign nationals which impair the sovereign rights of those countries; and in the dependent areas in this region we would wish to see the peoples given the opportunity to achieve a progressively larger measure of self-government.

During the past four hundred years the Western Powers—and more recently Japan—by war, threat of war, and exploitation of ignorance on the part of Oriental Governments, extended Western sovereignty, economic and political control, or exceptional semi-sovereign rights over great areas of Asia and the Pacific—areas which produce a substantial part of the world's supply of many critically important primary commodities and contain more than half of the human race.

In the past half century, however, the rising nationalism in Asia has led to a demand for freedom from this political and economic subjection, and the demand has increased in strength and in insistence, and has been intensified by Japanese propaganda during the present war. The fact that each Far Eastern people was suffering under disabilities maintained by the Western Powers provided the Far Eastern nations with a bond of kinship over and beyond common membership among the peoples of Asia.

Aside from the traditional American belief in the right of all peoples to independence, the largest possible measure of political freedom for the countries of Asia consistent with their ability to assume the responsibility thereof is probably necessary in order to achieve the chief objective of the United States in the Far East and the Pacific: continuing peace and security.

Another condition on which peace and security depend is cooperation among the peace-minded states of the world. One of the foremost policies of the United States is to maintain the unity of purpose and action of all the United Nations, especially of the leading powers. Two of these leading powers are Great Britain and France, each of which has dependencies in the Far East in which there is an insistent demand for a greater measure of self-government than the parent states have yet been willing to grant.

A problem for the United States is to harmonize, so far as possible, its policies in regard to the two objectives: increased political freedom for the Far East and the maintenance of the unity of the leading United Nations in meeting this problem. The United States Government may properly continue to state the political principle which it has frequently announced, that dependent peoples should be given the opportunity, if necessary after an adequate period of preparation, to achieve an increased measure of self-government, but it should avoid any course of action which would seriously impair the unity of the major United Nations.

The United States, also, may utilize either the force of its example or its influence or both. Its treatment of the Philippines has earned a rich reward for this country in the attitude and conduct of both the Filipinos and the nationals of other Far Eastern states. The American Government influenced the British Government to take parallel action with it in the renunciation of extraterritoriality and other exceptional rights in China.

The solution which would best harmonize these two policies of the United States would be a Far East progressively developing into a group of self-governing states—independent or with Dominion status—which would cooperate with each other and with the Western powers on a basis of mutual self-respect and friendship. The interests of the United States and of its European Allies require that the Far East be removed as a source of colonial rivalry and conflict, not only between the Great Powers, but between the Great Powers and the peoples of Asia. . . .

3

Declaration of Independence of the Democratic Republic of Vietnam, September 2, 1945

The Declaration came after the collapse of Japan, at a time when Ho's forces possessed as much power and legitimacy as existed in Vietnam. This version in English contains words identical to the famous phrases in the Declaration of Independence of the United States. That may be seen as a sincere homage to the first of the modern statements of national independence and individual rights, or as a play for American support of Ho's ambitions. Given the complexity of personal psychology and political strategy, the two interpretations are not necessarily incompatible.

Source: Vietnam: The Definitive Documentation of Human Decisions, I, edited with commentary and introduction by Gareth Porter (Stanfordville, N.Y.: Earl M. Coleman Enterprises, 1979), 64–66.

"We hold truths that all men are created equal, that they are endowed by their Creator with certain unalienable Rights, among these are Life, Liberty and the pursuit of Happiness."

This immortal statement is extracted from the Declaration of Independence of the United States of America in 1776. Understood in the broader sense, this means: "All peoples on the earth are born equal; every person has the right to live to be happy and free."

The Declaration of Human and Civic Rights proclaimed by the French Revolution in 1791 likewise propounds: "Every man is born equal and enjoys free and equal rights."

These are undeniable truths.

Yet, during and throughout the last eighty years, the French imperialists, abusing the principles of "Freedom, equality and fraternity," have violated the integrity of our ancestral land and oppressed our countrymen. Their deeds run counter to the ideals of humanity and justice.

In the political field, they have denied us every freedom. They have enforced upon us inhuman laws. They have set up three different political regimes in Northern, Central and Southern Viet Nam (Tonkin, Annam, and Cochinchina) in an attempt to disrupt our national, historical and ethnical unity.

They have built more prisons than schools. They have callously ill-treated our fellow-compatriots. They have drowned our revolutions in blood.

They have sought to stifle public opinion and pursued a policy of obscurantism on the largest scale; they have forced upon us alcohol and opium in order to weaken our race.

In the economic field, they have shamelessly exploited our people, driven them into the worst misery and mercilessly plundered our country.

They have ruthlessly appropriated our rice fields, mines, forests, and raw materials. They have arrogated to themselves the privilege of issuing banknotes, and monopolised all our external commerce. They have imposed hundreds of unjustifiable taxes, and reduced our countrymen, especially the peasants and petty tradesmen, to extreme poverty.

They have prevented the development of native capital enterprises; they have exploited our workers in the most barbarous manner.

In the autumn of 1940, when the Japanese fascists, in order to fight the Allies, invaded Indochina and set up new bases of war, the French imperialists surrendered on bended knees and handed over our country to the invaders.

Subsequently, under the joint French and Japanese yoke, our people were literally bled white. The consequences were dire in the extreme. From Quang Tri up to the North, two millions of our countrymen died from starvation during the first months of this year.

Vo Nguyen Giap (on the left), the military strategist of the Vietminh, standing with Ho Chi Minh, the leading Vietnamese political tactician. The photo was taken in September 1945 shortly after Ho had read the Vietnamese Declaration of Independence and had established the Democratic Republic of Vietnam. *(Courtesy, Wide World Photo)*

On March 9th, 1945, the Japanese disarmed the French troops. Again the French either fled or surrendered unconditionally. Thus, in no way have they proved capable of "protecting" us; on the contrary, within five years they have twice sold our country to the Japanese.

Before March 9th, many a time did the Viet Minh League invite the French to join in the fight against the Japanese. Instead of accepting this offer, the French, on the contrary, let loose a wild reign of terror with rigour worse than ever before against Viet Minh's partisans. They even slaughtered a great number of our *"condamnes politiques"* imprisoned at Yen Bay and Cao Bang.

Despite all that, our countrymen went on maintaining, vis-à-vis the French, a humane and even indulgent attitude. After the events of March 9th, the Viet Minh League helped many French to cross the borders, rescued others from Japanese prisons and, in general, protected the lives and properties of all the French in their territory.

In fact, since the autumn of 1940, our country ceased to be a French colony and became a Japanese possession.

After the Japanese surrender, our people, as a whole, rose up and proclaimed their sovereignty and founded the Democratic Republic of Viet Nam.

The truth is that we have wrung back our independence from Japanese hands and not from the French.

The French fled, the Japanese surrendered. Emperor Bao Dai abdicated, our people smashed the yoke which pressed hard upon us for nearly one hundred years, and finally made our Viet Nam an independent country. Our people at the same time overthrew the monarchical regime established tens of centuries ago, and founded the Republic.

For these reasons, we, the members of the Provisional Government representing the entire people of Viet Nam, declare that we shall from now on have no more connections with imperialist France; we consider null and void all the treaties France has signed concerning Viet Nam, and we hereby cancel all the privileges that the French arrogated to themselves on our territory.

The Vietnamese people, animated by the same common resolve, are determined to fight to the death against all attempts at aggression by the French imperialists.

We are convinced that the Allies who have recognized the principles of equality of peoples at the Conferences of Teheran and San Francisco cannot but recognize the Independence of Viet Nam.

A people which has so stubbornly opposed the French domination for more than 80 years, a people who, during these last years, so doggedly ranged itself and fought on the Allied side against Fascism, such a people has the right to be free, such a people must be independent.

For these reasons, we, the members of the Provisional Government of the Democratic Republic of Viet Nam, solemnly declare to the world:

"Viet Nam has the right to be free and independent and, in fact, has become free and independent. The people of Viet Nam decide to mobilise all their spiritual and material forces and to sacrifice their lives and property in order to safeguard their right of Liberty and Independence."

4

A Moment of Contact

As a member of the Office of Strategic Services—the organization that preceded the Central Intelligence Agency as an instrument of secret American activity abroad—Archimedes Patti was in touch with Ho Chi Minh in 1945. In this interview with Michael Charlton conducted over three decades later, Patti gives an account of friendly dealings with Ho, and touches on the phrasings of the Vietnamese Declaration taken from the American document.

PATTI: I was telling my Headquarters in Chungking, with respect to Ho Chi Minh he was definitely a Communist, no question in my mind about it. But he was not a Moscow Communist. He was more of a nationalist who was using the Communist techniques and methods to achieve his ends.

CHARLTON: Did he specifically disavow his interest in and connections with the Soviet Union? Did you talk to him about Russia?

PATTI: Yes, there was a period of August and September while I was talking to Ho, he told me on several occasions that he had nothing to expect from, could expect nothing from Russia and the Soviet Union, since the Soviet Union was in a bad way, in a bad state after the war, so he could expect no help from them. With respect to his being a Communist he said: 'Yes, I put in fifteen years of service to the party and I believe I paid my debt. From now on I am independent, and I can do as I find best for my country.'

Source: Michael Charlton and Anthony Moncrieff, *Many Reasons Why: The American Involvement in Vietnam* (New York: Hill and Wang, 1978), 9–10, 12. Reprinted by permission.

CHARLTON: He had convinced you of an allegiance which conformed to the interests of the United States?

PATTI: Allegiance is a hard word really, but he asked me on a number of occasions during the period of August and September 1945 that if the United States would provide the expertise of American technology he was more than happy to receive the Americans. And I asked about the French; and he said the French could come too. 'I have no objection to the French coming as advisers and to help us set up our country, but I don't want them here as colonial rulers.'

CHARLTON: But he had made it clear to you, presumably, that he regarded you Americans at this time with your Mission in Kunming as the advanced guard of a power and an army which would help him to power in Indo-China. Is that correct?

PATTI: No, that is not correct. No. I am sorry, but he didn't regard us as a power to help him take over or to achieve independence, because he knew we were not going to provide him with unlimited arms and equipment to fight the French since the French were our allies. Actually he expected moral support. As a matter of fact he said to me on more than one occasion: 'Why can't you look at us as you do the filipinos, you promised them independence, you have given them independence and here they are.' He said: 'Why don't you live up to the provisions of the Atlantic Charter. Have you forgotten the Fourteen Points of Wilson? Why don't you just support us? All we want is moral support. We don't want money, arms or equipment from you, all we want is moral support.'

CHARLTON: Were you personally attracted by those arguments?

PATTI: Yes, I was personally attracted. I thought they were reasonable and I presented them as such to Chungking and to Washington and London to the point that I received a cable from my own offices: 'For God's sake stop sending any more wires to London and Washington on this subject.'

CHARLTON: Was it obvious to you that the Americans were vital to Ho Chi Minh in helping him to establish his authority as a leader? After all, the man was completely unknown inside Indo-China, do you agree with that?

PATTI: Yes, that is true. He did use us, and I know it. I knew he was using us, and I didn't mind frankly because the use he made of us was more one of image rather than substance. Really what he was trying to do was to say: 'Well look, even the Americans believe in my cause'— when speaking to the Vietnamese. But at the same time he did use us, yes. . . .

CHARLTON: Now, we're coming to the fascinating episode of the use by Ho Chi Minh, as he seized power in Hanoi, of the famous wording of the American Declaration of Independence.

PATTI: He actually called me in one afternoon and we discussed among many things the preparation of the text of the Declaration of Independence and he asked me to help him . . .

5

A Consummate Cold Warrior

Dean Acheson, Secretary of State in the Democratic adminis-
tration of President Harry Truman, was instrumental in shap-
ing the diplomacy and the thinking of the Cold War, the con-
frontation of the Communist world by the nations of the West
and their Asian allies. In this telegram of May 20, 1949, to the
American consulate at Hanoi, at a time when France was still
in Vietnam, Acheson takes the hard line that was typical of him
whenever there was a question of containing Communism.

In light Ho's known background, no other assumption possible but that he outright Commie so long as (1) he fails unequivocally repudiate Moscow connections and Commie doctrine and (2) remains personally singled out for praise by internatl Commie press and receives its support. Moreover, US not impressed by nationalist character red flag with yellow stars. Question whether Ho as much nationalist as Commie is irrelevant. All Stalinists in colonial areas are nationalists. With achievement natl aims (i.e., independence) their objective necessarily becomes subordination state to Commie purposes and ruthless extermination not only opposition groups but all elements suspected even slightest deviation. On basis examples eastern Eur it must be assumed such wld be goal Ho and men his stamp if included Baodai Govt. To include them in order achieve reconciliation opposing polit elements and "national unity" wld merely postpone settlement issue whether Vietnam to be independent nation or Commie satellite until circumstances probably even less favorable nationalists than now. It must of course be conceded theoretical possibility exists estab National Communist state on pattern Yugoslavia in any area beyond reach Soviet army. However, US attitude cld take acct such

Source: U.S. Department of State, *Foreign Relations of the United States, 1949,* VII, pt. 1, The Far East and Australasia (Washington, D.C.: Government Printing Office, 1975), 29.

possibility only if every other possible avenue closed to preservation area from Kremlin control. Moreover, while Vietnam out of reach Soviet army it will doubtless be by no means out of reach Chi Commie hatchet men and armed forces. . . .

6

The American Interest in Indochina

This statement released by the State Department in October 1951 is an early effort by the United States government to persuade the public that defeating Communism in Indochina was an essential task of the Cold War. At the time of the statement, the French were still in Indochina, but the three nations of Vietnam, Laos, and Cambodia were defined as autonomous Associated States within the French Union.

A bitter and bloody struggle between Communist forces and French Union troops has been racking Indochina for 6 years. Civil war has raged throughout the former French colonies as the people of Indochina endeavor to mold themselves into three sovereign nations.

Fostered by a violent decade of Japanese conquest, Allied reoccupation, and civil war, Indochinese nationalism has come into its own. From the old French colony arose the states of Vietnam, Cambodia, and Laos, to become associate members of the French Union and recognized citizens of the world community.

In assuming the sponsorship of these new states, France has recognized the legitimacy of their claims to a greater role in developing their own future. The Associated States, in return, recognize their continuing need for close association with the Republic of France.

But many Indochinese have been disaffected by the policies of colonialism—which France has since renounced—and still want to see the French leave. The Communists use this sentiment as a rallying cry and around it have organized a popular front. It is this organization, with its high (but decreasing) percentage of genuine nationalists dominated by

Source: Background, Department of State Publication 4381, Far Eastern Series 50, October 1951, 1–2, 5, 7.

its Communist leaders, which is conducting warfare against the governments of the three Associated States and France.

The issue is control over the great emerging force of Indochinese nationalism. The question is whether the natural desire of the Indochinese to control their own destiny will be subverted by communism or whether it will be guided to success by the ideals of the free world.

The battle for control of Indochina would be of moment to the world at any time. Thousands of lives have been taken in the struggle, and the lives of 27 million people will be affected by its outcome. But a glance at the map shows that the importance of the war for Indochina goes beyond this.

To the north lies China, which ruled its weaker neighbor to the south for 1,200 years. For another 1,000 years Indochina fought constantly to prevent being reabsorbed. Given this history and the large numbers of Chinese who have settled in Indochina, it is obvious that the Communist revolution in China could not fail to create stirrings to the south.

West of Indochina is the independent kingdom of Thailand, one-sixth of whose population of 18 million is Chinese. Burma adjoins both these states, and there 3 years of three-cornered civil war could be ended disastrously by the advance of Communist forces from the north or east. The fall of these countries would cut off hope that British troops in Malaya could break the Communist revolt there.

Thus the independence of six countries—Vietnam, Laos, Cambodia, Thailand, Burma, and Malaya—depends on holding the line in Indochina. A break-through would not only add another satellite to the Soviet orbit but would also pave the way for aggression against Indochina's neighbors. These countries together comprise the greatest rice-producing area in the world. They are the source of 80 percent of the free world's supply of natural rubber and half of its tin. The loss of these resources would be serious to the free world and would enormously increase the military capabilities of the Communist bloc.

The urgent problem faced by the Associated States is to assert their authority throughout Indochina. It is impossible to do this without outside military aid. Such aid comes primarily from France. French Union forces in Indochina total 240,000, of which 160,000 are regular troops. In addition, France is paying the major share of maintenance costs for the three Indochinese national armies, which now number some 120,000 men. The French military budget for Indochina is approximately 1 billion dollars each year. A large part of the material needed by these soldiers is provided by the United States under its Mutual Defense Assistance Program. In addition, through the Economic Cooperation Administration, we are aiding in the rehabilitation of rural areas which have been recently pacified.

The military situation in Indochina today is critical. In Tonkin (north Vietnam), French Union forces control the important Red River Delta. But throughout large areas of Vietnam, bands of Communists roam the countryside, burning crops, arduously dismantling buildings, and fighting government patrols. In Cambodia and Laos, the small French garrisons and the National Army are barely adequate to maintain security against the Communists and border pirates who historically have preyed on traffic there.

The Communists' war has been conducted with both open and guerrilla tactics, with heavy dependence on infiltration, terrorism, propaganda, and sabotage. Military supplies are being channeled into the country from China to arm and sustain these forces—and there is the constant threat that troops may be obtained from the same source.

Until last year, French and Indochinese troops, well trained but limited in number, were losing ground in the seesaw battles with the less well equipped but more numerous Communist forces. In mid-December of 1950, Gen. Jean de Lattre de Tassigny took over as High Commissioner of France in Indochina and Commander in Chief of French forces in the Far East. Under his spirited command and through the use of United States military aid, Government forces repelled further Communist advances and provided hope that a positive solution might be reached. . . .

Ho is a Moscow-trained Communist. Having joined the French Communist Party in 1920, he spent long periods in Moscow during the ensuing decade. In 1930 in Hong Kong he founded the Indochinese Communist Party, which was recognized as an independent section of the Communist International (Comintern).

As chief of the Viet Minh, Ho took great pains to play down his Communist background and to capitalize on the reputation he had built up as an uncompromising anticolonialist. He even contrived, in 1945, a "dissolution" of the Indochinese Communist Party.

Ho's initial program was socially moderate and similar to the expressions of other nationalist groups. He proclaimed the Indochinese peasant's desire for relief from arbitrary taxation, usury, and (in Cochinchina) exploitation by absentee landlords. He also proposed a democratic system of popular education and a considerable degree of political liberty. None of these demands are Communist in character; on the contrary, their fulfillment would strengthen the traditional forms of private and village ownership of land and encourage the growth of democratic political institutions.

The strength of Ho and his officers is based on their leadership of the underground struggle against both the French and the Japanese and on their experience in clandestine techniques. Some of Ho's advisers have been fighting French colonial rule for 30 years in the name of nationalism. . . .

It is important to the security of the United States that Indochina remain among the free nations of the world. The six nations of the Indochinese peninsula depend upon the freedom of each of their neighbors for the maintenance of their own freedom. Their fall would complete Communist domination of Asia east of India.

The withdrawal of these countries from the free world would deprive us of much-needed rice, rubber, and tin—while adding these goods to the stock of Communist resources. Another result would be the closing of the port of Singapore to free world trade.

Perhaps even more important would be the psychological effect of the fall of Indochina. It would be taken by many as a sign that the force of communism is irresistible and would lead to an attitude of defeatism. The successful defense of Indochina, on the other hand, would hearten those who man the defenses against communism all over the world.

If Indochina is to remain among the free nations, the Communist forces there must be decisively conquered down to the last pocket of resistance which may at some time become a center for further attacks or sabotage.

For this purpose substantial United States military assistance is being extended to the Associated States and to the armies of the French Union. Without this aid, which is authorized under the Mutual Defense Assistance Program, it is doubtful whether they could hold their ground against the Communists.

7

An Alliance for Southeast Asia

This letter from President Dwight D. Eisenhower to the British statesman Winston Churchill, which reflects Eisenhower's concern about the failing position of the French in Indochina, projects an alliance for the defense of Southeast Asia against Communism. The letter is dated April 4, 1954. In less than

Source: Peter G. Boyle, ed., *The Churchill-Eisenhower Correspondence, 1953–1955* (Chapel Hill, N.C.: The University of North Carolina Press, 1990), 136–38.

a year emerged the Southeast Asia Treaty Organization, or
SEATO, a parallel to the North Atlantic Treaty Organization
(NATO).

I am sure that like me you are following with the deepest interest
and anxiety the daily reports of the gallant fight being put up by the
French at Dien Bien Phu. Today, the situation there does not seem
hopeless.

But regardless of the outcome of this particular battle, I fear that
the French cannot alone see this thing through, this despite the very
substantial assistance in money and material that we are giving them. It
is no solution simply to urge the French to intensify their efforts, and if
they do not see it through, and Indochina passes into the hands of the
Communists, the ultimate effect on our and your global strategic position
with the consequent shift in the power ratio throughout Asia and the
Pacific could be disastrous and, I know, unacceptable to you and me. It
is difficult to see how Thailand, Burma and Indonesia could be kept
out of Communist hands. This we cannot afford. The threat to Malaya,
Australia and New Zealand would be direct. The offshore island chain
would be broken. The economic pressure on Japan which would be
deprived of non-Communist markets and sources of food and raw material would be such, over a period of time, that it is difficult to see how
Japan could be prevented from reaching an accommodation with the
Communist world which would combine the manpower and natural
resources of Asia with the industrial potential of Japan. This has led us
to the hard conclusion that the situation in Southeast Asia requires us
urgently to take serious and far-reaching decisions.

Geneva is less than four weeks away. There the possibility of the
Communists driving a wedge between us will, given the state of mind in
France, be infinitely greater than at Berlin. I can understand the very
natural desire of the French to seek an end to this war which has been
bleeding them for eight years. But our painstaking search for a way out
of the impasse has reluctantly forced us to the conclusion that there is
no negotiated solution of the Indochina problem which in its essence
would not be either a face-saving device to cover a French surrender or
a face-saving device to cover a Communist retirement. The first alternative is too serious in its broad strategic implications for us and for you to
be acceptable. Apart from its effects in Southeast Asia itself, where you
and the Commonwealth have direct and vital interests, it would have the
most serious repercussions in North Africa, in Europe and elsewhere.
Here at home it would cause a wide-spread loss of confidence in the
cooperative system. I think it is not too much to say that the future of

France as a great power would be fatally affected. Perhaps France will never again be the great power it was, but a sudden vacuum wherever French power is, would be difficult for us to cope with.

Somehow we must contrive to bring about the second alternative. The preliminary lines of our thinking were sketched out by [Secretary of State John Foster Dulles] in his speech last Monday night when he said that under the conditions of today the imposition on Southeast Asia of the political system of Communist Russia and its Chinese Communist ally, by whatever means, would be a grave threat to the whole free community, and that in our view this possibility should now be met by united action and not passively accepted. He has also talked intimately with Roger Makins.

I believe that the best way to put teeth in this concept and to bring greater moral and material resources to the support of the French effort is through the establishment of a new ad hoc grouping or coalition composed of nations which have a vital concern in the checking of Communist expansion in the area. I have in mind in addition to our two countries, France, the Associated States, Australia, New Zealand, Thailand and the Philippines. The United States Government would expect to play its full part in such a coalition. The coalition we have in mind would not be directed against Communist China. But if, contrary to our belief, our efforts to save Indochina and the British Commonwealth position to the south should in any way increase the jeopardy to Hong Kong, we would expect to be with you there. I suppose that the United Nations should somewhere be recognized, but I am not confident that, given the Soviet veto, it could act with needed speed and vigor.

I would contemplate no role for Formosa or the Republic of Korea in the political construction of this coalition.

The important thing is that the coalition must be strong and it must be willing to join the fight if necessary. I do not envisage the need of any appreciable ground forces on your or our part. If the members of the alliance are sufficiently resolute it should be able to make clear to the Chinese Communists that the continuation of their material support to the Viet Minh will inevitably lead to the growing power of the forces arrayed against them.

My colleagues and I are deeply aware of the risks which this proposal may involve but in the situation which confronts us there is no course of action or inaction devoid of dangers and I know of no man who has firmly grasped more nettles than you. If we grasp this one together I believe that we will enormously increase our chances of bringing the Chinese to believe that their interests lie in the direction of a discreet disengagement. In such a contingency we could approach the Geneva conference with the position of the free world not only unimpaired but strengthened.

Today we face the hard situation of contemplating a disaster brought on by French weakness and the necessity of dealing with it before it develops. This means frank talk with the French. In many ways the situation corresponds to that which you describe so brilliantly in the second chapter of "Their Finest Hour," when history made clear that the French strategy and dispositions before the 1940 breakthrough should have been challenged before the blow fell.

I regret adding to your problems. But in fact it is not I, but our enemies who add to them. I have faith that by another act of fellowship in the face of peril we shall find a spiritual vigor which will prevent our slipping into the quagmire of distrust.

If I may refer again to history, we failed to halt Hirohito, Mussolini and Hitler by not acting in unity and in time. That marked the beginning of many years of stark tragedy and desperate peril. May it not be that our nations have learned something from the lesson?

So profoundly do I believe that the effectiveness of the coalition principle is at stake that I am prepared to send Foster or Bedell to visit you this week, at the earliest date convenient to you. Whoever comes would spend a day in Paris to avoid French pique. The cover would be preparation for Geneva.

8

Hell in a Very Small Place

Bernard B. Fall, a Frenchman who was to be one of the early opponents of the American war in Vietnam, here describes the effect in France of the fall of its fortress at Dien Bien Phu. That defeat did not leave France in a hopeless military position in Vietnam but confirmed the opinion that the time had arrived for a negotiated withdrawal. This edition of Fall's work

Source: Bernard B. Fall, *Hell in a Very Small Place: The Siege of Dien Bien Phu* (Philadelphia: J. B. Lippincott Company, 1967), 414–18. Reprinted by permission.

was published after the author was killed by a land mine in Vietnam.

At 0150, the command aircraft picked up the very last message a Frenchman would send from Dien Bien Phu:

> Sortie failed—Stop—Can no longer communicate with you— Stop and end.

It was the end, indeed. The end of the Indochina War. The end of France as a colonial power.

Later that night, a *Privateer* four-engine bomber of French Navy Squadron No. 28-F was shot down while bombing Viet-Minh communication lines along Road 41. Its pilot, Ensign Monguillon, and its crew of eight warrant officers and petty officers were the last Frenchmen killed in combat in the Battle of Dien Bien Phu.

Outside, May 7, 1954

There is a time-zone difference of seven hours between Paris and Dien Bien Phu. It was 1030, Paris time, on May 7, when the red flag was hoisted atop de Castries' command bunker at Dien Bien Phu. The news probably reached the French government around noon.

At 1630, the French government informed the National Assembly, France's major legislative body, that the Prime Minister would present it with an important communication. At 1645, the sixty-five-year-old Joseph Laniel, the bull-necked Norman who had become prime minister in June, 1953, mounted the tribune, escorted by several of his cabinet ministers. The Prime Minister was dressed entirely in black. The news of the disaster already had reached Paris and the hemicycle was filled with legislators. Every seat in the visitors' gallery and in the press section was taken.

The Prime Minister said in a voice which he vainly attempted to control and which was at first so low as to be barely audible even with the help of the public address system:

> The Government has been informed that the central position of Dien Bien Phu has fallen after twenty hours of uninterrupted violent combat.

As he said those words, his voice broke. There was an audible gasp in the audience, and in a clatter of seats, the legislators, the visitors, and the press rose to their feet, with the exception of the ninety-five Communists and M. Charles de Chambrun, a legislator from the Progressive Party allied with the Communists.

In the dead silence which followed, punctuated only by the loud sobs of a woman legislator, Laniel continued:

> Strongpoint Isabelle is still holding. The enemy has wanted to obtain the fall of Dien Bien Phu prior to the opening of the conference on Indochina. He believes that he could strike a decisive blow against the morale of France. He has responded to our goodwill, to France's will for peace, by sacrificing thousands of [his] soldiers to crush under their number the heroes who, for fifty-five days, have excited the admiration of the world . . .
>
> . . . France must remind her allies that for seven years now the Army of the French Union has unceasingly protected a particularly crucial region of Asia and has alone defended the interests of all. All of France shares the anguish of the families of the fighters of Dien Bien Phu. Their heroism has reached such heights that universal conscience should dictate to the enemy—in favor of the wounded and of those whose courage entitles them to the honors of war—such decisions as will contribute more than anything to establish a climate favorable to peace.

The news of the disaster covered France like a thick blanket. Maurice Cardinal Feltin, the Archbishop of Paris, ordered a solemn Mass to be said for the dead and prisoners of Dien Bien Phu. The Paris Opéra, which was to be the host for the first time since the end of World War II to the Moscow Opera Ballet, canceled the whole series of Russian performances. French television—in France both radio and television are government-controlled—canceled its programs for the evening and the three radio networks canceled all entertainment shows and replaced them with programs of French classical music, and notably Hector Berlioz' *Requiem*. It was the only Requiem which the thousands of dead of Dien Bien Phu were ever going to get.

In Nice, on the French Riviera, the Chief of State of the non-Communist Vietnamese regime, Bao Dai (whose name, in translation, means "Keeper of Greatness," but who preferred the life of the French Riviera to the chores of facing a war in Viet-Nam), issued a statement of his own in which he thanked the French for the sacrifices they had made:

> Now that France has recognized the independence of Viet-Nam, no one can have any doubts as to the unselfish nobleness of

A French soldier watches as reinforcements and supplies land at Dien Bien Phu, near the Laotian border. The Vietminh's ability to put artillery on top of the hills (shown in the background) led to the French defeat in a decisive battle in the spring of 1954. *(Courtesy, U.P.I.)*

her defense of the Vietnamese people and of the Free World . . .
The French can be assured that Viet-Nam shall not forget the sacrifices of France.

In Saigon, there was a double rush. On one hand, a call-up of
120,000 young Vietnamese had brought in only 7,000 draftees, of whom
5,000 were declared unfit for service. And the news of the defeat brought
an avalanche of Vietnamese and French bank transfers to Hong Kong,
where the Vietnamese piaster suddenly rose from a black market rate of
about sixty to the U.S. dollar to eighty-five.

The news of the fall of Dien Bien Phu hit the United States too late
for the morning newspapers of May 7—but that is precisely what makes
them doubly interesting. For Dien Bien Phu had in fact disappeared as
front-page news a great deal earlier. While the French were dying on
the Elianes, America was glued to its television sets, watching the now-
deceased junior senator from Wisconsin grilling the Secretary of the
Army and an Army general as to why an obscure Army dentist with
alleged left-wing leanings had been routinely promoted from captain to
major. At the very moment when the Viet-Minh mine gallery blew up
Eliane 2, Dien Bien Phu made page 6 of America's most respected
newspaper.

On the day that Dien Bien Phu fell, Senator McCarthy challenged
the right of the Executive to keep secret data from Congress, and Dien
Bien Phu rated page 3. However, a senator from Texas, Lyndon B.
Johnson, made a speech before the annual Jefferson-Jackson Day Democratic dinner in Washington, in the course of which he clearly showed
the beginnings of a deep interest in Viet-Nam, which was to grow after
he became President:

What is American policy on Indochina?

All of us have listened to the dismal series of reversals and
confusions and alarms and excursions which have emerged from
Washington over the past few weeks.

It is apparent only that American foreign policy has never in
all its history suffered such a stunning reversal.

We have been caught bluffing by our enemies, our friends and
Allies are frightened and wondering, as we do, where we are
headed.

We stand in clear danger of being left naked and alone in a
hostile world.

. . . This picture of our country needlessly weakened in the
world today is so painful that we should turn our eyes from abroad
and look homeward.

Coming after his crucial intervention of April 3, the May 6 speech of the future president committed him to a certain position on the Viet-Nam problem. Once president, Lyndon B. Johnson, contrary to the opinions of those who have denied him a deep knowledge of foreign affairs, acted in accordance with the lessons he had learned from Dien Bien Phu: there would be no American Dien Bien Phu as long as he could help it.

At 2130, EDT, Secretary of State Dulles gave an account of recent events to the American people, in which he paid brief homage to de Castries and his men:

> The French soldiers showed that they have not lost either the will or the skill to fight even under the most adverse conditions. It shows that Viet-Nam produces soldiers who have the qualities to enable them to defend their country.

In his speech, Secretary Dulles was also careful to lay the blame for American failure to act both on British Prime Minister Churchill's failure to agree to united action in Viet-Nam prior to the Geneva Conference, and upon the U.S. Congress as well. Here again, what Dulles had to say was of crucial importance in the shaping of the American commitment to Viet-Nam a decade later:

> In making commitments which might involve the use of armed force, the Congress is a full partner. Only the Congress can declare war. President Eisenhower has repeatedly emphasized that he would not take military action in Indochina without the support of Congress. Furthermore, he has made clear that he would not seek that unless, in his opinion, there would be an adequate collective effort based on genuine mutuality of purpose in defending vital interests.

In other words, the French defeat at Dien Bien Phu would be written off and the negotiations at Geneva would be allowed to take their pre-ordained course.

It was left to *Life* magazine to find at least something of a bright aspect to the end of the fortress. "The single ray of hope over the graves of Dien Bien Phu," said the periodical in its issue of May 17, 1954, "is the fact that one obstacle to united action—the heroic stubbornness of France—has been removed."

9

A Tough Line on Geneva

In a memorandum of May 9, 1954, to President Dwight D. Eisenhower's Secretary of Defense Charles E. Wilson, Brigadier General C. H. Bonesteel III as a member of the National Security Council planning board argues against compromise with the Vietminh at the Geneva conference.

1. In light of the French having tabled an armistice proposal at Geneva, the United States must now decide whether:

    a. To intervene actively in the Indo-China war to redeem the situation.

    b. To exercise all feasible pressure to require the French Government to avoid all compromise at Geneva and to take increased effective military and political action against the Viet Minh in Indo-China. This appears realistically possible only if the decision to implement *a* above is also made.

    c. To adopt a passive policy toward the negotiations at Geneva while endeavoring to organize hastily a regional grouping, with U.S. participation, to hold what remains of Southeast Asia.

2. Decisions *a* plus *b* offer the only sure way to stop the Communist advance. They involve substantial risk of war with Red China and increased risk of general war. However, recognizing the steadily increasing Soviet capabilities in nuclear warfare and the consequent steady diminution of the present military advantage of the U.S. over the USSR, these increased risks can more surely and safely be accepted now than ever again.

3. Decision *c* would be a compromise involving clear possibilities for piecemeal advancement of Communist control over the balance of free Asia despite the best efforts of the U.S. to the contrary. The likelihood of further such advancement would be somewhat diminished if the U.S. made publicly clear that the further support by Moscow and Peiping of Communist aggression or subversion, as judged by the U.S., would

Source: The Senator Gravel Edition, The Pentagon Papers: The Defense Department History of United States Decisionmaking in Vietnam (Boston: Beacon Press, 1971), I, Document 46, 506.

entail direct military action by the U.S. against the source or sources of this support. However, it might be months or years before further subversion would enable such a U.S. judgment. By then the increased Soviet nuclear capability might well inhibit the U.S. Government from implementing its announced intention. Asia could thus be lost.

4. Therefore, it would appear that the U.S. Government must decide whether to take the steps necessary to contain Communism in Asia within Red China by intervention in Indo-China or accept the probable loss of Asia to Communism.

10

Another Cold Warrior in the State Department

Dean Acheson of President Truman's Democratic administration had been instrumental in setting the tone and the terms of the Cold War. John Foster Dulles, Acheson's successor in the State Department under the Republican President Eisenhower, continued the mood, as he reveals in this message of July 10, 1954, to French President Pierre Mendès-France arguing against giving too much at Geneva to Ho Chi Minh's Vietminh.

President Eisenhower (who has been kept closely informed) and I have been greatly moved by your earnest request that I or General Bedell Smith should return next week to Geneva for what may be the conclusion of the Indochina phase of the Conference. I can assure you that our attitude in this respect is dictated by a desire to find the course which will best preserve the traditional friendship and cooperation of our countries. . . . We also attach great value to preserving the united front of France, Great Britain and the United States which has during this postwar period so importantly served all three of us in our dealings with the Communists.

What now concerns us is that we are very doubtful as to whether there is a united front in relation to Indochina, and we do not believe that the mere fact that the high representatives of the three nations physically reappear together at Geneva will serve as a substitute for a clear agreement on a joint position which includes agreement as to what will happen if that position is not accepted by the Communists. We fear that unless

Source: Pentagon Papers, I, Document 77, 550–51.

there is the reality of such a united front, the events at Geneva will expose differences under conditions which will only serve to accentuate them with consequent strain upon the relations between our two countries . . .

. . . [We] greatly fear that the seven points which constitute a minimum as far as the US is concerned will constitute merely an optimum solution so far as your Government and perhaps the UK are concerned, and that an armistice might be concluded on terms substantially less favorable than those we could respect.

We gather that there is already considerable French thinking in terms of the acceptability of departures from certain of the seven points. For example:

Allowing Communist forces to remain in Northern Laos; accepting a Vietnam line of military demarcation considerably south of Donghoi; neutralizing and demilitarizing Laos, Cambodia and Vietnam so as to impair their capacity to maintain stable, non-Communist regimes; accepting elections so early and so ill-prepared and ill-supervised as to risk the loss of the entire area to Communism; accepting international supervision by a body which cannot be effective because it includes a Communist state which has veto power.

These are but illustrations of a whittling-away process, each stroke of which may in itself seem unessential, but which cumulatively could produce a result quite different from that envisaged by the seven points. Also, of course, there is the danger that the same unacceptable result might come about through the Communist habit of using words in a double sense and destroying the significance of good principles with stultifying implementations. . . .

11

The Communists Want the World

Walter S. Robertson was Assistant Secretary for Far Eastern Affairs under President Eisenhower. In an address on July 30, 1954, before the Virginia state convention of the American Legion, he speaks in a language that was typical of the Cold

Source: *The Department of State Bulletin*, XXXI, No. 791, August 23, 1954, 260, 262–63.

War in its earlier days. In the course of his argument that Communist China should not be admitted to the United Nations, he describes the Chinese Communists as being behind the insurgency in Vietnam. For years cold warriors would continue to believe that a victory for the Vietnamese Communists would be a victory for China. The idea that the Vietnamese Communists were prepared to put themselves under China, which historically had been a threat to Vietnam, was one of the larger errors of the period of American involvement in Indochina.

. . . What do the Communists want? The answer is "the world"—their world, our world, everything. Aside from their ideological dedication, which fires their objective of communizing the world, they have two compelling and practical reasons for striving constantly to extend their domain: (1) they need the resources of other countries and (2) they do not feel safe while any country adjoining their empire is not 100 percent Communist. If only one country in the world remained outside their grasp, the Communists would still complain that they were encircled and threatened. This is not a baseless neurosis. Tyranny has never felt secure and has never been secure as long as freedom existed anywhere. The Soviet tyranny differs from previous tyrannies only in being immeasurably more thorough. Inside the Soviet Union every effort has been made to destroy the very concept of freedom, to produce a new type of man and woman—the Soviet man and Soviet woman—who would not know what to do with freedom if they had it, any more than a member of a colony of ants or a hive of bees would know what to do with freedom. Controls over life within Soviet Russia are matched by the barriers that are maintained around Soviet Russia, which hermetically seal it off from the outside world. The aim of Soviet policy is to proceed with the "communization" of the peoples within the bounds of the Soviet empire and, at the same time, to push the bounds of that empire constantly forward to incorporate additional countries.

What the Communists mean by "peaceful coexistence"—a phrase which you hear much these days—is a state of nonwar between their world and ours, in which the process of detaching pieces of our world and absorbing them in theirs can continue with minimum risk to themselves. . . .

The Communists are dedicated to advancing their cause with a determination and single-mindedness that is hard for us even to visualize, let alone to equal. We are accustomed to seeing two sides to a case, or even three or four. And this is our pride. The Communists never see but one side. We have seen nothing in history to equal Communist fanaticism and bigotry, not even in the religious wars which at various times in the past came near to drowning various parts of the human race in blood. In the case of the Communists, however, fanaticism and bigotry are matched by a calculating, ruthless cunning. . . .

The recognition and seating of Red China in the United Nations is the cornerstone of Communist policy today—a policy aided and abetted by many free nations plus a subdued but active minority in this country. Why is our Government opposed? For the best of all reasons—

The U.N. is *not* an organization of *de facto* governments. It is an organization of nations which under its charter have renounced war as an instrument of national policy and have pledged themselves to take collective action to oppose aggression and preserve the peace. Red China is at war in Korea today. With whom? The United Nations. The war in Indochina was inflamed, supplied, and captained by Red China. The truce just concluded was negotiated with Mendès-France by Chou En-lai, the Red China Foreign Minister, not by Pham Van Dong, representing the Ho Chi Minh regime. Red China has also flagrantly violated the international obligations assumed by responsible governments. It has confiscated our properties and, incidentally, the properties of the British as well, despite Britain's prompt recognition in 1950. It has imprisoned our nationals without trial, tortured and brain-washed our soldiers. It is an outlaw-gangster regime, unpurged of its crimes and aggressions, and unfit to sit in any respectable family of nations. . . .

We shall always be under the temptation to let down our guard, to surrender our advantages, to demonstrate how amiable and accommodating we really are. For us to do so would, of course, mean the end of us all. Every day since my first intimate contact with the Communists back in 1945 I have had continuing reason to become convinced of one simple truth. That is that the only successful resistance to Communist expansionism is strength. Just as only strong societies achieve democratic self-government, only weak societies fall victim to communism. The weakness may be military or it may be political. In June 1950 we saw what happens when a country in the path of Communist expansionism is militarily weak. The Communists had tried by every artifice of subversion and penetration to undermine the Republic of Korea but had failed. They resorted, in consequence, to their military advantage and launched an attack of overwhelming force upon their victim. In Indochina we have seen the consequences of political weakness on the anti-Communist side. The Communists there were able to turn to their advantage the strongest political force of our times—the force of nationalism. They achieved ascendancy in the anticolonial movement because for so long the choice for the Vietnamese seemed to be between siding with Communists who were native or with the French, who were not. But military or political, it is always weakness that leads to Communist success. The free world must see to it that there are no more Koreas and no more Indochinas. . . .

12

The Geneva Accords of 1954

This version in English is of the final declaration of the Geneva Conference dated July 21, 1954. The United States was not a signatory. The agreements, of which this entry was in part a summary, were intended to provide not a final arrangement but a transition to a permanent settlement. The elections scheduled for July 1956 never took place, and the hopes vested in the Geneva accords went unfulfilled.

Final declaration, dated July 21, 1954, of the Geneva Conference on the problem of restoring peace in Indochina, in which the representatives of Cambodia, the Democratic Republic of Viet-Nam, France, Laos, the People's Republic of China, the State of Viet-Nam, the Union of Soviet Socialist Republics, the United Kingdom, and the United States of America took part.

   1. The Conference takes note of the agreements ending hostilities in Cambodia, Laos, and Viet-Nam and organizing international control and the supervision of the execution of the provisions of these agreements.

   2. The Conference expresses satisfaction at the ending of hostilities in Cambodia, Laos, and Viet-Nam. The Conference expresses its conviction that the execution of the provisions set out in the present declaration and in the agreements on the cessation of hostilities will permit Cambodia, Laos, and Viet-Nam henceforth to play their part, in full independence and sovereignty, in the peaceful community of nations.

   3. The Conference takes note of the declarations made by the Governments of Cambodia and of Laos of their intention to adopt measures permitting all citizens to take their place in the national community, in particular by participating in the next general elections, which, in

Source: The Department of State Bulletin, XXXI, No. 788, August 2, 1954, 164.

conformity with the constitution of each of these countries, shall take place in the course of the year 1955, by secret ballot and in conditions of respect for fundamental freedoms.

4. The Conference takes note of the clauses in the agreement on the cessation of hostilities in Viet-Nam prohibiting the introduction into Viet-Nam of foreign troops and military personnel as well as of all kinds of arms and munitions. The Conference also takes note of the declarations made by the Governments of Cambodia and Laos of their resolution not to request foreign aid, whether in war material, in personnel, or in instructors except for the purpose of effective defense of their territory and, in the case of Laos, to the extent defined by the agreements on the cessation of hostilities in Laos.

5. The Conference takes note of the clauses in the agreement on the cessation of hostilities in Viet-Nam to the effect that no military base at the disposition of a foreign state may be established in the regrouping zones of the two parties, the latter having the obligation to see that the zones allotted to them shall not constitute part of any military alliance and shall not be utilized for the resumption of hostilities or in the service of an aggressive policy. The Conference also takes note of the declarations of the Governments of Cambodia and Laos to the effect that they will not join in any agreement with other states if this agreement includes the obligation to participate in a military alliance not in conformity with the principles of the charter of the United Nations or, in the case of Laos, with the principles of the agreement on the cessation of hostilities in Laos or, so long as their security is not threatened, the obligation to establish bases on Cambodian or Laotian territory for the military forces of foreign powers.

6. The Conference recognizes that the essential purpose of the agreement relating to Viet-Nam is to settle military questions with a view to ending hostilities and that the military demarcation line should not in any way be interpreted as constituting a political or territorial boundary. The Conference expresses its conviction that the execution of the provisions set out in the present declaration and in the agreement on the cessation of hostilities creates the necessary basis for the achievement in the near future of a political settlement in Viet-Nam.

7. The Conference declares that, so far as Viet-Nam is concerned, the settlement of political problems, affected on the basis of respect for the principles of independence, unity, and territorial integrity, shall permit the Vietnamese people to enjoy the fundamental freedoms, guaranteed by democratic institutions established as a result of free general elections by secret ballot.

In order to ensure that sufficient progress in the restoration of peace has been made, and that all the necessary conditions obtain for free expression of the national will, general elections shall be held in July 1956, under the supervision of an international commission composed of representatives of the member states of the International Supervisory Commission referred to in the agreement on the cessation of hostilities. Consultations will be held on this subject between the competent representative authorities of the two zones from April 20, 1955, onwards.

8. The provisions of the agreements on the cessation of hostilities intended to ensure the protection of individuals and of property must be most strictly applied and must, in particular, allow everyone in Viet-Nam to decide freely in which zone he wishes to live.

9. The competent representative authorities of the northern and southern zones of Viet-Nam, as well as the authorities of Laos and Cambodia, must not permit any individual or collective reprisals against persons who have collaborated in any way with one of the parties during the war, or against members of such persons' families.

10. The Conference takes note of the declaration of the French Government to the effect that it is ready to withdraw its troops from the territory of Cambodia, Laos, and Viet-Nam, at the request of the governments concerned and within a period which shall be fixed by agreement between the parties except in the cases where, by agreement between the two parties, a certain number of French troops shall remain at specified points and for a specified time.

11. The Conference takes note of the declaration of the French Government to the effect that for the settlement of all the problems connected with the reestablishment and consolidation of peace in Cambodia, Laos, and Viet-Nam, the French Government will proceed from the principle of respect for the independence and sovereignty, unity, and territorial integrity of Cambodia, Laos, and Viet-Nam.

12. In their relations with Cambodia, Laos, and Viet-Nam, each member of the Geneva Conference undertakes to respect the sovereignty, the independence, the unity and the territorial integrity of the above-mentioned states, and to refrain from any interference in their internal affairs.

13. The members of the Conference agree to consult one another on any question which may be referred to them by the International Supervisory Commission, in order to study such measures as may prove necessary to ensure that the agreements on the cessation of hostilities in Cambodia, Laos, and Viet-Nam are respected.

Part 2
INVOLVEMENT

The question of how or why the United States became involved in Vietnam will doubtless be an issue for years to come, particularly for people who believe that learning the mistakes of American involvement will aid in avoiding similar mistakes in the future. A common error, however, is to read history backward: to assume, for example, that because the American enterprise in Vietnam turned out to be a disaster, it could have been predicted to be a disaster and future Vietnams will have a similar predictability.

Dean Acheson in 1949, John Foster Dulles in 1954, John Kennedy in 1963, and Lyndon Johnson in 1964 had no way of foreseeing the Tet offensive of 1968 or the surrender of the Saigon government to the Communists in 1975. One thing they did know about was the vicious repressiveness of Communist regimes, which argued for opposing the spread of Communism in South Vietnam. Another thing they knew about was the extraordinary wealth of the West, more especially the United States, and the enormous sophistication of American warfare and weaponry. That gave some plausibility to the belief that in a clash of arms with the Vietnamese Communists, the French in 1954 or the Americans in the 1960s could be successful.

There is, however, at least one fact that was available to Acheson and later cold warriors that might have dissuaded them from attributing so much importance to the defeat of Ho Chi Minh. Ho in his years of struggle had acted not only as a Communist but as a Vietnamese nationalist and a potent personal symbol of the independence of the Vietnamese nation. He and the forces that gathered to him did not owe their primary allegiance to Moscow, or the Chinese Communists, or the abstractions of Karl Marx. They represented the desire of countless Vietnamese to be free both of foreign domination and of crushing poverty. If the United States had understood this—and the evidence making possible an understanding of it was accessible well before 1949—very much pain and death could have been spared.

That may provide the best and only lesson out of the American experience in Vietnam that has any permanence to it. Before you go to war, find out in careful detail what your prospective enemies are like and what they want. Then you can better decide whether going to war has any point.

Each of the selections here is intended to mark off a moment in which the American involvement in Vietnam deepened or to define the reasons that government officials gave to one another for continuing or modifying that involvement.

President Ngo Dinh Diem (second from right), dressed in his customary white suit, seen with his Finance Minister, Tan Huu Phuong, after receiving an American aid check for $11,720,000. U.S. Ambassador G. Frederick Reinhardt stands at the right in this 1955 photo while Justice William O. Douglas and Leland Barrows of the U.S. Aid Mission look on from the left. *(Courtesy, Wide World Photo)*

13

A Plea for Aid

This letter of December 7, 1961, to President Kennedy from South Vietnamese President Ngo Dinh Diem condemning Communist aggression in cold-war fashion also presents the claim that the anticommunist forces represent genuine Vietnamese nationalism. This fusion of arguments is an indication of the nationalist alternatives to Communism that cold warriors tried to find in Third-World regions.

DEAR MR. PRESIDENT: Since its birth, more than six years ago, the Republic of Viet-Nam has enjoyed the close friendship and cooperation of the United States of America.

Like the United States, the Republic of Viet-Nam has always been devoted to the preservation of peace. My people know only too well the sorrows of war. We have honored the 1954 Geneva Agreements even though they resulted in the partition of our country and the enslavement of more than half of our people by Communist tyranny. We have never considered the reunification of our nation by force. On the contrary, we have publicly pledged that we will not violate the demarcation line and the demilitarized zone set up by the agreements. We have always been prepared and have on many occasions stated our willingness to reunify Viet-Nam on the basis of democratic and truly free elections.

The record of the Communist authorities in the northern part of our country is quite otherwise. They not only consented to the division of Viet-Nam, but were eager for it. They pledged themselves to observe the Geneva Agreements and during the seven years since have never ceased to violate them. They call for free elections but are ignorant of the very meaning of the words. They talk of "peaceful reunification" and wage war against us.

From the beginning, the Communists resorted to terror in their efforts to subvert our people, destroy our government, and impose a

---

Source: The Department of State Bulletin, XLVI, No. 1175, January 1, 1962, 13–14.

Communist regime upon us. They have attacked defenseless teachers, closed schools, killed members of our anti-malarial program and looted hospitals. This is coldly calculated to destroy our government's humanitarian efforts to serve our people. . . .

In the course of the last few months, the Communist assault on my people has achieved high ferocity. . . . They have struck occasionally in battalion strength and they are continually augmenting their forces by infiltration from the North. . . .

A disastrous flood was recently added to the misfortunes of the Vietnamese people. The greater part of three provinces was inundated, with a great loss of property. We are now engaged in a nationwide effort to reconstruct and rehabilitate this area. The Communists are, of course, making this task doubly difficult, for they have seized upon the disruption of normal administration and communications as an opportunity to sow more destruction in the stricken area.

In short, the Vietnamese nation now faces what is perhaps the gravest crisis in its long history. For more than 2,000 years my people have lived and built, fought and died in this land. We have not always been free. Indeed, much of our history and many of its proudest moments have arisen from conquest by foreign powers and our struggle against great odds to regain or defend our precious independence. But it is not only our freedom which is at stake today, it is our national identity. For, if we lose this war, our people will be swallowed by the Communist Bloc, all our proud heritage will be blotted out by the "Socialist society" and Viet-Nam will leave the pages of history. We will lose our national soul.

Mr. President, my people and I are mindful of the great assistance which the United States has given us. Your help has not been lightly received, for the Vietnamese are proud people, and we are determined to do our part in the defense of the free world. It is clear to all of us that the defeat of the Viet Cong demands the total mobilization of our government and our people, and you may be sure that we will devote all of our resources of money, minds, and men to this great task.

But Viet-Nam is not a great power and the forces of International Communism now arrayed against us are more than we can meet with the resources at hand. We must have further assistance from the United States if we are to win the war now being waged against us.

We can certainly assure mankind that our action is purely defensive. Much as we regret the subjugation of more than half of our people in North Viet-Nam, we have no intention, and indeed no means, to free them by use of force.

I have said that Viet-Nam is at war. War means many things, but most of all it means the death of brave people for a cause they believe in. Viet-Nam has suffered many wars, and through the centuries we have always had patriots and heroes who were willing to shed their blood for Viet-Nam. We will keep faith with them.

When Communism has long ebbed away into the past, my people will still be here, a free united nation growing from the deep roots of our Vietnamese heritage. They will remember your help in our time of need. This struggle will then be a part of our common history. And your help, your friendship, and the strong bonds between our two peoples will be a part of Viet-Nam, then as now.

14

President Kennedy Replies

In this White House press release dated December 14 for release the next day, President Kennedy replies favorably to President Diem's request. It is reasonable to assume that the two letters were preplanned between Washington and Saigon as a way of presenting the public with an argument for aid that Kennedy had already decided to send.

DEAR MR. PRESIDENT: I have received your recent letter in which you described so cogently the dangerous condition caused by North Viet-Nam's efforts to take over your country. The situation in your embattled country is well known to me and to the American people. We have been deeply disturbed by the assault on your country. Our indignation has mounted as the deliberate savagery of the Communist program of assassination, kidnapping and wanton violence became clear.

Your letter underlines what our own information has convincingly shown—that the campaign of force and terror now being waged against your people and your Government is supported and directed from the outside by the authorities at Hanoi. They have thus violated the provisions of the Geneva Accords designed to ensure peace in Viet-Nam and to which they bound themselves in 1954.

At that time, the United States, although not a party to the Accords, declared that it "would view any renewal of the aggression in violation

Source: The Department of State Bulletin, XLVI, No. 1175, January 1, 1962, 13.

of the agreements with grave concern and as seriously threatening international peace and security.'' We continue to maintain that view.

In accordance with that declaration, and in response to your request, we are prepared to help the Republic of Viet-Nam to protect its people and to preserve its independence. We shall promptly increase our assistance to your defense effort as well as help relieve the destruction of the floods which you describe. I have already given the orders to get these programs underway.

The United States, like the Republic of Viet-Nam, remains devoted to the cause of peace and our primary purpose is to help your people maintain their independence. If the Communist authorities in North Viet-Nam will stop their campaign to destroy the Republic of Viet-Nam, the measures we are taking to assist your defense efforts will no longer be necessary. We shall seek to persuade the Communists to give up their attempts of force and subversion. In any case, we are confident that the Vietnamese people will preserve their independence and gain the peace and prosperity for which they have sought so hard and so long.

An American military adviser on patrol with South Vietnamese troops. By 1968, over half a million U.S. troops were fighting the unconventional war against Vietcong guerrilla forces. *(Courtesy, U.S. Army)*

15

A Warning

Here, in a memorandum to President Kennedy dated April 4, 1962, the economist and United States ambassador to India John Kenneth Galbraith warns against rash commitments in Vietnam. The memo is an instance of a cautionary note sounded from time to time within the government.

The following considerations influence our thinking on Viet-Nam:

1. We have a growing military commitment. This could expand step by step into a major, long-drawn out indecisive military involvement.

2. We are backing a weak and, on the record, ineffectual government and a leader who as a politician may be beyond the point of no return.

3. There is consequent danger we shall replace the French as the colonial force in the area and bleed as the French did.

4. The political effects of some of the measures which pacification requires or is believed to require, including the concentration of population, relocation of villages, and the burning of old villages, may be damaging to those and especially to Westerners associated with it.

5. We fear that at some point in the involvement there will be a major political outburst about the new Korea and the new war into which the Democrats as so often before have precipitated us.

6. It seems at least possible that the Soviets are not particularly desirous of trouble in this part of the world and that our military reaction with the need to fall back on Chinese protection may be causing concern in Hanoi.

In the light of the foregoing we urge the following:

1. That it be our policy to keep open the door for political solution. We should welcome as a solution any broadly based non-Communist government that is free from external interference. It should have the requisites for internal law and order. We should not require that it be militarily identified with the United States.

2. We shall find it useful in achieving this result if we seize any good opportunity to involve other countries and world opinion in settlement and its guarantee. This is a useful exposure and pressure on the Commu-

Source: Pentagon Papers, II, Document 112, 670.

nist bloc countries and a useful antidote for the argument that this is a private American military adventure.

3. We should measurably reduce our commitment to the particular present leadership of the government of South Viet-Nam. . . .

16

A Reply

Caution such as Galbraith urges in the selection preceding this one was not to prevail in American policy. This reply to Galbraith by Admiral L. L. Lemnitzer, chairman of the Joint Chiefs of Staff, represents the more conventional government thought about Vietnam. Lemnitzer's note to Secretary of Defense Robert S. McNamara bears the date April 13, 1962.

1. Reference is made to a memorandum by the Assistant Secretary of Defense (ISA) dated 10 April 1962, requesting comments on a memorandum to the President by the Honorable J. K. Galbraith, US Ambassador to India, wherein he proposes changes to the present US policy toward Vietnam and the government of President Diem.

2. The burden of Mr. Galbraith's proposals appears to be that present US policy toward Vietnam should be revised in order to seek a political solution to the problem of communist penetration in the area. The effect of these proposals is to put the United States in a position of initiating negotiations with the communists to seek disengagement from what is by now a well-known commitment to take a forthright stand against Communism in Southeast Asia.

3. The President of the United States and the Secretary of Defense both have recently and publicly affirmed the intention of the US Government to support the government of President Diem and the people of South Vietnam to whatever extend may be necessary to eliminate the Viet Cong threat. In his letter of 14 December 1961 to President Diem, President Kennedy said:

Source: Pentagon Papers, II, Document 113, 671–72.

Your (President Diem's) letter underlines what our own information has convincingly shown—that the campaign of force and terror now being waged against your people and your Government is supported and directed from the outside by the authorities at Hanoi. They have thus violated the provisions of the Geneva Accords designed to ensure peace in Vietnam and to which they bound themselves in 1954.

At that time, the United States, although not a party to the Accords, declared that it would view any renewal of the aggression in violation of the agreements with grave concern and as seriously threatening international peace and security. We continue to maintain that view.

In accordance with that declaration, and in response to your request, we are prepared to help the Republic of Vietnam to protect its people and to preserve its independence.

4. The various measures approved for implementation by the United States in support of our objectives in South Vietnam have not yet been underway long enough to demonstrate their full effectiveness. Any reversal of US policy could have disastrous effects, not only upon our relationship with South Vietnam, but with the rest of our Asian and other allies as well.

5. The problems raised by Mr. Galbraith with regard to our present policy have been considered in the coordinated development of that policy. The Joint Chiefs of Staff are aware of the deficiencies of the present government of South Vietnam. However, the President's policy of supporting the Diem regime while applying pressure for reform appears to be the only practicable alternative at this time. In this regard, the views of the Joint Chiefs of Staff as expressed in JCSM-33-62 are reaffirmed.

6. It is the opinion of the Joint Chiefs of Staff that the present US policy toward South Vietnam, as announced by the President, should be pursued vigorously to a successful conclusion.

17

Dissent Among the Buddhists

A high-ranking air force officer and President of South Viet-
nam especially known for military swagger, Nguyen Cao Ky
as an exile from Vietnam describes Diem's trouble with the
Buddhists. The Nhu referred to here is Ngo Dinh Nhu, Diem's
brother and a powerful member of his government, whose
beautiful and publicly aggressive wife was a figure by herself.
The clash between the Buddhists and Diem's government—he
and his brother were Roman Catholic—constituted one of the
major sources of turmoil during the later days of his regime.

. . . Roughly eleven million of the country's fifteen million people
were Buddhists but only about one in four of them—about four million—were practicing followers of the Buddha. As a Catholic who at
one time had been intended for the priesthood, Diem had spent much
of his time in Catholic retreats in the United States before his return to
government in Vietnam. The million Catholic refugees who crossed the
17th parallel from North Vietnam at the time of partition were among
his strongest supporters. They established themselves in Catholic communities, principally in central Vietnam, which was also the stronghold
of Buddhism. Soon the Buddhists became envious, claiming that the
newly arrived Catholics were being allotted the most fertile land and
receiving the biggest grants for schools and hospitals.

The friction between Buddhists and Catholics came to a head in 1963
in Hue, traditional seat of Buddhism in Vietnam, when rival celebrations
clashed. The Buddhists were celebrating the anniversary of the Buddha's
birth; the Catholics were commemorating the anniversary of the conse-
cration of the Archbishop of Hue. The Catholics were allowed to fly
the Vatican flag and parade sacred objects; the Buddhists were refused
permission to do the same.

On May 8, the Buddha's birthday, Buddhists converged outside the
radio station in Hue. When ordered to disperse they refused. Fire hoses
and tear gas failed to drive them away. On [Ngo Dinh] Nhu's orders
Major Dang Sy, deputy chief of the province and a Catholic, ordered
live ammunition and grenades to be issued. Nine Buddhists died, killed

Source: Nguyen Cao Ky, *Twenty Years and Twenty Days* (New York: Stein and Day,
1976), 34–36. Reprinted by permission.

by Sy's forces according to the Buddhist leaders, by Communist grenades according to Nhu.

The fuse was lit. In Saigon a saffron-robed priest had himself soaked in gasoline and then committed sacrificial suicide by fire at a busy road junction. Six more were to follow his example. The dramatic newsreel and press pictures went around the world and the world was horrified. Students in Saigon and Hue, not notably militant before, took to the streets in demonstrations. Diem acceded to certain Buddhist demands, including their right to fly flags, but Nhu called him a coward for these concessions.

It was at this moment that Madame Nhu uttered the words that made her one of the most despised women of our age, when she cried, "I would clap my hands at seeing another monk barbecue show."

According to Nhu, the Buddhists were merely seeking publicity and were influenced by Communists. Dying for a cause did not make it just, he declared, and determined to teach the Buddhists a lesson. On August 21, 1963, he acted ferociously. Using white-uniformed Special Forces and combat police—largely paid for by American money—he stormed the Xa Loi and other venerated Buddhist pagodas throughout the country. In all, 1,400 men, mostly monks, were dragged to jails where they

A Buddhist priest immolates himself in protest against the Diem regime's religious persecution. Buddhist protests were a leading factor in toppling the Diem regime in 1963. *(Courtesy, United Press International Photos)*

were beaten, half starved, sometimes subjected to electric shock torture. The American embassy was horrified, and taken completely by surprise. This was no accident. To make sure the Americans could not interfere during the long hours of the night, Nhu's men cut all the phone wires to the embassy.

That was the night of the pagodas. The following evening Henry Cabot Lodge arrived as American ambassador, succeeding Ambassador Frederick Nolting. That was the week when finally the Americans decided to get rid of their protégé, not by ordering Diem out of office, which would smack of colonialism (and would have outraged the Vietnamese) but by the simpler method of backing a group of generals who had long been planning a coup.

18

A Veiled Suggestion

This telegram of August 24, 1963, from the State Department to Henry Cabot Lodge, who was then American ambassador to South Vietnam, contains what must be one of the most remarkable suggestions in American diplomatic history. In effect, the document proposes that Lodge speak to the South Vietnamese military about the possibility of arranging a coup against the government of which Lodge was a guest. The unrest brought on by the actions Diem's brother Ngo Dinh Nhu was taking against the Buddhists was perceived as obstructing the effort to contain the Communists. On November 2, elements in the military overthrew Diem's regime and executed him and Nhu.

It is now clear that whether military proposed martial law or whether Nhu tricked them into it, Nhu took advantage of its imposition to smash pagodas with police and Tung's Special Forces loyal to him, thus placing onus on military in eyes of world and Vietnamese people. Also clear that Nhu has maneuvered himself into commanding position.

Source: Pentagon Papers, II, Document 126, 734–35.

US Government cannot tolerate situation in which power lies in Nhu's hands. Diem must be given chance to rid himself of Nhu and his coterie and replace them with best military and political personalities available.

If, in spite of all of your efforts, Diem remains obdurate and refuses, then we must face the possibility that Diem himself cannot be preserved.

We now believe immediate action must be taken to prevent Nhu from consolidating his position further. Therefore, unless you in consultation with Harkins perceive overriding objections you are authorized to proceed along following lines:

1. First, we must press on appropriate levels of GVN following line:

   a. USG cannot accept actions against Buddhists taken by Nhu and his collaborators under cover martial law.
   b. Prompt dramatic actions redress situation must be taken, including repeal of decree 10, release of arrested monks, nuns, etc.

2. We must at same time also tell key military leaders that US would find it impossible to continue support GVN militarily and economically unless above steps are taken immediately which we recognize requires removal of Nhus from the scene. We wish give Diem reasonable opportunity to remove Nhus, but if he remains obdurate, then we are prepared to accept the obvious implication that we can no longer support Diem. You may also tell appropriate military commanders we will give them direct support in any interim period of breakdown central government mechanism.

3. We recognize the necessity of removing taint on military for pagoda raids and placing blame squarely on Nhu. You are authorized to have such statement made in Saigon as you consider desirable to achieve this objective. We are prepared to take same line here and to have Voice of America make statement along lines contained in next numbered telegram whenever you give the word, preferably as soon as possible.

Concurrently, with above, Ambassador and country team should urgently examine all possible alternative leadership and make detailed plans as to how we might bring about Diem's replacement if this should become necessary.

Assume you will consult with General Harkins re any precautions necessary protect American personnel during crisis period.

You will understand that we cannot from Washington give you detailed instructions as to how this operation should proceed, but you will also know we will back you to the hilt on actions you take to achieve our objectives.

Needless to say we have held knowledge of this telegram to minimum essential people and assume you will take similar precautions to prevent premature leaks.

19

Gulf of Tonkin Resolution, August 7, 1964

This resolution, which passed the Senate with only two dissenting votes and the House of Representatives with no opposing votes, gave President Johnson a degree of legal cover for his subsequent escalation of the American presence in Vietnam. The occasion for it was the military clash between the United States and North Vietnam that had just taken place in the Gulf. Opponents were later to argue not only that the resolution was unwise but also that it was of no legal force.

To promote the maintenance of international peace and security in southeast Asia.

Whereas naval units of the Communist regime in Vietnam, in violation of the principles of the Charter of the United Nations and of international law, have deliberately and repeatedly attacked United States naval vessels lawfully present in international waters, and have thereby created a serious threat to international peace; and

Whereas these attacks are part of a deliberate and systematic campaign of aggression that the Communist regime in North Vietnam has been waging against its neighbors and the nations joined with them in the collective defense of their freedom; and

Whereas the United States is assisting the peoples of southeast Asia to protect their freedom and has no territorial, military or political ambitions in that area, but desires only that these peoples should be left in peace to work out their own destinies in their own way: Now, therefore, be it

Resolved by the Senate and House of Representatives of the United States of America in Congress assembled, That the Congress approves

Source: The Department of State Bulletin, LI, No. 1313, August 24, 1964, 268.

and supports the determination of the President, as Commander in Chief, to take all necessary measures to repel any armed attack against the forces of the United States and to prevent further aggression.

SEC. 2. The United States regards as vital to its national interest and to world peace the maintenance of international peace and security in southeast Asia. Consonant with the Constitution of the United States and the Charter of the United Nations and in accordance with its obligations under the Southeast Asia Collective Defense Treaty, the United States is, therefore, prepared, as the President determines, to take all necessary steps, including the use of armed force, to assist any member or protocol state of the Southeast Asia Collective Defense Treaty requesting assistance in defense of its freedom.

SEC. 3. This resolution shall expire when the President shall determine that the peace and security of the area is reasonably assured by international conditions created by action of the United Nations or otherwise, except that it may be terminated earlier by concurrent resolution of the Congress.

20

An Argument for Involvement

William P. Bundy of the State Department was chairman of a working group of the National Security Council charged with considering possible courses of action in Southeast Asia. Bundy submitted to Vice Admiral L. M. Mustin, a member of the group, a draft of a statement on the subject. Mustin found it insufficiently committed to sustaining the anticommunist cause in Indochina. In this document of November 10, 1964, Mustin includes statements from the draft, interspersed with his own comments about them.

US Objectives and the Present Basis of US Action

In South Viet-Nam we are helping a government defend its independence. In Laos, we are working to preserve, in its essence, an inter-

Source: Pentagon Papers, III, Document 228, 622–24.

national neutralized settlement willfully flouted by the communist side. Paradoxically, while American opinion weights the former well ahead of the latter, there are some quarters—such as Britain and India—where the latter is a more appealing cause both legally and practically. But our basic rationale is defensible in both cases.

> *Comment:* I believe the United States is committed in the eyes of the world to both of these tasks as matters of national prestige, credibility, and honor with respect to world-wide pledges. Later material in the paper seems to agree. This then would not appear to be a subject on which we should permit ourselves to be swayed unduly by other nations' views, paradoxical or other, and possibly more useful than noting that our rationale "is defensible" would be to affirm that it needs no defense.

Behind our policy have been three factors:

a. The general principle of helping countries that try to defend their own freedom against communist subversion and attack.

b. The specific consequences of communist control of South Viet-Nam and Laos for the security of, successively, Cambodia, Thailand (most seriously), Malaysia, and the Philippines—and resulting increases in the threat to India and—more in the realm of morale effects in the short term—the threat to South Korea and perhaps the GRC, and the effect on Japanese attitudes through any development that appears to make Communist China and its allies a dominant force in Asia that must be lived with.

c. South Viet-Nam, and to a lesser extent, Laos, as test cases of communist "wars of national liberation" world-wide.

> *Comment:* The third factor above, which is broadly stated, is related to but appears distinguishable from what may be considered a fourth, more specific issue: Now that we are publicly, officially, and heavily committed in SVN, US prestige has been rather specifically put at issue, and requires successful defense if we are to retain a measure of free-world leadership. This thought is brought out later in the paper; it could well be listed here as part of the subject introduction.

In other words, our policy toward South Viet-Nam and Laos is an integral part of our over-all policy of resisting Communist expansion world-wide, and a particularly close part of our policy of resisting the expansion of Communist China and its allies, North Viet-Nam and North Korea.

Thus, the loss of South Viet-Nam to Communist control, in any form, would be a major blow to our basic policies. US prestige is heavily committed to the maintenance of a non-Communist South Viet-Nam, and only less heavily so to a neutralized Laos.

Yet we must face the fact that, on any analysis we can now make, we cannot guarantee to maintain a non-Communist South Viet-Nam short of committing ourselves to whatever degree of military action would be required to defeat North Viet-Nam and probably Communist China militarily. Such a commitment would involve high risks of a major conflict in Asia, which could not be confined to air and naval action but would almost inevitably involve a Korean-scale ground action and possibly even the use of nuclear weapons at some point. Even if all these things were done, South Vietnam might still come apart under us.

> *Comment:* The above paragraph appears to overstate rather markedly the degree of difficulty associated with success for our objectives in SVN. Our first objective is to cause the DRV to terminate support of the SEA insurgencies. Once this is done, then we have a period of stabilization and maturing in SVN, during which we can consider what next we need do. To achieve this objective does not necessarily require that we "defeat North Viet-Nam," and it almost certainly does not require that we defeat Communist China. Hence our commitment to SVN does not involve a high probability let alone "high risks," of a major conflict in Southeast Asia. One reason it does not is our capability to show the CHICOMs that if there's a "risk" of such a war, the main "risk" is theirs. Certainly no responsible person proposes to go about such a war, if it should occur, on a basis remotely resembling Korea. "Possibly even the use of nuclear weapons at some point" is of course why we spend billions to have them. If China chooses to go to war against us she has to contemplate their possible use, just as does anyone else—this is more of the "risk" to *them*. And of course SVN *might* nevertheless come apart under us, but an alert initiative commensurate with the stakes should make the likelihood of this quite remote.

Hence, we must consider realistically what our over-all objectives and stakes are, and just what degree of risk and loss we should be prepared to make to hold South Vietnam, or alternatively to gain time and secure our further lines of defense in the world and specifically in Asia.

> *Comment:* Here again is emphasis on "risk" and "loss" to us, as though the harder we try the more we stand to risk and to lose.

On the contrary, a resolute course of action in lieu of half measures, resolutely carried out instead of dallying and delaying, offers the best hope for minimizing *risks, costs,* and *losses* in achieving our objectives. The paragraph also implies there is some alternative to our holding South Viet-Nam. There is none. . . .

21

A Gloomy Assessment

General Maxwell Taylor was ambassador to South Vietnam after Lodge (who was later to return for another ambassadorial term). Ambassador Taylor, in remarks dated November 27, 1964, offers a depressing analysis of conditions in South Vietnam. It was the sense that Saigon's war was going terribly that soon prompted the full entrance of the United States into the war. The alternative conclusion, that the feebleness of the Saigon government was reason for disengagement, got no serious hearing.

After a year of changing and ineffective government, the counter-insurgency program country-wide is bogged down and will require heroic treatment to assure revival. Even in the Saigon area, in spite of the planning and the special treatment accorded the Hop Tac plan, this area also is lagging. The northern provinces of South Vietnam which a year ago were considered almost free of Viet Cong are now in deep trouble. In the Quang Ngai–Binh Dinh area, the gains of the Viet Cong have been so serious that once more we are threatened with a partition of the country by a Viet-Cong salient driven to the sea. The pressure on this area has been accompanied by continuous sabotage of the railroad and of Highway 1 which in combination threaten an economic strangulation of the northern provinces.

This deterioration of the pacification program has taken place in spite of the very heavy losses inflicted almost daily on the Viet-Cong and the increase in strength and professional competence of the Armed Forces of South Vietnam. Not only have the Vietcong apparently made

Source: Pentagon Papers, III, Document 242, 666–68.

good their losses, but of late, have demonstrated three new or newly expanded tactics: The use of stand-off mortar fire against important targets, as in the attack on the Bien Hoa airfield; economic strangulation on limited areas; finally, the stepped-up infiltration of DRV military personnel moving from the north. These new or improved tactics employed against the background of general deterioration offer a serious threat to the pacification program in general and to the safety of important bases and installations in particular.

Perhaps more serious than the downward trend in the pacification situation, because it is the prime cause, is the continued weakness of the central government. Although the Huong government has been installed after executing faithfully and successfully the program laid out by the Khanh government for its own replacement, the chances for the long life and effective performance of the new line-up appear small. Indeed, in view of the factionalism existing in Saigon and elsewhere throughout the country, it is impossible to foresee a stable and effective government under any name in anything like the near future. Nonetheless, we do draw some encouragement from the character and seriousness of purpose of Prime Minister Huong and his cabinet and the apparent intention of General Khanh to keep the Army out of politics, at least for the time being.

As our programs plod along or mark time, we sense the mounting feeling of war weariness and hopelessness which pervade South Vietnam, particularly in the urban areas. Although the provinces for the most part appear steadfast, undoubtedly there is chronic discouragement there as well as in the cities. Although the military leaders have not talked recently with much conviction about the need for "marching North," assuredly, many of them are convinced that some new and drastic action must be taken to reverse the present trends and to offer hope of ending the insurgency in some finite time.

The causes for the present unsatisfactory situation are not hard to find. It stems from two primary causes, both already mentioned above, the continued ineffectiveness of the central government, the increasing strength and effectiveness of the Vietcong and their ability to replace losses. . . .

The ability of the Vietcong continuously to rebuild their units and to make good their losses is one of the mysteries of this guerrilla war. We are aware of the recruiting methods by which local boys are induced or compelled to join the Viet Cong ranks and have some general appreciation of the amount of infiltration of personnel from the outside. Yet taking both of these sources into account, we still find no plausible explanation of the continued strength of the Vietcong if our data on Viet Cong losses are even approximately correct. Not only do the Viet Cong units have the recuperative powers of the phoenix, but they have an amazing ability to maintain morale. Only in rare cases have we found evidences of bad morale among Viet Cong prisoners or recorded in captured Viet Cong documents.

Undoubtedly one cause for the growing strength of the Viet Cong is the increased direction and support of their campaign by the government of North Vietnam. This direction and support take the form of endless radioed orders and instructions, and the continuous dispatch to South Vietnam of trained cadre and military equipment, over infiltration routes by land and by water. While in the aggregate, this contribution to the guerrilla campaign over the years must represent a serious drain on the resources of the DRV, that government shows no sign of relaxing its support of the Viet Cong. In fact, the evidence points to an increased contribution over the last year, a plausible development, since one would expect the DRV to press hard to exploit the obvious internal weaknesses in the south.

If, as the evidence shows, we are playing a losing game in South Vietnam, it is high time we change and find a better way. To change the situation, it is quite clear that we need to do three things: first, establish an adequate government in SVN; second, improve the conduct of the counter insurgency campaign; and, finally, persuade or force the DRV to stop its aid to the Viet Cong and to use its directive powers to make the Viet Cong desist from their efforts to overthrow the government of South Vietnam. . . .

22

The San Antonio Formula

By the spring of 1965, the question of whether the United States should be further involved in South Vietnam had become obsolete. The United States was fully engaged militarily, and troop levels were going to increase. In time, the question became, to the contrary, that of whether the country should in some degree disengage from the conflict, and if so how. In this speech of

Source: U.S. President, *Public Papers of the Presidents of the United States* (Washington, D.C.: United States Government Printing Office, 1968), Lyndon B. Johnson, 1967, 876–77, 879–80.

*September 29, 1967, before the National Legislative Confer-
ence in San Antonio, Texas, Johnson refers to the willingness
of the United States to halt the bombing of North Vietnam
whenever that would lead to negotiations. The offer became
known as the San Antonio formula.*

. . . Why should three Presidents and the elected representatives of
our people have chosen to defend this Asian nation more than 10,000
miles from American shores?

We cherish freedom—yes. We cherish self-determination for all
people—yes. We abhor the political murder of any state by another,
and the bodily murder of any people by gangsters of whatever ideology.
And for 27 years—since the days of lend-lease—we have sought to
strengthen free people against domination by aggressive foreign powers.

But the key to all that we have done is really our own security.
At times of crisis—before asking Americans to fight and die to resist
aggression in a foreign land—every American President has finally had
to answer this question:

Is the aggression a threat—not only to the immediate victim—but
to the United States of America and to the peace and security of the
entire world of which we in America are a very vital part?

That is the question which Dwight Eisenhower and John Kennedy
and Lyndon Johnson had to answer in facing the issue in Vietnam.

That is the question that the Senate of the United States answered
by a vote of 82 to 1 when it ratified and approved the SEATO treaty
in 1955, and to which the Members of the United States Congress
responded in a resolution that it passed in 1964 by a vote of 504 to 2,
". . . the United States is, therefore, prepared, as the President determines, to take all necessary steps, including the use of armed force, to
assist any member or protocol state of the Southeast Asia Collective
Defense Treaty requesting assistance in defense of its freedom."

Those who tell us now that we should abandon our commitment—
that securing South Vietnam from armed domination is not worth the
price we are paying—must also answer this question. And the test they
must meet is this: What would be the consequences of letting armed
aggression against South Vietnam succeed? What would follow in the
time ahead? What kind of world are they prepared to live in 5 months
or 5 years from tonight? . . .

I know there are other questions on your minds, and on the minds
of many sincere, troubled Americans: "Why not negotiate now?" so
many ask me. The answer is that we and our South Vietnamese allies
are wholly prepared to negotiate tonight.

I am ready to talk with Ho Chi Minh, and other chiefs of state concerned, tomorrow.

I am ready to have Secretary Rusk meet with their foreign minister tomorrow.

I am ready to send a trusted representative of America to any spot on this earth to talk in public or private with a spokesman of Hanoi.

We have twice sought to have the issue of Vietnam dealt with by the United Nations—and twice Hanoi has refused.

Our desire to negotiate peace—through the United Nations or out—has been made very, very clear to Hanoi—directly and many times through third parties.

As we have told Hanoi time and time and time again, the heart of the matter is really this: The United States is willing to stop all aerial and naval bombardment of North Vietnam when this will lead promptly to productive discussions. We, of course, assume that while discussions proceed, North Vietnam would not take advantage of the bombing cessation or limitation.

But Hanoi has not accepted any of these proposals.

So it is by Hanoi's choice—and not ours, and not the rest of the world's—that the war continues.

Why, in the face of military and political progress in the South, and the burden of our bombing in the North, do they insist and persist with the war?

From many sources the answer is the same. They still hope that the people of the United States will not see this struggle through to the very end. As one Western diplomat reported to me only this week—he had just been in Hanoi—"They believe their staying power is greater than ours and that they can't lose." A visitor from a Communist capital had this to say: "They expect the war to be long, and that the Americans in the end will be defeated by a breakdown in morale, fatigue, and psychological factors." The Premier of North Vietnam said as far back as 1962: "Americans do not like long, inconclusive war. . . . Thus we are sure to win in the end."

Are the North Vietnamese right about us?

I think not. No. I think they are wrong. I think it is the common failing of totalitarian regimes that they cannot really understand the nature of our democracy:

—They mistake dissent for disloyalty.

—They mistake restlessness for a rejection of policy.

—They mistake a few committees for a country.

—They misjudge individual speeches for public policy.

They are no better suited to judge the strength and perseverance of America than the Nazi and the Stalinist propagandists were able to judge it. It is a tragedy that they must discover these qualities in the American people, and discover them through a bloody war.

And, soon or late, they will discover them.

In the meantime, it shall be our policy to continue to seek negotiations—confident that reason will some day prevail; that Hanoi will realize that it just can never win; that it will turn away from fighting and start building for its own people. . . .

23

Johnson Will Not Seek Re-election

In 1968, after the startling Communist Tet offensive, President Johnson and his government were thinking with increasing seriousness about disengagement. In the famous nationwide address of March 31, 1968, reproduced here, Johnson announced measures inviting negotiation with North Vietnam. What most startled the public, however, was his announcement at the end of the speech that he would not run for re-election that November. Johnson here was no doubt reacting sincerely to the demands of the war and to his own conscience. Yet he was also facing a stark political reality. In the New Hampshire Democratic primary held on March 12, Eugene McCarthy had polled just slightly fewer votes than the President (who was not officially on the ballot, but received a write-in vote). For an incumbent President to do no better than Johnson had done in a primary in his own party amounted to a defeat. Robert Kennedy's announcement shortly afterward of his candidacy for the Democratic nomination gave Johnson further reason to recognize that his power base in his party had eroded. The announcement of March 31 followed.

Tonight I want to speak to you of peace in Vietnam and Southeast Asia.

No other question so preoccupies our people. No other dream so

Source: U.S. President, *Public Papers of the Presidents of the United States* (Washington, D.C.: United States Government Printing Office, 1970), Lyndon B. Johnson, 1968–69, 469–70, 474–76.

Peace demonstration at the Pentagon in the fall of 1967. President Johnson was pictured as a war criminal on one placard and was the subject of numerous chants and catcalls from the crowd. *(Courtesy, U.P.I.)*

absorbs the 250 million human beings who live in that part of the world. No other goal motivates American policy in Southeast Asia.

For years, representatives of our Government and others have traveled the world—seeking to find a basis for peace talks.

Since last September, they have carried the offer that I made public at San Antonio.

That offer was this:

That the United States would stop its bombardment of North Vietnam when that would lead promptly to productive discussions—and that we would assume that North Vietnam would not take military advantage of our restraint.

Hanoi denounced this offer, both privately and publicly. Even while the search for peace was going on, North Vietnam rushed their preparations for a savage assault on the people, the government, and the allies of South Vietnam.

Their attack—during the Tet holidays—failed to achieve its principal objectives.

It did not collapse the elected government of South Vietnam or shatter its army—as the Communists had hoped.

It did not produce a "general uprising" among the people of the cities as they had predicted.

The Communists were unable to maintain control of any of the more than 30 cities that they attacked. And they took very heavy casualties.

But they did compel the South Vietnamese and their allies to move certain forces from the countryside into the cities.

They caused widespread disruption and suffering. Their attacks, and the battles that followed, made refugees of half a million human beings.

The Communists may renew their attack any day.

They are, it appears, trying to make 1968 the year of decision in South Vietnam—the year that brings, if not final victory or defeat, at least a turning point in the struggle.

This much is clear:

If they do mount another round of heavy attacks, they will not succeed in destroying the fighting power of South Vietnam and its allies.

But tragically, this is also clear: Many men—on both sides of the struggle—will be lost. A nation that has already suffered 20 years of warfare will suffer once again. Armies on both sides will take new casualties. And the war will go on.

There is no need for this to be so.

There is no need to delay the talks that could bring an end to this long and this bloody war.

Tonight, I renew the offer I made last August—to stop the bombardment of North Vietnam. We ask that talks begin promptly, that they be serious talks on the substance of peace. We assume that during those talks Hanoi will not take advantage of our restraint.

We are prepared to move immediately toward peace through negotiations.

So, tonight, in the hope that this action will lead to early talks, I am taking the first step to de-escalate the conflict. We are reducing—substantially reducing—the present level of hostilities.

And we are doing so unilaterally, and at once.

Tonight, I have ordered our aircraft and our naval vessels to make no attacks on North Vietnam, except in the area north of the demilitarized zone where the continuing enemy buildup directly threatens allied forward positions and where the movement of their troops and supplies are clearly related to that threat.

The area in which we are stopping our attacks includes almost 90 percent of North Vietnam's population, and most of its territory. Thus there will be no attacks around the principal populated areas, or in the food-producing areas of North Vietnam.

Even this very limited bombing of the North could come to an early end—if our restraint is matched by restraint in Hanoi. But I cannot in good conscience stop all bombing so long as to do so would immediately and directly endanger the lives of our men and our allies. Whether a complete bombing halt becomes possible in the future will be determined by events.

Our purpose in this action is to bring about a reduction in the level of violence that now exists.

It is to save the lives of brave men—and to save the lives of innocent women and children. It is to permit the contending forces to move closer to a political settlement. . . .

At Johns Hopkins University, about 3 years ago, I announced that the United States would take part in the great work of developing Southeast Asia, including the Mekong Valley, for all of the people of that region. Our determination to help build a better land—a better land for men on both sides of the present conflict—has not diminished in the least. Indeed, the ravages of war, I think, have made it more urgent than ever.

So, I repeat on behalf of the United States again tonight what I said at Johns Hopkins—that North Vietnam could take its place in this common effort just as soon as peace comes. . . .

Fifty-two months and 10 days ago, in a moment of tragedy and trauma, the duties of this office fell upon me. I asked then for your help and God's, that we might continue America on its course, binding up our wounds, healing our history, moving forward in new unity, to clear the American agenda and to keep the American commitment for all of our people.

United we have kept that commitment. United we have enlarged that commitment.

Through all time to come, I think America will be a stronger nation, a more just society, and a land of greater opportunity and fulfillment because of what we have all done together in these years of unparalleled achievement.

Our reward will come in the life of freedom, peace, and hope that our children will enjoy through ages ahead.

What we won when all of our people united just must not now be lost in suspicion, distrust, selfishness, and politics among any of our people.

Believing this as I do, I have concluded that I should not permit the Presidency to become involved in the partisan divisions that are developing in this political year.

With America's sons in the fields far away, with America's future under challenge right here at home, with our hopes and the world's hopes for peace in the balance every day, I do not believe that I should devote an hour or a day of my time to any personal partisan causes or to any duties other than the awesome duties of this office—the Presidency of your country.

Accordingly, I shall not seek, and I will not accept, the nomination of my party for another term as your President.

But let men everywhere know, however, that a strong, a confident, and a vigilant America stands ready tonight to seek an honorable peace—and stands ready tonight to defend an honored cause—whatever the price, whatever the burden, whatever the sacrifice that duty may require.

Thank you for listening.

Good night and God bless all of you.

24

Cambodia

*In this nationwide address of April 30, 1970, President Richard
Nixon announced that he was ordering a military attack on
Vietnamese Communist positions in the neighboring nation of
Cambodia, where they had previously enjoyed virtual immunity from American and South Vietnamese assault but could
launch operations into Vietnam. Nixon's action brought widespread public demonstrations, in the course of which Ohio
national guard troops sent to Kent State University shot and
killed four students there. Shortly afterwards in a campus disturbance at Jackson State, a black college in Mississippi, police
killed two students.*

Ten days ago, in my report to the Nation on Vietnam, I announced
a decision to withdraw an additional one hundred and fifty thousand
American troops over the next year. I said then that I was making that
decision despite our concern over increased enemy activity in Laos, in
Cambodia, and in South Vietnam.

At that time, I warned that if I concluded that increased enemy
activity in any of these areas endangered the lives of Americans remaining in Vietnam, I would not hesitate to take strong and effective measures to deal with that situation.

Despite that warning, North Vietnam has increased its military
aggression in all these areas—particularly in Cambodia.

After full consultation with the National Security Council, Ambassador Bunker, General Abrams and my other advisers, I have concluded
that the actions of the enemy in the last 10 days clearly endanger the
lives of Americans who are in Vietnam now and would constitute an
unacceptable risk to those who will be there after withdrawal of another
150,000.

To protect our men who are in Vietnam and to guarantee the continued success of our withdrawal and Vietnamization programs, I have concluded the time has come for action.

Tonight, I shall describe the actions of the enemy, the actions I have
ordered to deal with that situation, and the reasons for my decision.

Source: U.S. President, *Public Papers of the Presidents of the United States* (Washington,
D.C.: United States Government Printing Office, 1971), Richard Nixon, 1970, 405–08.

Cambodia, a small country of 7 million people has been a neutral nation since the Geneva Agreement of 1954—an agreement, incidentally, which was signed by the Government of North Vietnam.

American policy since then has been to scrupulously respect the neutrality of the Cambodian people. We have maintained a skeleton diplomatic mission of fewer than 15 in Cambodia's capital, and that only since last August. For the previous 4 years, from 1965 to 1969, we did not have any diplomatic mission whatever. For the past 5 years, we have provided no military assistance whatever and no economic assistance to Cambodia.

North Vietnam, however, has not respected that neutrality.

For the past 5 years—as indicated on this map that you see here— North Vietnam has occupied military sanctuaries all along the Cambodian frontier with South Vietnam. Some of these extend up to 20 miles into Cambodia. These sanctuaries are in red and, as you note, they are on both sides of the border. They are used for hit-and-run attacks on American and South Vietnamese forces in South Vietnam.

These Communist occupied territories contain major base camps, training sites, logistics facilities, weapons and amnunition factories, airstrips and prisoner-of-war compounds.

For 5 years, neither the United States nor South Vietnam has moved against those enemy sanctuaries because we did not wish to violate the territory of a neutral nation. Even after the Vietnamese Communists began to expand these sanctuaries 4 weeks ago, we counseled patience to our South Vietnamese allies and imposed restraints on our own commanders.

In contrast to our policy, the enemy in the past 2 weeks has stepped up his guerrilla actions and he is concentrating his main forces in these sanctuaries that you see on this map where they are building up to launch massive attacks on our forces and those of South Vietnam.

North Vietnam in the last 2 weeks has stripped away all pretense of respecting the sovereignty or neutrality of Cambodia. Thousands of their soldiers are invading the country from the sanctuaries; they are encircling the capital of Phnom Penh. . . .

. . . [I]f this enemy effort succeeds, Cambodia would become a vast enemy staging area and a springboard for attacks on South Vietnam along 600 miles of frontier—and a refuge where enemy troops could return from combat without fear of retaliation.

North Vietnamese men and supplies could then be poured into that country, jeopardizing not only the lives of our own men but the people of South Vietnam as well. . . .

. . . [T]his is the decision I have made.

In cooperation with the armed forces of South Vietnam, attacks are

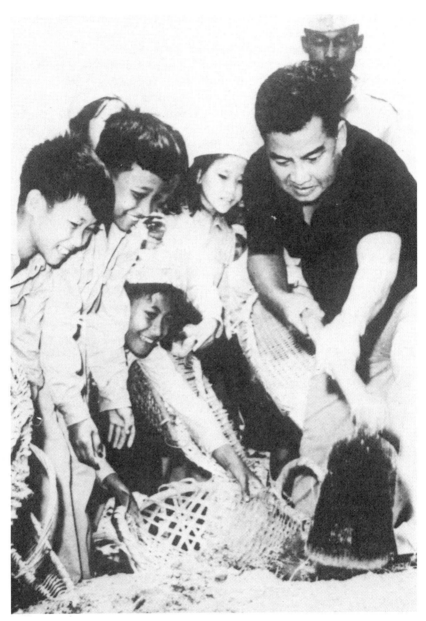

Prince Norodom Sihanouk of Cambodia was often photographed pitching in to help build a better Cambodia. Here he helps rural youth in a community project. *(Courtesy, U.P.I.)*

being launched this week to clean out major enemy sanctuaries on the Cambodian-Vietnam border. . . .

Tonight, American and South Vietnamese units will attack the headquarters for the entire Communist military operation in South Vietnam. This key control center has been occupied by the North Vietnamese and Vietcong for 5 years in blatant violation of Cambodia's neutrality.

This is not an invasion of Cambodia. The areas in which these attacks will be launched are completely occupied and controlled by North Vietnamese forces. Our purpose is not to occupy the areas. Once enemy forces are driven out of these sanctuaries and once their military supplies are destroyed, we will withdraw.

These actions are in no way directed to the security interests of any nation. Any government that chooses to use these actions as a pretext for harming relations with the United States will be doing so on its own responsibility, and on its own initiative, and we will draw the appropriate conclusions. . . .

25

The Decision on Cambodia

Here Henry Kissinger, at the time of the American invasion of Cambodia President Nixon's national security adviser, gives the case for that most controversial of Nixon's actions in Indochina. The Sihanouk to whom Kissinger refers was Prince Norodom Sihanouk, a powerful figure in Cambodian politics; Le Duc Tho conducted negotiations for North Vietnam in the peace talks at Paris that Kissinger attended for the United States.

Revisionist history has painted a picture of a peaceful, neutral Cambodia wantonly assaulted by American forces and plunged into a civil war that could have been avoided but for the American obsession with military solutions. The facts are different. Sihanouk declared war on the new Cambodian government as early as March 20, two days after his overthrow, throwing in his lot with the Communists he had held at bay

Source: Henry Kissinger, *White House Years* (Boston: Little, Brown and Company, 1979), 484–86. Reprinted by permission.

and locating himself in Peking, then still considered the most revolutionary capital in the world and with which, moreover, we had no means of communication whatever. April saw a wave of Communist attacks to overthrow the existing governmental structure in Cambodia. Le Duc Tho on March 16 had rejected all suggestions of de-escalation of military activities and on April 4 had rejected all suggestions of neutralization. He had asserted that the Cambodian, Laotian, and Vietnamese peoples were one and would fight shoulder to shoulder to win the whole of Indochina. By the second half of April, the North Vietnamese were systematically expanding their sanctuaries and merging them into a "liberated zone." They were surrounding Phnom Penh and cutting it off from all access—using the very tactics that five years later led to its collapse.

If these steps were unopposed, the Communist sanctuaries, hitherto limited to narrow unpopulated areas close to the Vietnamese border, would be organized into a single large base area of a depth and with a logistics system which would enable rapid transfer of units and supplies. . . .

There was no serious doubt that Hanoi's unopposed conquest of Cambodia would have been the last straw for South Vietnam. In the midst of a war, its chief ally was withdrawing forces at an accelerating rate and reducing its air support. Saigon was being asked to take the strain at the very moment Hanoi was increasing reinforcements greatly over the level of the preceding year. If Cambodia were to become a single armed camp at this point, catastrophe was inevitable. Saigon needed time to consolidate and improve its forces; the United States had to pose a credible threat for as long as possible; and Hanoi's offensive potential had to be weakened by slowing down its infiltration and destroying its supplies. It was a race between Vietnamization, American withdrawal, and Hanoi's offensives.

Strategically, Cambodia could not be considered a country separate from Vietnam. The indigenous Cambodian Communist forces—the murderous Khmer Rouge—were small in 1970 and entirely dependent on Hanoi for supplies. The forces threatening the South Vietnamese and Americans from Cambodia were *all* North Vietnamese; the base areas were part of the war in Vietnam. North Vietnamese forces that were busy cutting communications had already seized a quarter of the country. The danger of being "bogged down in a new war in Cambodia" was a mirage; the enemy in Cambodia and Vietnam was the same one. Whatever forces we fought in Cambodia we would not have to fight in Vietnam and vice versa. The war by then was a single war, as Le Duc Tho had proclaimed; there was turmoil in Cambodia precisely because Hanoi was determined to use it as a base for its invasion of South Vietnam and to establish its hegemony over Indochina.

26

The American Involvement Ends

*In this agreement signed in Paris on January 27, 1973, the
United States in effect ended its military involvement in Vietnam. More than two years of fighting among the Vietnamese
followed this agreement before the Saigon government fell to
the Communists at the end of April 1975.*

The Parties participating in the Paris Conference on Vietnam,

With a view to ending the war and restoring peace in Vietnam on
the basis of respect for the Vietnamese people's fundamental national
rights and the South Vietnamese people's right to self-determination,
and to contributing to the consolidation of peace in Asia and the world,

Have agreed on the following provisions and undertake to respect
and to implement them:

Chapter I
The Vietnamese People's Fundamental National Rights

Article 1

The United States and all other countries respect the independence,
sovereignty, unity, and territorial integrity of Vietnam as recognized by
the 1954 Geneva Agreements on Vietnam.

Chapter II
Cessation of Hostilities—Withdrawal of Troops

Article 2

A cease-fire shall be observed throughout South Vietnam as of 2400
hours G.M.T., on January 27, 1973.

At the same hour, the United States will stop all its military activities
against the territory of the Democratic Republic of Vietnam by ground,
air and naval forces, wherever they may be based, and end the mining of
the territorial waters, ports, harbors, and waterways of the Democratic
Republic of Vietnam. The United States will remove, permanently de-

---

Source: Weekly Compilation of Presidential Documents, Vol. 9, Number 4, January 29,
1973, 45–46, 49.

Henry Kissinger (background left), National Security Adviser to President Nixon, and North Vietnamese Politburo Member Le Duc Tho (seated foreground) initial the peace agreement in Paris in January 1973. The men shared the Nobel Peace Prize for bringing an end to one stage of the conflict in Southeast Asia. *(Courtesy, Wide World Photo)*

activate or destroy all the mines in the territorial waters, ports, harbors, and waterways of North Vietnam as soon as this Agreement goes into effect.

The complete cessation of hostilities mentioned in this Article shall be durable and without limit of time.

Article 3

The parties undertake to maintain the cease-fire and to ensure a lasting and stable peace.

As soon as the cease-fire goes into effect:

a. The United States forces and those of the other foreign countries allied with the United States and the Republic of Vietnam shall remain in-place pending the implementation of the plan of troop withdrawal. The Four-Party Joint Military Commission described in Article 16 shall determine the modalities.

b. The armed forces of the two South Vietnamese parties shall remain in-place. The Two-Party Joint Military Commission described in Article 17 shall determine the areas controlled by each party and the modalities of stationing.

c. The regular forces of all services and arms and the irregular forces of the parties in South Vietnam shall stop all offensive activities against each other and shall strictly abide by the following stipulations:

—All acts of force on the ground, in the air, and on the sea shall be prohibited;

—All hostile acts, terrorism, and reprisals by both sides will be banned.

Article 4

The United States will not continue its military involvement or intervene in the internal affairs of South Vietnam.

Article 5

Within sixty days of the signing of this Agreement, there will be a total withdrawal from South Vietnam of troops, military advisers, and military personnel, including technical military personnel and military personnel associated with the pacification program, armaments, munitions, and war material of the United States and those of the other foreign countries mentioned in Article 3 (a). Advisers from the above-mentioned countries to all paramilitary organizations and the police force will also be withdrawn within the same period of time.

Article 6

The dismantlement of all military bases in South Vietnam of the United States and of the other foreign countries mentioned in Article 3 (a) shall be completed within sixty days of the signing of this Agreement.

Article 7

From the enforcement of the cease-fire to the formation of the government provided for in Articles 9 (b) and 14 of this Agreement, the two South Vietnamese parties shall not accept the introduction of troops, military advisers, and military personnel including technical military personnel, armaments, munitions, and war material into South Vietnam.

The two South Vietnamese parties shall be permitted to make periodic replacement of armaments, munitions and war material which have been destroyed, damaged, worn out or used up after the cease-fire, on the basis of piece-for-piece, of the same characteristics and properties, under the supervision of the Joint Military Commission of the two South Vietnamese parties and of the International Commission of Control and Supervision.

Chapter III
The Return of Captured Military Personnel and Foreign Civilians, and Captured and Detained Vietnamese Civilian Personnel

Article 8

a. The return of captured military personnel and foreign civilians of the parties shall be carried out simultaneously with and completed not later than the same day as the troop withdrawal mentioned in Article 5. The parties shall exchange complete lists of the above-mentioned captured military personnel and foreign civilians on the day of the signing of this Agreement.

b. The parties shall help each other to get information about those military personnel and foreign civilians of the parties missing in action, to determine the location and take care of the graves of the dead so as to facilitate the exhumation and repatriation of the remains, and to take any such other measures as may be required to get information about those still considered missing in action.

c. The question of the return of Vietnamese civilian personnel captured and detained in South Vietnam will be resolved by the two South Vietnamese parties on the basis of the principles of Article 21 (b) of the Agreement of the Cessation of Hostilities in Vietnam of July 20, 1954.

The two South Vietnamese parties will do so in a spirit of national reconciliation and concord, with a view to ending hatred and enmity, in order
to ease suffering and to reunite families. The two South Vietnamese
parties will do their utmost to resolve this question within ninety days
after the cease-fire comes into effect. . . .

Chapter VII
Regarding Cambodia and Laos

Article 20

a. The parties participating in the Paris Conference on Vietnam shall
strictly respect the 1954 Geneva Agreements on Cambodia and the 1962
Geneva Agreements on Laos, which recognized the Cambodian and the
Lao peoples' fundamental national rights, i.e., the independence, sovereignty, unity, and territorial integrity of these countries. The parties shall
respect the neutrality of Cambodia and Laos.

The parties participating in the Paris Conference on Vietnam undertake to refrain from using the territory of Cambodia and the territory of
Laos to encroach on the sovereignty and security of one another and of
other countries.

b. Foreign countries shall put an end to all military activities in Cambodia and Laos, totally withdraw from and refrain from reintroducing
into these two countries troops, military advisers and military personnel,
armaments, munitions and war material.

c. The internal affairs of Cambodia and Laos shall be settled by the
people of each of these countries without foreign interference.

d. The problems existing between the Indochinese countries shall
be settled by the Indochinese parties on the basis of respect for each
other's independence, sovereignty, and territorial integrity, and non-
interference in each other's internal affairs.

27

Vietnam Visited

The three articles here were published in The Washington Post *in May 1994. They are the result of a visit to Vietnam by Robert G. Kaiser, managing editor of the paper. The third indicates that on the Vietnamese side, reconciliation between that nation and the United States may come easily.*

Ho Chi Minh City, Vietnam—Americans and South Vietnamese foresaw "a bloodbath" if the Communists won the Vietnam War. One calculation publicized by the United States Information Agency in 1970 predicted that 3 million people could lose their lives after a Communist victory.

Nguyen Huu Co was one of the predicted victims. Co was briefly South Vietnam's defense minister in 1965, and was for many years a general in the army—positions that made him a prime candidate for a bloodbath.

Co actually held no important job after 1965, because he and Nguyen Van Thieu, South Vietnam's last president, did not get along. Co was a retired general by the time the Communists took over the south in 1975. Nevertheless, he was one of 32 South Vietnamese generals who were taken as a group to "reeducation camp."

The euphemism was an important one to the Vietnamese authorities in Hanoi. They have insisted since 1975 that they killed no one who fought against them in the war and did not use prison camps to punish their old enemies. Instead they "reeducated" the men once known as "puppets" in their propaganda. In fact, thousands are thought to have died in the camps, but there have been no reports of systematic execution of prisoners.

It is difficult to keep in mind the distinction that the Vietnamese made about the treatment of their former enemies while listening to Co describe his 12 years of reeducation, which he remembers almost month by month. He told the story with care recently while sitting at a small table on a terrace in his large house in Ho Chi Minh City, formerly Saigon. He spoke carefully in French while members of his large extended family bustled about.

Source: Washington Post, May 15, 1994, A 33; May 16, 1994, A 12; May 22, 1994, C 7.

Co's first stop after his arrest was a military camp not far from Saigon, where the generals were rigorously lectured by instructors sent from Hanoi. Conditions in those first three years were not too bad; his family could send a 22-pound parcel of food or clothing once a month.

The reeducators gave seven, week-long political lessons, Co recalled, following each with reading and discussion among the generals. The instructors were not interested in back talk. "We couldn't say frankly that we had not fought against our homeland," he said.

"Or the instructor said the Americans came to South Vietnam as invaders. I couldn't say, 'No, the Americans came to help protect South Vietnam.' Well, I could insist on my point of view, even for two or three months, but the instructor would never give in. . . . He would agree to discuss, but never to agree with me. Eventually I had to agree, yes, I collaborated with the Americans who invaded Vietnam."

Was he or any of his fellow South Vietnamese generals ever really convinced by the lecturer? "No, not once," Co replied.

After the first three years, Co's situation deteriorated sharply. He and his fellow generals were moved to a new camp in northern Vietnam, near the border with China. There they faced forced labor and short rations. No packages from home were allowed for the first year in the new camp; one every other month was permitted in the second. Letters were permitted once every two months. "That camp was the hardest," he said.

Then the generals were moved to a succession of camps run not by the military but by Hanoi's Interior Ministry. Conditions improved; occasional family visits were permitted. But the dreary reeducation continued, with no end in sight. It was difficult to know what to make of the situation.

"At the outset I was sure I'd be killed," Co said. Survival was better than that—but life in the camp was profoundly depressing.

Several of the 32 generals died in camp, but there were 28 alive when Co was released in 1987. Eight of them were held until 1993, when the last of the camps was closed. Some 300,000 people had spent from a few weeks to 18 years in them.

When Co was released he thought he would move to the United States, as many former South Vietnamese officers had. The government would let him go, but only with his wife.

The other 21 members of Co's immediate family would not be allowed to accompany them, at least initially. "We discussed it in the family," Co said. "We decided to stay."

He still had his fine house in Ho Chi Minh City, and a number of his children could work for foreign firms just coming to Vietnam after the government changed its economic policies. Now he enumerates their employers: "Two for French companies, one for a Japanese, one for a Taiwanese. . . ."

Co is now an old man, his hair nearly gone, his eyes surrounded by circles of darkened skin. His biography tells an extraordinary story: born in the Mekong River Delta in 1925, recruited into the French army at 18, drafted into service to the occupying Japanese in 1944, escaped and returned to the Delta, recruited by the Communist Vietminh in September 1945, fought against the French but rejoined the French army when it prevailed in the south.

"I was young, I had no ideals—I didn't reflect on it," Co said when asked if it was hard to switch loyalties so often. "I went where the wind blew me."

In 1954, he was at Dien Bien Phu—on the losing side when Vietnamese divisions routed the French. Then he fought for the new South Vietnam.

Looking around now at visiting Americans, at his family, at the young woman from the Vietnamese Foreign Ministry who arranged this interview and who sat passively through Co's account of his years in the camps, the old general smiled.

"Now the world has changed so much!" he observed. "It's time to turn the page, to start a new page."

*   *   *

BEN TRE, Vietnam—For an American reporter covering the Vietnam War a generation ago, the greatest mystery was the enemy. Who were these resourceful, courageous and utterly determined men who could fight so well and absorb such losses? Now it is easy to find out.

One of them was Nguyen Huu Vy, now 64. He grew up near here, fought against the French near here, was arrested here in 1955 in the new South Vietnamese government's "Denunciation of Communists" campaign, got out of prison in 1959 and in 1960—responding to an order from the Communist Party—organized a military unit here to begin a new war.

He had no weapons, he recalled in an animated interview. His first squad of 11 recruits armed itself with fake rifles carved from the heavy, butt ends of coconut palm fronds. With them they ambushed soldiers of the Ngo Dinh Diem regime, who were apparently too frightened to look closely at the weapons. Vy built up an arsenal by stealing the weapons of Diem's forces, usually in ambushes. With the new weapons he could expand his force—to a platoon, then a company, then a battalion.

Vy told his story with an enthusiastic body language unusual in Vietnamese. He gestured vigorously, and his eyebrows moved up and down his forehead. It was easy to see why other men were willing to follow him into battle.

When he realized that his American visitor had spent time in the Ben Tre area during the war, he asked if the American knew the names of any local Viet Cong units. "Did you ever hear of Battalion 516?" he asked. It was a famous unit, and Vy was clearly proud to announce that he created it.

Did the visitor remember the battle in 1964 when Battalion 516 cut up two South Vietnamese battalions, killing their four American advisers? The visitor did not. Vy was disappointed.

What about the Tet Offensive of the Year of the Monkey, in 1968? Yes, this was well known. Ben Tre City, the provincial capital, won an odd sort of notoriety as the city of which an American officer was quoted as saying after Tet, "We had to destroy the city in order to save it." In fact Ben Tre wasn't destroyed, but it was badly shot up by the American 9th Infantry Division, which had to pry Vy and his men out of the town.

Vy said he was given his orders to attack the city just 24 hours ahead of time. Sappers began the battle at 2 a.m.—just as Viet Cong guerrillas were moving on the U.S. Embassy in Saigon, now known as Ho Chi Minh City, and other targets all over the country.

Vy's sappers came across the river in sampans and began setting off explosives in the city. They were followed by three battalions, known as 516 A, B and C. Altogether Vy threw 2,000 men into the Tet Offensive.

They held their ground for two days, when the Americans landed several miles east of town and began to fight their way toward the city, supported by heavy artillery and fighter-bombers. Seventeen Americans in the first U.S. unit to advance on the town were killed, Vy remembered. His own losses were heavy in the fierce combat, and at the end of the day's fighting he had run out of ammunition. At midnight he withdrew silently from Ben Tre.

How heavy were his casualties? The proud commander refused to give a number—hundreds, he acknowledged, "but we didn't lose our effectiveness."

How could that be? The losses were obviously grievous, but he insisted that his units remained effective fighting forces. His visitor challenged that conclusion; it didn't seem possible. What was Vy's definition of an effective force? "Unless we suffered more than 40 percent casualties, we considered our forces were still intact," he replied. Forty percent of 2,000 was 800 men.

Vietnamese losses during the war were huge—at least 2 million killed out of a wartime population of less than 40 million. The United States would have to lose 12 million to suffer comparably.

Vy and other veterans interviewed across southern Vietnam never suggested that they considered these losses excessive. Tran Bach Dang, leader of the underground Communist Party in Saigon during the entire American war, put it most bluntly in discussing his losses from the 1968 Tet Offensive.

"More than 5,000 were sacrificed," he said of those killed in the attacks on Saigon. "More than 10,000 were wounded. Seven thousand were taken prisoner."

"Wasn't that a very high price?" he was asked.

"No, we considered it not a very high price," he replied. "We wanted to make a political statement. And that led to the Paris peace talks and to the end of the war. Without the Tet Offensive, the killing would have been greater."

Dang was an original member of the National Liberation Front and one of the highest-ranking southern Communists during the war. Ironically, he now lives in a house in Ho Chi Minh City that was famous during the war as the residence of a series of young American diplomats who, by reputation, gave the best parties in the capital.

For many years on New Year's Eve, a "Light at the End of the Tunnel" party was held in the house at 47 Phan Tan Gian St. (now renamed Dien Bien Phu Street). Diplomats, CIA agents, journalists and American officers gathered there to drink and gossip about whether that light was yet visible—whether, or how, the war could ever end. Now No. 47 is Dang's house. His Mercedes, an old model, is in the garage.

Dang was born in Saigon in 1926. He fought against the French in the first Indochina war and was captured. He tells his story now out of the right side of his mouth; the left side is paralyzed—"tortured by the French, in prison," he explained.

In 1957, he was called into the jungle to help form the National Liberation Front and was a member of its first presidium, or executive committee. In 1965, he was sent to Saigon as first secretary of the city's Communist Party. He came in the guise of a professor. "I had suits, shirts and ties, a car to go back and forth as though I was a professor," he recalled with a grin.

Eventually his identity did become known, Dang said; spies in his organization or members who defected or were taken prisoner saw to that. "I used to see my own face on posters around the city," he said, so he grew a mustache and wore sunglasses.

Dang became one of the South Vietnamese Communists who openly criticized the leadership in Hanoi over its clumsy efforts to absorb the south after 1975. He opposed reeducation, believing that "good people" could be converted to the revolution in a few days, and that hard cases could not be convinced in 15 or 20 years.

"We deluded ourselves," he said. "Personally, I would have just let the people go who wanted to go." For several years Dang has spoken out for greater freedoms and more liberalization.

Writing for the official newspapers, pressing his views and meeting with foreign journalists constitute Dang's principal activities these days.

He expressed satisfaction with new economic policies that have turned the country toward individual enterprise. There's even something in it for Dang. The Foreign Ministry's press department—which requires "capitalist" journalists to pay a fee for assistance in setting up interviews here—in turn pays those who give the interviews. For spending two hours with The Washington Post, Dang was paid 50,000 dong—roughly the weekly salary of a mid-level civil servant, equal to $4.50.

*   *   *

Ho Chi Minh City, Vietnam—An American reporter who lived and worked here a quarter-century ago returned last month with trepidation. What sort of reception could I expect from the Vietnamese who boast of their victory over the United States, who built museums to memorialize American "war atrocities," who lost 2 million of their countrymen in a decade of war?

Trepidation was unnecessary. Some bitterness and anger must survive here, but they are well hidden. Those who remember the war seem eager to bury the memory, to start afresh with the United States. And a huge number of Vietnamese don't remember the war at all—the 30 million born since it ended.

I encountered about 50 of those young Vietnamese on a recent afternoon along a path in their native village of Song Phu in the flat, emerald-green rice-growing country of the Mekong Delta. School was getting out. A crowd of young Vietnamese walked by, looking curiously at the visitor. A girl of about 11 said knowingly, "Soviet." She was corrected by another visitor who spoke her language—not Soviet, American. American? That stopped the parade of students in its tracks. A growing crowd gathered to gape at the American—their first American, evidently. With the new generation, Americans get a clean slate.

Even their parents and grandparents give Americans a warm welcome. Vietnamese have found a path to reconciliation, perhaps because they had to find it first in their own families. Most Vietnamese families, it seems, were divided by conflicting allegiances during three decades of civil war. But that really is over now, long over.

Preparing for this visit I found it hard to imagine southern Vietnam without Americans. During the war Americans were everywhere, nearly always in a superior position to the natives. The curfew in Saigon didn't apply to us; customs officials at Ton Son Nhut airport gave us special consideration; merchants in the markets charged us specially high prices, on the (correct) theory that we had a lot more money than the locals.

We built massive installations in Vietnam. If you had told us in 1970 that most of them could simply disappear, we would have laughed. But most of them have disappeared. The mammoth army base at Long Binh, perhaps the biggest Army base the United States ever constructed on foreign soil, a vast collection of bunkers, buildings and tents covering hundreds of acres, is now a vacant lot. The Third Field Hospital in Saigon, where American civilians went for medical care and often saw wounded GIs being helicoptered in from the field for emergency treatment, is also gone—a vacant piece of ground now used as a depot for air freight for nearby Ton Son Nhut airport. At the airport, the old helicopter terminal known to generations of war correspondents as Hotel Three, from which we flew off to see the war and to visit every corner of South Vietnam, is now Ho Chi Minh City Heliport, according to a sign. But there are no helicopters visible—the place looks vacant too.

Helicopters were part of the landscape of wartime South Vietnam. Their thwoketa-thwoketa rumble was nearly always in the air. Now there are no helicopters anywhere. The loudest noise in the countryside is the two-cycle hum of Honda motorbikes, which is ubiquitous.

The recent end of the American economic boycott of Vietnam is a source of great excitement here—and of many rumors, too. A recent visitor to Hanoi reports intense speculation there about the impending sale of entire city blocks to American businessmen. In Ho Chi Minh City people speculate about the fate of the old American Embassy, a strange structure built behind a concrete screen to deter rocket-propelled grenades. It's now used by Vietnam's state oil company. Vietnamese from all walks of life ask a visiting American when the Americans will come in force to take advantage of Vietnam's new openness to foreign investment.

Advance parties have already landed. Pepsi and Coke are both here. American corporations, law firms, accounting firms and more have established beachheads. There's even a bar on Hy Ba Trung Street here owned by an American war veteran from San Jose, Calif., named Bob Shibley, and his Vietnamese wife, Hien—"Bob and Hien's Place." It offers a real ham and cheese sandwich and, at night, the company of young women who look painfully familiar—a new generation of bar girls, alas.

English is well established as the preferred foreign language. French, which was still a useful reporter's tool here during the war, is fast disappearing—French tourists visiting this remnant of their colonial empire have to use English to be understood by waiters in the restaurants here. Russian, briefly the most popular foreign language after the war, has all but disappeared. Vietnamese with just a smattering of English can make extra money tutoring the many others who are eager to learn what they perceive as the official language of commerce.

When America was important here, South Vietnamese mimicked American ways and American institutions. The South Vietnamese government we helped create had a president, a vice president, a legislature, a supreme court and so on. That government failed. So did the Marxist-Leninist state that succeeded it after 1975. Now, as the Vietnamese search for a new model, they talk a lot about Taiwan, South Korea and Singapore—Asian neighbors that started, as Vietnam does, with authoritarian power structures, built thriving free-market economies, then began to evolve into real democracies. Might that be the right path for Vietnam? Many here obviously hope so.

Dean Rusk, secretary of state to John F. Kennedy and Lyndon B. Johnson, argued eloquently that the United States had to fight the war in Vietnam to contain China. It was an appealing argument at the time, but it was historically flawed. In fact Vietnam and China have been rivals for centuries, something we failed to grasp 30 years ago. Now that rivalry is much discussed by Vietnamese nervous about China's vibrant growth. The Vietnamese are palpably eager for deeper American involvement in their affairs now because they see a large American presence as a way to . . . contain China!

A two-week visit to Vietnam after a 24-year interval was cathartic. Many of the Americans who fought or worked here took away a lot of psychological baggage that hasn't been easy to carry. To discover now that here, where it happened, the war really is a closed chapter, is a comfort, a relief.

So I recommend a visit. The restaurants are terrific, and it's hard to spend $15 on a splendid dinner for two. (Yes, the airplane ticket here isn't cheap, but a good travel agent can find one for less than $1,500 round trip.) Vietnam is a lot more crowded than it used to be, but remains beautiful, even beguiling—the more so for the absence of guns firing. And if you buy mangoes in the market, you'll still be charged a premium for being a rich foreigner.

This applies even to Americans who look like Vietnamese and speak their language—Vietnamese Americans, of whom there are more than a million. For America, this new Vietnamese diaspora will be the most permanent consequence of the war. Already the Viet Khieu, or overseas Vietnamese, have an enormous influence here, and it will certainly grow. History has knit a Vietnamese strand into the American fabric, and has made America a permanent part of Vietnam.

Part 3

ARGUMENTS

Much of the argument for resistance to Communism in Indochina reflected the more general suppositions of American cold warriors. Advocates of opposition to the Indochinese Communists made the entirely accurate assumption that Communism wherever it reigned was a system of oppression. They also held to the considerably less demonstrable proposition that the appetite on the part of Communists for further and further conquests was insatiable. By that reasoning, a Communist victory in South Vietnam would invite Asian Communism, or Communism in all its forms, to seek triumphs elsewhere. Cold warriors more specifically held to what goes by the name of the domino theory, the idea that if one Asian nation fell, the collapse would set neighboring countries to tumbling like the chips in a stack of upright dominoes.

Other arguments had to do less with Communism and the Cold War than with convictions about the proper character and behavior of the United States in general. Running through American statements of the era is a concern for the strength of the American will and an insistence that it must prove itself by its resoluteness. Another preoccupation was over the keeping of commitments. Once Americans had encouraged a nation to rely on their backing, so the claim went, it would be a betrayal to fail to live up to that commitment in all that it implied in the way of military support. The problem with this is that it allowed for no disengagement or any other change of course. The slightest increase in military aid constituted a commitment, that commitment was unbreakable, living up to its implications might require a further expansion in aid, and so forth.

Among arguments against the American presence in Vietnam, the most obvious was that the justification for any warfare whatsoever must be absolutely convincing, which the American engagement in Vietnam was not. Typical among opponents was a perception of the North Vietnamese and the Vietcong as nationalists and homegrown social radicals rather than agents of a single international Communist movement. Anti-

war activists denied that the United States could ever make the South Vietnamese regime permanent and workable. They pointed to the unimaginable destruction the war was effecting on the Vietnamese people: the very scale of American weaponry, which supporters of the war were convinced could bring victory, constituted for opponents the criminality of the American enterprise. Some critics also connected the war to other issues—but these we shall touch on in the section entitled Meanings.

Secretary of Defense Robert McNamara seen with South Vietnamese head of state General Nguyen Khanh, who had overthrown General Minh in January 1964. McNamara made frequent trips to South Vietnam to meet with the many South Vietnamese leaders and to get a firsthand picture of American progress in the war.

28

"Freedom Is Truly Indivisible"

This address by President Dwight D. Eisenhower at Gettysburg College on April 4, 1959, embraces the range of moral arguments and claims of American national self-interest that would reappear in later defenses of American involvement. In this address the President, without using the phrase, articulates a version of the domino theory.

. . . What are the facts?

The first and most important fact is the implacable and frequently expressed purpose of imperialistic communism to promote world revolution, destroy freedom, and communize the world. Its methods are all-inclusive, ranging through the use of propaganda, political subversion, economic penetration, and the use or the threat of force.

The second fact is that our country is today spending an aggregate of about $47 billion annually for the single purpose of preserving the Nation's position and security in the world. This includes the costs of the Defense Department, the production of nuclear weapons, and mutual security. All three are mutually supporting and are blended into one program for our safety. The size of this cost conveys something of the entire program's importance—to the world and, indeed, to each of us.

And when I think of this importance to us—think of it in this one material figure—this cost annually for every single man, woman, and child of the entire Nation is about $275 a year.

The next fact we note is that, since the Communist target is the world, every nation is comprehended in their campaign for domination. The weak and the most exposed stand in the most immediate danger.

Another fact, that we ignore to our peril, is that, if aggression or subversion against the weaker of the free nations should achieve successive victories, communism would step by step overcome once-free areas. The danger, even to the strongest, would become increasingly menacing.

Source: The Department of State Bulletin, XL, No. 1035, April 27, 1959, 579–83.

Clearly the self-interest of each free nation impels it to resist the loss to imperialistic communism of the freedom and independence of any other nation.

Freedom is truly indivisible.

To apply some of these truths to a particular case, let us consider briefly the country of Viet-Nam and the importance to us of the security and progress of that country. It is located, as you know, in the southeastern corner of Asia, exactly halfway round the world from Gettysburg College.

Viet-Nam is a country divided into two parts, like Korea and Germany. The southern half, with its 12 million people, is free but poor. It is an underdeveloped country; its economy is weak, average individual income being less than $200 a year. The northern half has been turned over to communism. A line of demarcation running along the 17th parallel separates the two. To the north of this line stand several Communist divisions. These facts pose to south Viet-Nam two great tasks: self-defense and economic growth.

Understandably the people of Viet-Nam want to make their country a thriving, self-sufficient member of the family of nations. This means economic expansion.

For Viet-Nam's economic growth, the acquisition of capital is vitally necessary. Now, the nation could create the capital needed for growth by stealing from the already meager rice bowls of its people and regimenting them into work battalions. This enslavement is the commune system, adopted by the new overlords of Red China. It would mean, of course, the loss of freedom within the country without any hostile outside action whatsoever.

Another way for Viet-Nam to get the necessary capital is through private investments from the outside and through governmental loans and, where necessary, grants from other and more fortunately situated nations.

In either of these ways the economic problem of Viet-Nam could be solved. But only the second way can preserve freedom.

And there is still the other of Viet-Nam's great problems—how to support the military forces it needs without crushing its economy.

Because of the proximity of large Communist military formations in the north, Free Viet-Nam must maintain substantial numbers of men under arms. Moreover, while the Government has shown real progress in cleaning out Communist guerrillas, those remaining continue to be a disruptive influence in the nation's life.

Unassisted, Viet-Nam cannot at this time produce and support the military formations essential to it or, equally important, the morale—the hope, the confidence, the pride—necessary to meet the dual threat of aggression from without and subversion within its borders.

Still another fact! Strategically south Viet-Nam's capture by the Communists would bring their power several hundred miles into a hitherto free region. The remaining countries in Southeast Asia would be menaced by a great flanking movement. The freedom of 12 million people would be lost immediately and that of 150 million others in adjacent lands would be seriously endangered. The loss of south Viet-Nam would set in motion a crumbling process that could, as it progressed, have grave consequences for us and for freedom.

Viet-Nam must have a reasonable degree of safety now—both for her people and for her property. Because of these facts, military as well as economic help is currently needed in Viet-Nam.

We reach the inescapable conclusion that our own national interests demand some help from us in sustaining in Viet-Nam the morale, the economic progress, and the military strength necessary to its continued existence in freedom.

Viet-Nam is just one example. One-third of the world's people face a similar challenge. All through Africa and Southern Asia people struggle to preserve liberty and improve their standards of living, to maintain their dignity as humans. It is imperative that they succeed.

But some uninformed Americans believe that we should turn our backs on these people, our friends. Our costs and taxes are very real, while the difficulties of other peoples often seem remote from us.

But the costs of continuous neglect of these problems would be far more than we must now bear—indeed more than we could afford. The added costs would be paid not only in vastly increased outlays of money but in larger drafts of our youth into the military establishment and in terms of increased danger to our own security and prosperity.

No matter what areas of Federal spending must be curtailed—and some should—our safety comes first. Since that safety is necessarily based upon a sound and thriving economy, its protection must equally engage our earnest attention. . . .

A free America can exist as part of a free world, and a free world can continue to exist only as it meets the rightful demands of people for security, progress, and prosperity. That is why the development of south Viet-Nam and Southeast Asia is important, why Japanese export trade is important, why firmness in Berlin is important.

It is why Communist challenges must always be answered by the free world standing on principle, united in strength and in purpose.

This is the true meaning of mutual security.

It is the idea that, by helping one another build a strong, prosperous world community, free people will not only win through to a just peace but can apply their wonderful, God-given talents toward creating an ever-growing measure of man's humanity to man.

But this is something that will come only out of the hard intellectual effort of disciplined minds. For the future of our country depends upon enlightened leadership, upon the truly understanding citizen.

We look to the citizen who has the ability and determination to seek out and to face facts, who can place them in logical relationship one to another, who can attain an understanding of their meaning and then act courageously in promoting the cause of an America that can live, under God, in a world of peace and justice. These are the individuals needed in uncounted numbers in your college, your country, and your world.

Over the 127 years of Gettysburg College's existence, its graduates have, in many ways, served the cause of freedom and of justice. May the years ahead be as fruitful as those which you now look back upon with such pride and with such satisfaction.

29

"Only the Determined . . . Can Possibly Survive"

In its stressing of determination and courage, President Kennedy's address of April 20, 1961, before the American Society of Newspaper Editors catches both a theme of cold-war thinking and a part of the public image of the Kennedy presidency. For all its usual caution, that presidency represented for portions of the public the qualities of energy, activity, and resoluteness.

. . . [I]t is clearer than ever that we face a relentless struggle in every corner of the globe that goes far beyond the clash of armies or even nuclear armaments. The armies are there, and in large number. The nuclear armaments are there. But they serve primarily as the shield behind which subversion, infiltration, and a host of other tactics steadily advance, picking off vulnerable areas one by one in situations which do not permit our own armed intervention.

Power is the hallmark of this offensive—power and discipline and deceit. The legitimate discontent of yearning people is exploited. The legitimate trappings of self-determination are employed. But once in power, all talk of discontent is repressed, all self-determination disap-

Source: U.S. President, *Public Papers of the Presidents of the United States* (Washington, D.C.: United States Government Printing Office, 1962), John F. Kennedy, 1961, 305–06.

pears, and the promise of a revolution of hope is betrayed, as in Cuba, into a reign of terror. Those who on instruction staged automatic "riots" in the streets of free nations over the efforts of a small group of young Cubans to regain their freedom should recall the long roll call of refugees who cannot now go back—to Hungary, to North Korea, to North Viet-Nam, to East Germany, or to Poland, or to any of the other lands from which a steady stream of refugees pours forth, in eloquent testimony to the cruel oppression now holding sway in their homeland.

We dare not fail to see the insidious nature of this new and deeper struggle. We dare not fail to grasp the new concepts, the new tools, the new sense of urgency we will need to combat it—whether in Cuba or South Viet-Nam. And we dare not fail to realize that this struggle is taking place every day, without fanfare, in thousands of villages and markets—day and night—and in classrooms all over the globe.

The message of Cuba, of Laos, of the rising din of Communist voices in Asia and Latin America—these messages are all the same. The complacent, the self-indulgent, the soft societies are about to be swept away with the debris of history. Only the strong, only the industrious, only the determined, only the courageous, only the visionary who determine the real nature of our struggle can possibly survive.

No greater task faces this country or this administration. No other challenge is more deserving of our every effort and energy. Too long we have fixed our eyes on traditional military needs, on armies prepared to cross borders, on missiles poised for flight. Now it should be clear that this is no longer enough—that our security may be lost piece by piece, country by country, without the firing of a single missile or the crossing of a single border.

We intend to profit from this lesson. We intend to reexamine and reorient our forces of all kinds—our tactics and our institutions here in this community. We intend to intensify our efforts for a struggle in many ways more difficult than war, where disappointment will often accompany us.

For I am convinced that we in this country and in the free world possess the necessary resource, and the skill, and the added strength that comes from a belief in the freedom of man. And I am equally convinced that history will record the fact that this bitter struggle reached its climax in the late 1950's and the early 1960's. Let me then make clear as the President of the United States that I am determined upon our system's survival and success, regardless of the cost and regardless of the peril!

30

"Our Purpose Is Peace"

Addressing Congress on August 5, 1964, just after the clash in the Gulf of Tonkin, President Johnson asks for a resolution expressing support for whatever action might be necessary in Southeast Asia. He got his wish.

Last night I announced to the American people that the North Vietnamese regime had conducted further deliberate attacks against U.S. naval vessels operating in international waters, and that I had therefore directed air action against gunboats and supporting facilities used in these hostile operations. This air action has now been carried out with substantial damage to the boats and facilities. Two U.S. aircraft were lost in the action.

After consultation with the leaders of both parties in the Congress, I further announced a decision to ask the Congress for a resolution expressing the unity and determination of the United States in supporting freedom and in protecting peace in southeast Asia.

These latest actions of the North Vietnamese regime have given a new and grave turn to the already serious situation in southeast Asia. Our commitments in that area are well known to the Congress. They were first made in 1954 by President Eisenhower. They were further defined in the Southeast Asia Collective Defense Treaty approved by the Senate in February 1955.

This treaty with its accompanying protocol obligates the United States and other members to act in accordance with their constitutional processes to meet Communist aggression against any of the parties or protocol states.

Our policy in southeast Asia has been consistent and unchanged since 1954. I summarized it on June 2 in four simple propositions:

1. *America keeps her word.* Here as elsewhere, we must and shall honor our commitments.

2. *The issue is the future of southeast Asia as a whole.* A threat to any nation in that region is a threat to all, and a threat to us.

3. *Our purpose is peace.* We have no military, political, or territorial ambitions in the area.

4. *This is not just a jungle war, but a struggle for freedom on every*

Source: The Department of State Bulletin, LI, No. 1313, August 24, 1964, 261–62.

front of human activity. Our military and economic assistance to South Vietnam and Laos in particular has the purpose of helping these countries to repel aggression and strengthen their independence.

The threat to the free nations of southeast Asia has long been clear. The North Vietnamese regime has constantly sought to take over South Vietnam and Laos. This Communist regime has violated the Geneva accords for Vietnam. It has systematically conducted a campaign of subversion, which includes the direction, training, and supply of personnel and arms for the conduct of guerrilla warfare in South Vietnamese territory. In Laos, the North Vietnamese regime has maintained military forces, used Laotian territory for infiltration into South Vietnam, and most recently carried out combat operations—all in direct violation of the Geneva agreements of 1962.

In recent months, the actions of the North Vietnamese regime have become steadily more threatening. In May, following new acts of Communist aggression in Laos, the United States undertook reconnaissance flights over Laotian territory, at the request of the Government of Laos. These flights had the essential mission of determining the situation in territory where Communist forces were preventing inspection by the International Control Commission. When the Communists attacked these aircraft, I responded by furnishing escort fighters with instructions to fire when fired upon. Thus, these latest North Vietnamese attacks on our naval vessels are not the first direct attack on armed forces of the United States.

As President of the United States I have concluded that I should now ask the Congress, on its part, to join in affirming the national determination that all such attacks will be met, and that the United States will continue in its basic policy of assisting the free nations of the area to defend their freedom.

As I have repeatedly made clear, the United States intends no rashness, and seeks no wider war. We must make it clear to all that the United States is united in its determination to bring about the end of Communist subversion and aggression in the area. We seek the full and effective restoration of the international agreements signed in Geneva in 1954, with respect to South Vietnam, and again in Geneva in 1962, with respect to Laos.

I recommend a resolution expressing the support of the Congress for all necessary action to protect our Armed Forces and to assist nations covered by the SEATO Treaty. At the same time, I assure the Congress that we shall continue readily to explore any avenues of political solution that will effectively guarantee the removal of Communist subversion and the preservation of the independence of the nations of the area. . . .

31

"We Have a Promise to Keep"

In a talk at Johns Hopkins University on April 7, 1965, President Johnson argues for the American presence in Vietnam that he had recently greatly expanded. Note that Johnson sees Communist China as the power looming behind Hanoi. This was a common perception at the time. After Hanoi's victory, in fact, China would fight Vietnam in a border war. The speech is also notable for its projection of economic aid for the region: the concept of exporting economic progress along with the political ideas of the West was a component of liberal cold-war thought.

. . . Why are we in South Viet-Nam?

We are there because we have a promise to keep. Since 1954 every American President has offered support to the people of South Viet-Nam. We have helped to build, and we have helped to defend. Thus, over many years, we have made a national pledge to help South Viet-Nam defend its independence.

And I intend to keep that promise.

To dishonor that pledge, to abandon this small and brave nation to its enemies, and to the terror that must follow, would be an unforgivable wrong.

We are also there to strengthen world order. Around the globe, from Berlin to Thailand, are people whose well-being rests in part on the belief that they can count on us if they are attacked. To leave Viet-Nam to its fate would shake the confidence of all these people in the value of an American commitment and in the value of America's word. The result would be increased unrest and instability, and even wider war.

We are also there because there are great stakes in the balance. Let no one think for a moment that retreat from Viet-Nam would bring an end to conflict. The battle would be renewed in one country and then another. The central lesson of our time is that the appetite of aggression is never satisfied. To withdraw from one battlefield means only to prepare for the next. We must say in Southeast Asia—as we did in Europe—in the words of the Bible: "Hitherto shalt thou come, but no further."

Source: The Department of State Bulletin, LII, No. 1348, April 26, 1965, 607–09.

There are those who say that all our effort there will be futile—that China's power is such that it is bound to dominate all Southeast Asia. But there is no end to that argument until all of the nations of Asia are swallowed up.

There are those who wonder why we have a responsibility there. Well, we have it there for the same reason that we have a responsibility for the defense of Europe. World War II was fought in both Europe and Asia, and when it ended we found ourselves with continued responsibility for the defense of freedom.

Our objective is the independence of South Viet-Nam and its freedom from attack. We want nothing for ourselves—only that the people of South Viet-Nam be allowed to guide their own country in their own way. We will do everything necessary to reach that objective. And we will do only what is absolutely necessary.

In recent months attacks on South Viet-Nam were stepped up. Thus, it became necessary for us to increase our response and to make attacks by air. This is not a change of purpose. It is a change in what we believe that purpose requires.

We do this in order to slow down aggression.

We do this to increase the confidence of the brave people of South Viet-Nam who have bravely borne this brutal battle for so many years with so many casualties.

And we do this to convince the leaders of North Viet-Nam—and all who seek to share their conquest—of a simple fact:

We will not be defeated.

We will not grow tired.

We will not withdraw, either openly or under the cloak of a meaningless agreement.

We know that air attacks alone will not accomplish all of these purposes. But it is our best and prayerful judgment that they are a necessary part of the surest road to peace. . . .

This war, like most wars, is filled with terrible irony. For what do the people of North Viet-Nam want? They want what their neighbors also desire—food for their hunger, health for their bodies, a chance to learn, progress for their country, and an end to the bondage of material misery. And they would find all these things far more readily in peaceful association with others than in the endless course of battle.

These countries of Southeast Asia are homes for millions of impoverished people. Each day these people rise at dawn and struggle through until the night to wrest existence from the soil. They are often wracked by disease, plagued by hunger, and death comes at the early age of 40.

Stability and peace do not come easily in such a land. Neither independence nor human dignity will ever be won, though, by arms alone.

It also requires the works of peace. The American people have helped generously in times past in these works, and now there must be a much more massive effort to improve the life of man in that conflict-torn corner of our world.

The first step is for the countries of Southeast Asia to associate themselves in a greatly expanded cooperative effort for development. We would hope that North Viet-Nam would take its place in the common effort just as soon as peaceful cooperation is possible.

The United Nations is already actively engaged in development in this area, and as far back as 1961 I conferred with our authorities in Viet-Nam in connection with their work there. And I would hope tonight that the Secretary-General of the United Nations could use the prestige of his great office and his deep knowledge of Asia to initiate, as soon as possible, with the countries of that area, a plan for cooperation in increased development.

For our part I will ask the Congress to join in a billion-dollar American investment in this effort as soon as it is underway. And I would hope that all other industrialized countries, including the Soviet Union, will join in this effort to replace despair with hope and terror with progress.

The task is nothing less than to enrich the hopes and the existence of more than a hundred million people. And there is much to be done.

The vast Mekong River can provide food and water and power on a scale to dwarf even our own TVA. The wonders of modern medicine can be spread through villages where thousands die every year from lack of care. Schools can be established to train people in the skills that are needed to manage the process of development. And these objectives, and more, are within the reach of a cooperative and determined effort.

I also intend to expand and speed up a program to make available our farm surpluses to assist in feeding and clothing the needy in Asia. We should not allow people to go hungry and wear rags while our own warehouses overflow with an abundance of wheat and corn, rice and cotton. . . .

32

"Cutting Our Losses"

*Under Secretary of State George Ball in a memorandum of
June 29, 1965, to Secretary of State Dean Rusk, Secretary of
Defense Robert McNamara, and others argues in effect against
administration policy.*

1. Plan for Cutting Our Losses

In essence, what we should seek to achieve is a posture *vis-à-vis* the
various leaders in Saigon that will appear to the world as reasonable and
lacking any suggestion of arbitrariness. What I have proposed is that we
make it a condition of continued assistance that the various elements in
Saigon put aside their petty differences and organize themselves to fight
the war. The only argument against the reasonableness of this proposition is that we have not insisted on such performance in the past. This
is not persuasive. From the point of view of legitimacy, effective representation of the major elements of opinion, and social and economic
progressiveness, the present government seems even worse than its predecessors.

2. The Task of Re-education

It should by now be apparent that we have to a large extent created our own predicament. In our determination to rally support, we
have tended to give the South Vietnamese struggle an exaggerated and
symbolic significance (Mea culpa, since I personally participated in this
effort).

The problem for us now—if we determine not to broaden and
deepen our commitments—is to re-educate the American people and
our friends and allies that:

a. The phasing out of American power in South Vietnam should not
be regarded as a major defeat—either military or political—but a tactical redeployment to more favorable terrain in the overall cold war
struggle;

b. The loss of South Vietnam does not mean the loss of all of Southeast Asia to the Communist power. Admittedly, Thailand is a special
problem that will be dealt with later in this memo;

Source: Pentagon Papers, IV, Document 258, 609–10.

c. We have more than met our commitments to the South Vietnamese people. We have poured men and equipment into the area, and run risks and taken casualties, and have been prepared to continue the struggle provided the South Vietnamese leaders met even the most rudimentary standards of political performance;

d. The Viet Cong—while supported and guided from the North—is largely an indigenous movement. Although we have emphasized its cold war aspects, the conflict in South Vietnam is essentially a civil war within that country;

e. Our commitment to the South Vietnamese people is of a wholly different order from our major commitments elsewhere—to Berlin, to NATO, to South Korea, etc. We ourselves have insisted the curtailment of our activities in South Vietnam would cast doubt on our fidelity to the other commitments. Now we must begin a process of differentiation being founded on fact and law. We have *never* had a treaty commitment obligating us to the South Vietnamese people or to a South Vietnamese government. Our only treaty commitment in that area is to our SEATO partners, and they have—without exception—viewed the situation in South Vietnam as not calling a treaty into play. To be sure, we *did* make a promise to the South Vietnamese people. But that promise is conditioned on their own performance, and they have not performed.

33

"There Is *So Much* of Everything"

Bernard Fall, whose work on Dien Bien Phu this anthology has already cited, was an early critic of the American war. The essay presented here is significant for its concentration on what became a common observation among opponents of the American effort: the extravagant, wasteful power of American weaponry.

. . . Today in Vietnam, there is *so much* of everything available that almost any kind of military error, no matter how stupid, can be retrieved

Source: Bernard B. Fall, "Vietnam Blitz: A Report on the Impersonal War," *The New Republic,* October 9, 1965, 18–19. Reprinted by permission.

on the rebound. In the case of the recent battle near Ankhé the mis-dropped unit was reinforced by other helicopter outfits and progressively surrounded by a protective wall of American firepower until the enemy, unable to maintain his position, broke off contact. At Bongson, on September 24, the VC overran a government outpost, but in the "reaction" operation they allegedly lost 600 men—500 of whom were killed by American aircraft. Against that kind of slaughter, the teachings of Mao Tse-tung, superior tactics, popular support for the VC, or, conversely, poor motivation among the Arvins and patent ineptness among many of their officers, and even the "mess in Saigon" are totally irrelevant. If tomorrow morning Mickey Mouse became prime minister of South Vietnam it would have precious little influence on the men of US Army Task Force Alfa (in fact, a full US Army Corps in everything but name) or on the fighting ability of the 3d US Marine Division.

Much has been said about the use of B-52's in a counterinsurgency operation or, as it should properly be called, a revolutionary war. [Columnist] Joseph Alsop, always willing to swallow uncritically every official handout on Vietnam, has again assured us in a recent column that the B-52's are necessary to destroy "deeply dug-in" VC installations, thus making a few underground bunkers covered with sandbags and bamboo look like the Siegfried Line.

His words had hardly appeared in print when the Air Force switched targets on Alsop and flew three raids into the Mekong Delta, followed by several raids along the Central Vietnam shore. The trouble with the Mekong Delta is that it is so flat, and the water table so high that one cannot dig a pit privy in the place without hitting water. It is well-nigh impossible to build underground positions in it. And, as official population density maps of Vietnam clearly show, the Delta has (with the exception of one single district out of perhaps thirty) an average population density of about 250 people per square mile, with one belt of districts across the whole Delta reaching the fantastic density of *one thousand people* per square mile! With an average bomb load of 500 tons per thirty-plane raid and a known bomb dispersion pattern of about 2,000 yards by 1,000 yards for such a raid, the effects of such a bombardment on a heavily-populated area can be readily guessed.

The point is that this consideration, too, has become irrelevant because it presupposes that hate or love for Saigon or the acquiescence of the Vietnamese population in its own fate, is important. In the view of many of the *realpolitiker* in Saigon and Washington, this is no longer true. Even the old-fashioned military view that a given target must be attained or destroyed before the operation can be called a success no longer holds. The B-52 raids (or "in-country" raids by smaller aircraft) do one thing regardless of whether they hit a VC installation or a totally innocent and even pro-government village—they keep the Viet Cong on the move, day and night, in constant fear of being hit. Gone are the days of large and even comfortable jungle hospitals above ground; of the VC rest camp with warm food, clean clothes and a good swimming hole; of the large ammunition depot and weapons repair plant with electric generators chugging away peacefully. The heavy bombers have changed all that. The VC is hunted down like an animal. His wounded die un-attended. A VC combat unit returns from an operation only to find its camp area destroyed and its painfully-amassed rice and ammunition reserve shattered.

And now there are research figures (for this is the most operations-researched conflict in human history) to back up the allegations of success through fire-power. Before February 1965—that is, before the United States began to use jets inside South Vietnam—only about two percent of VC deserters cited air action as a reason for leaving their side. Since then the rate has risen to 17 percent. Indeed, as many an informed observer in Saigon will concede, what changed the character of the Vietnam war was *not* the decision to bomb North Vietnam; *not* the decision to use American ground troops in South Vietnam; but the decision to wage unlimited aerial warfare inside the country at the price of literally pounding the place to bits.

There are hundreds of perfectly well-substantiated stories to the effect that this merciless bombing hurt thousands of innocent bystanders and that one of the reasons why few weapons are found in many cases is that the heaps of dead in the battle zone include many local villagers who didn't get away in time. And every observer in Vietnam meets several American officers who will curse loudly every time they hear a jet overhead, because it again means an invisible objective hit blindly—for an F-105 travels far too fast to see what he hits and must be guided on his target by a "FAC"—a Forward Air Controller in a spotter plane. The same goes for the incredible wastage of artillery ammunition. "In my area," said an American provincial adviser to me, "we shot a half-million dollars' worth of howitzer ammunition last month on unob-served targets. Yet the whole provincial budget for information- and intelligence-gathering is $300."

In another instance known personally to me, a plantation hospital had been pilfered by the VC. When informed of that fact by a plantation official, the immediate reaction of the local command was *not* to pursue the retreating VC with troops—always a tiresome and risky affair—but to propose the laying-down of an artillery barrage on the plantation area. "I had the devil's own time dissuading them from it," said the plantation official later. "After all, we have 9,000 workers and 22,000 women and children here.". . .

34

"If We Were Not Already Involved . . . "

George F. Kennan had been one of the first of the cold warriors, a theoretician who argued for the necessity of blocking the ambitions of the Soviet Union. But in these excerpts from his testimony before the Senate Foreign Relations Committee on February 10, 1966, reprinted soon after in The New Republic, *he argues against the wisdom of American intervention in South Vietnam. At one point here he touches on the dilemma of our involvement. It was bad to get entangled in Vietnam at all, he observes, but since we are there it would be harmful to us suddenly to leave. Involvement itself, in other words, makes further involvement a necessity. Disapproving of our being in Vietnam at all, but recognizing that we cannot merely get out, Kennan proposes moderating our presence.*

. . . The first point I would like to make is that if we were not already involved as we are today in Vietnam, I would know of no reason why we should wish to become so involved, and I could think of several reasons why we should wish not to.

Vietnam is not a region of major military, industrial importance. It is difficult to believe that any decisive developments of the world situation would be determined in normal circumstances by what happens on that territory. If it were not for the considerations of prestige that arise precisely out of our present involvement, even a situation in which South Vietnam was controlled exclusively by the Viet Cong, while regrettable, and no doubt morally unwarranted, would not, in my opinion, present dangers great enough to justify our direct military intervention.

Given the situation that exists today in the relations among the leading Communist powers, and by that I have, of course, in mind primarily the Soviet-Chinese conflict, there is every likelihood that a Communist regime in South Vietnam would follow a fairly independent course.

There is no reason to suspect that such a regime would find it either necessary or desirable in present circumstances to function simply as a passive puppet and instrument of Chinese power. And as for the danger that its establishment there would unleash similar tendencies in neigh-

---

Source: George F. Kennan, *The New Republic*, February 26, 1966, 20–21. Reprinted by permission.

boring countries, this, I think, would depend largely on the manner in which it came into power. . . .

From the long-term standpoint, therefore, and on principle, I think our military involvement in Vietnam has to be recognized as unfortunate, as something we would not choose deliberately, if the choice were ours to make all over again today, and by the same token, I think it should be our government's aim to liquidate this involvement just as soon as this can be done without inordinate damage to our own prestige or to the stability of conditions in that area.

It is obvious on the other hand that this involvement is today a fact. It creates a new situation. It raises new questions ulterior to the long-term problem which have to be taken into account; a precipitate and disorderly withdrawal could represent in present circumstances a disservice to our own interests, and even to world peace greater than any that might have been involved by our failure to engage ourselves there in the first place.

This is a reality which, if there is to be any peaceful resolution of this conflict, is going to have to be recognized both by the more critical of our friends and by our adversaries.

But at the same time, I have great misgivings about any deliberate expansion of hostilities on our part directed to the achievement of something called "victory"—if by the use of that term we envisage the complete disappearance of the recalcitrance with which we are now faced, the formal submission by the adversary to our will, and the complete realization of our present stated political aims.

I doubt that these things can be achieved even by the most formidable military successes.

There seems to be an impression about that if we bring sufficient military pressure to bear there will occur at some point something in the nature of a political capitulation on the other side. I think this is a most dangerous assumption. I don't say that it is absolutely impossible, but it is a dangerous assumption in the light of the experience we have had with Communist elements in the past. . . .

Our motives are widely misinterpreted, and the spectacle, the spectacle emphasized and reproduced in thousands of press photographs and stories that appear in the press of the world, the spectacle of Americans inflicting grievous injury on the lives of a poor and helpless people, and particularly a people of different race and color, no matter how warranted by military necessity or by the excesses of the adversary our operations may seem to us to be or may genuinely be, this spectacle produces reactions among millions of people throughout the world profoundly detrimental to the image we would like them to hold of this country. I am not saying that this is just or right. I am saying that this is so, and that it is bound in the circumstances to be so, and a victory purchased at the price of further such damage would be a hollow one in terms of our world interests, no matter what advantages it might hold from the standpoint of developments on the local scene.

Now, these are the reasons, gentlemen, why I hope that our government will restrict our military operations in Vietnam to the minimum necessary to assure the security of our forces, and to maintain our military presence there until we can achieve a satisfactory peaceful resolution of the conflict, and these are the reasons why I hope that we will continue to pursue vigorously, and I may say consistently, the question—the questions for such a peaceful resolution of the conflict—even if this involves some moderation of our stated objectives, and even if the resulting settlement appears to us as something less than ideal. . . .

35

The Arrogance of Power

Senator J. William Fulbright, though a sponsor of the Gulf of Tonkin Resolution giving support to President Johnson's efforts in Vietnam, since became one of the leading opponents of the course of the war, which he interpreted as a destructive act of American power. Fulbright here argues that nations act on an urge to possess and express power.

Many of the wars fought by man—I am tempted to say most—have been fought over . . . abstractions. The more I puzzle over the great wars of history, the more I am inclined to the view that the causes attributed to them—territory, markets, resources, the defense or perpetuation of great principles—were not the root causes at all but rather explanations or excuses for certain unfathomable drives of human nature. For lack of a clear and precise understanding of exactly what these motives are, I refer to them as the "arrogance of power"—as a psychological need that nations seem to have in order to prove that they are bigger, better, or stronger than other nations. Implicit in this drive is the assumption, even

Source: J. William Fulbright, *The Arrogance of Power* (New York: Random House, 1966), 5, 106–08. Reprinted by permission.

on the part of normally peaceful nations, that force is the ultimate proof of superiority—that when a nation shows that it has the stronger army, it is also proving that it has better people, better institutions, better principles, and, in general, a better civilization. . . .

Why are Americans fighting in Vietnam? For much the same reason, I think, that we intervened militarily in Guatemala in 1954, in Cuba in 1961, and in the Dominican Republican in 1965. In Asia as in Latin America we have given our opposition to communism priority over our sympathy for nationalism because we have regarded communism as a kind of absolute evil, as a totally pernicious doctrine which deprives the people subjected to it of freedom, dignity, happiness, and the hope of ever acquiring them. I think that this view of communism is implicit in much of American foreign policy; I think it is the principal reason for our involvement in Vietnam and for the emergence of an "Asian Doctrine" under which the United States is moving toward the role of policeman for all of Southeast Asia.

It is said that we are fighting against North Vietnam's aggression rather than its ideology and that the "other side" has only to "stop doing what it is doing" in order to restore peace. But what are the North Vietnamese doing, except participating in a civil war, not in a foreign country but on the other side of a demarcation line between two sectors of the same country, a civil war in which Americans from ten thousand miles across the ocean are also participating? What are they doing that is different from what the American North did to the American South a hundred years ago, with results that few of my fellow Southerners now regret?

What exactly is their crime? They are harsh in their treatment of their own people and cruel in their conduct of the war, but these attributes hardly distinguish them from the South Vietnamese for whom we are fighting. The crime of the North Vietnamese that makes them America's enemy is that they are communists, practitioners of a philosophy we regard as evil. When all the official rhetoric about aggression and the defense of freedom and the sanctity of our world has been cited and recited, we are still left with two essential reasons for our involvement in Vietnam: the view of communism as an evil philosophy and the view of ourselves as God's avenging angels, whose sacred duty it is to combat evil philosophies.

The view of communism as an evil philosophy is a distorting prism through which we see projections of our own minds rather than what is actually there. Looking through the prism, we see the Viet Cong who cut the throats of village chiefs as savage murderers but American flyers who incinerate unseen women and children with napalm as valiant fighters for freedom; we see Viet Cong defections as the rejection of communism but the much greater number of defections from the Saigon Army as expressions of a simple desire to return to the farm; we see the puritan discipline of life in Hanoi as enslavement but the chaos and corruption of life in Saigon as liberty; we see Ho Chi Minh as a hated tyrant but Nguyen Cao Ky as the defender of freedom; we see the Viet Cong as Hanoi's puppet and Hanoi as China's puppet but we see the Saigon government as America's stalwart ally; and finally, we see China, with no troops in South Vietnam, as the real aggressor while we, with hundreds of thousands of men, are resisting foreign intervention.

These perceptions are not patently wrong but they are distorted and exaggerated. It is true that whatever the fault may be on our side, the greater fault is with the communists, who have indeed betrayed agreements, subverted unoffending governments, and generally done a great deal to provoke our hostility. It is *our* shortcoming, however, that we have the power to overcome and, in so doing, to set a constructive example for our adversaries. As the more powerful belligerent by far, we are better able to take the initiative in showing some magnanimity, but we are not doing so. Instead we are treading a strident and dangerous course, a course that is all but unprecedented in American history.

36

The Nation and the World

Eugene V. Rostow, Under Secretary of State for Political Affairs, in this address of October 17, 1967, at the University of Kansas argues for the American commitment to the effort in Vietnam. What is distinctive here is Rostow's placing of the Vietnam issue within the larger and continuing American debate between isolationists, who wished for the United States to turn inward, and advocates of the nation's connecting itself to the world at large.

My topic today is the great debate which is going on over every breakfast table of the nation. Viet-Nam is the focal point of the controversy. But the issue is broader. For many who disagree with the Govern-

Source: Department of State Publication 8322, East Asian and Pacific Series 171, released November 1967, 1–5.

ment about Viet-Nam, the real question is whether the United States should abandon its whole postwar foreign policy—a policy which four Presidents of both parties and a bipartisan majority in Congress have believed vital to our national security.

The basic issue in the debate has been posed often and well by high-minded and sincere critics of our Viet-Nam policy.

Their arguments follow this approximate pattern: They start with the premise that the main purpose of our foreign policy is to foster a world environment in which we can with reasonable security devote our main energies to building a good society for our own citizens at home. No one disputes this premise. It has always described the goal of our foreign policy since the war. In this period, confronting new conditions, we have sought with others to organize a reliable peace—to help build a peaceful world of wide horizons in which we can live with assurance as a free and democratic community and not as an autarchic fortress or a garrison state.

But the critics proceed from this universally accepted premise to the startling conclusion that the main contribution the United States should make to the stability of the world environment is the service of her own domestic example. They often recall a comment by John Quincy Adams, one of our greatest Secretaries of State. At a time when the immediate neighborhood of the United States was measured by the speed of sailing vessels and patrolled by the British Navy, Adams said that America should be "the well-wisher of the freedom and independence of all" but "the champion and vindicator only of her own."

In marching as they do from a universally accepted premise to a highly debatable conclusion, the critics of our foreign policy evade the really difficult question in the middle: how to maintain a world environment in which American democracy can continue to be safe. The answer to this question must face up to conditions in the world as it is, not as we would wish it to be. We live today not in the age of John Quincy Adams but in a world of intercontinental ballistic missiles, one-third occupied by ambitious and energetic Communist regimes; a world in which another third of the people live in developing countries, groping their way toward modernity under conditions of weakness which tempt agression; and a world in which Europe and Japan have not yet fully joined us as stabilizing influences in world politics.

It is of course true that our primary national mission is the improvement of our own society. But it is equally true that a responsible government must protect the safety of the nation. We cannot expect to be allowed to pursue our domestic goals, vital as they are, in a world that is not reasonably safe for our democracy.

The challenge to our four postwar Presidents has been something completely new in American history—and a challenge for which we have not been particularly well prepared, intellectually or psychologically, by our earlier experience as a nation. The essence of that challenge can be summed up in this way:

In the small, unstable, nuclear world in which we live, the security of the United States depends on maintaining a tolerably stable balance of power not merely in the Western Atlantic or the Hemisphere but in the world as a whole. If we do not take the lead in maintaining that balance, no one else will. We have had to take an active part in world politics since the war only because those who used to undertake the vital tasks of maintaining an international equilibrium of power have lost the capacity to do so. This is the fact which the critics of our foreign policy ignore or evade. It is the key to our security problem today. . . .

When the Soviet Union breached the Yalta and Potsdam agreements calling for free elections in Eastern Europe and Germany and began to push outward toward Iran, Turkey, and Greece, our instinct for self-preservation was stirred. Our response, in 1947, was the Truman doctrine and the Marshall Plan, expressing the two key themes of our postwar foreign policy.

The essence of the Truman doctrine has been a simple rule designed to minimize risks and miscalculations: that there be no unilateral change in the relevant frontiers of the Communist and free-world systems, no change that is achieved by force directly or indirectly applied.

This rule does not make us and our allies the universal gendarmes of the world. There are, and will doubtless continue to be, local conflicts that do not threaten the general peace and can therefore safely be left to run their course.

But in areas of significance to political geography, major conflicts and extensions of the Communist sphere achieved by force do carry with them a threat to the world equilibrium and the possibility of escalation into general war. Such acts would therefore directly concern the national interests of the United States and other free nations.

Since President Truman's decision, the United States has followed what few democracies have been able to maintain: a measured, flexible policy combining firmness and restraint.

The goal of that policy is nothing less than a stable world peace. We have a national interest in world peace because wide disturbance in world politics inevitably threatens us. To achieve that goal, our foreign policy has employed four basic means to the end of stability: resistance to aggression which threatens our particular interests or the general peace; respect for the vital interests of the other side; zeal in searching for common areas of agreement and cooperation; and support for national and international programs that could lead to a more stable and decent world. . . .

37

Authors Take Sides on Vietnam

These solicited remarks taken from a collection represent a range of views on Vietnam by well-known writers. William F. Buckley, Jr., is a leading conservative commentator. Norman Mailer is a novelist. Susan Sontag is a literary and cultural critic.

William F. Buckley, Jr.

I am in favor of it. America's commitment is to a beleaguered people. It is a commitment originally made by a man who knew a great deal about dying, and about war making, and about war prevention, that having been Eisenhower's professional training and professional concern back when he swore, with the backing of the people's representatives, to defend Southeast Asia against the Communists. That pledge was reaffirmed by his successor, who knew war from the heroic isolation of a long night in the Pacific Ocean spent retrieving the broken bodies of companions who had gone down under enemy fire. That pledge has been reaffirmed, once again, by Lyndon Johnson. As a Christian, I consider it fantastic to urge acquiescence in a Communist takeover, or on grounds of "conscience" to commend an entire population to the superintendence of the Vietcong.

What are we doing in South Vietnam, if not trying to save Southeast Asia from the Communists? Yet if this is our purpose, how long can we put off facing the strategic realities? That situation is simply this, that we cannot keep South Vietnam free without taking action against North Vietnam, whose capacity to extravasate terrorists into Free Vietnam is beyond our capacity, or the free Vietnamese's, to cope with. It is all very well for us to distribute literature to South Vietnamese hamlets about

Source: Cecil Woolf and John Bagguley, eds., *Authors Take Sides on Vietnam: Two Questions on the War in Vietnam Answered by the Authors of Several Nations* (New York: Simon and Schuster, 1967), 26–27, 49, 69–70. Reprinted by permission.

the glories of democratic government. It is something else to reply persuasively to the arguments used by the Vietcong Communist guerrillas. Their favorite form of cajolery is to descend on pro-Western hamlets, pick out the leaders, and publicly disembowel them. The effect on putative freedom lovers is said to be considerable. How can we hope, under the circumstances, to have the people of South Vietnam with us? Why should they be "with us" when we permit our fear of world opinion to count more heavily than their fear of the Vietcong guerrillas with their bloody pangas?

What the President needs is a first-class balky Congress, a Congress of dug-in naysayers, who will by gawd wrest information from Mr. Johnson about matters of public concern, or refuse to continue blank-checking him along his tortured odysseys. It is not merely to play politics to demand from a Chief Executive in a mature democracy the right to participate in the decision-making.

LBJ has not yet told Congress, or the people: a) Why do we not encourage the use of Asians in the battlefield? b) How can we hope to win an enduring peace so long as the Red Chinese are left free to continue to develop their atom bombs?

America's primary responsibility is, surely, to supply what preemi-

A protest rally in New York City.

nently it is in a position to supply, namely, the materiel of war. That and, most important of all, the ultimate resolution, which is our determination to use our total resources if necessary in order to protect the freedom fighters there. In a word, to provide the South Vietnamese with the shelter of our nuclear umbrella.

Initial steps should be taken, leading, ideally, to the day when the American presence in South Vietnam would be purely advisory and logistical: and when the peoples of Free Asia could join hands together, as was done so often by the peoples of Europe, to repel the common oppressor.

Norman Mailer

The truth is, maybe we need a war. It may be the last of the tonics. From Lydia Pinkham to Vietnam in sixty years, or bust. We're the greatest country ever lived for speeding up the time. So, let's do it right. Let's cease all serious wars, kids. Let's leave Asia to the Asians. Let us, instead, have wars which are like happenings. Let us have them every summer. Let us buy a tract of land in the Amazon, two hundred million acres will do, and throw in Marines and Seabees and Air Force, Scuba divers for the river bottom, motor-cyclists for the mud-races, carrier pilots landing on bounce-all decks in typhoons, invite them all, the Chinks and the Aussies, the Frogs and the Gooks and the Wogs, the Wops and the Russkies, the Yugos, the Israelis, the Hindus, the Pakistanis. We'll have war games with real bullets and real flamethrowers, real hot-wire correspondents on the spot, TV with phone-in audience participation, amateur war movie film contests for the soldiers, discotheques, Playboy Clubs, pictures of the corpses for pay TV, you know what I mean—let's get the hair on the toast for breakfast. So a write-in campaign (all of us) to King Corporation Exec Mr. Pres; let us tell him to get the boys back home by Christmas, back from Vietnam and up the Amazon for summer. Yours—readers—till the next happening.

Unless Vietnam is the happening. Could that be? Could that really be? Little old Vietnam just a happening? Cause if it is, Daddy Warbucks, couldn't we have the happening just with the Marines and skip all that indiscriminate roast tit and naked lunch, all those bombed-out civilian ovaries, Mr. J., Mr. LBJ, Boss Man of Show Biz—I salute you in your White House Oval; I mean America will shoot all over the shithouse wall if this jazz goes on, Jim.

Susan Sontag

A small nation of handsome people, ravished by twenty years of civil war, is being brutally and self-righteously slaughtered—in the name of freedom!—by the richest, most grotesquely overarmed, most powerful country in the world. America has become a criminal, sinister country— swollen with priggishness, numbed by affluence, bemused by the monstrous conceit that she has the mandate to dispose of the destiny of the world, *of life itself,* in terms of her own interests and jargon.

America's war on Vietnam makes me, for the first time in my life, ashamed of being an American. But that's unimportant.

I am in complete agreement with Bertrand Russell's statement that "Vietnam is an acid test for this generation of Western intellectuals."

38

"For the Health of Our Land"

When the great civil rights leader Martin Luther King, Jr., was turning against the conflict in Vietnam, there were complaints that he was injuring the rights cause by joining it to the antiwar movement. Here, addressing a meeting of clergy against the war held at Riverside Church in New York City on April 4, 1967, he discusses the similarities between the two movements.

. . . There is . . . a very obvious and almost facile connection between the war in Vietnam and the struggle I, and others, have been waging in America. A few years ago there was a shining moment in that struggle. It seemed as if there was a real promise of hope for the poor—both black and white—through the poverty program. There were experiments, hopes, new beginnings. Then came the buildup in Vietnam and I watched the program broken and eviscerated as if it were some idle political plaything of a society gone mad on war, and I knew that America would never invest the necessary funds or energies in rehabilitation of its poor so long as adventures like Vietnam continued to draw men and skills and money like some demonic destructive suction tube. So I was increasingly compelled to see the war as an enemy of the poor and to attack it as such.

Source: James Melvin Washington, ed., *A Testament of Hope: The Essential Writings of Martin Luther King, Jr.* (San Francisco: Harper and Row Publishers, 1986), 232–34, 240–41. Reprinted by permission.

Perhaps the more tragic recognition of reality took place when it became clear to me that the war was doing far more than devastating the hopes of the poor at home. It was sending their sons and their brothers and their husbands to fight and to die in extraordinarily high proportions relative to the rest of the population. We were taking the black young men who had been crippled by our society and sending them eight thou-

Antiwar protests.

sand miles away to guarantee liberties in Southeast Asia which they had not found in southwest Georgia and East Harlem. So we have been repeatedly faced with the cruel irony of watching Negro and white boys on TV screens as they kill and die together for a nation that has been unable to seat them together in the same schools. So we watch them in brutal solidarity burning the huts of a poor village, but we realize that they would never live on the same block in Detroit. I could not be silent in the face of such cruel manipulation of the poor. . . .

For those who ask the question, "Aren't you a civil rights leader?" and thereby mean to exclude me from the movement for peace, I have this further answer. In 1957 when a group of us formed the Southern Christian Leadership Conference, we chose as our motto: "To save the soul of America." We were convinced that we could not limit our vision to certain rights for black people, but instead affirmed the conviction that America would never be free or saved from itself unless the descendants of its slaves were loosed completely from the shackles they still wear. In a way we were agreeing with Langston Hughes, the black bard of Harlem, who had written earlier:

O, yes,
I say it plain,
America never was America to me,
And yet I swear this oath —
America will be!

Now, it should be incandescently clear that no one who has any concern for the integrity and life of America today can ignore the present war. If America's soul becomes totally poisoned, part of the autopsy must read Vietnam. It can never be saved so long as it destroys the deepest hopes of men the world over. So it is that those of us who are yet determined that America *will* be are led down the path of protest and dissent, working for the health of our land.

As if the weight of such a commitment to the life and health of America were not enough, another burden of responsibility was placed upon me in 1964; and I cannot forget that the Nobel Prize for Peace was also a commission—a commission to work harder than I had ever worked before "the brotherhood of man." This is a calling that takes me beyond national allegiances, but even if it were not present I would yet have to live with the meaning of my commitment to the ministry of Jesus Christ. To me the relationship of this ministry to the making of peace is so obvious that I sometimes marvel at those who ask me why I am speaking against the war. Could it be that they do not know that the good news was meant for all men—for Communist and capitalist, for their children and ours, for black and for white, for revolutionary and conservative? Have they forgotten that my ministry is in obedience to the one who loved his enemies so fully that he died for them? What then can I say to the "Vietcong" or to Castro or to Mao as a faithful minister of this one? Can I threaten them with death or must I not share with them my life?

Finally, as I try to delineate for you and for myself the road that leads from Montgomery to this place I would have offered all that was most valid if I simply said that I must be true to my conviction that I share with all men the calling to be a son of the living God. Beyond the calling of race or nation or creed in this vocation of sonship and brotherhood, and because I believe that the Father is deeply concerned especially for his suffering and helpless and outcast children, I come tonight to speak for them.

This I believe to be the privilege and the burden of all of us who deem ourselves bound by allegiances and loyalties which are broader and deeper than nationalism and which go beyond our nation's self-defined goals and positions. We are called to speak for the weak, for the voiceless, for victims of our nation and for those it calls enemy, for no document from human hands can make these humans any less our brothers. . . .

I am convinced that if we are to get on the right side of the world revolution, we as a nation must undergo a radical revolution of values. We must rapidly begin the shift from a "thing-oriented" society to a "person-oriented" society. When machines and computers, profit motives and property rights are considered more important than people, the giant triplets of racism, materialism, and militarism are incapable of being conquered.

A true revolution of values will soon cause us to question the fairness and justice of many of our past and present policies. On the one hand we are called to play the good Samaritan on life's roadside; but that will be only an initial act. One day we must come to see that the whole Jericho road must be transformed so that men and women will not be constantly beaten and robbed as they make their journey on life's highway. True compassion is more than flinging a coin to a beggar; it is not haphazard and superficial. It comes to see that an edifice which produces beggars needs restructuring. A true revolution of values will soon look uneasily on the glaring contrast of poverty and wealth. With righteous indignation, it will look across the seas and see individual capitalists of the West investing huge sums of money in Asia, Africa and South America, only to take the profits out with no concern for the social betterment of the countries, and say: "This is not just." It will look at our alliance with the landed gentry of Latin America and say: "This is not just." The Western arrogance of feeling that it has everything to teach others and nothing to learn from them is not just. A true revolution of values will lay hands on the world order and say of war: "This way of settling differences is not just." This business of burning human beings with napalm, of filling our nation's homes with orphans and widows, of injecting poisonous drugs of hate into veins of peoples normally humane, of sending men home from dark and bloody battlefields physically handicapped and psychologically deranged, cannot be reconciled with wisdom, justice and love. A nation that continues year after year to spend more money on military defense than on programs of social uplift is approaching spiritual death.

America, the richest and most powerful nation in the world, can well lead the way in this revolution of values. There is nothing, except a tragic death wish, to prevent us from reordering our priorities, so that the pursuit of peace will take precedence over the pursuit of war. There is nothing to keep us from molding a recalcitrant status quo with bruised hands until we have fashioned it into a brotherhood. . . .

39

The Media Begin to Question

The Tet offensive, though crushed by American and South Vietnamese forces, showed more strength on the part of the Communists than Washington had calculated and brought conventional journalism to questioning the progress of the war. Walter Cronkite was among the first to express doubts and did so in this report for CBS television on February 27, 1968.

. . . Tonight, back in more familiar surroundings in New York, we'd like to sum up our findings in Vietnam, an analysis that must be speculative, personal, subjective. Who won and who lost in the great Tet offensive against the cities? I'm not sure. The Viet Cong did not win by a knockout, but neither did we. The referees of history may make it a draw. Another stand-off may be coming in the big battles expected south of the Demilitarized Zone. Khe Sanh could well fall, with a terrible loss in American lives, prestige and morale, and this is a tragedy of our

Source: CBS Television, "Who, What, When, Where, Why: Report from Vietnam by Walter Cronkite," February 27, 1968, in Peter Braestrup, *Big Story: How the American Press and Television Reported and Interpreted the Crisis of Tet 1968 in Vietnam and Washington,* 2 (Boulder, Colorado: Westview Press, 1977), 188–89. Reprinted by permission.

stubbornness there; but the bastion no longer is a key to the rest of the northern regions, and it is doubtful that the American forces can be defeated across the breadth of the DMZ with any substantial loss of ground. Another stand-off. On the political front, past performance gives no confidence that the Vietnamese government can cope with its problems, now compounded by the attack on the cities. It may not fall, it may hold on, but it probably won't show the dynamic qualities demanded of this young nation. Another stand-off.

We have been too often disappointed by the optimism of the American leaders, both in Vietnam and Washington, to have faith any longer in the silver linings they find in the darkest clouds. They may be right, that Hanoi's winter-spring offensive has been forced by the communist realization that they could not win the longer war of attrition, and that the communists hope that any success in the offensive will improve their position for eventual negotiations. It would improve their position, and it would also require our realization, that we should have had all along, that any negotiations must be that—negotiations, not the dictation of peace terms. For it seems now more certain than ever that the bloody experience of Vietnam is to end in a stalemate. This summer's almost certain stand-off will either end in real give-and-take negotiations or terrible escalation; and for every means we have to escalate, the enemy can match us, and that applies to invasion of the North, the use of nuclear weapons, or the mere commitment of 100—, or 200—, or 300,000 more American troops to the battle. And with each escalation, the world comes closer to the brink of cosmic disaster.

To say that we are closer to victory today is to believe, in the face of the evidence, the optimists who have been wrong in the past. To suggest we are on the edge of defeat is to yield to unreasonable pessimism. To say that we are mired in stalemate seems the only realistic, yet unsatisfactory, conclusion. On the off chance that military and political analysts are right, in the next few months we must test the enemy's intentions, in case this is indeed his last gasp before negotiations. But it is increasingly clear to this reporter that the only rational way out then will be to negotiate, not as victors, but as an honorable people who lived up to their pledge to defend democracy, and did the best they could.

This is Walter Cronkite. Good night.

40

"To Them, Warfare Is . . . No Reality"

Photographer David Douglas Duncan here registers, in a piece entitled I Protest!, *a plea both for American marines and for the Vietnamese the American military was killing. The South Vietnamese and American post at Khe Sanh was under a major siege by Communist forces that began shortly before the Tet offensive. Hue was a city occupied by the Communists during that offensive. There they carried out a butchery of civilians. An especially ferocious battle drove the occupiers out of Hue.*

The significance of our frustrations at Khe Sanh goes beyond discredited military strategy. It goes beyond the fact that the three senior government civilians who originated America's *war* policy for Vietnam—President Johnson, Secretary of State Rusk and former Secretary of Defense McNamara—lack any kind of field combat experience and so, to them, warfare is a matter of top-secret papers and maps and briefings—and no reality. Judging by evidence from around the rest of the world—the non-Communist world—one conclusion is now inescapable regarding this war. Despite all of the Hanoi oil depots in flames, all of the dropped bridges, every MiG-21 shot down, all of our lost fighter-bomber pilots and those boots of dead paratroopers, and even my heroic, trapped friends at Khe Sanh—despite all of this, there is one fact that must be faced. By standing up to us Americans, with our incredible military power, industrial wealth and men under arms, and with reserves of more of everything still uncommitted to battle . . . by just standing up to us and absorbing each body punch we throw, the Viet Cong and the North Vietnamese have beaten us in the eyes of the rest of the world—even if every one of their soldiers should die in his sandals, tonight. We may destroy them and their slender jungle land beyond recall of the slightest glimmer of life for a hundred years—and they still will be the victors. Because they stood—forget their credo—against the most powerful nation ever to exist on the face of the earth, and, in the end, it was they, the simple rice farmers and fishermen and their children, who were stronger. . . .

The concept of hanging American prestige and honor and military

Source: David Douglas Duncan, *I Protest!* (New York: A Signet Broadside, The New American Library, 1968), no pagination. Reprinted by permission.

valor on the defense of Khe Sanh is sad indeed. Equally tragic was the White House–Saigon method of freeing Hué from the North Vietnamese Army and Viet Cong political cadres who occupied the most ancient Vietnamese cultural shrine during the first days of the *Tet* offensive. Prior to *Tet,* and the disaster it brought upon the entire countryside, Hué was viewed as little more than a tourist attraction for American troops based in Vietnam. The students at its university appeared to sympathize with Ho Chi Minh more than Marshal Ky, but that was true in many towns other than Hué. It was a fine place to take Instamatic color shots for the folks at home, proving that a guy really was serving his country in exotic Asia. Hué was of no recorded military importance. Then the Communists grabbed it and dug in, with their own flag unfurled over

This photo, showing South Vietnamese National Police Chief Brigadier General Nguyen Ngoc Loan killing an enemy soldier with a single pistol shot to the head, vividly demonstrated the horrors of the war. Caught on camera, the summary execution was shown on nationwide American television and reported in the newspapers. *(Courtesy, Wide World Photo)*

the city's historic Citadel. And that spelled the destruction of Hué and the death of untold hundreds of its civilians. We Americans pounded the Citadel and surrounding city almost to dust with air strikes, napalm runs, artillery and naval gunfire and the direct cannon fire of tanks and recoilless rifles—a total effort to root out and kill every enemy soldier. Christ! The mind reels at the carnage, cost—and almost fanatical ruthlessness of it all. Wouldn't a siege-blockade have been a more effective, and less wasteful, military tactic? It had been employed only since before the Crusades—those earlier religious wars to the death.

It seemed that so long as a single Communist survived to shoot back at the attacking Marines and South Vietnamese Rangers, Westmoreland would continue to order counter-battery fire, punching every red button in his Saigon command post. Apparently it was intolerable to contemplate having the Viet Cong flag flutter over Hué during the lengthy weeks of blockade that would surely have ensued until a surrender was forced upon the enemy troopers holed up in the once sleepy old city. When Kyoto, the religious heart of Japan, was marked for destruction by our Army Air Force during World War II, it was saved at the last moment by Secretary of War Stimson. He had visited Kyoto's shrines long before the war, and he held a protective hand over the tiny pinhead marking just another target on a war room wall map. Assistant Secretary of War John J. McCloy saved classic Rothenberg, Germany, in like manner. As a child in Philadelphia he had fallen in love with an engraving of the romantic medieval town which his mother had brought home from her first trip to Europe. Poor Hué! It had no friends or protectors in Saigon—or anywhere. Now it is gone; scattered Communists still snipe from the rubble, and our Marine dead are on their way home. Now, too, a fresh North Vietnamese division is reportedly moving toward Hué— seemingly bent upon besieging the Americans setting up housekeeping in the ruins. . . .

[A]s the worst example of the Vietnam war rhetoric, there is something so fundamentally offensive to Marines everywhere that it is rarely discussed with outsiders. It was forced upon them by the Department of Defense—and they feel it is degrading and humiliating them as Marines and as human beings. Their shame—and it should be our national shame—rests on the only two words being used to distinguish between victory and defeat in the war in Vietnam: "Body Count."

Every "Free World Forces" press conference reeks with these two words; each American Armed Forces broadcast is prefaced by the "Body Count" of that day's action; all records of every skirmish or major campaign feature, above everything else, "Body Count." It is inescapable, insidious, corrosive—even among veterans of other wars, where victory was represented by hilltops overrun, sea walls breached then bypassed, islands secured and cities captured and whole armies taken prisoner. Who, in the name of God and decency, can remember anyone posting daily "Body Count" scores during the battles for Salerno, Iwo Jima, Omaha Beach, Remagen Bridge, Stalingrad or even Berlin. But, now! Someone, apparently in Washington, decided that there *must* be a way to keep score in a war where there are no victories, ever, in the conventional meaning of the word as related to combat. If "Body Count" is considered victory, does it mean we threaten genocide to all who oppose us and our arms and our political philosophy? . . .

By comparison to what is happening to *us,* the future of the war in Vietnam seems simple, and a solution easy. The President of the United States has asked us all, "What would you do if you were here in my place, as President?" Well, Mr. President, I would do three things without delay:

1. I would immediately order the complete cessation of bombing of North Vietnam, *with whom we are not at war.* We might still regain a fraction of our lost respect in this world community while, I hope, there is something left to salvage.

2. I would order all fighter and bomber crews to concentrate on Viet Cong and North Vietnamese Army installations and routes of supply in *South* Vietnam until a cease-fire is secured. One might imagine the relief of our pilots at being assigned targets reasonably uncluttered by such operational inconveniences as SAMs and antiaircraft fire, and even air-to-air missiles fired by the few surviving MiGs in North Vietnam.

3. I would ask the United Nations to sponsor and police a referendum to be held throughout all of South Vietnam. The referendum would pose only three questions of the South Vietnamese populace:

    a. Do you wish to unite into a single state with North Vietnam?

    b. Do you wish to remain a separate and independent state?

    c. If you wish to remain a separate and independent state, do you wish the assitance of the Americans in your task of nation-building?

Upon these answers, Mr. President, I would base my future policy and conduct of the war in South Vietnam. I would then concentrate on finding an honorable and stable role for the United States of America in the world of tomorrow.

But there is very little time.

41

The Challenger

In receiving in the New Hampshire Democratic primary a vote nearly equal to President Johnson's, Senator Eugene McCarthy of Minnesota was instrumental in changing the course of Democratic politics. Here he recounts some of the reasons he turned against the President's policies in Vietnam.

As the year 1966 wore on and criticism of the war mounted, the Administration became more defensive and the language of its response more violent.

The motives of those who spoke out were questioned. Critics of the war were called "nervous Nellies" and "special pleaders." At a Medal of Honor ceremony in December 1966, the President had a word for dissenters:

> [The war] is a cause which deserves not only the bravery of our soldiers, but the patience and fortitude of all of our citizens.
>
> And all of these we have in good supply.
>
> It far outweighs the reluctance of men who exercise so well the right of dissent, but let others fight to protect them from those whose very philosophy is to do away with the right of dissent. . . .

At the same time, reassuring and optimistic reports on the war itself continued to be issued. . . .

In January 1967, our Ambassador to Vietnam, Henry Cabot Lodge, had predicted "sensational" military gains in 1967. He added that open peace negotiations would probably never take place; rather, the enemy would merely fade away.

On April 28, 1967, the Commanding General, William C. Westmoreland, at the request of the Administration, appeared before a joint meeting of the Congress. Much of General Westmoreland's statement dealt with his estimate of the military situation and his anticipation of the enemy's possible future strategy. He said that our forces and those of the other free world allies had grown in strength and profited from experience.

Source: Eugene J. McCarthy, *The Year of the People* (Garden City, New York: Doubleday and Company, 1969), 37–40. Reprinted by permission.

Of the South Vietnamese army, he asserted:

> What I see now in Vietnam is a military force that performs with growing professional skill. During the last six months, Vietnamese troops have scored repeated successes against some of the best Vietcong and North Vietnamese army units.

We were fighting a war with no front lines, he pointed out, and we could not measure progress by lines on a map. We had to use other means to chart progress. As examples of progress:

> Two years ago . . . there were three jet-capable runways in South Vietnam. Today there are fourteen. . . . Then there was one deep-water port for sea-going ships. Now there are seven. . . .
> During 1965 the Republic of Vietnam Armed Forces and its allies killed 36,000 of the enemy at a cost of approximately 12,000 friendly killed, and 90 percent of these were Vietnamese. During recent months this 3 to 1 ratio in favor of the allies has risen significantly and in some weeks has been as high as 10 or 20 to 1 in our favor.

The Westmoreland statement did not move the critics of the war. The escalation continued through 1967: the bombing was expanded steadily; casualties, both civilian and military, continued to mount.

In January and February of 1967, our military forces in Vietnam conducted "Operation Cedar Falls" and "Operation Junction City," uprooting large numbers of Vietnamese from their homes and lands and removing them to resettlement villages surrounded by barbed wire. American artillery in South Vietnam began shelling North Vietnam, and we started to mine North Vietnamese rivers. By April, we were bombing power plants inside Haiphong, and we attacked North Vietnamese MIG bases for the first time.

We moved troops into the demilitarized zone and bombed a power plant a mile north of the center of Hanoi. Twice we accidentally struck Soviet ships in North Vietnamese ports. In June, our troop strength in Vietnam reached 463,000.

In August, United States planes destroyed Vietnam's most important railway bridge linking Hanoi with Haiphong and China. We admitted we had been bombing in Laos since 1964. Also in August, a "maximum limit" of 525,000 American troops was authorized for Vietnam.

In his address to the Congress, Westmoreland had cited the help of our allies:

It is also worthy of note that 30 other nations are providing noncombat support. . . . Their exploits deserve recognition, not only for their direct contribution to the overall effort, but for their symbolic reminder that the whole of free Asia opposes communist expansion.

Westmoreland neglected to mention that, with the exception of a few nations such as Korea for whose assistance we are paying, assistance to Vietnam by most governments is largely of a humanitarian nature, aimed at relieving the suffering and rebuilding the war damage.

42

A Liberal Supports the War

Vietnam had been to a large extent the liberals' war, an expression of the Cold War that had been in good part the work of liberals. Yet as the war continued, liberals became disaffected from it, and conservatives remained as its more energetic supporters. John A. Roche, a columnist and former president of the liberal Americans for Democratic Action, maintained the older liberal view of Southeast Asia. On December 18, 1969, the conservative Republican Senator Robert Dole of Congress requested that Roche's article in The Washington Post *be included in the* Congressional Record.

The poor old Democratic Party is in worse shape today than it has been in some time—since perhaps 1956. When the Republicans have problems—as they did in 1964—there is always a good simple remedy. But the Democrats, alas, are not so easily doctored: too many of their troubles are, as my father would have put it, "in the head." The GOP can go out and get a few stitches—the Democrats need a psychiatrist.

Take the cross pressures at work on, say, Hubert Humphrey, or Ed Muskie, or Fred Harris. A tremendously articulate constituency is at

Source: Congressional Record, 91st Cong., 1st Sess. (December 18, 1969), vol. 115, pt. 29, 40068.

work on them day and night telling them that unless the party makes Vietnam the issue, and comes out for instant withdrawal, the Democrats are through. These are mostly fine sincere people. Though the Communist Party and other sects have undoubtedly played an important organizational role in the antiwar movement, the great majority of the protesters are there on their own. (Unfortunately, the Attorney General does not seem to understand that these two propositions are not inconsistent.)

I admit that I am fundamentally baffled by the wildly irrational response to Vietnam in intellectual circles, but there it is. So we have a situation where leading academic and cultural figures—who will always get press and media coverage—are socking it to Humphrey, Muskie, Harris, et al. And they can not be dismissed automatically as "Commies," "dupes," or just fanatics. Many of them have worked hard and loyally in past campaigns. And, I repeat (despite the fact that some of the scars on my back ache) they are fundamentally decent people, driven by a deep concern for American national interest as they see it.

I, for example, spent 21 years as a member of Americans for Democratic Action—three years as national chairman. Throughout that period ADA was the nesting place of Cold War liberals, a designation that I am proud to accept though it has recently become a term of abuse. Hubert Humphrey is also a former national chairman of ADA and— even though we left the organization—many personal ties and warm memories of past campaigns remain.

But, even making personal allowances, what can one make of an ADA decision to oppose Senate Resolution No. 280? The key section of the resolution reads that the Senate "affirms its support for the President in his efforts to negotiate a just peace in Vietnam, expresses the earnest hope of the (American) people . . . for such a peace, . . . approves and supports the principles . . . that the people of South Vietnam are entitled to choose their own government by means of free elections . . . and that the U.S. is willing to abide by the results of such elections and requests the President to call upon (Hanoi) to join in a proclamation of a mutual cease-fire and to announce its willingness to honor such elections and abide by the results. . . ."

Regrettably, opposition to this resolution can only be founded on one premise: ADA has a vested interest in an American catastrophe in Vietnam. Having predicted disaster so long and stridently (national chairman John K. Galbraith, for example, announced shortly after the Tet offensive in 1968 that the Saigon government would collapse in two weeks!), ADA has reached the point of no return.

But what sense can this position make to a liberal politician? In immediate terms, he knows that if things go well in Vietnam, President Nixon wins—and if they go badly, the liberals (who got us there) lose.

In broader terms, however, the impact of liberal catastrophe politics would be a long-run disaster—if the American people ever get it through their heads that liberal Democrats are rooting for an American defeat in Southeast Asia, we will be through politically for the rest of the century.

Humphrey, of course, knows this—it helps to account for his occasionally schizophrenic political behavior. As chief psychiatrist of the Democratic Party—a fearful job—he deserves considerably more sympathy and understanding than he has received.

43

A War on Nonwhites?

Noam Chomsky, known for his studies on the origin and character of language, has also gained recognition for relentless opposition to American foreign policy. Here he connects atrocities in Vietnam to an American tradition. "Pinkville" was slang for Song My or Son My, within which occurred the massacre at My Lai.

And now there is Song My—"Pinkville." More than two decades of indoctrination and counterrevolutionary interventions have created the possibility of a name like "Pinkville"—and the acts that may be done in a place so named. Orville and Jonathan Schell have pointed out what any literate person should realize, that this was no isolated atrocity but the logical consequence of a virtual war of extermination directed against helpless peasants: "enemies," "reds," "dinks." But there are, perhaps, still deeper roots. Some time ago, I read with a slight shock the statement by Eqbal Ahmad that "America has institutionalized even its genocide," referring to the fact that the extermination of the Indians "has become the object of public entertainment and children's games." Shortly after, I was thumbing through my daughter's fourth-grade social science reader. The protagonist, Robert, is told the story of the extermination of the Pequot tribe by Captain John Mason:

Source: Noam Chomsky, *At War With Asia* (New York: Pantheon Books, 1970), 102–03. Reprinted by permission.

His little army attacked in the morning before it was light and took the Pequots by surprise. The soldiers broke down the stockade with their axes, rushed inside, and set fire to the wigwams. They killed nearly all the braves, squaws, and children, and burned their corn and other food. There were no Pequots left to make more trouble. When the other Indian tribes saw what good fighters the white men were, they kept the peace for many years.

"I wish I were a man and had been there," thought Robert.

Nowhere does Robert express, or hear, second thoughts about the matter. The text omits some other pertinent remarks: for example, Cotton Mather, who said that "It was supposed that no less than six hundred Pequot souls were brought down to hell that day." Is it an exaggeration to suggest that our history of extermination and racism is reaching its climax in Vietnam today? It is not a question that Americans can easily put aside.

44

"To Pacify Our Own Hearts"

In testimony before the Senate Foreign Relations Committee in late April 1971, Vietnam navy veteran John Kerry, who is now himself a Senator from Massachusetts, testified on behalf of other disaffected veterans. The participation of Vietnam veterans was one of the most convincing components of the anti-war movement.

    . . . I would like to talk on behalf of all those veterans and say that several months ago in Detroit we had an investigation at which over 150 honorably discharged, and many very highly decorated, veterans testified to war crimes committed in Southeast Asia. These were not isolated incidents but crimes committeed on a day to day basis with the full awareness of officers at all levels of command.

    It is impossible to describe to you exactly what did happen in Detroit—the emotions in the room and the feelings of the men who were

Source: Congressional Record, 92nd Cong., 1st Sess. (April 23, 1971), vol. 117, pt. 9, 11738–11739.

reliving their experiences in Vietnam. They relived the absolute horror of what this country, in a sense, made them do.

They told stories that at times they had personally raped, cut off ears, cut of[f] heads, taped wires from portable telephones to human genitals and turned up the power, cut off limbs, blown up bodies, randomly shot at civilians, razed villages in fashion reminiscent of Genghis Khan, shot cattle and dogs for fun, poisoned food stocks, and generally ravaged the countryside of South Vietnam in addition to the normal ravage of war and the normal and very particular ravaging which is done by the applied bombing power of this country.

We call this investigation the Winter Soldier Investigation. The term Winter Soldier is a play on words of Thomas Paine's in 1776 when he spoke of the Sunshine Patriots and summer time soldiers who deserted. . . .

We who have come here to Washington have come here because we feel we have to be winter soldiers now. We could come back to this country, we could be quiet, we could hold our silence, we could not tell what went on in Vietnam, but we feel because of what threatens this country, not the reds, but the crimes which we are committing that threaten it, that we have to speak out.

I would like to talk to you a little bit about what the result is of the feelings these men carry with them after coming back from Vietnam. The country doesn't know it yet but it has created a monster, a monster in the form of millions of men who have been taught to deal and to trade in violence and who are given the chance to die for the biggest nothing in history; men who have returned with a sense of anger and a sense of betrayal which no one has yet grasped.

As a veteran and one who feels this anger I would like to talk about it. We are angry because we feel we have been used in the worst fashion by the administration of this country.

In 1970 at West Point Vice President Agnew said "some glamorize the criminal misfits of society while our best men die in Asian rice paddies to preserve the freedom which most of those misfits abuse," and this was used as a rallying point for our effort in Vietnam.

But for us, as boys in Asia whom the country was supposed to support, his statement is a terrible distortion from which we can only draw a very deep sense of revulsion, and hence the anger of some of the men who are here in Washington today. It is a distortion because we in no way consider ourselves the best men of this country; because those he calls misfits were standing up for us in a way that nobody else in this country dared to; because so many who have died would have returned to this country to join the misfits in their efforts to ask for an immediate withdrawal from South Vietnam; because so many of those best men have returned as quadruplegics and amputees—and they lie forgotten in Veterans Administration Hospitals in this country which fly the flag which so many have chosen as their own personal symbol—and we cannot consider ourselves America's best men when we are ashamed of and hated for what we were called on to do in Southeast Asia.

In our opinion, and from our experience, there is nothing in South Vietnam which could happen that realistically threatens the United States of America. And to attempt to justify the loss of one American life in Vietnam, Cambodia or Laos by linking such loss to the preservation of freedom, which those misfits supposedly abuse, is to us the height of criminal hypocrisy, and it is that kind of hypocrisy which we feel has torn this country apart.

We are probably much more angry than that, but I don't want to go into the foreign policy aspects because I am outclassed here. I know that all of you talk about every possible alternative to getting out of Vietnam. We understand that. We know you have considered the seriousness of the aspects to the utmost level and I am not going to try to dwell on that. But I want to relate to you the feeling that many of the men who have returned to this country express because we are probably angriest about all that we were told about Vietnam and about the mystical war again[st] communism.

We found that not only was it a civil war, an effort by a people who had for years been seeking their liberation from any colonial influence whatsoever, but also we found that the Vietnamese whom we had enthusiastically molded after our own image were hard put to take up the fight against the threat we were supposedly saving them from.

We found most people didn't even know the difference between communism and democracy. They only wanted to work in rice paddies without helicopters strafing them and bombs with napalm burning their villages and tearing their country apart. They wanted everything to do with the war, particularly with this foreign presence of the United States of America, to leave them alone in peace, and they practiced the art of survival by siding with whichever military force was present at a particular time, be it Viet Cong, North Vietnamese or American.

We found also that all too often American men were dying in those rice paddies for want of support from their allies. We saw first hand how monies from American taxes were used for a corrupt dictatorial regime. We saw that many people in this country had a one-sided idea of who was kept free by our flag, and blacks provided the highest percentage of casualties. We saw Vietnam ravaged equally by American bombs and search and destroy missions, as well as by Viet Cong terrorism, and yet we listened while this country tried to blame all of the havoc on the Viet Cong.

We rationalized destroying villages in order to save them. We saw America lose her sense of morality as she accepted very coolly a My Lai and refused to give up the image of American soldiers who hand out chocolate bars and chewing gum.

We learned the meaning of free fire zones, shooting anything that moves, and we watched while America placed a cheapness on the lives of orientals.

We watched the United States falsification of body counts, in fact the glorification of body counts. We listened while month after month we were told the back of the enemy was about to break. We fought using weapons against "oriental human beings." We fought using weapons against those people which I do not believe this country would dream of using were we fighting in the European theater. We watched while men charged up hills because a general said that hill has to be taken, and after losing one platoon or two platoons they marched away to leave the hill for reoccupation by the North Vietnamese. We watched pride allow the most unimportant battles to be blown into extravaganzas, because we couldn't lose, and we couldn't retreat, and because it didn't matter how many American bodies were lost to prove that point, and so there were Hamburger Hills and Khe Sahns [sic] and Hill 81s and Fire Base 6s, and so many others. . . .

. . . [Y]ou think about a poster in this country with a picture of Uncle Sam and the picture says "I want you." And a young man comes out of high school and says, "that is fine, I am going to serve my country," and he goes to Vietnam and he shoots and he kills and he does his job. Or maybe he doesn't kill. Maybe he just goes and he comes back, and when he gets back to this country he finds that he isn't really wanted, because the largest corps of unemployed in the country—it varies depending on who you get it from, the Veterans Administration says 15 percent and various other sources 22 percent—but the largest corps of unemployed in this country are veterans of this war, and of those veterans 33 percent of the unemployed are black. That means one out of every ten of the nation's unemployed is a veteran of Vietnam.

The hospitals across the country won't, or can't meet their demands. It is not a question of not trying; they haven't got the appropriations. A man recently died after he had a tracheotomy in California, not because of the operation but because there weren't enough personnel to clean the mucus out of his tube and he suffocated to death.

Another young man just died in a New York VA Hospital the other day. A friend of mine was lying in a bed two beds away and tried to help him but he couldn't. He rang a bell and there was nobody there to service that man and so he died of convulsions.

I understand 57 percent of all those entering the VA hospitals talk about suicide. Some 27 percent have tried, and they try because they come back to this country and they have to face what they did in Vietnam, and then they come back and find the indifference of a country that doesn't really care. . . .

An American Indian friend of mine who lives in the Indian Nation of Alcatraz put it to me very succinctly. He told me how as a boy on an Indian reservation he had watched television and he used to cheer the cowboys when they came in and shot the Indians, and then suddenly one day he stopped in Vietnam and he said "my God, I am doing to these people the very same thing that was done to my people," and he stopped. And that is what we are trying to say, that we think this thing has to end.

We are also here to ask, and we are here to ask vehemently, where are the leaders of our country? Where is the leadership? We are here to ask where are McNamara, Rostow, Bundy, Gilpatrick and so many others? Where are they now that we, the men whom they sent off to war, have returned? These are commanders who have deserted their troops, and there is no more serious crime in the law of war. The Army says they never leave their wounded. The Marines say they never leave even their dead. These men have left all the casualties and retreated behind a pious shield of public rectitude. They have left the real stuff of their reputations bleaching behind them in the sun in this country.

Finally, this administration has done us the ultimate dishonor. They have attempted to disown us and the sacrifices we made for this country. In their blindness and fear they have tried to deny that we are veterans or that we served in Nam. We do not need their testimony. Our own scars and stumps of limbs are witness enough for others and for ourselves.

We wish that a merciful God could wipe away our own memories of that service as easily as this administration has wiped away their memories of us. But all that they have done and all that they can do by this denial is to make more clear than ever our own determination to undertake one last mission—to search out and destroy the last vestige of this barbaric war, to pacify our own hearts, to conquer the hate and the fear that have driven this country these last ten years and more. And more. And so when 30 years from now our brothers go down the street without a leg, without an arm, or a face, and small boys ask why, we will be able to say "Vietnam" and not mean a desert, not a filthy obscene memory, but mean instead the place where America finally turned and where soldiers like us helped it in the turning.

Thank you.

45

"Never Before Has a Land Been So . . . Mutilated"

The Congressional Record *for January 28, 1972, carries a speech by Senator Gaylord Nelson of Wisconsin introducing a bill for assessing the ecological damage to South Vietnam, Laos, and Cambodia by the American military. The devastation of the land of Vietnam was one of the most spectacular effects of the war.*

. . . [S]uppose we took gigantic bulldozers and scraped the land bare of trees and bushes at the rate of 1,000 acres a day or 44 million square feet a day until we had flattened an area the size of Rhode Island, 750,000 acres.

Suppose we flew huge planes over the land and sprayed 100 million pounds of poisonous herbicides on the forests until we had destroyed an area of prime forests the size of Massachusetts or 5½ million acres.

Suppose we flew B-52 bombers over the land, dropping 500-pound bombs until we had dropped almost 3 pounds per person for every man, woman and child on earth—8 billion pounds—and created 23 million craters on the land measuring 26 feet deep and 40 feet in diameter.

Suppose the major objective of the bombing is not enemy troops but rather a vague and unsuccessful policy of harassment and territorial denial called pattern or carpet bombing.

Suppose the land destruction involves 80 percent of the timber forests and 10 percent of all the cultivated land in the Nation.

We would consider such results a monumental catastrophe. That is what we have done to our ally, South Vietnam.

While under heavy pressure the military finally stopped the chemical defoliation war and has substituted another massive war against the land itself by a program of pattern or carpet bombing and massive land clearing with a huge machine called Rome Plow.

The huge areas destroyed[,] pockmarked, scorched, and bulldozed resemble the moon and are no longer productive.

This is the documented story from on-the-spot studies and pictures done by two distinguished scientists, Prof. E. W. Pfeiffer and Prof. Arthur H. Westing. These are the same scientists who made the defoliation studies that alerted Congress and the country to the grave implica-

---

Source: Congressional Record, 92nd Cong., 2nd Sess. (January 28, 1972), vol. 118, pt. 2, 1634–1635.

Mangrove forests in Vietnam before and after defoliation. *(Courtesy, U.P.I.)*

tions of our chemical warfare program in Vietnam, which has now been terminated.

The story of devastation revealed by their movies, slides, and statistics is beyond the human mind to fully comprehend. We have senselessly blown up, bulldozed over, poisoned and permanently damaged an area so vast that it literally boggles the mind.

Quite frankly . . . I am unable adequately to describe the horror of what we have done there.

There is nothing in the history of warfare to compare with it. A "scorched earth" policy has been a tactic of warfare throughout history but never before has a land been so massively altered and mutilated that vast areas can never be used again or even inhabited by man or animal.

This is impersonal, automated and mechanistic warfare brought to its logical conclusion—utter, permanent, total destruction.

The tragedy of it all is that no one knows or understands what is happening there, or why, or to what end. We have simply unleashed a gigantic machine which goes about its impersonal business, destroying whatever is there without plan or purpose. The finger of responsibility points everywhere but nowhere in particular. Who designed this policy of war against the land, and why? Nobody seems to know and nobody rationally can defend it.

Those grand strategists who draw the lines on the maps and order the B-52 strikes never see the face of that innocent peasant whose land has been turned into a pock-marked moon surface in 30 seconds of violence without killing a single enemy soldier because none were there.

If they could see and understand the result, they would not draw the lines or send the bombers.

If Congress knew and understood, we would not appropriate the money.

If the President of the United States knew and understood, he would stop it in 30 minutes.

If the people of America knew and understood, they would remove from office those responsible for it, if they could ever find out who is responsible. But they will never know, because nobody knows.

By any conceivable standard of measurement, the cost benefit ratio of our program of defoliation, carpet bombing with B-52's, and bulldozing is so negative that it simply spells bankruptcy. It did not protect our soldiers or defeat the enemy, and it has done far greater damage to our ally than to the enemy.

These programs should be halted immediately before further permanent damage is done to the landscape.

The cold, hard, and cruel irony of it all is that South Vietnam would have been better off losing to Hanoi than winning with us. Now she faces the worst of all possible worlds with much of her land destroyed and her chances of independent survival after we leave in grave doubt at best.

This has been a hard speech to give and harder to write because I did not know what to say and how to say it—and I still do not know. But I do know that when the members of Congress finally understand what we are doing there, neither they nor the people of this Nation will sleep well that night.

For many reasons I did not want to make this speech but someone has to say it, somewhere, sometime. . . .

46

Born on the Fourth of July

Ron Kovic came back from Vietnam confined to a wheelchair. His book, Born on the Fourth of July, *has been rendered into a film. Here he describes the protest that he and other antiwar veterans carried out at the Republican Convention of 1972.*

People had begun to sit down all around me. They all had Four More Years buttons and I was surprised to see how many of them were young. I began speaking to them, telling them about the Last Patrol and why veterans from all over the United States had taken the time and effort to travel thousands of miles to the Republican National Convention. "I'm a disabled veteran!" I shouted. "I served two tours of duty in Vietnam and while on my second tour of duty up in the DMZ I was wounded and paralyzed from the chest down." I told them I would be that way for the rest of my life. Then I began to talk about the hospitals and how they treated the returning veterans like animals, how I, many nights in the Bronx, had lain in my own shit for hours waiting for an aide. "And they never come," I said. "They never come because that man that's going to accept the nomination tonight has been lying to all of us and spending the money on war that should be spent on healing and helping the wounded. That's the biggest lie and hypocrisy of all—that we had to

Source: Ron Kovic, *Born on the Fourth of July* (New York: Signet Books, 1977), 178–80, 183–84. Reprinted by permission.

March on the Pentagon.

go over there and fight and get crippled and come home to a government and leaders who could care less about the same boys they sent over."

I kept shouting and speaking, looking for some kind of reaction from the crowd. No one seemed to want to even look at me.

"Is it too real for you to look at? Is this wheelchair too much for you to take? The man who will accept the nomination tonight is a liar!" I shouted again and again, until finally one of the security men came back and told me to be quiet or they would have to take me to the back of the hall.

I told him that if they tried to move me or touch my chair there would be a fight and hell to pay right there in front of Walter Cronkite and the national television networks. I told him if he wanted to wrestle me and beat me to the floor of the convention hall in front of all those cameras he could.

By then a couple of newsmen, including Roger Mudd from CBS, had worked their way through the security barricades and begun to ask me questions.

"Why are you here tonight?" Roger Mudd asked me. "But don't start talking until I get the camera here," he shouted.

It was too good to be true. In a few seconds Roger Mudd and I would be going on live all over the country. I would be doing what I had come here for, showing the whole nation what the war was all about. The camera began to roll, and I began to explain why I and the others had come, that the war was wrong and it had to stop immediately. "I'm a Vietnam veteran," I said. "I gave America my all and the leaders of this government threw me and the others away to rot in their V.A hospitals. What's happening in Vietnam is a crime against humanity, and I just want the American people to know that we have come all the way across this country, sleeping on the ground and in the rain, to let the American people see for themselves the men who fought their war and have come to oppose it. If you can't believe the veteran who fought the war and was wounded in the war, who can you believe?"

"Thank you," said Roger Mudd, visibly moved by what I had said. "This is Roger Mudd," he said, "down on the convention floor with Ron Kovic, a disabled veteran protesting President Nixon's policy in Vietnam." . . .

President Nixon began to speak and all three of us took a deep breath and shouted at the top of our lungs, "Stop the bombing, stop the war, stop the bombing, stop the war," as loud and as hard as we could, looking directly at Nixon. The security agents immediately threw up their arms, trying to hide us from the cameras and the president. "Stop the bombing, stop the bombing," I screamed. For an instant Cronkite looked down, then turned his head away. They're not going to show it,

I thought. They're going to try and hide us like they did in the hospitals. Hundreds of people around us began to clap and shout "Four more years," trying to drown out our protest. They all seemed very angry and shouted at us to stop. We continued shouting, interrupting Nixon again and again until Secret Service agents grabbed our chairs from behind and began pulling us backward as fast as they could out of the convention hall. "Take it easy," Bobby said to me. "Don't fight back."

I wanted to take a swing and fight right there in the middle of the convention hall in front of the president and the whole country. "So this is how they treat their wounded veterans!" I screamed.

A short guy with a big Four More Years button ran up to me and spat in my face. "Traitor!" he screamed, as he was yanked back by police. Pandemonium was breaking out all around us and the Secret Service men kept pulling us out backward.

"I served two tours of duty in Vietnam!" I screamed to one newsman. "I gave three-quarters of my body for America. And what do I get? Spit in the face!" I kept screaming until we hit the side entrance where the agents pushed us outside and shut the doors, locking them with chains and padlocks so reporters wouldn't be able to follow us out for interviews.

All three of us sat holding on to each other shaking. We had done it. It had been the biggest moment of our lives, we had shouted down the president of the United States and disrupted his acceptance speech. What more was there left to do but go home?

I sat in my chair still shaking and began to cry.

47

"Laos: The Furtive War"

On September 13, 1972, Senator Thomas Eagleton of Missouri requested the printing in the Congressional Record *of an article, "Laos, the Furtive War," that Senator Stuart Symington of Missouri had published in* World *magazine.*

The United States has been involved for more than a decade in an undeclared and largely unnoticed war in northern Laos. From the

Source: Congressional Record, 92nd Cong., 2nd Sess. (September 13, 1972), vol. 118, pt. 23, 30413–30414.

beginning, and as of today, this war has been characterized by a degree of secrecy never before true of a major American involvement abroad in which many American lives have been lost and billions of American tax dollars spent.

A perversion of the processes of government has been going on, a perversion inimical to our democratic system and to the nation's future.

Who is responsible? The Constitution has been bypassed by a small group of men in various departments of the Executive Branch who, under the direction of four Presidents, initiated and carried out policies without any real Congressional knowledge and thus any true Congressional authorization. Needless to say, these policies were also carried out without the knowledge and approval of the American people, on whose consent our government is supposed to rest.

The war in northern Laos, in which the United States has been a principal party, has been pursued without a declaration of war by the Congress. Moreover, in the past few years, the U.S. government has financed Thai troops fighting in northern Laos despite a clear legislative prohibition against such activity.

It has been possible for successive administrations to ignore the normal processes of government because, until recently, the Executive Branch has succeeded in concealing from the people and the Congress the true facts of our involvement in this little country. As long as Congress and the people did not know what the United States was doing, as long as there was no public debate on the issues involved, Executive Branch policymakers were free to do as they pleased without having to explain or justify their actions. John Foster Dulles, Secretary of State under President Eisenhower and an arch proponent of the Domino Theory, considered Laos a key domino that then stood between China and North Vietnam on the Communist side and Thailand, Cambodia, and South Vietnam on the free world side.

By an exchange of diplomatic notes in July 1955, the U.S. and the Royal Government of Laos called for economic cooperation and the defense of the Kingdom of Laos. During the late Fifties, U.S. aid to Laos was running $40-million a year, and 80 per cent of that went to the support of the Royal Laotian Army.

To guide the Lao Army, the State Department organized an incognito American military mission with headquarters in Vientiane. This group was attached to the U.S. Operations Mission, or more popularly, the PEO. Its members were called technicians and wore civilian clothes. At its head was an equally disguised American general. When the general assumed command of this force his name was erased from the list of active American army officers.

Thus for many years this war was a well-kept secret. When John F.

Kennedy became President in 1961, there were 700 American military personnel in Laos as well as 500 Soviet operatives whose mission was to provide logistic support to local Communist forces. These forces included at least 10,000 North Vietnamese. . . .

With the outbreak of serious hostilities in 1963, the United States secretly began to train Lao pilots and ground crews in Thailand. In June 1964, American tactical fighter bombers began, again secretly, to strike targets in northern Laos far from the Ho Chi Minh Trail area in the south.

When these strikes were reported by the press, the Executive Branch clung to the story, even after it was no longer true, that the United States was flying reconnaissance missions at the request of the Lao government and that our planes were authorized to fire back if they were fired upon.

The United States also began to provide greater amounts of war material and other assistance and to transport Lao supplies and military personnel, using the airplanes and the services of Air America and Continental Air.

In 1965, as the war in South Vietnam intensified, American aircraft began to attack North Vietnamese supply routes in the southern panhandle region of Laos. These attacks were not officially acknowledged until 1970.

In 1966, about fifty U.S. Air Force officers and enlisted men, nominally assigned to the air attaché's office, were stationed at Lao air force bases as advisers to the local command.

In 1967, about the same number of U.S. Army personnel were assigned to the Lao regional headquarters for similar duty, and about twenty U.S. Air Force pilots stationed in Laos and others stationed in Thailand began to fly as forward air controllers directing tactical aircraft to their targets.

American air attacks on North Vietnam intensified in 1967 and 1968. Following the bombing halt in North Vietnam in 1968, a large part of the U.S. air effort there was redirected at Laos. During this period, the United States installed several navigational aid facilities in Laos, some manned by American Air Force personnel, and U.S. air strikes in Laos increased. By 1969, more than 100 sorties a day were being flown in northern Laos in addition to those being flown over the Ho Chi Minh Trail area in southern Laos, which was considered to be an adjunct of the battlefield in South Vietnam.

Since the Executive Branch, during the Kennedy, Johnson, and Nixon administrations, obviously intended not to give the Congress all the facts, it was necessary for the Legislative Branch to seek the information on its own. It determined to find out what the United States is doing now in northern Laos and which of its activities are still surrounded by secrecy. It did so by holding hearings and through staff reports of the United States Security Agreements and Commitments Abroad Subcommittee of the Committee on Foreign Relations.

As a result of these hearings and reports originally secret but subsequently made public after they had been sanitized by the Executive Branch, the American people now know that the United States, through Defense Department-funded military assistance, is training, arming, and feeding the Royal Lao Army and Air Force; that the United States, through the CIA, is training, advising, paying for, supporting, and organizing a 30,000-man Lao irregular force; and that the United States is also paying for, training, advising, and supporting a force of Thai troops in Laos, at a cost last year in the neighborhood of $100 million. . . .

The American involvement in Laos continues to grow. In the past few months, we have begun a program to support Thai who fly helicopter gunships in northern Laos. It is claimed by the Executive Branch that these gunships, now being flown for the first time in northern Laos, will be used only to support medical evacuations. The force of Thai irregulars in Laos will also be increased this year. There are preliminary indications that the Executive Branch will ask for more money for Thai and Lao irregulars and will insist that the $350-million ceiling be raised in the fiscal year 1973.

Certain aspects of the Thai irregulars' program in Laos are still kept secret by the Executive Branch. The size of the Thai force remains classified. The Lao Prime Minister, however, in an interview with a Voice of America reporter last January 14, put the limit at twenty-five or twenty-six battalions of volunteers. It has been more than half a year since he acknowledged that the battalion had arrived, and that the remainder were on the way.

The war in northern Laos is thus still secret in some respects, although far less secret than it has been in the past. Congress now examines the appropriation requests instead of blindly appropriating the money.

The Executive Branch is still reluctant, however, to place the question of U.S. involvement in Laos squarely before the Congress, and it continues to circumvent existing laws. Meanwhile the war continues, at a terrible cost in Lao lives and American money.

This war in northern Laos, furtive and secret, will perhaps teach us all a lesson about the dangers of creeping involvements, hidden from the Congress and the public, that make a mockery of our governmental processes. It is a lesson we cannot afford to be taught again.

48

A Protest in Congress

On February 26, 1975, Representative Bob Carr of Michigan requested inclusion in the Congressional Record *of a letter to President Gerald R. Ford signed by eighty-five Senators and Representatives protesting the idea of aid to the South Vietnamese regime over two years after the United States had militarily disengaged from the region. About two months later, the Communists won complete victory.*

DEAR MR. PRESIDENT: We, the undersigned Members of Congress for Peace through Law, write to you on a matter of very great concern—the extent and direction of the continuing U.S. involvement in Indochina.

What particularly disturbs us is the clear implication in remarks made by the Secretary of State and the Vice President and by yourself in a recent news conference that this only partly resolved issue—one of the most divisive in the nation's history—is being reopened for debate. We had thought that the American military withdrawal, the Peace Agreements negotiated by the Administration and the clearly and repeatedly expressed Congressional mandate to gradually eliminate the American role in Indochina had settled the matter. Apparently, that is not the case.

We remain resolute in our conviction, supported by the legislation passed in the 93rd Congress, that continuing American military and economic involvement in Indochina will not bring that unhappy region closer to a lasting peace. While continuing high levels of American assistance may perhaps prolong the life of the incumbent South Vietnamese and Cambodian governments, we can see no humanitarian or national interest that justifies the cost of this assistance to our country. Although the phased withdrawal of American support will not in itself bring peace to the region, it is equally clear that its continuation will not do so either.

Another prolonged disagreement over events in Vietnam and our policy there may well lead to acrimonious accusations over who "lost" Indochina, reminiscent of the China debate over two decades ago. The result of that earlier experience was to freeze U.S. options in Asia for a

Source: Congressional Record, 94th Cong., 1st Sess. (February 26, 1975), vol. 121, pt. 4, 4514–4515.

American soldiers walking through a destroyed countryside. *(Courtesy, U.P.I. Radio-photo)*

quarter of a century. We must at all costs avoid a repetition of such a struggle which would set the Congress against the Executive.

It is especially unfortunate that the internal debate over Indochina should resume at a time when we are confronted by so many pressing domestic and international problems. These problems do not have easy solutions. They require an extraordinary degree of accord between our two branches of government and among the industrialized and developing nations.

This is not the time for another divisive debate that can only impede the development of the cooperation so necessary in dealing with the complex problems of global inflation, domestic recession, and growing shortages of necessary raw materials. Instead, we need to work together.

We believe the time is now at hand when our government must make a decision, too long postponed at a tragically high cost to both the people of Indochina and to our own citizens, as to how we will extricate ourselves from the situation in Southeast Asia once and for all.

We write to ask you and your most senior advisers to accept this expression of our views in a spirit of conciliation. We should get on with the important work ahead of us. Innovative leadership both from you and the Congress will be needed more than ever.

Accordingly, we are prepared for a serious, unemotional dialogue on the immediate problem of ending our involvement in Indochina responsibly and honorably. We are not prepared for it to continue indefinitely.

49

The South Vietnamese Regime Cannot Hold

This editorial in The New York Times *for April 6, 1975, rejects the notion that the United States had a large commitment to provide aid to the South Vietnamese government then under heavy attack by the Communists (later that month they would attain complete victory). The* Times *piece reflects the frustration and exhaustion that Americans had felt for some time over the involvement in Vietnam.*

What, if anything, do the people and Government of the United States now owe to the people and Government of South Vietnam? This question does not admit of any easy answer, entangled as it is in considerations of ethical responsibility, political commitment, and strategic self-interest, as well as the ambiguities of a shared history between a very powerful nation and a very weak one.

Beyond the clear call of human fellow feeling, there resides the hard and complex political question of the relationship between the United States and South Vietnam. The South Vietnamese Ambassador to Washington stated bitterly that the world could draw "only one possible conclusion: . . . that is, it is safer to be an ally of the Communists, and it looks like it is fatal to be an ally of the United States."

At his news conference last week, President Ford implicitly criticized the Democratic-controlled Congress for its failure to appropriate all the funds he had requested for Vietnamese military aid. Secretary of Defense Schlesinger meanwhile has repeatedly stated his view that this country has a moral—though not a legal—commitment to continue aid indefinitely to South Vietnam, a commitment allegedly given before Saigon agreed to sign the Paris peace protocols in 1973.

"I think that it was strongly stated to the South Vietnamese Government that the United States Government intended to see to it that the Paris accords were indeed enforced," Secretary Schlesinger said a few days ago.

It is clear that any such commitment, if it was ever made, has no legal basis. The Paris accords permit one-for-one replacement of military equipment but do not obligate the United States to provide such help. If Secretary of State Kissinger, the chief negotiator of those accords,

---

Source: New York Times, April 6, 1975, section 4, 18. Reprinted by permission.

offered private assurances of aid or, more ambitiously, intimated that the United States would respond to North Vietnamese violations with renewed bombing or the reintroduction of ground troops, he has never acknowledged doing so. At this news conference explaining the Paris agreements on Jan. 24, 1973, Mr. Kissinger said categorically: "There are no secret understandings."

If such understandings ever existed the Government of South Vietnam has been on notice for more than a year and a half that they would not be fulfilled. Effective Aug. 15, 1973, the Nixon Administration accepted a ban imposed by Congress against further bombing anywhere in Vietnam or Cambodia.

That leaves open the question of military aid, which has continued but on a declining basis. It has been the position of this newspaper, particularly in view of the intensified North Vietnamese attacks of recent months in open violation of the Paris agreements, that the United States should continue to provide military aid to South Vietnam for a definitely limited period, but possibly as much as the next three years. Legal commitments and diplomatic hints aside, there is always an implicit responsibility not to abandon a military ally if it has any prospect of making a go of it.

The sudden collapse of much of South Vietnam's army, however, makes the military aid question moot. Poor generalship and a breakdown in morale—not an immediate shortage of equipment and ammunition— caused the rout of recent days. Unless the Saigon Government can soon achieve a remarkable reversal of the military situation, the fate of the country will have been settled before further American equipment could make any difference.

It is never easy to come to terms with failure and disappointment, even if it is the failure of an effort that was mistaken in its basic premises, as America's involvement in Vietnam was. The United States made a fundamental miscalculation of its own national interests in intervening on a large-scale in 1965 and fighting there for three years. It then spent the next five years trying to extricate itself while at the same time hoping that "Vietnamization" of the war would gradually enable South Vietnam to fight successfully on its own. That gamble appears now to have failed.

If challenged, a nation's sense of its own honor can never much exceed its perception of its own vital interests. Southeast Asia has never been an area of vital American interest. Only the gratuitous American intervention made it appear to be such an area. The lives, money and energy expended were out of all proportion to any discernible American interest. When means and ends are so disproportionate, a shift in policy sooner or later becomes inevitable. For seven years since President Johnson withdrew as a candidate for re-election and initiated the Paris peace talks, the United States has been trying to withdraw from that over-commitment and yet create conditions in which South Vietnam could continue on its own. The events of recent weeks have sadly proved that South Vietnam could not prevail militarily unless helped by American bombing and probably also by American ground troops. Regardless of their lingering sense of obligation, the American people long ago rightly determined that those are heavy costs that they would not pay again in Southeast Asia.

50

The Khmer Rouge Cannot Be Blamed on the United States

When the victorious Communist forces in Cambodia, the Khmer Rouge, launched a national program that amounted to extermination, the claim was made that the American invasion of Cambodia had so conditioned the Khmer Rouge as to make them later a murderous force. This editorial attacks that argument.

Time magazine's account of genocide in Cambodia is reminiscent of the horrors of Stalinist Russia and Nazi Germany; in Cambodia the horrors have taken the form of mass forced marches and forced labor, political purges and assassinations and massacres of entire villages, with people sometimes buried alive by bulldozers or clubbed to death to save ammunition.

The magazine estimates that upwards of 600,000 Cambodians, roughly one-tenth of the population, have died from mistreatment at the hands of the Communist Khmer Rouge. Even that estimate may be low. The French newspaper Le Monde, which has a center-left political orientation, recently published two detailed articles on Cambodia, translated by the Library of Congress and introduced into the Congressional Record by Senator Robert Griffin. Le Monde puts the casualties from the organized slaughter to close to 800,000.

Source: Wall Street Journal, April 16, 1976, 6. Reprinted by permission.

The enormity of this kind of atrocity, conducted by a party in power against the people, is mind numbing. A generous person might hold that simple shock explains the relatively weak outcry from the usual wellsprings of moral outrage around the world. But while that may have some validity, we would guess that it is much too generous. There are undoubtedly other reasons, both puzzling and complex.

One answer could be that the crimes of the Khmer Rouge, even though they dwarf some other state crimes of our time—tortures in Brazil and Chile, for example—have attracted less attention because they are inflicted in the name of revolution. In our world, the wellsprings of moral outrage and the wellsprings of revolution are often the same.

The pain and discomfort experienced by revolutionary moralists in even discussing Cambodia are reflected in some recent remarks we heard from an Eastern college professor. In his view, the Khmer Rouge is murdering people in 1976 because the U.S. bombed Cambodia in 1970. That may well be the record extension to date of the politics of guilt.

But going more deeply, such a tortuous reasoning reflects the notion, not at all uncommon, that there is some inherent nobility in those of our world who would create a new man and thereby reform mankind. And that concept of nobility seems to remain untarnished even when the would-be reformers commit despicable acts in pursuit of their utopian dreams. Fervent moralism is no stranger to naked power.

It seems to be only after the fact, when those dreams collapse, that their admirers have second thoughts. Stalin, Hitler and Mussolini were men of such dreams, ruthless in their drives to create a new order and a new man. And while they were committing their wholesale cruelties, they did not lack for admirers.

The Khmer Rouge have had, as an immediate example, Hanoi. Scholar Robert F. Turner in his recent book "Vietnamese Communism: Its Origins and Development" (Hoover Institution), notes that when the Viet Minh first moved into Hanoi in 1954, they at first followed a policy of "moderation."

But he observes that later they conducted a reign of terror, executing perhaps 100,000 and were probably responsible for upwards of 500,000 deaths. The use of terror as a weapon continued throughout that long struggle to put all of Vietnam under Hanoi's control.

It remains an open question whether South Vietnam will escape a new genocide. Currently, there is the same moderation first employed in Hanoi. But there also are spreading controls over personal affairs, "re-education" classes, people's courts and public tribunals, the organization of families into manageable cells, and threats to ferret out enemies who owe a "blood debt to the people." Just last week, the official Saigon press announced the roundup of 110 "reactionaries" who failed to register with the government and are charged with "spreading false news designed to stir up confusion among the population."

We suspect that world opinion, if employed, could have some influence even on the revolutionaries of Hanoi. The best way that opinion could be registered would be through a world-wide outcry against the atrocities being committed in Cambodia.

But here again—not for the first time in the world's history—world opinion seems to be stupefied in the face of truly colossal crimes. When there is no censure from self-professed authorities on morality, is there any wonder that those hard-eyed men who would slaughter thousands to fulfill their dreams so often think they are right?

51

A Conservative's View of the American Failure

Louis A. Fanning writes here a right-wing explanation of the loss of Vietnam. Even Republican President Richard Nixon does not meet Fanning's standards: conservatives were disturbed at Nixon's opening to Communist China. Fanning's discussion of the actress Jane Fonda's highly publicized trip to North Vietnam is typical of his treatment of antiwar activism. But Ms. Fonda's action met with disfavor even among numbers of American opponents of the war.

President Nixon's July 15, 1971 announcement that he had accepted an invitation to visit the People's Republic of China the following year astounded a great many Americans. The surprise was probably greatest among the political conservatives who had supported Nixon through his many trials and tribulations. Their astonishment soon turned to chagrin, which then became a deep feeling of defeat and revulsion.

The bewilderment that the conservatives felt was based primarily upon the reversal of what had appeared to be the President's solid anti-Communist credentials. This record had been developed over a long period of time from Nixon's public statements and actions against the

Source: Louis A. Fanning, *Betrayal in Vietnam* (New Rochelle, N.Y.: Arlington House Publishers, 1976), 95–96, 120–22. Reprinted by permission.

Communist movement throughout his entire career. The most galling part of the entire episode was that the President had won his first real acclaim as a member of the prosecution team that imprisoned Alger Hiss.

The conservatives need not have been surprised, had they merely read the revised doctoral dissertation of Henry Kissinger, the President's major foreign affairs adviser. Dr. Kissinger's scholarly magnum opus is entitled *A World Restored,* and it deals exclusively with the Congress of Vienna. Throughout this entire work the author's pragmatic approach to foreign affairs shines through. There is no question that Kissinger admired the work of the diplomats who had gathered in Vienna in 1815. While the handiwork of these statesmen was indeed admirable, their restoration of the balance of power in Europe was accomplished with little, if any, consideration for the wishes of the pawns. This formula, of course, has had a long and honorable tradition in European diplomatic circles. But it is not held in very high esteem among some Americans who approach their politics with a sense of ethics. For after all, what room is there in the practice of balance of power for principles, for morals, or even virtue? Though the Metternichs of the nineteenth century may have had no problem in adapting to their former enemies, in this Age of Ideology accommodation often means the death of allies.

A month after Nixon's startling announcement, Secretary of State William P. Rogers announced that the United States had adopted a new policy regarding Chinese Communist representation in the United Nations. On August 2, 1971, the secretary stated that America would support action to seat the People's Republic of China in the Security Council of the international organization. At the same time, Rogers said, the State Department would do everything in its power to maintain representation in the UN for the government of the Republic of China. Unfortunately for the Taiwan government, in spite of the "best efforts" of the United States, the Republic of China was excluded from the world organization, and on November 15 Communist China took its seat in the UN. The cold-blooded treatment and alienation of Nationalist China was one of the first results of the Kissinger policy of international pragmatism. In time, the tree of "practicalism in foreign affairs" would produce more bitter fruit for America. . . .

It was not until she became deeply involved with Hanoi's effort to defeat United States forces in Vietnam . . . that Fonda's hatred for America really reached its greatest depths. Her opportunity to contribute to the demise of the country she so detested arrived when the actress was invited to visit Hanoi in the summer of 1972.

Fonda arrived in North Vietnam on July 8 in the possession of American passport number C1478434, which had not been validated for travel in that country. Over the next few days, she was taken on the standard tour, which included visits to "war museums" displaying evidence of alleged American "war crimes," trips to hospitals containing war casualties, and a bomb-damaged dike.

Following her visits to the countryside, the actress made a series of broadcasts over Radio Hanoi. These speeches included a strong condemnation of the United States and the American war effort in Vietnam. The first broadcast was made on July 14 over the Voice of Vietnam Radio. In this address, she appealed to United States servicemen who were engaged in bombing North Vietnam and said:

> All of you in the cockpits of your planes, on the aircraft carriers, those who are loading the bombs, those who are repairing the planes, those who are working on the Seventh Fleet, please think what you are doing.
>
> Are these people your enemy? What will you say to your children years from now who may ask you why you fought the war? What words will you be able to say to them?

Three days later, she made another broadcast particularly directed to "servicemen who are stationed on the aircraft carriers in the Gulf of Tonkin . . . and in the Anglico Corps in the south of Vietnam." In this speech Fonda said:

> I don't know what your officers tell you that you are dropping on this country. I don't know what your officers tell you, you are loading, those of you who load the bombs on the planes . . . The men who are ordering you to use these weapons are war criminals according to international law, and in the past, in Germany and in Japan, men who were guilty of these kind of crimes were tried and executed.

She continued:

> Now I know you are not told these kind of things, but, you know, history changes. We've witnessed incredible changes, for example, in the United States in the last five years. The astounding victory that has just been won by George McGovern, for example, who was nominated by the Democratic party, is an example of the kind of changes that are going on—an example of the overwhelming, overwhelming feeling in the United States among people to

end the war. McGovern represents all that is good to these people. He represents an end to the war, an end to the bombing.

To several congressmen, Fonda's statements smacked of high treason, and on September 19 and September 25, 1972, the House Committee on Internal Security conducted hearings regarding her activities in North Vietnam. During the testimony concerning Fonda's disloyalty, the Committee listened attentively while William Olson, a Department of Justice lawyer, defined the term "treason." In Olson's opinion:

> The treason statute, 18 U.S.C. 2381, provides that whoever levies war against the United States or adheres to their enemies, giving them aid and comfort, is guilty of treason. Additionally, Section III, Article 3 of the constitution provides that no person shall be convicted of treason except on the testimony of two witnesses to the same overt act or a confession in open court.

He further stated that "a country with whom the United States is engaged in open hostility would qualify as an enemy." However, Olson directed the Committee's attention to the procedural difficulties the Justice Department would have in prosecuting Fonda. These legal technicalities were based on the simple fact that the government was unable to produce two witnesses who had seen her make the broadcasts.

Later in the hearing Edward Hunter, a former propaganda specialist with the OSS during World War II, was questioned as to the value of Fonda's actions to the enemy. The psychological warfare veteran answered that in his opinion, her broadcasts had produced an effect on American military morale in Vietnam that was "bad to devastating." Hunter added that the Fonda performance was merely a part of an overall "black" propaganda effort of the Communists to destroy the defenses of the United States. He described the first goal of this operation as the elimination of the legal means to combat subversion in America. According to the former intelligence officer, once these laws have been removed or rendered ineffective, Communist propaganda experts would be free to ply their trade.

52

We Went to Help

In a news conference for February 18, 1982, President Ronald Reagan answered a question involving operations by the Central Intelligence Agency in Vietnam and later in Latin America. The President's answer continues the defense of the American effort in Vietnam.

Q. In the 1960's the CIA came up with a secret plan to get us involved in Vietnam in a surreptitious, covert manner. Is it possible that you can tell us that there is no secret plan now devised by the CIA or any other agency in government to surreptitiously involve Americans in similar activities in Latin America? . . .

The President. . . . If I recall correctly, when France gave up Indochina as a colony, the leading nations of the world met in Geneva with regard to helping those colonies become independent nations. And since North and South Vietnam had been, previous to colonization, two separate countries, provisions were made that these two countries could, by a vote of all their people together, decide whether they wanted to be one country or not.

And there wasn't anything surreptitious about it, that when Ho Chi Minh refused to participate in such an election—and there was provision that people of both countries could cross the border and live in the other country if they wanted to. And when they began leaving by the thousands and thousands from North Vietnam to live in South Vietnam, Ho Chi Minh closed the border and again violated that part of the agreement.

And openly, our country sent military advisers there to help a country which had been a colony have such things as a national security force, an army, you might say, or a military to defend itself. And they were doing this, if I recall correctly, also in civilian clothes, no weapons, until they began being blown up where they lived and walking down the street by people riding by on bicycles and throwing pipe-bombs at them. And then they were permitted to carry sidearms or wear uniforms.

But it was totally a program until John F. Kennedy—when these attacks and forays became so great that John F. Kennedy authorized the sending in of a division of Marines. And that was the first move toward combat troops in Vietnam.

Source: U.S. President, *Public Papers of the Presidents of the United States* (Washington, D.C.: United States Government Printing Office, 1983), Ronald Reagan, 1982, 184–85.

United States marines under attack while withdrawing from Southeast Asia. *(Courtesy, AP/Wide World Photos)*

53

A Retrospective Look in Defense of the War

Norman Podhoretz, a neoconservative commentator, here argues in retrospect for the justice of the war as a battle against a brutal Communist regime and movement.

But what about indiscriminate and excessive firepower resulting in an unusually high number of civilian casualties? Here, too, the charge can be characterized as "a bit grotesque." According to [historian Guenter] Lewy's calculations—which are generous in their definition of civil-

Source: Norman Podhoretz, *Why We Were in Vietnam* (New York: Simon and Schuster, 1982), 187, 195–98. Reprinted by permission.

ian and extremely cautious in their reliance on official "body counts"—
"the Vietnam War during the years of active American involvement was
no more destructive of civilian life, both North and South, than other
armed conflicts of this century and a good bit less so than some, such as
the Korean War." Whereas as many as 70 percent of those killed in
Korea were civilians, in Vietnam the proportion was at most 45 percent,
which was approximately the level of civilian casualties in World War II.
And of course a substantial percentage of these civilians were killed not
by the Americans or the South Vietnamese but by the Vietcong and the
North Vietnamese, especially after 1969, when there was a steady decline
in American bombing and shelling and combat increasingly occurred
farther away from areas in which the rural population lived. . . .

The United States sent half a million men to fight in Vietnam. More
than 50,000 of them lost their lives, and many thousands more were
wounded. Billions of dollars were poured into the effort, damaging the
once unparalleled American economy to such an extent that the country's competitive position was grievously impaired. The domestic disrup-
tions to which the war gave rise did perhaps even greater damage to a
society previously so self-confident that it was often accused of entertain-
ing illusions of its own omnipotence. Millions of young people growing
to maturity during the war developed attitudes of such hostility toward
their own country and the civilization embodied by its institutions that
their willingness to defend it against external enemies in the future was
left hanging in doubt.

Why did the United States undertake these burdens and make these
sacrifices in blood and treasure and domestic tranquillity? What was in
it for the United States? It was a question that plagued the antiwar movement from beginning to end because the answer was so hard to find. If
the United States was simply acting the part of an imperialist aggressor
in Vietnam, as many in the antiwar movement professed to believe, it
was imperialism of a most peculiar kind. There were no raw materials
to exploit in Vietnam, and there was no overriding strategic interest
involved. To Franklin Roosevelt in 1941 Indochina had been important
because it was close to the source of rubber and tin, but this was no
longer an important consideration. Toward the end of the war, it was
discovered that there was oil off the coast of Vietnam and antiwar radicals happily seized on this news as at last providing an explanation for
the American presence there. But neither Kennedy nor Johnson knew
about the oil, and even if they had, they would hardly have gone to war
for its sake in those pre-OPEC days when oil from the Persian Gulf could
be had at two dollars a barrel.

In the absence of an economic interpretation, a psychological version of the theory of imperialism was developed to answer the maddening

question: *Why are we in Vietnam?* This theory held that the United States was in Vietnam because it had an urge to dominate—"to impose its national obsessions on the rest of the world," in the words of a piece in the *New York Review of Books,* one of the leading centers of antiwar agitation within the intellectual community. But if so, the psychic profits were as illusory as the economic ones, for the war was doing even deeper damage to the national self-confidence than to the national economy.

Yet another variant of the psychological interpretation, proposed by the economist Robert L. Heilbroner, was that "the fear of losing our place in the sun, of finding ourselves at bay, . . . motivates a great deal of the anti-Communism on which so much of American foreign policy seems to be founded." This was especially so in such underdeveloped countries as Vietnam, where "the rise of Communism would signal the end of capitalism as the dominant world order, and would force the acknowledgment that America no longer constituted the model on which the future of world civilization would be mainly based."

All these theories were developed out of a desperate need to find or invent selfish or self-interested motives for the American presence in Vietnam, the better to discredit it morally. In a different context, proponents of one or another of these theories—Senator Fulbright, for example—were not above trying to discredit the American presence politically by insisting that *no* national interest was being served by the war. This latter contention at least had the virtue of being closer to the truth than the former. For the truth was that the United States went into Vietnam for the sake not of its own direct interests in the ordinary sense but for the sake of an ideal. The intervention was a product of the Wilsonian side of the American character—the side that went to war in 1917 to "make the world safe for democracy" and that found its contemporary incarnations in the liberal internationalism of the 1940s and the liberal anti-Communism of the 1950s. One can characterize this impulse as naive; one can describe it, as Heilbroner does (and as can be done with any virtuous act), in terms that give it a subtly self-interested flavor. But there is no rationally defensible way in which it can be called immoral.

Why, then, were we in Vietnam? To say it once again: because we were trying to save the Southern half of that country from the evils of Communism. But was the war we fought to accomplish this purpose morally worse than Communism itself? Peter L. Berger, who at the time was involved with Clergy and Laymen Concerned About Vietnam (CALCAV), wrote in 1967: "All sorts of dire results might well follow a reduction or a withdrawal of the American engagement in Vietnam. Morally speaking, however, it is safe to assume that none of these could be worse than what is taking place right now." Unlike most of his fellow members of CALCAV, Berger would later repent of this statement.

Writing in 1980, he would say of it: "Well, it was *not* safe to assume. . . . I was wrong and so were all those who thought as I did." For "contrary to what most members (including myself) of the antiwar movement expected, the peoples of Indochina have, since 1975, been subjected to suffering far worse than anything that was inflicted upon them by the United States and its allies."

54

The Domino Fell

James S. Olson and Randy Roberts here give a summary evaluation of the blunders of American involvement in Vietnam.

For the generation after the fall of Saigon in 1975, the American people wondered how it had happened, how the Vietnam War had gone out of control, how the richest country in the world could sacrifice hundreds of billions of dollars and tens of thousands of young men in a military effort that seemed, in the end, to have so little significance. Vietnam, Laos, and Cambodia fell to communism, but the rest of Asia survived. Only three dominoes went down. During the 1970s and 1980s the victorious Socialist Republic of Vietnam slipped into stupefying poverty, while the United States recovered from its malaise and enjoyed a period of unprecedented growth and prosperity. Around the world there were nearly 60,000 graves covering the bodies of Americans who lost their lives, but few people in the United States knew whether their sacrifice meant anything at all. Communism had taken over Indochina in the end, and the United States was just fine anyway.

Back in the late 1940s, when the American crusade began, it had all seemed so simple, so clear, the threat so real and the sacrifice so necessary. Communism was on the march—in Europe and in Asia—and it appeared to be enjoying great success. Much of Eastern Europe was under Soviet domination, and in 1949 China fell to Mao Zedong's cadres. Ho Chi Minh threatened to do the same to Vietnam, Laos, and Cambodia. In the United States, the fear of communist expansion became a paranoia, and American leaders vowed to hold the line, to fight the

Source: James S. Olson and Randy Roberts, *Where the Domino Fell: America and Vietnam, 1945 to 1990* (New York: St. Martin's Press, 1991), 281–83.

Marxist menace at home and abroad. The policy became known as containment, and the United States looked to apply it all around the world. Because Southeast Asia seemed crucial to the economic recovery of Japan and Western Europe, United States policymakers committed themselves to the survival of the French empire, even though it left a bad taste in the mouths of many. Given a choice between European colonialism and communism, they chose the former. Nationalism and democracy took a backseat to anticommunism.

For most American policymakers in the Truman and Eisenhower administrations, Vietnam was like Eastern Europe and Korea—just a blatant case of communist military aggression that had to be stopped. The memories of Munich were still clear. European leaders had given Adolf Hitler an inch in Czechoslovakia, and he had taken hundreds of thousands of square miles of territory across the continent. Ho Chi Minh was just another dictator who needed his bluff called. The United States assumed it would be a relatively simple task. Surely no poor Southeast Asian guerrilla could stand up to the American killing machine. American leaders did not see Ho Chi Minh for what he was—a communist who also happened to be a Vietnamese hero.

In order to stand up to Ho Chi Minh, however, the United States committed itself to upholding a tiny elite in South Vietnam—an urban, Roman Catholic minority that had nothing in common with the masses of rural, Buddhist and Confucian peasants. The government of South Vietnam—with its arrogance and corruption—was never able to win the loyalties of its own people, and large numbers of them gravitated instead to the Vietcong. When the United States tried to win the war militarily by bludgeoning the Vietcong and North Vietnamese with massive firepower, there were inordinately large numbers of civilian casualties, which only made the problem of winning political loyalty more acutely difficult.

Throughout most of the war, however, the United States did not worry much about peasant loyalties. The Kennedy and Johnson administrations decided to fight a war of attrition, to kill so many enemy troops and inflict so much damage on North Vietnam that continuation of the war would be impossible. Long before there was any hope of finally converting the peasants, Kennedy and Johnson expected the war to be over, with the communists licking their wounds and retreating back across the seventeenth parallel. What the Americans did not know was the extent of the communists' commitment to reunification and independence. They were fighting a war to the death, an open-ended commitment to risk everything, including annihilation, for victory. The United States commitment fell far short of that, and the Vietcong and North Vietnamese were willing to wait until the American public reached its political and economic limit.

Slowly but surely the United States found itself getting deeper and deeper into the war, not out of any forthright commitment to military victory but out of compromise and moderation, taking the middle road between those Neanderthals who wanted to bomb the enemy back into the stone age and the weak-kneed pacifists who wanted out at any cost. Each escalation of the conflict was undertaken as a compromise, and each step was taken with the conviction that just a little more firepower would win the day. None of the presidents who increased the volume of American assets in Indochina viewed himself as an extremist. On the contrary, each was acting prudently, carefully, and moderately. But the sum total of dozens of small escalations was the dreaded land war in Asia.

Even when American policymakers began to see Vietnam for the quagmire it was, disengagement was excruciatingly difficult. Presidents Eisenhower, Kennedy, Johnson, and Nixon all expressed the fear of becoming the first American president to lose a war. Each of them remembered the political abuse Harry Truman had taken from the Republican right wing over the "loss" of China to the Reds, and none of them wanted to be the target of similar abuse for "losing" Vietnam. Domestic politics, as much as the perceived need to stop communism in Vietnam, kept the United States in the war against the better judgment of a number of prominent leaders. Even in the early 1970s, when the war had become an albatross to the Nixon administration, blanket withdrawal was not an option because of the need to maintain "American credibility" around the world. What started out as a righteous crusade in the late 1940s to save Southeast Asia and ultimately the rest of the world from global communism ended up in the 1970s as a face-saving game to get out of an impossible mess without looking too bad. The war was a colossal blunder born of an odd mixture of paranoia and arrogance. Blind to history, the United States saw only communism, not nationalism, in Vietnam, and, naively confident about its role as the premier power on earth, the United States applied military solutions to a problem that was essentially political and cultural. Vietnam was the wrong war in the wrong place at the wrong time for the wrong reason.

> And the end of the fight is a tombstone white with
>   the name of the late deceased,
> In the epitaph drear: "A fool lies here who tried
>   to hustle the East."

And the end of the Vietnam War is a black wall in Washington with 58,175 names, an epitaph to a loss that is every American's.

Part 4

FIGHTING

Much of the commentary, fictional and reportorial, on the war in Vietnam tells of conditions that survivors of other conflicts have remembered: the boredom, the small daily miseries, the fear, the suffering of civilians, the peculiar intensity and exhilaration of combat. Vietnam, however, brought its own characteristics.

It was a war fought in the midst of civilians any of whom might be friendly or hostile. The difficulties that this brought to the conduct of the war, the killings of Americans by Vietnamese they thought they could trust, the atrocities that Americans committed against the innocent: all this fomented among the troops both hostility and guilt.

Another impression that reminiscences of Vietnam combat carry is that Americans needed to be notably inventive and skillful. Ground troops operated in small units, sometimes far from larger bases, and had to learn the ways of enemy guerrilla warfare. They had as well to practice methods of coordinating artillery and air weaponry with the intimate ground combat of infantry troops. Beyond these considerations were the demands for self-control: in the mastery of technical skills, in resistance to fear, in resistance to the downward pull into primitive impulse. Above all, the war compelled the more introspective among American soldiers to discover for themselves a right conduct, a right relation to a conflict waged in a foreign unfamiliar ground and with no clear indication from the American government or society of what the war was all about.

An American soldier thinking about the future.

55

Planting Rumors

This report on covert activities during 1954 and 1955 of the Saigon Military Mission headed by Edward G. Lansdale tells of one of the more startling devices for waging war.

. . . There was deepening gloom in Vietnam. Dien Bien Phu had fallen. The French were capitulating to the Vietminh at Geneva. The first night in Saigon, Vietminh saboteurs blew up large ammunition dumps at the airport, rocking Saigon throughout the night. . . .

Working in close cooperation with George Hellyer, USIS [United States Information Service] Chief, a new psychological warfare campaign was devised for the Vietnamese Army and for the government in Hanoi. Shortly after, a refresher course in combat psywar was constructed and Vietnamese Army personnel were rushed through it. A similar course was initiated for the Ministry of Information. Rumor campaigns were added to the tactics and tried out in Hanoi. It was almost too late.

The first rumor campaign was to be a carefully planted story of a Chinese Communist regiment in Tonkin taking reprisals against a Vietminh village whose girls the Chinese had raped, recalling Chinese Nationalist troop behavior in 1945 and confirming Vietnamese fears of Chinese occupation under Vietminh rule; the story was to be planted by soldiers of the Vietnamese Armed Psywar Company in Hanoi dressed in civilian clothes. The troops received their instructions silently, dressed in civilian clothes, went on the mission, and failed to return. They had deserted to the Vietminh. Weeks later, Tonkinese told an excited story of the misbehavior of the Chinese Divisions in Vietminh territory. Investigated, it turned out to be the old rumor campaign, with Vietnamese embellishments. . . .

Towards the end of the month, it was learned that the largest printing establishment in the north intended to remain in Hanoi and do business with the Vietminh. An attempt was made by SMM [Saigon Military Mission] to destroy the modern presses, but Vietminh security agents

---

Source: Pentagon Papers, I, Document 95, 575, 578–79.

already had moved into the plant and frustrated the attempt. . . . Earlier in the month they had engineered a black psywar strike in Hanoi: leaflets signed by the Vietminh instructing Tonkinese on how to behave for the Vietminh takeover of the Hanoi region in early October, including items about property, money reform, and a three-day holiday of workers upon takeover. The day following the distribution of these leaflets, refugee registration tripled. Two days later Vietminh currency was worth half the value prior to the leaflets. The Vietminh took to the radio to denounce the leaflets; the leaflets were so authentic in appearance that even most of the rank and file Vietminh were sure that the radio denunciations were a French trick. . . .

56

"No Other Road to Take"

Mrs. Nguyen Thi Dinh was a founder of the South Vietnamese insurgent National Liberation Front, the Vietcong. This English translation of an account she gave of her activities in Ben Tre province in 1960 describes a combination of military and political action. Passages here are especially illustrative of how the Vietcong acted.

. . . Sau Duong gave a report on the current situation and the policy adopted by the higher levels. The moment he mentioned this policy I felt an immense joy and happiness. It clearly called for the mobilization of the people all over the South to carry out political struggle in conjunction with military action. The moment they heard military action mentioned the conference burst out in stormy applause. The higher levels had followed exactly the aspirations of the lower levels in an extraordinary manner. Seeing that the comrades were too enthusiastic about military action, Sau Duong had to remind them over and over again:

—Comrades, please remember that political struggle is the main

---

Source: Mrs. Nguyen Thi Dinh, translated by Mai Elliott, *No Other Road to Take, Memoir of Mrs. Nguyen Thi Dinh,* Data Paper: Number 102, Southeast Asia Program, Department of Asian Studies, Cornell University (Ithaca, New York, June 1976), 62, 65–66, 68–72, 75–77.

policy, armed action only supplements it and is aimed at mobilizing the peasants to rise up and destroy the enemy's suffocating control in order to become masters of the countryside, of their villages and hamlets. . . .

In the political field, we planned to set up a hard-core force which would operate openly under legal cover to mobilize the people over a wide area. We should lose no time in recruiting good people into revolutionary organizations so as to expand our military and political forces quickly and strongly in order to create conditions for continuous attacks and to achieve continuous success. We would make preparations to win over the soldiers' families and mobilize and motivate them—once the uprising started—to go into the posts and appeal to their husbands or sons to turn around and join the revolution. The most serious difficulty confronting us at this juncture was the shortage of cadres at a time when there were so many tasks to attend to. So, we decided to recall all the [cadres operating underground] and to mobilize all the cadres in the province and district agencies and send them to the villages and hamlets to directly motivate the people. Finally before parting we unanimously adopted the following slogans: (a) the attacks should be relentless, (b) once the movement was set in motion, it should be developed to its utmost capacity, without constraints, and (c) once the storm and wind started to blow, the boats should boldly hoist their sails and glide over the waves. (The intention here was to counteract hesitation and reluctance to boldly move forward.) . . .

January 17th, 1960, was a day full of hope and worry for the patriotic people in Ben Tre province. I waited for the attack on the canton militia unit, composed of two squads stationed in Dinh Thuy village, to occur. The comrades had decided to attack while the militiamen were sleeping and off their guards. At the appointed time, a hard-core youth who knew the militia commander entered in a panic to look for him concerning an urgent matter. This fellow was still awake while his troops were sound asleep. Our forces, disguised as ordinary merchants, lay in ambush around the communal house. Being suspicious by nature, the commander pulled out his Sten pistol and came to the door of the communal house. His arms akimbo, he tilted his bearded chin and asked haughtily:

— What's the matter?

Our comrade obsequiously bent down to whisper in his ear, as though to transmit something important, then suddenly raised his arm and hit him hard on the nape of the neck. He collapsed right away. Our forces poured in and called on the troops to surrender. A number of them bolted and fled in disorder, while the rest surrendered. We captured enough weapons to equip about a squad of men. The Dinh Thuy post was only about one kilometer from here. Hai Thuy was afraid that the soldiers belonging to the unit of the canton militia commander would go and warn the post which would then take precautions, so he ordered the immediate capture of the post at 3:00 p.m. There were sympathizers among the soldiers in this post, and before the news [of the attack on the militia unit] reached the post, our infiltrators rose up and burned it down. The flames billowed high in the sky. The brothers brought back about ten additional rifles. . . .

As the situation evolved successfully, the leadership of the committee of the Concerted Uprising right that night drafted a military order which was then posted everywhere in the areas under the temporary control of the enemy to heighten the prestige of the revolution. The contents of the military order included the following points:

— All soldiers, no matter how serious their crimes were, if they repented and rejoined the ranks of the people with their weapons, would be forgiven.

— Village and hamlet officials, heads of inter-family groups, security policemen and informers who resigned and surrendered to the people would be forgiven by the people.

— Landlords who had relied on the power of the enemy to seize the land of the peasants and increase their rents should return what they had taken to the peasants.

This military order would remain in force from January 17th to 25th, 1960. Anyone who disobeyed it would be condemned to death by the people and had their properties confiscated. This order was written in large letters and posted in strategic areas and in the towns.

In the first night of the concerted uprising, the enemy's machinery of control in a number of villages crumbled. In some villages, the officials went to hand in their resignations even before our arrival. The villagers then forced them to issue the order to have the flags torn and family registers burned. The reactionaries with blood debts and the tyrannical landlords whom we had not managed to capture fled. The people became the complete masters of a number of hamlets and villages. Our task on January 18th and the following days was to track down and arrest the remaining tyrants, besiege the posts, take over the remaining hamlets and villages, destroy the roads, cut down trees to build roadblocks, and get ready to fight if the enemy brought in troops to attack us. We organized meetings of peasants to discuss the equal distribution of the rice fields we had seized. The people were extremely encouraged. . . .

That whole week, the enemy stayed put in their positions. They trembled before the power and prestige of the revolution. Since we had eliminated their machinery of control in the villages—their eyes and arms—they had no way of knowing what the real situation was. Two days after Dinh Thuy and Binh Khanh posts fell, the enemy abandoned Phuoc Hiep post and fled. These three villages were completely liberated. On the 19th, Mo Cay district dispatched a column of troops to Dinh Thuy post to check the situation. Forewarned, comrade Hai Thuy organized a "trick" ambush—complete with crisscrossing communication trenches, foxholes, mortars, submachine gun and machine gun emplacements, and positioned a cell to fire on landing crafts. When the clash occurred, the moment we opened fire the soldiers fled toward Mo Cay and then sent reconnaissance agents back to check. Seeing the grandiose defense network, they became frightened and reported to their superiors:

—It's true that large units are involved. It's true that liberation forces from the North have arrived!

Emboldened, the villagers stepped up their efforts to eliminate village officials and tyrants, surround the posts, call on the soldiers to surrender, and seize weapons. In some places, whenever the soldiers manning the posts wanted to go to the latrine or to fetch fresh water, they had to ask permission from the guerrillas, otherwise if they took the liberty of doing so without asking they would be shot at by the guerrillas—this was the same tactic of sniping that had been employed at Dien Bien Phu. A week after the concerted uprising began, we reviewed the results and found that we had captured about ten posts and that the apparatus of control which the enemy had spent six years consolidating had either been shaken to the foundations or had disintegrated. The enemy, however, remained completely ignorant of our strength, as though they were deaf and blind. . . .

The people of Ben Tre province who had endured untold miseries during the past six years could now laugh, sing and live. A new spirit was burning all over the countryside. The political forces held animated discussions about the struggle. Carpenters and blacksmiths raced to produce knives and machetes to kill the enemy. The workshops improved the sky-horse rifles, making them more lethal, and produced a batch of new weapons called "mút nhét" (primed rifles). At this time, the armed forces of the province were over one company in strength and each district had from one to two squads. Each village had from one to three rifles, but the majority of these were French muskets. Young girls stayed up many nights to sew "Main Force" green uniforms for the troops. An information office was set up in each hamlet in Giong Trom, Mo Cay and Chau Thanh districts. On each side of the road, slogans were drawn on tree trunks and caught everyone's eyes. On some days people from the province town came by the hundreds to visit the liberated areas. . . .

I looked at the large popular force and felt overjoyed. The armed units had expanded rapidly. Ben Tre province now had close to a battalion of adequately armed troops. This was a real battalion, not a "fake" one. As for the strong and large "long haired" force, I did not even know how many battalions of them there were. From now on, on the road of resisting the Americans and their lackeys, our people would stand firm on the two powerful legs of military and political strength to fight and achieve victory. There was no other road to take.

57

Counterinsurgency

The fortunes of counterinsurgency, the effort to combat guerrilla warfare especially of the kind that drew on popular support, were central to anticommunism in South Vietnam. Noteworthy in this National Security Action Memorandum of March 13, 1962, discussing training for counterinsurgency is the inclusion of instruction in the problems of underdeveloped countries and means of meeting them. It is an instance of the concept among some cold warriors of combining military action with social progress.

. . . a. *The Historical Background of Counter-Insurgency.* Personnel of all grades will be required to study the history of subversive insurgency movements, past and present, in order to familiarize themselves with the nature of the problems and characteristics of Communist tactics and techniques as related to this particular aspect of Communist operations. This kind of background historical study will be offered throughout the school systems of the responsible departments and agencies, beginning at the junior level of instruction and carrying forward to the senior level.

b. *Study of Departmental Tactics and Techniques to Counter Subversive Insurgency.* Junior and middle grade officers will receive instructions in the tactics and techniques of their particular departments which have an application in combating subversive insurgency. This level of instruction will be found in the schools of the Armed Services at the company/field officer level. In the case of the Central Intelligence Agency, this kind of instruction will be offered at appropriate training installations. The State Department will be responsible for organizing appropriate courses in this instructional area for its own officers and for

Source: *Pentagon Papers*, II, Document 111, 668–69.

Pfc. Bernard A. Roe, Durango, Colo., chats with a trio of Vietnamese boys, one of whom wears a Robin Hood-style hat. Roe is a member of C Co., 1st Bn. (Abn), 327th Inf. of the 1st Brigade, 101st Airborne Division. This photograph represents the American effort to win the hearts and minds of the Vietnamese.

representatives of the Agency for International Development and the United States Information Agency. Schools of this category will make available spaces in agreed numbers for the cross-training of other U.S. agencies with a counter-insurgency responsibility.

c. *Instruction in Counter-Insurgency Program Planning.* Middle grade and senior officers will be offered special training to prepare them for command, staff, country team and departmental positions involved in the planning and conduct of counter-insurgency programs. At this level the students will be made aware of the possible contributions of all departments, and of the need to combine the departmental assets into effective programs. This type of instruction will be given at the Staff College–War College level in the Armed Services. The State Department will organize such courses as may be necessary at the Foreign Service Institute for officials of State, Agency for International Development and United States Information Agency. All schools of this category will make available spaces in agreed numbers for the cross-training of other U.S. agencies with a counter-insurgency responsibility.

d. *Specialized Preparations for Service in Underdeveloped Areas.* There is an unfulfilled need to offer instruction on the entire range of problems faced by the United States in dealing with developing countries, including special area counter-insurgency problems, to middle and senior grade officers (both military and civilian) who are about to occupy important posts in underdeveloped countries. A school will accordingly be developed at the national level to meet this need, to teach general (including counter-insurgency) policy and doctrine with respect to underdeveloped areas, to offer studies on problems of the underdeveloped world keyed to areas to which the students are being sent, and to engage in research projects designed to improve the U.S. capability for guiding underdeveloped countries through the modernization barrier and for countering subversive insurgency. In addition, this school would undertake to assist other more specialized U.S. Government institutions engaged in underdeveloped area problems (i.e., those conducted by the Foreign Service Institute, Agency for International Development, the Joint Chiefs of Staff and the Services, including the Military Assistance Institute and the Central Intelligence Agency) to develop curricula on the nontechnical aspects of their courses of instruction. . . .

58

The Difficulties of Combat in Vietnam

This analysis in 1965 by G. Etzel Pearcy, the Geographer of the Department of State, presents considerations of a kind that might profitably have guided Washington planners as they moved the nation deeper into the war.

. . . Geopoliticians cite compact shape as a decided asset for defense purposes and refer to France, with its hexagonal form, as approaching the ideal. South Vietnam represents the opposite extreme: a narrow ledge of land clinging to the great interior mountain system of Asia and presenting a classic example of exposed territory. So lengthy are the country's boundaries in relation to its size that those who would infiltrate have a rich choice of spots from which to select for entry.

. . . About 60 percent of South Vietnam consists of relatively high mountains and plateau lands. While not comparable to the Himalayas or Rockies in grandeur or broad dimension, the South Vietnamese mountains are higher than the Appalachians and present greater difficulty for movement. Maximum elevation is 8,500 feet, about 1,500 feet lower than in North Vietnam. Lowlands with little or no relief make up most of the remaining 40 percent of the country and are located chiefly in the Mekong Delta area.

Thus it can be seen that well over half of the countryside presents obstacles to penetration and movement but offers protection to offensive forces engaged in guerrilla-type warfare. And even in the lowlands, swamps and heavy vegetative growth afford the invaders a certain immunity against government security forces. . . .

While fine for the rice crop, heavy rainfall handicaps security measures in several ways. Mobility is reduced, equipment becomes difficult to maneuver, and better protection is offered the aggressor. Air action may be limited by the poor visibility resulting from high humidity and low cloud cover during the rainy season. . . .

Heavy rainfall, together with high temperatures, encourages the growth of a dense, barrier-like vegetation. Over five-sixths of South Vietnam has a cover of natural vegetation—rain forests, monsoon forests, and some savanna lands. When the original forest is cut away or burned,

Source: The Department of State Bulletin, LIII, No. 1369, September 20, 1965, 488, 490, 492, 495–96.

Young boy in South Vietnamese uniform ready to fight.

a secondary forest cover takes over in many places, poorer in timber but with heavier undergrowth.

Without doubt, these tangles of vegetation are a marked disadvantage for forces seeking out an enemy which moves quickly on foot, with a good knowledge of the terrain. For example, roadways cleared through heavy vegetative growth must be maintained or they soon revert to the jungle. In contrast, dense foliage offers excellent concealment from both air and land observation. From such terrain guerrillas may operate with relative safety and on a time schedule of their own making. . . .

The obstacles of inaccessibility also handicap those fighting against the guerrilla aggressors from the North. Inadequate lines of communication allow guerrillas to infiltrate large areas and remain under cover while at the same time they prevent effective offensive action to rout them. American military operations, ordinarily geared to efficient transportation systems, contrast markedly with those of the Viet Cong along the infiltration routes, where guerrillas slip in with their less-than-complex supplies and equipment. . . .

From a geographic point of view there can be no doubt that the U.S. faces disadvantages in Vietnam that far outweigh the advantages. While factors of relief, climate, and vegetation which handicap the defenders are not necessarily in themselves assets to the guerrillas, the guerrillas, of course, take advantage of the landscape as it is. They turn heavy foliage into camouflage, use light arms on terrain too rough for most conventional weapons, and seek strategic advantages during the monsoon season, when aircraft cannot be fully effective.

Tactics of the Viet Cong are likewise tailored to the cultural environment, including the abstract struggle for the minds and sympathies of the inhabitants. A recent estimate identifies well over a million villagers as dominated by Communists, with other millions subjected to some degree of Viet Cong control or pressure. Methods of obtaining cooperation from these rural inhabitants vary—from terrorism to the promise of concession. By holding small, scattered areas, the Viet Cong can erode government control more than they could if they gained larger but fewer blocks of territory. Hit-and-run tactics can be extended in more widespread fashion for greater psychological effect. Also, control of areas as close as possible to Saigon tends to give the impression that a rice-roots rebellion is closing in on the capital.

Since the South Vietnam conflict takes place on the real estate of that country and within its administrative jurisdiction, American military measures must be molded to the geography of the land—political, economic, and social. To appreciate these circumstances, difficult though they be, is to lessen the jeopardy of fighting in a strange land.

59

As the Communists View the Fighting

*This assessment, put out by Hanoi analysts, is heavy with ideo-
logical pronouncements, heavier even than an American governmental document of like intention would have been. It also
assumes, incorrectly, that the American military was losing the
battle on the ground. But beneath the vocabulary are some
fairly accurate considerations of problems plaguing the Americans, such as the necessity of dispersing forces and of fighting
an enemy who could easily disappear.*

. . . Behind the enemy's apparent might, his deep weakness should
be perceived. The U.S. imperialists intervened not in the wake of a
victorious campaign, but in an attempt to rescue half a million puppet
troops from disaster. Their expeditionary corps was sent unprepared to
a theatre of operations where their adversary was entrenched on all combat fronts, and his forces deployed in all strategic zones: the Mekong
delta, the coastal plains, the mountain regions and even the cities.

A long experience of over twenty years of political and armed struggle against the imperialist aggressor—ever since November 1940, the
South Vietnam population had practically not ceased fighting—had
given the population absolute confidence in themselves and organizational abilities equal to all situations. Political forces, like armed forces
of all categories, were ready for action. By taking direct part in combat,
the Americans only threw away their mask, further exasperated the Vietnamese people's anger and strengthened their unanimous will to struggle
for national independence and freedom. This struggle was growing more
and more vigorous. Long years of experience had shown the immense
possibilities of the people's revolutionary war. . . .

The U.S. command wants to concentrate its forces for big offensives,
but is forced to disperse them, not only to occupy more and more diverse
and numerous positions, but also to assume increasingly exacting tasks.
This strategic contradiction between concentration and dispersal makes
the U.S. expeditionary corps more and more incapable of putting into
practice the offensive strategy elaborated by the Pentagon.

Source: Tran Duc Thao and Nguyen Van Ba, "U.S. Military Failure in Vietnam: Why and
How?" in Nguyen Khac Vien, ed., *In Face of American Aggression: 1965–1967* (Hanoi:
Xunhasaba, 1968), 7–8, 15–18.

The Ho Chi Minh Trail was a series of footpaths which North Vietnamese troops took to the South. The trails, some of which traveled through the neighboring countries of Laos and Cambodia, were, as seen here, often quite narrow and primitive, but were modernized as the war went on. *(Courtesy, Wide World Photo)*

Besides, the U.S. war machine is too heavy. It requires considerable technical means, huge supplies of munitions, fuel, spare parts, and a complex infrastructure; its bases are constantly exposed; U.S. troops must be provided with living conditions of unequalled "comfort," and this puts a heavy strain on supply services. During his last inspection tour, McNamara remarked that only one G.I. out of seven was engaged in combat duties. The one-year tour of duty in Vietnam results in quick rotation of troops and limited combat power not proportionate to their number. . . .

Right from the beginning, it has been clear that it is not the U.S. expeditionary corps which could choose on what battlefields and terrains to fight, but the L.A.F. and the population of South Vietnam who can draw the enemy to wherever they want and force him to fight on their own terms. This results in a war with no clear front line, no precise objectives, so much so that G.I.'s never find their adversary when they look for him, but only at the most unexpected moments, and are thus inevitably destroyed.

In those conditions, the great firepower of U.S. planes and artillery loses almost all its effectiveness, this war machine being designed for conflicts opposing modern armies fighting on clear-cut frontlines, with easily detected objectives. The most modern means of detection become inoperative against an extremely mobile adversary, dispersed in countless small units which may disappear and reappear at any moment, which are everywhere and yet nowhere.

The huge American machine is one designed to be used against an enemy facing U.S. lines at a distance. But in South Vietnam, the L.A.F. are in the rear as well as the flanks of U.S. troops, and when they do come out, they are so close that U.S. planes and artillery become dangerous to the Americans themselves. G.I.s are frequently hit by U.S. bombs and shells. "Avoid close-range fighting," such is an American general's advice to his men, but he does not say how.

The U.S. command each time tries to draw lessons from experience, in order to improve combat tactics. However, the elaboration of U.S. tactics suffers from an inherent, irremediable defect: it is entirely based on blind reliance upon technique, and does not take into account man's abilities. For the Yankee generals, all combat problems can be solved by firepower, mobility, and ingenious detection apparatuses. They throw into battle the most diversified engines, fire countless bombs and shells, resort to innumerable manoeuvres: motorized, airborne, etc. On the battlefield, their junction and encirclement manoeuvres are carried out with rapidity and precision.

But most of the time, for want of accurate information, bombs and shells fall on empty places, pincers and traps close on a vacuum. . . .

60

The Tet Offensive

The Tet offensive of early 1968 is often described as the decisive event of the war against the Americans. That is not because the Communists were victorious: as is commonly observed, the offensive was crushed. The gain that the Communists achieved at Tet—and it was not their primary objective—was political. The analysis here is by a scholar, James J. Wirtz.

On 31 January 1968, during the Tet holiday, communist forces simultaneously attacked urban areas, military installations, and government facilities throughout South Vietnam. By the time the offensive's intensity began to wane on 13 February, 1100 Americans had been killed in action, and members of the Johnson administration and the American public had been stunned by the fury of the Tet attacks. Following the offensive, the official U.S. government investigation into the circumstances surrounding the Tet attacks concluded that, "although warning had . . . been provided, the intensity, coordination, and timing of the enemy attack were not fully anticipated." U.S. and South Vietnamese officers and intelligence analysts failed to anticipate the nature of the Tet offensive. This failure not only contributed to the initial military gains enjoyed by the communists but also increased the shock produced by the attack. Ultimately, it was the surprise, not the short-term military advantages, that reduced the willingness of the American public and political elite to continue to prosecute the war in Vietnam. . . .

As the Tet offensive approached, communist diversionary attacks along the borders of South Vietnam, especially on the U.S. firebase at Khe Sanh, increased in intensity. While high-quality indications of an imminent attack on southern cities became apparent, so did increasing noise generated by the diversionary attacks. Because this deception took the form of actual combat, the noise it generated made the signals about impending urban attacks appear pale in comparison. The difference between the intensity of the noise generated by the ongoing diversion and the signals created by preparations for urban attacks produced a dilemma that contributed to the surprise suffered by the allies. Most U.S. commanders considered the attack on southern cities a diversion

Source: James J. Wirtz, *The Tet Offensive: Intelligence Failure in War* (Ithaca, N.Y.: Cornell Univerity Press, 1991), 1, 254–56.

and expected the primary blow to fall along the DMZ, probably at Khe Sanh.

The communists paid a price for this successful diversion. To be convincing, the diversion along the DMZ and border areas had to be intense. The effort to stage major attacks throughout South Vietnam, however, ultimately strained communist capabilities beyond their limit. Because of a remarkable communist miscalculation, the offensive violated the principle of concentration of forces. By simultaneously attacking everywhere, the NVA and VC lacked the numerical superiority they needed to succeed; as a result, they were defeated piecemeal. If the offensive had unfolded as planned, the principle of concentration of forces would not have been violated. But as the attacks developed, a large portion of the force the communists included in their plans failed to materialize on the battlefield; South Vietnamese civilians did not stage a general uprising in support of the offensive. A general uprising might have allowed the communists to secure their primary objective, a quick and successful conclusion of the war. Faced with the disintegration of ARVN and isolated by a hostile and partially armed population, the United States might have been left with no alternative but to abandon South Vietnam. In such a situation, NVA commanders might have attempted to hasten U.S. forces on their way by accepting the tremendous costs of storming Khe Sanh. But without the added strain on allied resources created by a general uprising, such an NVA effort would have been suicidal.

Communist miscalculation about the likelihood of a general uprising added an extremely difficult element to the problem faced by U.S. intelligence analysts. Because they possessed superior information about the sympathies of the southern population, they interpreted communist calls for a general uprising as incredible. In fact, analysts and officers even claimed that propaganda calling for a general uprising was an encouraging development, since the communists would be discredited when the revolt failed to materialize. U.S. analysts accurately estimated that, without the manpower provided by a general uprising, the communists would lack the resources needed to pose overwhelming multiple threats throughout the country. The communist plan made no sense from the allied perspective; it violated the principle of concentration of forces. Communist miscalculation about the likelihood of a general uprising thus created an interesting irony. On the one hand, it greatly contributed to the successful diversion of U.S. forces toward the border and maximized the element of surprise in the attacks against urban areas. On the other hand, it ultimately doomed these urban attacks to failure.

The communists also used cover operations in the strategy of deception, especially as preparations reached an advanced stage. Perhaps they recognized that secrecy and diversionary attacks could not prevent the allies from detecting the burst of signals generated by the final preparations for the offensive. They apparently realized that cover operations were needed to create confusion and hesitancy among the allies as they attempted to respond to indications of impending attack. The Tet holiday itself constituted the primary cover. The possibility exists that the North Vietnamese realized that they had established a pattern of activity during previous truce periods, leading to a sense of security among the allies about the likelihood of a major attack during the Tet truce. It was no coincidence that the communists, not the allies, proposed an extended truce for the 1968 Tet holidays. Even though attacking during a truce constitutes a classic cover operation, the communists also may have anticipated that the allies would expect them to conduct final preparations for the offensive during the truce. The communists probably expected to catch the allies off guard by attacking during the truce, abandoning their standard practice of using truces to resupply. The Trinh initiative was also a successful cover operation, even though its basic purpose was to lay the groundwork for a negotiated end to the war following a successful offensive. Because the offensive failed to destroy ARVN or spark a general uprising, the Trinh initiative also failed in its main objective. But it still achieved its secondary objective, by provoking a highly cooperative, albeit unanticipated, allied response. In reaction to the initiative, the United States restricted its bombing of North Vietnam. The Trinh initiative can also be linked to the 50 percent reduction in ARVN strength during the Tet truce. In comparison to other allied acts of omission or commission, the absence of these ARVN forces contributed most to the military setbacks suffered by the allies during Tet.

In sum, the communist plans for the Tet offensive constituted a military tour de force in identifying and exploiting allied weaknesses. They exploited divisions in the allied command structure, differences in the missions of various allied forces, and the distance that usually separated U.S. units from their ARVN counterparts. Thus, the communists responded to U.S. intervention in the ground war by tying down and isolating powerful U.S. units in order to attack directly the government infrastructure and relatively weak ARVN units. The communists succeeded in circumventing the shield provided by U.S. units, leaving them to play a peripheral role during the Tet offensive. Communist miscalculation about civilian sympathies helped to gain the element of surprise during Tet, but it also doomed the offensive to failure. Ironically, the communists, like the Americans, were far better at identifying the vulnerabilities of their enemy than the weaknesses in their own alliance.

61

"Saigon Under Fire"

This report by Mike Wallace and Dan Rather on CBS television for January 31, 1968, deals with one of the most startling facts of the Tet offensive: the ability of the Communists to fight within Saigon itself.

WALLACE: Good evening. I'm Mike Wallace.

With a bold series of raids during the last three days the enemy in Vietnam has demolished the myth that Allied military strength controls that country. The Communists hit the very heart of Saigon, the capital of South Vietnam, and at least ten cities which correspond to state capitals here in the United States. And then, as if to demonstrate that no place in that war-torn nation is secure they struck at least nine American military strongholds and unnumbered field positions. Tonight the magnitude of those raids became apparent in the U.S. Command's report on casualties. The Communists paid a heavy toll for their strikes, almost 5,000 dead, including 660 in Saigon alone, and almost 2,000 captured. But Allied casualties also are high: 232 Americans killed, 929 wounded; 300 South Vietnamese killed, 747 wounded, and that toll is expected to climb.

The enemy's well-coordinated attacks occurred throughout South Vietnam, but the most dramatic demonstration of his boldness and capability came at the very symbol of America's presence in Vietnam, the brand new U.S. Embassy building there. CBS NEWS Correspondent Robert Schakne reports.

SCHAKNE: The American Embassy is under siege; only the besiegers are Americans. Inside, in part of the building, are the Vietcong terror squads that charged in during the night. Military Police got back into the compound of the $2½ million Embassy complex at dawn. Before that a platoon of Vietcong were in control. The Communist raiders never got into the main chancery building; a handful of Marines had it blocked and kept them out. But the raiders were everywhere else. By daylight (voice drowned out by gunfire) No one, unless identified, was allowed in the street. An Australian Military Policeman was standing guard, firing warning shots to keep the street clear.

Source: CBS NEWS SPECIAL REPORT: "Saigon Under Fire," CBS, Inc., January 31, 1968. Reprinted by permission.

Saigon burning.

Outside the building knots of Military Policemen held positions. There were bursts of wild shooting in the streets, perhaps snipers in other buildings and there had been casualties. The bodies of two Military Policemen who died as they tried to assault the compound lay near their jeep across the boulevard. But even after the Military Police fought their way back inside, there was more fighting to do. The raiders were still about the compound. They may have been a suicide cadre. In the end none of them were to surrender.

This is where the Vietcong raiders broke in. They sneaked up and blasted a hole in the reinforced concrete fence surrounding the compound. They were inside before anyone knew it. They had the big Embassy wall to protect them. But none of the raiders lived to tell of their exploit. By 8:00 o'clock, five hours after they first broke in, almost all of them were dead. Nineteen bodies were counted. All in civilian clothes, they had been armed with American M-16 rifles and also rocket-launchers and rockets. They had explosives, their purpose apparently to destroy the Embassy. In that purpose they did not succeed.

The fighting went on for a total of six hours before the last known Vietcong raider was killed. They were rooted out of bushes, from outlying buildings, and then the last one, the 19th, from the small residence of the Embassy's Mission Coordinator, George Jacobson, who had been hiding out all alone, all morning. . . .

Saigon had been on the alert for Vietcong terror attacks during the night, but for some reason the Embassy guard was not increased. Just two Military Policemen at one gate, a handful of Marines inside. There wasn't anyone to stop the Vietcong when they came. General William Westmoreland came by soon after. His version was that all this represented a Vietcong defeat.

WESTMORELAND: In some way the enemy's well-laid plans went afoul. Some superficial damage was done to the building. All of the enemy that entered the compound as far as I can determine were killed. Nineteen bodies have been found on the premises—enemy bodies. Nineteen enemy bodies have been found on the premises.

SCHAKNE: General, how would you assess yesterday's activities and today's? What is the enemy doing? Are these major attacks?

(Sound of explosions)

WESTMORELAND: That's POD setting off a couple of M-79 duds, I believe.

SCHAKNE: General, how would you assess the enemy's purposes yesterday and today?

WESTMORELAND: The enemy very deceitfully has taken advantage of the Tet truce in order to create maximum consternation within South Vietnam, particularly in the populated areas. In my opinion this is diversionary to his main effort, which he had planned to take place in Quang Tri Province, from Laos, toward Khesanh and across the Demilitarized Zone. This attack has not yet materialized; his schedule has probably been thrown off balance because of our very effective air strikes.

Now yesterday the enemy exposed himself by virtue of this strategy and he suffered great casualties. When I left my office late yesterday, approximately 8:00 o'clock, we—we had accounted for almost 700 enemy killed in action. Now we had suffered some casualties ourselves, but they were small by comparison. My guess is, based on my conversations with my field commanders, that there were probably—there were probably far more than 700 that were killed. Now by virtue of this audacious action by the enemy, he has exposed himself, he has become more vulnerable. As soon as President Thieu, with our agreement, called off the truce, U.S. and American [ARVN?] troops went on the offensive and pursued the enemy aggressively.

SCHAKNE: When they built this Embassy it was first to be a secure building. This Embassy was designed as a bomb-proof, attack-proof building, but it turned out, when the VC hit us, it wasn't attack-proof enough. Robert Schakne, CBS NEWS, Saigon.

WALLACE: Washington regards the enemy raids as the first step in a strategy aimed at strengthening their hand for any peace talks which may develop, and captured Communist documents lend weight to the theory.

CBS NEWS White House Correspondent Dan Rather reports.

RATHER: We knew this was coming—a well-coordinated series of enemy raids against South Vietnamese cities. Our intelligence even pinpointed the exact day it would happen. What we did not know was where. This is the official story, as given out by White House news secretary George Christian, who went on to say there was no way to completely insulate yourself against this kind of thing if the enemy is willing to sacrifice large numbers of men.

But if we knew it was coming, even to the exact day, Christian was asked, why wasn't extra protection placed around such an obvious place as the Saigon Embassy? The White House spokesman paused, then said, "I just don't know." At the Pentagon a high-ranking source said, "There simply were more of them and they were better than we expected."

Washington is startled but not panicked by the latest series of events. President Johnson privately is warning Congressmen that intelligence reports indicate the whole month of February will be rough in Southeast Asia. Mr. Johnson is emphasizing that the enemy's winter offensive is only beginning. Dan Rather, CBS NEWS, Washington.

WALLACE: The drama of the battle for Saigon captured most attention, but the South Vietnamese capital was only one of the Communist targets. In a moment we'll return with battle film from another city.

(ANNOUNCEMENT)

WALLACE: The U.S. Command's battle communique indicates that the Allies repulsed most of the enemy's attacks, but this success was not universal. In an assault today the Communists captured half of the Central Highlands city of Kontum and the Vietcong flag flies in the center of the northern city of Hue. The enemy claims also to control Quang Tri City, also in I Corps in the north, a claim as yet unconfirmed by the Allies.

But one place where American and South Vietnamese troops turned back the enemy was at Nhatrang, a coastal city about 190 miles northeast of Saigon. In peacetime a pleasant resort city, now Nhatrang is the headquarters for the Fifth Special Forces, the Green Berets; and the Green Berets were in the thick of the fighting. The Communist attack there had begun around midnight, and it developed into a street fight which, as you see here, carried over into the daylight hours. The enemy's apparent goal in this fight, down the street, was a provincial prison where many important Vietcong were held. During this battle many innocent civilians, friendly to the Allies, were trapped in their homes between the lines of fire between VC and the Green Berets. It was only after twelve hours of battle that the area was secure enough to call those civilians out to safety.

The Communist raids had a stunning impact, all of them, around the world, and the question is, what is it that the enemy is after in these attacks. Certainly he does not believe that these suicide assaults by terrorists squads are going to radically change the course of the war in Vietnam; but there can be no doubt that these attacks are calculated to impress indelibly on public opinion in North and South Vietnam and in the United States the resourcefulness and the determination of the Vietcong and his ability to strike almost at will any place in South Vietnam if he is willing to pay the price.

The story of the past three days, with heavy emphasis, of course, on American and South Vietnamese casualties will be trumpeted throughout Vietnam and around the world by Hanoi. Whether all of this is a prelude to an expression that Hanoi is willing now to go to the negotiation table remains to be seen, but there is little doubt that there will be more such stories from Khesanh and elsewhere in South Vietnam in the bitter month of February that lies ahead.

Mike Wallace, CBS NEWS, New York.

ANNOUNCER: This has been a CBS NEWS SPECIAL REPORT: "Saigon Under Fire."

62

Combat in the Midst of Civilians

Following the Tet offensive early in 1968, Patrick M. Trinkle of the American army was in the My Lai area, where the most publicized atrocity committed by American troops would soon take place. Here on April 15, 1970, Major Trinkle is testifying before a subcommittee of the Committee on Armed Services of the House of Representatives investigating the atrocity. The major was not at My Lai at the time of the incident. His testimony is significant for illustrating the care and discipline American troops had to follow in their encounters with civilians in Vietcong territory if any humane dealings were to take place.

Source: U.S. Congress, House, Armed Services Investigating Subcommittee of the Committee on Armed Services, *Investigation of the My Lai Incident: Hearings of the Armed Services Investigating Subcommittee,* 91st Cong., 2nd sess., April 15–June 22, 1970, 9–15, 19.

Vietnamese refugees fleeing the combat areas.

... MR. GUBSER. Major, what instructions did you give your command prior to an action with respect to what should be done about possible civilian casualties?

MAJOR TRINKLE. My standing operating procedures were, sir, that we weren't to have any civilian casualties if it could possibly be avoided. In other words, if there was any doubt, don't shoot, and if a civilian did happen to get hurt, which was the case when the girl was hurt in My Lai, they were evacuated immediately for medical attention.

MR. GUBSER. What would be the criteria upon which doubt would be resolved, whether they carried weapons, whether they fled, and what else?

MAJOR TRINKLE. The main thing was do they have a weapon. And if it were a military age male that took off running, you know, like as fast as he could, they were supposed to catch him. But if it was obviously a military age male and they couldn't catch him, then they were allowed to fire.

MR. GUBSER. A grenade is considered a weapon, isn't it?

MAJOR TRINKLE. Yes, sir.

MR. GUBSER. Did you ever find situations where women or children and people who under civilized warfare rules would ordinarily be noncombatants, carrying grenades?

MAJOR TRINKLE. I don't personally recall ever finding a woman with a grenade on her, but I am sure they must have, because we did have these three I know that were carrying carbines. I don't remember whether they had grenades or not. I found a lot of young boys carrying grenades.

MR. GUBSER. You have?

MAJOR TRINKLE. 14 years old.

MR. GUBSER. Of course this could be concealed more than a carbine could.

MAJOR TRINKLE. Yes, sir.

MR. GUBSER. In other words, would you say, though, that it would be a normal fear for a GI in that area to feel that he could be attacked with a grenade or some other weapon by a woman or a child at any point?

MAJOR TRINKLE. Yes, sir. . . .

MR. STRATTON. What rules did you have for reporting any atrocities or infractions of procedures with regard to civilians? Did you have any instructions as to what should be done, if you saw this happening?

MAJOR TRINKLE. I can only speak from the standpoint of my company, sir. But I constantly stressed with my platoon leaders to be careful, in other words, if they had to hurt somebody or had to kill somebody, to make sure that it was necessary, and the thought of atrocities never really entered my mind that much.

I remember talking to my whole company before we left from Hawaii—a lot of my men were brand new, and I was worried about this, because I had been there in 1965, and you know, I knew then when American units get there they don't always know who is good and who is bad. And at that particular time, I think there was a Marine being tried for some—he was being charged with murder in Da Nang. This was in 1967. Just about the time we deployed. And I used that example to talk to them about how important it was that we didn't do anything like this. But if it happened, my rule would have been to find the person responsible and prefer charges against him.

MR. STRATTON. You had been in Vietnam before, so you were aware of some of the problems that would occur in that kind of a war?

MAJOR TRINKLE. Yes, sir.

MR. STRATTON. Were there any periodic instructions from division headquarters with regard to this procedure? Did the division officers or the brigade officers make any effort to sort of remind company commanders, battalion commanders, platoon commanders, to take precautions of this sort?

MAJOR TRINKLE. I don't remember, sir. I really don't.

MR. STRATTON. Major, what was the impact of the Tet offensive on the troops? Let me just preface that. I remember I was in Vietnam in December, I think—several of the members of this committee were there, December of 1967. The situation looked good. We were assured that things were pretty well under control. And then you had this concerted attack that took place at Tet. Did this rather unexpected attack have some impact on the troops themselves?

MAJOR TRINKLE. The main effect it had on the American troops, sir, was it was just a little bit easier to find the VC for about a week. They came out of hiding, and you know, they fought like soldiers.

If you are talking about did it shake them up or scare them, no.

MR. STRATTON. Make them a little jittery.

MAJOR TRINKLE. No. Because the Tet offensive hurt mostly the civilians. It didn't really hurt the American troops that much.

MR. STRATTON. I see.

MAJOR TRINKLE. It just made our job easier for about a week because they came out of their tunnels and fought for a while.

MR. STRATTON. Thank you very much.

MAJOR TRINKLE. Yes, sir.

MR. HÉBERT. Mr. Dickinson.

MR. DICKINSON. Yes, just a couple of short questions.

What were your orders, your standing operating procedures when civilians were killed? What did you do? Was there any particular way that you were supposed to report it? Was there anything separate from this? I mean noncombatants.

MAJOR TRINKLE. Well, they would have been reported as civilians killed in a crossfire or something like that, yes, sir. If it did happen.

MR. DICKINSON. I know that this did happen occasionally, but could you give us an idea of the frequency and possibly the numbers that you experienced, where noncombatants or questionable combatants were killed, civilians?

MAJOR TRINKLE. I remember the girl that we evacuated there from My Lai. But very few other times, in my company. It happened in other companies once in a while.

MR. DICKINSON. I understand. But it was relatively rare?

MAJOR TRINKLE. Yes, sir.

MR. DICKINSON. Wasn't it? I am not really trying to lead you.

MAJOR TRINKLE. Well, I will put it this way, sir. Some companies reconned by fire, and you get more civilian casualties that way. It is not uncommon, and it has got a lot to be said for it. In other words, when they go into a village where they are real sure there are VC there, they lay down a heavy base of fire, and sometimes they kill civilians that way. I didn't use that technique.

MR. DICKINSON. All right. Well, now, in your experience, though, if you got two, three, four civilians killed, that would be an average number?

MAJOR TRINKLE. No.

MR. DICKINSON. An unusually large number or what?

MAJOR TRINKLE. From my company, there weren't any.

MR. DICKINSON. There weren't any?

MAJOR TRINKLE. Except for this girl.

MR. DICKINSON. But there was no particular reporting procedure or nothing in particular that you had to do if a noncombatant, or what you assumed to be a civilian, were killed?

MAJOR TRINKLE. You reported it to your next higher headquarters that you needed a medevac for a civilian. . . .

MR. HÉBERT. Major, I want to reconstruct some of your statements.

At the time up to your becoming a casualty—it was the end of February?

MAJOR TRINKLE. Yes, sir. I can't remember the exact date, but it was about the end of February.

MR. HÉBERT. And the alleged incident occurred on March 15 or 16?

MAJOR TRINKLE. Yes, sir.

MR. HÉBERT. The 16th of March, two weeks later.

MAJOR TRINKLE. Yes, sir.

MR. HÉBERT. How were you wounded?

MAJOR TRINKLE. Gunshot wound.

MR. HÉBERT. Where?

MAJOR TRINKLE. Once in the back and once in the leg.

MR. HÉBERT. Once in the leg. And you were evacuated?

MAJOR TRINKLE. Yes, sir.

MR. HÉBERT. And then you had no connection whatsoever with any activity, any action?

MAJOR TRINKLE. No connection with Task Force Barker again, sir.

MR. HÉBERT. No connection with Task Force Barker at all?

MAJOR TRINKLE. No.

MR. HÉBERT. Did you hear any conversation, or skuttlebutt, or rumors about something unusual taking place at My Lai 4 on March 16?

MAJOR TRINKLE. Yes, sir. I mentioned that to the Peers Board, too, and I can't remember the source.

MR. HÉBERT. Tell us.

MAJOR TRINKLE. I did hear a rumor.

MR. HÉBERT. Never mind the Peers Report. This is an independent investigation. We want to know from scratch.

MAJOR TRINKLE. Several weeks, or possibly as much as a couple of months after I got back from the hospital, I came back to my parent battalion. I did hear a rumor, and I don't—I think it might have been Captain Riggs, who took over the company from me. But I am not sure. I mean, he is just the most likely person I would have been talking to.

I heard that C Company had done a sloppy job on their operation at My Lai, in that some of the civilians were killed, but you know, in my mind at that time, it was just a rumor, and I had visions of this three to half a dozen or so killed in a crossfire.

MR. HÉBERT. Well, now, would it be a usual thing that just occupied a passing thought in your mind, or would this be an unusual operation? Or was this the usual modus operandi of troops?

MAJOR TRINKLE. It wasn't usual. I probably just had the opinion, well. Medina did a sloppy job.

MR. HÉBERT. Well, then, how long were you in Vietnam?

MAJOR TRINKLE. I have been there for a total of 2 years, sir.

MR. HÉBERT. Two years. And you engaged in many actions during that time?

MAJOR TRINKLE. Yes, sir.

MR. HÉBERT. And if this was not the usual thing, wouldn't it have an impression on you that this was a sloppy operation, and this was something that was unusual?

MAJOR TRINKLE. There are a lot of sloppy operations over there, sir.

MR. HÉBERT. Well, all right then. That is what I am trying to find out. I am not trying to lead you or anything. I am trying to find out what the general atmosphere was. Just another sloppy operation.

MAJOR TRINKLE. Yes, sir.

MR. HÉBERT. And there had been many sloppy operations?

MAJOR TRINKLE. Yes, sir.

MR. HÉBERT. And if anything happened, in your definition of sloppy, is where there is just —

MAJOR TRINKLE. Everybody shoots at everything that moves.

MR. HÉBERT. That's what you call it when you say "sloppy," you mean just "slop" them out?

MAJOR TRINKLE. Yes, sir.

MR. HÉBERT. We'll use that word. And did you hear it discussed any more except on that one occasion?

MAJOR TRINKLE. No, sir.

MR. HÉBERT. So then am I right in presuming that this was a regular type of action?

MAJOR TRINKLE. Yes, sir. . . .

MR. HÉBERT. All right. Now, then, this became a cause celebre, if we are going to describe it that way, in the summer of 1969, when the first formal attention was brought to Congress by this letter of this individual, Ridenhour. When did you become knowledgeable of this complaint?

MAJOR TRINKLE. When I read about it in the press.

MR. HÉBERT. When you read about it in the press.

MAJOR TRINKLE. Yes, sir.

MR. HÉBERT. Did this generate in your mind any recollection about what you had heard or what you knew about sloppy operations?

MAJOR TRINKLE. Well, I didn't believe it at all, sir. I was shocked that these accusations were being made. And I thought —

MR. HÉBERT. Now, you say you were shocked that these accusations would be made. Yet just a few minutes ago you said that sloppy operations were —

MAJOR TRINKLE. Sloppy operation doesn't include that many people being killed, sir. The first reports that came out were something like 500 people.

MR. HÉBERT. Five hundred people. In other words, you are defining sloppy by numbers?

MAJOR TRINKLE. When I first heard the rumor —

MR. HÉBERT. That's beyond sloppy.

MAJOR TRINKLE. When I first heard the rumor that some civilians had been killed, I thought they were talking about something less than a half dozen people.

MR. HÉBERT. And then?

MAJOR TRINKLE. When I read about it in the press, all these hundreds or 500's or 50, anything over half a dozen —

MR. HÉBERT. Then are we to understand when you say "sloppy operations," you are only talking about six civilians being killed? Six, seven, a dozen?

MAJOR TRINKLE. Certainly nothing like the numbers that are being talked about here.

MR. HÉBERT. Say a dozen, two dozen. That is what you are talking about. So when you say "sloppy operations," you mean just a handful of people being killed?

MAJOR TRINKLE. Yes, sir.

MR. HÉBERT. You are not talking about a number that's involved or suggested in this incident?

MAJOR TRINKLE. No, sir. . . .

MR. STRATTON. You did not—the rumor that you heard did not involve the rather coldblooded and deliberate lining up of civilians in a particular spot, presumably having surrendered, and unarmed, and then gunning them down in cold blood?

MAJOR TRINKLE. No, sir. There was no indication that anything like that happened at all.

MR. STRATTON. Now, I think—well, let me say this. If that thing were to have occurred, would you regard that as a sloppy job, or would you regard that as —

MAJOR TRINKLE. No, sir. I would regard that as murder. . . .

63

"Now They Only Kill and Rape Day After Day"

This propaganda message was in the wake of the killings at My Lai. In tone it differs little from what any nation or movement at war might produce. British accusations of German barbarities during the First World War were scarcely less shrill. For all its stridency, this statement also contains truth: the reference to the events in Son Tinh Province is to the killings at My Lai.

Source: U.S. Congress, House, Armed Services Investigating Subcommittee of the Committee on Armed Services, *Investigation of the My Lai Incident: Hearings of the Armed Services Investigating Subcommittee,* 91st Cong., 2nd sess., April 15–June 22, 1970, 305–06.

The American Devils Divulge Their True Form

The empire building Americans invade South Vietnam with war. They say that they came to Vietnam to help the Vietnamese people and that they are our friends.

When the US Soldiers first arrived in Vietnam they tried to conceal their cruel invasion. They gave orders to the US soldiers to be good to the Vietamese people thus employing psychological warfare. They also employed strict discipline which required US soldiers to respect the Vietnamese women and the customs of the Vietnamese people.

When the first US soldiers arrived in Vietnam they were good soldiers and they paid when they made purchases from the people. They would even pay a price in excess of the cost. When they did wrong they gave money to indemnify their deeds. They gave the people around their basecamps and in nearby hamlets medical aid. US newspapers often printed pictures of US troops embracing the Vietnamese people and giving candy to children. The American Red Cross also gave medical attention to the Vietnamese. This lead a small group of ARVN's to believe that the American man was a good friend and had continued pity for the people. The Army Republic of Vietnam was happy to have allies which are such good friends and who are rich.

But, it is a play and every play must come to an end and the curtain come down. The espionage was very professional and clever. If the plan is completed it will one day become saucy, because all the people will know what they are trying to hide and what they are really doing to the Vietnamese people.

They continue to produce this play but each year they receive fewer victorious responses. Each year they are attacked by the enemy in the south and they are being defeated more every day. This play lies to the people and will soon be disclosed to them. Today the Americans cannot cover anything. Now they only kill and rape day after day. Their animalistic character has been uncovered even by the American civilians. In Saigon there are some Americans that put their penis outside of their pants and put a dollar on it to pay the girls who sell themselves. The Americans get laid in every public place. This beast in the street is not afraid of the presence of the people.

In the American basecamps when they check the people they take their money, rings, watches, and the women's ear rings. The Americans know the difference between good gold and cheap bronze. If the jewelry is of bronze they do not take it.

Since the Americans heavy loss in the spring they have become like wounded animals that are crazy and cruel. They bomb places where many people live, places which are not good choices for bombings, such as the cities within the provinces, especially in Hue, Saigon, and Ben Tro. In Hue the US newspapers reported that 70% of the homes were destroyed and 10,000 people killed or left homeless. The newspapers and radios of Europe also tell of the killing of the South Vietnamese people by the Ameicans. The English tell of the action where the Americans are bombing the cities of South Vietnam. The Americans will be sentenced first by the Public in Saigon. It is there where the people will lose sentiment for them because they bomb the people and all people will soon be against them. The world public objects to this bombing including the American public and that of its Allies. The American often shuts his eye and closes his ear and continues his crime.

In the operation of 15 March 1968 in Son Tinh District the American enemies went crazy. They used machine guns and every other kind of weapons to kill 500 people who had empty hands, in Tinh Khe (Son My) Village (Son Tinh District, Quang Ngai Province). There were many pregnant women some of which were only a few days from childbirth. The Americans would shoot everybody they saw. They killed people and cows, burned homes. There were some families in which all members were killed.

When the red evil Americans remove their prayer shirts they appear as barbaric men.

When the American wolves remove their sheepskin their sharp meat-eating teeth show. They drink our peoples blood with animal sentimentality.

Our people must choose one way to beat them until they are dead, and stop wriggling.

For the ARVN officer and soldier, by now you have seen the face of the real American. How many times have they left you alone to defend against the National Liberation Front? They do not fire artillery or mortars to help you even when you are near them. They often bomb the bodies of ARVN soldiers. They also fire artillery on the tactical elements of the ARVN soldiers.

The location of the ARVN soldier is the American target. If someone does not believe this he may examine the 39th Ranger Battalion when it was sent to Khe Sanh where its basecamp was placed between the Americans and the Liberation soldiers. They were willing to allow this battalion to die for them. This activity was not armed toward helping South Vietnam as is the National Liberation Front but was to protect the 6,000 Americans that live in Khe Sanh.

Can you accept these criminal friends who slaughter our people and turn Vietnam into red blood like that which runs in our veins?

What are you waiting for and why do not you use your US Rifles to shoot the Americans in the head—for our people, to help our country and save your life too?

There is no time better than now
>The American Rifle is in your hands
>You must take aim at the Americans head and
>>>>Pull the trigger

64

Cover-up?

Ron Ridenhour was one of the first to bring to official attention the rumors of the atrocity at My Lai. Son My was the larger village area in which My Lai was located. The "Kally" to whom Ridenhour refers in this letter to Congress is Lieutenant William Calley, whose name is closely associated with the incident. The Army commissioned an investigation under General William R. Peers. Here is part of the report of the findings of the Peers Commission. Included is the Ridenhour letter. The discovery that members of the army hierarchy were slow to act on the rumors is a reflection on the self-protective instincts of institutions.

Gentlemen:

It was late in April, 1968 that I first heard of "Pinkville" and what allegedly happened there. I received that first report with some skepticism, but in the following months I was to hear similar stories from such a wide variety of people that it became impossible for me to disbelieve that something rather dark and bloody did indeed occur sometime in March, 1968 in a village called "Pinkville" in the Republic of Viet Nam. . . .

"Charlie" Company 1/20 had been assigned to Task Force Barker

---

Source: Joseph Goldstein, Burke Marshall, Jack Schwartz, *The My Lai Massacre and Its Cover-up: Beyond the Reach of Law? The Peers Commisssion Report with a Supplement and Introductory Essay on the Limits of Law* (New York: The Free Press, 1976), 34–37, 314–17. Reprinted by permission.

in late February, 1968 to help conduct "search and destroy" operations on the Batangan Peninsula, Barker's area of operation. The task force was operating out of L. F. Dottie, located five or six miles north of Quang Nhai city on Viet Namese National Highway 1. [Pfc "Butch"] Gruver said that Charlie Company had sustained casualties; primarily from mines and booby traps, almost every day from the first day they arrived on the peninsula. One village area was particularly troublesome and seemed to be infested with booby traps and enemy soldiers. It was located about six miles northeast of Quang Nhai city at approximate coordinates B.S. 728795. It was a notorious area and the men of Task Force Barker had a special name for it: they called it "Pinkville." One morning in the latter part of March, Task Force Barker moved out from its firebase headed for "Pinkville." Its mission: destroy the trouble spot and all of its inhabitants.

When "Butch" told me this I didn't quite believe that what he was telling me was true, but he assured me that it was and went on to describe what had happened. The other two companies that made up the task force cordoned off the village so that "Charlie" Company could move through to destroy the structures and kill the inhabitants. Any villagers who ran from Charlie Company were stopped by the encircling companies. I asked "Butch" several times if all the people were killed. He said that he thought they were, men, women and children. He recalled seeing a small boy, about three or four years old, standing by the trail with a gunshot wound in one arm. The boy was clutching his wounded arm with his other hand, while blood trickled between his fingers. He was staring around himself in shock and disbelief at what he saw. "He just stood there with big eyes staring around like he didn't understand; he didn't believe what was happening. Then the captain's RTO (radio operator) put a burst of 16 (M-16 rifle) fire into him." It was so bad, Gruver said, that one of the men in his squad shot himself in the foot in order to be medivac-ed out of the area so that he would not have to participate in the slaughter. Although he had not seen it, Gruver had been told by people he considered trustworthy that one of the company's officers, 2nd Lieutenant Kally (this spelling may be incorrect) had rounded up several groups of villagers (each group consisting of a minimum of 20 persons of both sexes and all ages). According to the story, Kally then machine-gunned each group. Gruver estimated that the population of the village had been 300 to 400 people and that very few, if any, escaped.

After hearing this account I couldn't quite accept it. Somehow I just couldn't believe that not only had so many young American men participated in such an act of barbarism, but that their officers had ordered it. There were other men in the unit I was soon to be assigned to, "E" Company, 51st Infantry (LRP), who had been in Charlie Company at the time that Gruver alleged the incident at "Pinkville" had occurred. I became determined to ask them about "Pinkville" so that I might compare their accounts with Pfc Gruver's.

When I arrived at "Echo" Company, 51st Infantry (LRP) the first men I looked for were Pfc's Michael Terry and William Doherty. Both were veterans of "Charlie" Company, 1/20 and "Pinkville." Instead of contradicting "Butch" Gruver's story they corroborated it, adding some tasty tidbits of information of their own. Terry and Doherty had been in the same squad and their platoon was the third platoon of "C" Company to pass through the village. Most of the people they came to were already dead. Those that weren't were sought out and shot. The platoon left nothing alive, neither livestock nor people. Around noon the two soldiers' squad stopped to eat. "Billy and I started to get out our chow," Terry said, "but close to us was a bunch of Vietnamese in a heap, and some of them were moaning. Kally (2nd Lt. Kally) had been through before us and all of them had been shot, but many weren't dead. It was obvious that they weren't going to get any medical attention so Billy and I got up and went over to where they were. I guess we sort of finished them off." Terry went on to say that he and Doherty then returned to where their packs were and ate lunch. He estimated the size of the village to be 200 to 300 people. Doherty thought that the population of "Pinkville" had been 400 people.

If Terry, Doherty and Gruver could be believed, then not only had "Charlie" Company received orders to slaughter all the inhabitants of the village, but those orders had come from the commanding officer of Task Force Barker, or possibly even higher in the chain of command. Pfc Terry stated that when Captain Medina (Charlie Company's commanding officer Captain Ernest Medina) issued the order for the destruction of "Pinkville" he had been hesitant, as if it were something he didn't want to do but had to. Others I spoke to concurred with Terry on this.

It was June before I spoke to anyone who had something of significance to add to what I had already been told of the "Pinkville" incident. It was the end of June, 1968 when I ran into Sarge[a]nt Larry La Croix at the USO in Chu Lai. La Croix had been in 2nd Lt. Kally's platoon on the day Task Force Barker swept through "Pinkville." What he told me verified the stories of the others, but he also had something new to add. He had been a witness to Kally's gunning down of at least three separate groups of villagers. "It was terrible. They were slaughtering the villagers like so many sheep." Kally's men were dragging people out of bunkers and hootches and putting them together in a group. The people in the group were men, women and children of all ages. As soon as he felt that the group was big enough, Kally ordered an M-60 (machine-gun) set up and the people killed. La Croix said that he bore witness to this procedure at least three times. The three groups were of different sizes, one of about twenty people, one of about thirty people, and one of about forty people. When the first group was put together Kally ordered Pfc Torres to man the machine-gun and open fire on the villagers that had been grouped together. This Torres did, but before everyone in the group was down he ceased fire and refused to fire again. After ordering Torres to recommence firing several times, Lieutenant Kally took over the M-60 and finished shooting the remaining villagers in that first group himself. Sarge[a]nt La Croix told me that Kally didn't bother to order anyone to take the machine-gun when the other two groups of villagers were formed. He simply manned it himself and shot down all villagers in both groups.

This account of Sarge[a]nt La Croix's confirmed the rumors that Gruver, Terry and Doherty had previously told me about Lieutenant Kally. It also convinced me that there was a very substantial amount of truth to the stories that all of these men had told. If I needed more convincing, I was to receive it.

It was in the middle of November, 1968 just a few weeks before I was to return to the United States for separation from the army that I talked to Pfc Michael Bernhardt. Bernhardt had served his entire year in Viet Nam in "Charlie" Company 1/20 and he too was about to go home. "Bernie" substantiated the tales told by the other men I had talked to in vivid, bloody detail and added this. "Bernie" had absolutely refused to take part in the massacre of the villagers of "Pinkville" that morning and he thought that it was rather strange that the officers of the company had not made an issue of it. But that evening "Medina (Captain Ernest Medina) came up to me ("Bernie") and told me not to do anything stupid like write my congressman" about what had happened that day. Bernhardt assured Captain Medina that he had no such thing in mind. He had nine months left in Viet Nam and felt that it was dangerous enough just fighting the acknowledged enemy.

Exactly what did, in fact, occur in the village of "Pinkville" in March, 1968 I do not know for *certain*, but I am convinced that it was something very black indeed. I remain irrevocably persuaded that if you and I do truly believe in the principles of justice and the equality of every man, however humble, before the law, that form the very backbone that this country is founded on, then we must press forward a widespread and public investigation of this matter with all our combined efforts. I think that it was Winston Churchill who once said "A country without a conscience is a country without a soul, and a country without a soul is a country that cannot survive." I feel that I must take some positive action on this matter. I hope that you will launch an investigation immediately and keep me informed of your progress. If you cannot, then I don't know what other course of action to take.

I have considered sending this to newspapers, magazines, and broadcasting companies, but I somehow feel that investigation and action by the Congress of the United States is the appropriate procedure, and as a conscientious citizen I have no desire to further besmirch the image of the American serviceman in the eyes of the world. I feel that this action, while probably it would promote attention, would not bring about the constructive actions that the direct actions of the Congress of the United States could.

Sincerely,
/s/ Ron Ridenhour

*   *   *

On the Basis of the Foregoing, the Findings of the Inquiry Are as Follows:

A. Concerning events surrounding the Son My operation of 16–19 March 1968

1. During the period 16–19 March 1968, US Army troops of TF Barker, 11th Brigade, Americal Division, massacred a large number of noncombatants in two hamlets of Son My Village, Quang Ngai Province, Republic of Vietnam. The precise number of Vietnamese killed cannot be determined but was at least 175 and may exceed 400.

2. The massacre occurred in conjunction with a combat operation which was intended to neutralize Son My Village as a logistical support base and staging area, and to destroy elements of an enemy battalion thought to be located in the Son My area.

3. The massacre resulted primarily from the nature of the orders issued by persons in the chain of command within TF Barker.

4. The task force commander's order and the associated intelligence estimate issued prior to the operation were embellished as they were disseminated through each lower level of command, and ultimately presented to the individual soldier a false and misleading picture of the Son My area as an armed enemy camp, largely devoid of civilian inhabitants.

5. Prior to the incident, there had developed within certain elements of the 11th Brigade a permissive attitude toward the treatment and safeguarding of noncombatants which contributed to the mistreatment of such persons during the Son My operation.

6. The permissive attitude in the treatment of Vietnamese was, on

16–19 March 1968, exemplified by an almost total disregard for the lives and property of the civilian population of Son My Village on the part of commanders and key staff officers of TF Barker.

7. On 16 March, soldiers at the squad and platoon level, within some elements of TF Barker, murdered noncombatants while under the supervision and control of their immediate superiors.

8. A part of the crimes visited on the inhabitants of Son My Village included individual and group acts of murder, rape, sodomy, maiming, and assault on noncombatants and the mistreatment and killing of detainees. They further included the killing of livestock, destruction of crops, closing of wells, and the burning of dwellings within several sub-hamlets.

9. Some attempts were made to stop the criminal acts in Son My Village on 16 March; but with few exceptions, such efforts were too feeble or too late.

10. Intensive interrogation has developed no evidence that any members of the units engaged in the Son My operation was under the influence of marijuana or other narcotics.

B. Concerning the adequacy of reports, investigations and reviews

11. The commanders of TF Barker and the 11th Brigade had substantial knowledge as to the extent of the killing of noncombatants but only a portion of their information was ever reported to the Commanding General of the Americal Division.

12. Based on his observations, WO1 Thompson made a specific complaint through his command channels that serious war crimes had been committed but through a series of inadequate responses at each level of command, action on his complaint was delayed and the severity of his charges considerably diluted by the time it reached the Division Commander.

13. Sufficient information concerning the highly irregular nature of the operations of TF Barker on 16 March 1968 reached the Commanding General of the Americal Division to require that a thorough investigation be conducted.

14. An investigation by the Commander of the 11th Brigade conducted at the direction of the Commanding General of the Americal Division, was little more than a pretense and was subsequently misrepresented as a thorough investigation to the CG, Americal Division in order to conceal from him the true enormity of the atrocities.

15. Patently inadequate reports of investigation submitted by the Commander of the 11th Brigade were accepted at face value and without an effective review by the CG, Americal Division.

16. Reports of alleged war crimes, noncombatant casualties, and serious incidents concerning the Son My operation of 16 March were received at the headquarters of the American Division but were not reported to higher headquarters despite the existence of directives requiring such action.

17. Reports of alleged war crimes relating to the Son My operation of 16 March reached Vietnamese government officials, but those officials did not take effective action to ascertain the true facts.

18. Efforts of the ARVN/GVN officials discreetly to inform the US commanders of the magnitude of the war crimes committed on 16 March 1968 met with no affirmative response.

C. Concerning attempts to suppress information

19. At every command level within the American Division, actions were taken, both wittingly and unwittingly, which effectively suppressed information concerning the war crimes committed at Son My Village.

20. At the company level there was a failure to report the war crimes which had been committed. This, combined with instructions to members of one unit not to discuss the events of 16 March, contributed significantly to the suppression of information.

21. The task force commander and at least one, and probably more, staff officers of TF Barker may have conspired to suppress information and to mislead higher headquarters concerning the events of 16–19 March 1968.

22. At the 11th Brigade level, the commander and at least one principal staff officer may have conspired to suppress information to deceive the division commander concerning the true facts of the Son My operation of 16–19 March.

23. A reporter and a photographer from the 11th Brigade observed many war crimes committed by C/1–20 Inf on 16 March. Both failed to report what they had seen; the reporter submitted a misleading account of the operation; and the photographer withheld and suppressed (and wrongfully misappropriated upon his discharge from the service) photographic evidence of such war crimes.

24. Efforts within the 11th Brigade to suppress information concerning the Son My operation were aided in varying degrees by members of US Advisory teams working with ARVN and GVN officials.

25. Within the American Division headquarters, actions taken to suppress information concerning what was purportedly believed to be the inadvertent killing of 20 to 28 noncombatants effectively served to conceal the true nature and scope of the events which had taken place in Son My Village on 16–19 March 1968.

26. Failure of the Americal Division headquarters to act on reports and information received from GVN/ARVN officials in mid-April served effectively to suppress the true nature and scope of the events which had taken place in Son My Village on 16–19 March 1968.

27. Despite an exhaustive search of the files of the 11th Brigade, Americal Division, GVN/ARVN advisory team files, and records holding centers, with few exceptions, none of the documents relating to the so-called investigation of the events of 16–19 March were located.

D. With respect to individuals

1. During the period March–June 1968 a number of persons assigned to the Americal Division and to US Advisory elements located in Quang Ngai Province had information as to the killing of noncombatants and other serious offenses committed by members of TF Barker during the Son My operation in March 1968 and did one or more of the following:

- a. Failed to make such official report thereof as their duty required them to make;
- b. Suppressed information concerning the occurrence of such offenses acting singly or in concert with others;
- c. Failed to order a thorough investigation and to insure that such was made, or failed to conduct an adequate investigation, or failed to submit an adequate report of investigation, or failed to make an adequate review of a report of investigation, as applicable;

or committed other derelictions related to the events of the Son My operation, some constituting criminal offenses.

65

Why My Lai?

The army's Lieutenant General William R. Peers headed the Peers Commission report just cited.

In drafting the initial outline for the final report I included a chapter entitled "Why My Lai?" When the writers got down to working on it, however, they encountered innumerable difficulties and were in favor of deleting it. But I felt strongly that if we were going to include the details of the operation we should provide some explanation of why it had developed into a massacre. . . .

We started making a list of the things that might have influenced the various soldiers, and after considerable give-and-take finally narrowed it down to what we felt were the principal causes. We decided to include these in the report not only to highlight the deficiencies in the My Lai operation but also to indicate some of the differences between this operation and those of other units in South Vietnam. Also, we wanted to point out problems of command and control that existed within the American Division, problems that would require vigorous corrective action by the Army in order to prevent repetition of such an incident in the future.

Lack of Proper Training

Neither units nor individual members of Task Force Barker and the 11th Brigade received the proper training in the Law of War (Hague and Geneva conventions), the safeguarding of noncombatants, or the Rules of Engagement. This was due to many factors—the decision to ship the brigade to South Vietnam earlier than had been planned, the large turnover of personnel shortly before the overseas movement, the shortened orientation period in South Vietnam, and the continuing arrival of new troops. While some men felt they had received adequate training, others could not remember having had any training at all in these matters. Undoubtedly part of the problem was rooted in the lackadaisical manner in which this training was handled. Several of the men testified that they were given MACV's "Nine Rules" and other pocket cards, but since there had been no accompanying instructions they had put the

Source: Lt. Gen. W. R. Peers, USA (Ret.), *The My Lai Inquiry* (New York: W. W. Norton and Company, 1979), 229–31. Reprinted by permission.

cards in their pockets unread and never had any idea of their contents. This, combined with the failure to disseminate division, brigade, and task force policies down to the individual soldier, created a significant void in many of the soldiers' minds as to what was expected of them.

Even accepting these training deficiencies as an important factor in the My Lai operation, however, the members of the Inquiry felt there were some things a soldier did not have to be told were wrong—such as rounding up women and children and then mowing them down, shooting babies out of mothers' arms, and raping.

Attitude Toward Vietnamese

The most disturbing factor we encountered was the low regard in which some of the men held the Vietnamese, especially rural or farming people. This attitude appeared to have been particularly strong in Charlie Company, some of whose men viewed the Vietnamese with contempt, considering them subhuman, on the level of dogs. Personally, I had great respect for the Vietnamese rice farmer or peasant; men and women alike worked in the fields from morning until night in all kinds of weather, often at the mercy of piastre-pinching landlords, and had little to show for it but callouses, wrinkles, and bent backs.

Some of the men never referred to Vietnamese as anything but "gooks," "dinks," or "slopes." During my time in Vietnam, I had never heard these terms used so universally, and I think I lived fairly close to the troops. To be sure, one heard them from time to time, as we did in Burma and China in World War II, but they were not used in hatred.

Undoubtedly, this attitude was partly the result of the mines and booby traps that had killed or maimed so many men in their units. Many of the men thought these devices had been laid by the women, children, and old men or that if Vietnamese civilians had not actually planted them they at least knew where the devices were, but never warned the American troops. Others thought some of the innocent-appearing youngsters tending the water buffalo in the fields served as scouts who warned of approaching U.S. forces.

Also, as in all units of any size in any army, there was a sprinkling of toughs—in Task Force Barker they were almost gangsters. In the absence of effective leadership by junior officers and NCOs some of the lower-ranking enlisted men probably followed along with these hoodlums.

Attempting to follow this line of analysis, we thought that perhaps the units had included an unusual number of men of inferior quality. When we thought only Charlie Company had been involved in the incident, we had requested the deputy chief of staff for personnel to make an analysis of the men in that company. The result was a fact sheet that in the main concluded that the men in Charlie Company were about average as compared with other units of the Army; 70 per cent were high school graduates and nineteen had some college credits. Later, we asked for a comparable analysis for Bravo Company, and its conclusions were about the same as those for Charlie Company. It seems to follow that if these men were average American soldiers, and if other units with the same kind of men did not commit atrocities of this order, there must have been other overriding causes.

It would not be true to say that all the men in Task Force Barker held the Vietnamese in low regard. Quite a few of them, even in Charlie Company, liked the Vietnamese people. They picked up some of the language, used their own money to buy gifts for children, and gave donations to orphanages, schools, and churches. But on the whole, we concluded that the attitude of at least some of the men contributed to the atrocities that occurred at My Lai-4 and My Khe-4.

66

"Sooner or Later . . . the Shock . . . Wore Off"

During the American phase of the war in Indochina, Truong Nhu Tang was a member of the group that considered itself the provisional government of Vietnam, an insurgent body hiding out in the Vietnamese jungle. Here he comments briefly on the difference between the attitude of North Vietnamese troops and that of South Vietnamese guerrillas toward heavy-handed Communist ideological indoctrination. He also describes at length the experience of being subjected to American bombing.

Among the Northern troops the curriculum differed considerably. Having grown to manhood in the austere Marxist climate of the DRV, they were used to taking their ideology straight, and their political cadres and instructors kept up a steady infusion of Marxist precepts and class

Source: Truong Nhu Tang with David Chanoff and Doan Van Toai, *A Vietcong Memoir* (New York: Harcourt Brace Jovanovich, 1985), 164, 166–68, 170–71. Reprinted by permission.

analysis. Had we attempted similar indoctrination of the Southern peasant guerrillas, they would have considered it worse torture than the regime could possibly devise for them. . . .

But for all the privations and hardships, nothing the guerrillas had to endure compared with the stark terrorization of the B-52 bombardments. During its involvement, the United States dropped on Vietnam more than three times the tonnage of explosives that were dropped during all of World War II in military theaters that spanned the world. Much of it came from the high altitude B-52s, bombs of all sizes and types being disgorged by these invisible predators. The statistics convey some sense of the concentrated firepower that was unleashed at America's enemies in both North and South. From the perspective of those enemies, these figures translated into an experience of undiluted psychological terror, into which we were plunged, day in, day out for years on end.

From a kilometer away, the sonic roar of the B-52 explosions tore eardrums, leaving many of the jungle dwellers permanently deaf. From a kilometer, the shock waves knocked their victims senseless. Any hit within a half kilometer would collapse the walls of an unreinforced bunker, burying alive the people cowering inside. Seen up close, the bomb craters were gigantic—thirty feet across and nearly as deep. In the rainy seasons they would fill up with water and often saw service as duck or fishponds, playing their role in the guerrillas' never-ending quest to broaden their diet. But they were treacherous then too. For as the swamps and lowland areas flooded under half a foot of standing water, the craters would become invisible. Not infrequently some surprised guerrilla, wading along what he had taken to be a familiar route, was suddenly swallowed up. . . .

Often the warnings would give us time to grab some rice and escape by foot or bike down one of the emergency routes. Hours later we would return to find, as happened on several occasions, that there was nothing left. It was as if an enormous scythe had swept through the jungle, felling the giant teak and go trees like grass in its way, shredding them into billions of scattered splinters. On these occasions—when the B-52s had found their mark—the complex would be utterly destroyed: food, clothes, supplies, documents, everything. It was not just that things were destroyed; in some awesome way they had ceased to exist. You would come back to where your lean-to and bunker had been, your home, and there would simply be nothing there, just an unrecognizable landscape gouged by immense craters.

Equally often, however, we were not so fortunate and had time only to take cover as best we could. The first few times I experienced a B-52 attack it seemed, as I strained to press myself into the bunker floor, that I had been caught in the Apocalypse. The terror was complete. One lost control of bodily functions as the mind screamed incomprehensible orders to get out. On one occasion a Soviet delegation was visiting our ministry when a particularly short-notice warning came through. When it was over, no one had been hurt, but the entire delegation had sustained considerable damage to its dignity—uncontrollable trembling and wet pants the all-too-obvious outward signs of inner convulsions. The visitors could have spared themselves their feelings of embarrassment; each of their hosts was a veteran of the same symptoms.

It was a tribute to the Soviet surveillance techniques that we were caught aboveground so infrequently during the years of the deluge. One of these occasions, though, almost put an end to all our endeavors. Taken by surprise by the sudden earthshaking shocks, I began running along a trench toward my bunker opening when a huge concussion lifted me off the ground and propelled me through the doorway toward which I was heading. Some of my Alliance colleagues were knocked off their feet and rolled around the ground like rag dolls. One old friend, Truong Cao Phuoc, who was working in the foreign relations division, had jumped into a shelter that collapsed on him, somehow leaving him alive with his head protruding from the ground. We extricated him, shoveling the dirt out handful by handful, carefully removing the supporting timbers that were crisscrossed in the earth around him. Truong had been trapped in one of the old U-shaped shelters, which became graves for so many. Later we learned to reinforce these dugouts with an A-frame of timbers that kept the walls from falling in. Reinforced in this manner, they could withstand B-52 bomb blasts as close as a hundred meters.

Sooner or later, though, the shock of the bombardments wore off, giving way to a sense of abject fatalism. The veterans would no longer scrabble at the bunker floors convulsed with fear. Instead people just resigned themselves—fully prepared to "go and sit in the ancestors' corner." The B-52s somehow put life in order. Many of those who survived the attacks found that afterward they were capable of viewing life from a more serene and philosophical perspective. It was a lesson that remained with me, as it did with many others, and helped me compose myself for death on more than one future occasion.

But even the most philosophical of fatalists were worn to the breaking point after several years of dodging and burrowing away from the rain of high explosives. During the most intense periods we came under attack every day for weeks running. At these times we would cook our rice as soon as we got out of our hammocks, kneading it into glutinous balls and ducking into the bunkers to be ready for what we knew was coming. Occasionally, we would be on the move for days at a time, stopping only to prepare food, eating as we walked. At night we would sling our hammocks between two trees wherever we found ourselves, collapsing into an exhausted but restless sleep, still half-awake to the inevitable explosions.

67

Pacification

Though this document, put out by the United States Depart-
ment of State in July 1969, emphasizes that the forms of pacifi-
cation it describes are essentially a Vietnamese effort, the meth-
ods had the strong urging of Americans. The combination of
military and social programs was of much the same mentality
as that which in the Kennedy administration had produced the
military Special Forces along with the social-reformist Peace
Corps. An added feature is the Phoenix Program. The docu-
ment describes it as an intelligence-gathering operation. But it
gained a reputation for killing individuals its operatives de-
fined as dangerous.

"The countryside, and the countryside alone, can provide the broad areas in which the revolutionaries can maneuver freely."

Communist Chinese Defense
Minister Lin Piao

More than half of the population of South Viet-Nam lives in the countryside. It is here that Viet Cong insurgency has taken root. It is here that shadow governments seek to rule over thousands of hamlets, inflicting terror on approximately 3 million peasant inhabitants.

To combat this threat in the countryside and at the same time defeat the enemy in the field, the Government of the Republic of Viet-Nam (GVN) has combined military operations and civil nation-building programs into a unified and coordinated process called "pacification." The aim:

Source: "Pacification in Viet-Nam," *Vietnam Information Notes,* No. 14, Department of State Publication 8473, East Asian and Pacific Series 181, July 1969, 1–4.

— to liberate the people from Communist control;

— to assist them in choosing their own government;

— to help them carry out various projects that will give them a better and more prosperous life.

Throughout the countryside of South Viet-Nam the daily results of pacification are reflected in a wide variety of activities. These may include such diverse incidents as:

— the arrest by the police of a 24-year-old knife grinder accused of being a tax collector for the Viet Cong;

— the opening of a health station featuring prenatal care;

— the issuance of a rifle to a young lad, no more than 16, who has volunteered to join the local militia;

— the installation by a U.S. civilian engineer of a generator which will bring electricity to a hamlet for the first time;

— a 20-year-old farmer who had defected from the Viet Cong ranks being welcomed home by his family;

— the nailing to a tree of a poster announcing forthcoming elections.

Hamlets where incidents such as these take place would be in the "relatively secure" category. How they got that way reflects the blending of military and civil operations to achieve the first essential of pacification—security.

Hamlet Protection

Without continuous local security to keep the Viet Cong (VC) away from the farmer, the rest of pacification cannot get underway. The farmer's first desire is for protection so that he can be left alone to tend to his crops in peace. Protection starts when the Army of Viet-Nam (ARVN) and its allies have eliminated from the area any existing VC or North Viet-Nam (NVA) enemy main force units. Thereafter, the main responsibility for insuring hamlet security rests with the Popular Forces (PF), the People's Self Defense Forces (PSDF), the Regional Forces (RF), and the National Police (NP).

Creating a secure environment is essentially a matter of people participating in their own defense. The hamlets of Viet-Nam illustrate the point dramatically. Here members of the Popular Forces, all of them volunteers, all with only a meager education, have been taught how to handle light weapons and perform modest military activity. They guard check points, warehouses, government installations, and key provincial buildings. They rarely go far from their own hamlet. They serve mostly at night when enemy activities are more intense, and are ready to engage guerrilla units if necessary.

The People's Self Defense Forces are a mixture of young and old, including women. They number 1.2 million, with about 200,000 armed and only moderately trained. The PSDF are utilized to gather intelligence and to report information to their superiors. More often they serve as a warning alert system. But the importance of the PSDF is perhaps less military than political. In a country where involvement of the people in their own behalf is only now beginning to assert itself, the role of the PSDF may be regarded as an expression of political awareness and responsibility. The fact that the Government of Viet-Nam plans this year to enlarge the PSDF to 2 million may be taken as evidence of growing rural support of the central government.

As distinct from the PF and PSDF, the Regional Force is a better educated, more mobile body whose responsibility for security and protection extends beyond hamlet limits. Also better trained and armed, and more highly organized, the RF continually seeks out and engages the Viet Cong in battle until relieved by superior ARVN or allied military forces. The RF is also called upon to support local actions of the popular

U.S. Marines often entered South Vietnamese hamlets to search for suspected Vietcong sympathizers and destroy the bunkers where they hid, a process that could inflict heavy damage on the village and sometimes led to civilian deaths. One soldier noted that such behavior hardly won over the local peasantry: "Their homes had been wrecked, their chickens killed, their rice confiscated—and if they weren't pro-Vietcong before we got there, they sure as hell were by the time we left."

forces and people's defense units, to serve as a shield for their operations.

The role of these hamlet defense units may be likened to a combined home guard/national guard militia, having the responsibility of dealing with external threats from VC local forces and guerrilla units.

Still, the threat from within is often more dangerous than the threat from without. To the National Police falls the responsibility not only of maintaining public order but of enforcing internal security—dealing with the threat from within. That means rooting out the Viet Cong infrastructure (VCI)—the Communists' shadow government. Together with all civil and military intelligence services, the NP is joined in a campaign to identify and eliminate the hardcore cadres who make up the VCI in the hamlets. The operation is known as *Phoenix*.

Operation Phoenix

VCI members are not soldiers. They are the leadership elements who run the Communist political apparatus, control the guerrilla bands, collect taxes, order assassinations, set up front organizations, draft young men and women as soldiers or laborers, disseminate propaganda, and direct terror campaigns.

American soldiers advancing through fields in hunt of the enemy.

Nobody knows yet exactly how many VCI are running this shadow government behind the bamboo hedges. But in December 1967, when *Operation Phoenix* was launched, it was estimated by intelligence sources that about 80,000 were in VCI jobs. In its first year, despite the Communist offensives in February and May 1968, *Phoenix* resulted in nearly 16,000 of these cadres being rooted out of their underground positions.

Operation Phoenix is not an organization but a program—a systematized method of intelligence-sharing among the already existing services, mainly the National Police elements assigned to the countryside and the numerous Vietnamese military intelligence services. It is a Vietnamese government program to cripple and eventually eliminate the VC political control structure by getting various intelligence and information services to work together. The VCI is tracked down by the pooling of information, shared on a regular basis, by all the intelligence services, civil and military.

The rural policeman on his remote hamlet beat, or the ARVN medic bandaging a villager's blisters, may feed valuable information into the *Phoenix* intelligence network. As much of [these] data originally must come from the people, *Phoenix* is coordinated with campaigns to encourage the people to identify the VCI who are disrupting their lives. . . .

Revolutionary Development

To liberate the countryside from Communist control, to destroy the VCI, and to maintain constant vigil against VC infiltration—these efforts by themselves are not enough. Hand in hand must go vigorous and sustained action to involve the people in creating their own local government and, beyond that, generating economic and social development programs. The name given to this activity is Revolutionary Development (RD).

Although essentially and predominantly a Vietnamese program, the RD effort is supported by United States and other free world assistance missions. Under the overall coordination of the Military Assistance Command in Vietnam (MACV), American aid and technical advice is funneled through U.S. Civil Operations and Revolutionary Development Support (CORDS)—an inter-agency management group which combines the efforts of the Agency for International Development (AID), the U.S. Information Agency (USIA), several U.S. Embassy offices, and the non-combat provincial advisory teams of the U.S. Armed Forces.

Carrying out the goals of the Revolutionary Development program are the RD Cadre—some 55,000 villagers, trained and organized in

30-man teams, and operating under the command of the Ministry of Revolutionary Development (MORD) in Saigon.

Soon after their recruitment, the RD Cadre teams are put through a 13-week course at a training center which specializes in political and psychological warfare techniques, local government administration, civic affairs, organization for self-defense, and development of self-help programs.

Most of the trainees are young men, although there is a scattering of female Cadre members. Clad in the simple black pajama that has become their familiar "uniform," the Cadre workers are assigned to a single village—usually their own—for an indefinite period.

Within each Cadre team there are Militia, Civic Affairs, and Development sections. RD workers are "cross-trained" to carry out duties in all these fields even though they are usually assigned to a specific section. At work in the village or hamlet, the Militia section develops a self-defense group of local people and takes police action against the VCI. The Civic Affairs section conducts a census, organizes citizen groups, and improves local government. The remaining section assists village officials in the implementation of development programs.

Since the establishment in 1966 of the RD concept, its subsequent programs have emphasized different directions. For example, the 1967 program stressed the political role of the RD effort—to build "bridges of understanding" between the population and the government. At that time it was felt the people needed a better sense of the GVN's concern for them. In 1968, the emphasis was on territorial and internal security—in recognition of the basic fact that no program in the rural areas of Vietnam could succeed without adequately coping with the ever present VC and NVA military threat. The 1969 program in effect combines both concepts—expansion of the GVN presence while pointing up the need for security and an understanding between the people and their government.

The point needs to be underscored that RD, like the war itself, is basically a Vietnamese effort. Nothing illustrates the principle more clearly than what the RD program is trying to accomplish in the area of self-help projects. The real objective is not merely to build schools, health stations, and market places in the hamlets and villages but to mobilize the rural population in a community effort under the security provided by the GVN and with the help of GVN-provided resources.

Projects implemented on a self-help basis by the villagers' own labor gives them a direct interest in the preservation of what they have built and the political system which permitted them to do so.

AID provides advisory and material assistance to the self-help projects in such fields as education, health, public works, and agriculture. Material assistance is mainly in the form of basic construction items—roofing and iron reinforcement bars.

Village Government Development

The village for centuries has been the basic social and political unit of Vietnamese society. It is that today. But never before has village government assumed such expanding authority and taken such long steps toward full representative democracy.

New and young leadership has emerged from hamlet and village elections held over the last two years. Self-governing communities are today exercising unprecedented responsibilities—administering local security forces, collecting their own taxes, preparing and adopting their own budgets, overseeing the activities of the 30-man RD teams, and generally taking measures to meet their own local needs.

Since the adoption of the Constitution in April 1967, elections have been held in 1,693 villages and in 7,867 hamlets. Before 1969 ends, elections are expected to be held in 130 more villages and another 889 hamlets. . . .

GI waiting for medical help for wounded buddy with Vietamese fleeing in background.

68

Fighting at Khe Sanh

Khe Sanh is remembered for the firepower that the Americans poured onto the attackers, at terrible loss of life to the Communists. But the firepower had meaning only in concert with troops on the ground. The materials here describe some of the ground fighting.

Hill 861-A was a fresh position. No Marines had ever occupied it before, so Echo had to start from scratch building defensive positions. Supply was also a problem, particularly water. [Larry E.] Jackson recalls:

> We started cutting bamboo trees around the surrounding area to drain the small amount of water from each section. We gathered probably eight or ten canteens of water which contained leech larvae that we had to strain off. We boiled the water and split it between the company. A couple of days later we received a load of water from a chopper which had to virtually drop it from about twenty feet in the air. We only salvaged five containers . . . [then] we were told by radio communication that they didn't know when we would receive water again. The five containers were kept in the CP area. We were [given] a half canteen cup of water a day for about five days. With this ½ cup of water you had to drink it, shave with it, and also brush your teeth with it.

Other features of life on 861-A were constant fog, damp mornings and evenings, and low morale, because the North Vietnamese seemed to be shooting often at the combat base but never bothering with the hill.

The Marines began stringing barbed wire around their perimeter. By February 4 they had four or five strands completed. It made Larry Jackson, for one, feel more secure, though he had sweated over the wire all day. A hot day degenerated into really dense fog in which Marines literally could not see past their wire barriers. The men were on three-hour watches. One man in each foxhole would be asleep, one awake. The attack came that night; it was the moment, Jackson recalls, "when my bad dreams started."

Source: John Prados and Ray W. Stubbe, *Valley of Decision: The Siege of Khe Sanh* (Boston: Houghton Mifflin Company, 1991), 305–09. Reprinted by permission.

The sole indication of anything untoward was a pungent smell that the Marines atop 861-A detected from about midnight on. Some likened it to marijuana, others to unwashed troops. Shortly after four o'clock on the morning of February 5 came a tremendous volley of 82mm mortar fire simultaneous with a battalion-size assault. The wire barriers were professionally blown. North Vietnamese troops quickly closed with Lieutenant Edmund R. Shanley's 1st Platoon. They seemed to know the locations of weapons pits and other support positions and fired into them. Echo Company was in trouble immediately.

Earle Breeding told debriefers later that most of his casualties occurred during the initial mortar barrage, primarily because Echo had not been in place long enough to have really good fortifications. Typical of this phase of the battle was the experience of Corporal Eugene J. Franklin, with the mortar squad of Shanley's platoon:

> All I heard was one shot go off, and I thought that was just somebody, like they thought they saw something in the wire and they just fired. And all of a sudden mortar rounds . . . dropped all around the gun pit and around my hootch. And I had one man that got trapped inside his hootch when they busted the lines. And myself, I was still inside my hootch. And I seen the flashes of light from the inside . . . 'cause I had a tunnel-way . . . leading from my hootch straight to the gun pit. And I seen different colors of light. I didn't know exactly what it was—come to find it was shrapnel flying around inside the gun pit. And as I tried to get out [of] my gun pit, I got right up in it and concussion from one of the rounds knocked me back. . . . Then I tried to get out again, that's when I see a couple of enemy troops coming up on [the] side of the hill.

Meanwhile the mortar section leader, Corporal Billy E. Drexel, braved the heavy fire to get another squad with a second 60mm mortar into the battle area. Private First Class Newton D. Lyle came with the reinforcing mortar:

> We went over there and you could actually see the Gooks running around on the lines, laughing and throwing [grenades] in bunkers, and you could hear the screams of your buddies, your friends, and we was running around out there firing mortar rounds out in front of the wires, and after a while they come and told us that all the men had been wiped out in the trenches directly in front of us and we was to fire directly into the trenches.

The mortar's targets finally were so close that the shell blasts sent shrapnel right back onto the Marine crew.

Then there was Tom Eichler, a machine gunner moving toward Shanley's platoon positions to provide more help:

> Making my way down the trench line I found three of my machine-gun crew lying severely wounded. Thinking they had been hit by a mortar shell, I took off my ammunition belt, laid down my rifle and placed one of the wounded Marines on my back. Making my way back through the trench line I suddenly came face to face with an NVA soldier. Instinctively I turned and began running down the trench. . . . The NVA soldier opened fire and I could feel the bullets striking me in the back, but they were not penetrating. The wounded Marine was absorbing the rounds in his flak jacket. I ran right into another NVA soldier who was firing a rocket down the trench line. With the wounded Marine on my back I strangled the NVA soldier with the strap from his rocket pouch. During this incident the young Marine on my back who was now close to death was whispering directions in my ear. Funny, I had started out saving his life, now he had saved mine. Then and only then did I realize that we had been overrun.

There were many harrowing moments, such as when Eichler saw bloody marks on the wall of a hole from a mortally wounded Marine trying to claw his way out. But there were humorous incidents too. Eichler recounts one that occurred with the Marines in their last defensive perimeter:

> I was in the process of throwing grenade after grenade out of the position when I thought, this is taking too long. So, in my haste to speed up the process I pulled the pin on two grenades and laid them behind the Lieutenant [Shanley] who was directing supporting fire from Hill 881. The Lieutenant turned around just as I came to my senses and had barely managed to get the grenades out of the trench line before they exploded. To this day he believes that I saved his life by throwing enemy grenades out of the position. At the time I was afraid to tell him what really happened.

Support meanwhile came to Echo Company in abundance. The mortars on 881 South were just the beginning of it. Those weapons technically lacked range for targets on 861-A, but they happened to be located at a relative altitude about twenty feet higher that provided them just enough extra range to shoot. By the end of the battle the mortars on 881 South, it is said, had just five shells left. Artillery also played a major role, with about two thousand shells fired in barrages boxing in 861-A, cutting the NVA assault battalion off from the estimated additional battalion behind it in reserve, and firing patterns designed to trap and eliminate the North Vietnamese. The long-range Army 175mm guns and Marine weapons from the combat base cooperated and coordinated their fire. Mortars and 106mm recoilless rifles from Hill 558 also contributed. Colonel Lownds put the combat base on red alert to guard against any NVA attack on Khe Sanh itself.

On top of 861-A North Vietnamese assault troops lost some of their momentum trying to loot Marine bunkers. Several Marines mentioned subsequently that NVA soldiers were caught sitting down looking at copies of *Playboy* and other magazines left behind by Marines out on the firing line. Captain Breeding also used CS gas grenades, although they did not seem to do much good—wind blew the gas back on the Marines, while the adversary seemed so excited that no effect could be observed; indeed some speculated that the North Vietnamese were drugged and thus avoided the effects of gas.

In the final contest it came down to hand-to-hand fighting, after Breeding gathered some troops and made a counterattack. Breeding recalled:

> The M-16 didn't come into play too much because of the hill we were on. There were really no fields of fire to speak of, and it turned out to be a hand grenade war. And then when Charlie got inside the wire it was just like a World War II movie with . . . knife-fighting, bayonet fighting, hitting people on the nose with your fist and all the rest of that, and Charlie didn't know how to cope with it at all. We just walked all over him once we were able to close with him.

Five Navy Crosses and many other awards were given for actions on 861-A that night. Lieutenant Don Shanley, who rallied his platoon in spite of a painful head wound, received a Bronze Star. The company lost seven Marines with another thirty-five wounded seriously enough to be evacuated.

The North Vietnamese tried a last gasp assault from the south at 6:10 A.M. on February 5 but were quickly beaten back. Behind them were left many bodies, 109 according to the official Marine monograph, as many as 150 by other counts. Larry Jackson, put on a burial detail, had to toss nineteen bodies of North Vietnamese soldiers into one hole, but Captain Breeding allowed policing of the battlefield only within the Marine positions. No one was permitted outside the perimeter, either to count bodies or to do anything else. As the sun burned off the fog that morning, it looked as if Captain Breeding had redeemed the promise he had made to Colonel Lownds that his company would successfully defend Khe Sanh.

69

What Was the Point of Khe Sanh?

When John S. Carroll of the Baltimore Sun *revealed that Khe Sanh (also spelled "Khesanh") was being abandoned, he raised an embarrassing question. How could the military casually leave a base that when it was under attack had been presented as a vital point in the defense of South Vietnam? Had American officials exaggerated for reasons of drama and propaganda the importance of Khe Sanh? For his revelation, Carroll temporarily lost his official accreditation. Here he discusses the issue.*

It was in January that public concern about Khesanh began to build. The military command knew it had problems. Some high-ranking officers had opposed holding Khesanh at all. Militarily, the base was simply not worth it, they believed. But there were problems in pulling out. One was the fact that many of the guns would have to be destroyed if the Marines fought their way out on the ground. The guns had been flown in, and the prime movers—the machines that tow the guns and carry the ammunition and crews—had been left behind.

Another problem, the decisive one, was that a withdrawal under pressure would have all the earmarks of a defeat. By the last ten days of January the world was watching Khesanh, and the first grim parallels with Dienbienphu had been drawn. So to withdraw at this time would be to take a terrific drubbing before a huge audience.

What was needed, then, was a good, solid, military sound explanation of why we were holding Khesanh. The American public could be counted upon to take a dim view of it all if the military were to announce frankly: "Your sons are at Khesanh to win a psychological victory, or at least to prevent a psychological defeat."

The military explanation that finally emerged was twofold. It goes as follows: Khesanh is critical to American military interests in Vietnam because it sits "astride" major infiltration routes from North Vietnam and Laos. Moreover, it is the "western anchor" of the defensive line of bases along the demilitarized zone.

Source: John S. Carroll, "Report: Khesanh," in Robert Manning and Michael Janeway, eds., *Who We Are: An Atlantic Chronicle of the United States and Vietnam* (Boston: An Atlantic Monthly Press Book, Little, Brown and Company, 1969), 313–18. Reprinted by permission.

In reality, Khesanh sat astride nothing but Khesanh. To the North Vietnamese Army, which can do without valleys or roads in making its way into the south, Khesanh was merely a speck of flotsam—an irritating speck, to be sure—in a sea of infiltration routes.

The "western anchor" concept was equally fallacious, based as it was on a simplistic Maginot scheme for keeping the North Vietnamese out of South Vietnam. One might think that if our *western anchor* were lost, the enemy would be able to turn our flank. Of course the flank was being turned every day, Khesanh or no, by means of the Ho Chi Minh Trail in the mountains of nearby Laos.

It has been put forth in defense of the decision to hold Khesanh that, as it turned out, the cost was not inordinately high, as battles go: fewer than a hundred Marines killed on the base, with roughly another hundred deaths in the surrounding hills, and 1600 Marines wounded, in addition to South Vietnamese and Special Forces casualties. The cost of a withdrawal under fire might have been as great. But to figure the real cost of Khesanh, one must take into account the forces held in reserve, ready to move into the base. Add to this the cost of mounting the most intensive aerial bombardment in the history of warfare (commanders in some parts of the country practically wrote off their chances of getting any air support during the Khesanh bombing). The logistic effort, too, was costly in terms of man-hours, casualties, and aircraft lost.

While all these resources were being poured into a remote outpost in the farthest corner of South Vietnam, the enemy turned up at the gate of the Presidential Palace, in the front yard of the United States Embassy, and in Vietnam's old imperial throne room in Hué. . . .

The withdrawal from Hué signaled the end of the Tet offensive, but there was still Khesanh. By this time it was evident that the bombing was taking a high toll. This massive bombardment is where we won our victory, according to those who consider Khesanh a victory. Our success was in terms of enemy forces tied down and enemy soldiers killed. General Westmoreland stated later: "With only one percent of my forces, I tied down two enemy divisions and seriously defeated them. It was a major victory."

Certainly we were successful in keeping the North Vietnamese from massing and overrunning the base as, it appears, was their intention. But tied down? This claim ignores the obvious fact that only one party to the Khesanh battle retained his options: General Vo Nguyen Giap, the North Vietnamese commander. His forces could leave any time they felt their losses were outweighing their gains. We, on the other hand, were committed for the duration.

In terms of enemy forces destroyed, no doubt terrible losses were inflicted on the North Vietnamese at Khesanh. By American standards, such losses would simply be unacceptable; the North Vietnamese are far more willing to sacrifice men, and there has been no strong sign that they are having trouble replacing the thousands who fall in battle.

Giap's withdrawal finally came late in March, when the monsoon clouds were growing thin and the Army's First Air Cavalry was about to mount Operation Pegasus to relieve the base. Reporters on the scene started picking up signs of the withdrawal a week or two before Pegasus started, as did one or two Pentagon reporters with sources outside the official briefing circle. The briefers, for their part, denied any knowledge of the enemy's withdrawal. For this reason some members of the Saigon press corps strongly suspected the image-conscious command of attempting to conceal the withdrawal so that it would appear that Operation Pegasus rather than any decision by Giap had cleared the Khesanh area of North Vietnamese forces.

To those expecting a big battle, Pegasus was an anticlimax. The Air Cavalry sliced through to Khesanh like a knife through butter. At the end of the operation, George Wilson, the Washington *Post*'s military writer, and I wandered through the rolling country near the base, inspecting the battered North Vietnamese bunkers and the shallow trenches that snaked their way toward Khesanh's perimeter.

The force of the bombing defied comprehension: where the 2000-pounders had hit soft dirt the craters were big enough to contain a small house. The ground was littered with torn North Vietnamese and shattered supplies. On one hillside we found what we believed to be the remains of the last Marine patrol to go any distance outside the perimeter wire. Marines are fond of writing slogans on their helmets, and on one scorched and battered helmet was an ironic touch of Marine bravado: "To really live you must nearly die." . . .

Portions of the base that had been crowded with sandbagged bunkers and antennae were now broad fields of raw, red earth. Marines were tearing down bunkers, and bulldozers were filling the remaining holes with rubble and dirt. Big tandem-rotor helicopters were shuttling in and out, carrying slings full of cargo east to Landing Zone Stud and returning empty. The unloading tarmac of the metal runway was being peeled up and stacked in strips, ready to be hauled out.

In talking to the Marines on the ground, I learned that the North Vietnamese Army had seen everything I had. Patrols had encountered enemy troops on the hills overlooking the base, and there had been sniper fire within only a few hundred yards of the perimeter. It was clear that the news of the withdrawal was being held up for political, not military, reasons. The North Vietnamese Army knew about the withdrawal; the American public did not.

Writing the story would mean trouble from the command, for stories about troop movements and future plans are embargoed until released by the Saigon headquarters. For the command, releasing the story at this time would have meant headache after headache. Correspondents would flock to the base to file eyewitness accounts of the last days of Khesanh. Instead of disposing of the issue in a single day after the completion of the move, the command would have to answer questions every day for nearly two weeks. Television watchers and newspaper readers would want answers. What would happen when our forces no longer sat *astride* those infiltration routes? What would become of the defensive line of bases along the demilitarized zone if the *western anchor* was hauled in? Above all, why was Khesanh worth all that effort a few months ago and not now?

As things worked out, the command ultimately faced the questions with its lame answers, and I lost my press card. At first the suspension was indefinite, then it was set at six months. At that point the whole issue was hashed over publicly, and after some protests, the command agreed to reduce the suspension to sixty days, leaving neither of us entirely satisfied. My own hassle was one of the less significant unresolved questions about the military's role in political and propaganda aspects of the war which remain as the Khesanh episode passes into history, and the trenches and crumbled bunkers become overgrown with the lush foliage of Southeast Asia.

70

Bloods

These excerpts from an oral history of the war reflect on the particular problems black Americans experienced in Vietnam. But they and the rest of Wallace Terry's Bloods *also constitute a valuable account of the gritty business of fighting itself in the peculiar conditions presented by Vietnam. The first materials are from the reminiscences of Archie "Joe" Biggers, a marine first lieutenant, the second from the recollections of army captain Norman Alexander McDaniel, who had been a prisoner of war.*

Source: Wallace Terry, ed., *Bloods: An Oral History of the Vietnam War by Black Veterans* (New York: Random House, 1984), 113–16, 119–22, 141–43. Reprinted by permission.

. . . The enemy would do anything to win. You had to respect that. They believed in a cause. They had the support of the people. That's the key that we Americans don't understand yet. We can't do anything in the military ourselves unless we have the support of the people.

Sometimes we would find the enemy tied to trees. They knew they were going to die. I remember one guy tied up with rope and bamboo. We didn't even see him until he shouted at us and started firing. I don't know whether we killed him or some artillery got him.

One time they had a squad of sappers that hit us. It was like suicide. They ran at us so high on marijuana they didn't know what they were doing. You could smell the marijuana on their clothes. Some of the stuff they did was so crazy that they had to be high on something. In the first place, you don't run through concertina wire like that. Nobody in his right mind does. You get too many cuts. Any time you got a cut over there, it was going to turn to gangrene if it didn't get treated. And they knew we had the place covered.

Another time this guy tried to get our attention. I figured he wanted to give up, because otherwise, I figured he undoubtedly wanted to die. We thought he had started to *chu hoi*. And we prepared for him to come in. But before he threw his weapon down, he started firing and we had to shoot him.

And, you know, they would walk through our minefields, blow up, and never even bat their heads. Weird shit.

But I really thought they stunk.

Like the time we were heli-lifted from Vandergrift and had to come down in Dong Ha. There was this kid, maybe two or three years old. He hadn't learned to walk too well yet, but he was running down the street. And a Marine walked over to talk to the kid, touched him, and they both blew up. They didn't move. It was not as if they stepped on something. The kid had to have the explosive around him. It was a known tactic that they wrapped stuff around kids. That Marine was part of the security force around Dong Ha, a lance corporal. He was trying to be friendly. . . .

I learned a lot about people in my platoon. I learned you have to take a person for what he feels, then try to mold the individual into the person you would like to be with. Now my platoon had a lot of Southerners, as well as some Midwesterners. Southerners at the first sign of a black officer being in charge of them were somewhat reluctant. But then, when they found that you know what's going on and you're trying to keep them alive, then they tried to be the best damn soldiers you've got. Some of the black soldiers were the worse I had because they felt that they had to jive on me. They wanted to let me know, Hey, man. Take care of me, buddy. You know I'm your buddy. That's bull.

As long as a black troop knows he's going to take a few knocks like everybody else, he can go as far as anybody in the Corps. Our biggest problem as a race is a tendency to say that the only reason something didn't go the way it was programmed to go is because we are black. It may be that you tipped on somebody's toes. We as blacks have gotten to the place now where we want to depend on somebody else doing something for us. And when we don't measure up to what the expectations are—the first thing we want to holler is racial discrimination. My philosophy is, if you can't do the job—move. . . .

It never got better. It seemed like everyday somebody got hurt. Sometimes I would walk point. Everybody was carrying the wounded. We had 15 wounded in my platoon alone. And the water was gone.

Then on the twelfth day, while we were following this trail through the jungle, the point man came running back. He was all heated up. He said, "I think we got a tank up there." I told him, "I don't have time for no games." The enemy had no tanks in the South.

Then the trail started converging into a really well-camouflaged road, about 12 feet wide and better made than anything I had ever seen in Vietnam. Then I saw the muzzle of this gun. It was as big as anything we had. And all hell broke open. It was like the sun was screaming.

I thought, my God, if I stay here, I'm going to get us all wiped out.

In front of us was a reinforced platoon and two artillery pieces all dug into about 30 real serious bunkers. And we were in trouble in the rear, because a squad of snipers had slipped in between us and the rest of Charlie Company. My flanks were open. All the NVA needed to finish us off was to set up mortars on either side.

Someone told me the snipers had just got Joe. He was my platoon sergeant.

That did it. I passed the word to call in napalm at Danger Close, 50 meters off our position. Then I turned to go after the snipers. And I heard this loud crash. I was thrown to the ground. This grenade had exploded, and the shrapnel had torn into my left arm.

The Phantoms were doing a number. It felt like an earthquake was coming. The ground was just a-rumbling. Smoke was everywhere, and then the grass caught fire. The napalm explosions had knocked two of my men down who were at the point, but the NVA were running everywhere. The flames were up around my waist. That's when I yelled, "Charge. Kill the gooks. Kill the motherfuckers."

We kept shooting until everything was empty. Then we picked up the guns they dropped and fired them. I brought three down with my .45. In a matter of minutes, the ridge was ours. We had the bunkers, an earth mover, bunches of documents, tons of food supplies. We counted 70 dead NVA. And those big guns, two of them. Russian-made. Like our 122, they had a range of 12 to 15 miles. They were the first ones captured in South Vietnam.

Well, I ordered a perimeter drawn. And since I never ask my men to do something I don't do, I joined the perimeter. Then this sniper got me. Another RPG. I got it in the back. I could barely raise myself up on one elbow. I felt like shit, but I was trying to give a command. The guys just circled around me like they were waiting for me to tell them something. I got to my knees. And it was funny. They had their guns pointed at the sky.

I yelled out, "I can walk. I can walk."

Somebody said, "No, sir. You will *not* walk."

I slumped back. And two guys got on my right side. Two guys got on my left side. One held me under the head. One more lifted my feet. Then they held me high above their shoulders, like I was a Viking or some kind of hero. They formed a perimeter around *me*. They told me feet would never touch ground there again. And they held me high up in the air until the chopper came.

I really don't know what I was put in for. I was told maybe the Navy Cross. Maybe the Medal of Honor. It came down to the Silver Star. One of those guns is at Quantico in the Marine Aviation Museum. And the other is at Fort Sill in Oklahoma. And they look just as horrible today as they did when we attacked them. . . .

But the thing that really hurt me more than anything in the world was when I came back to the States and black people considered me as a part of the establishment. Because I am an officer. Here I was, a veteran that just came back from a big conflict. And most of the blacks wouldn't associate with me. You see, blacks are not supposed to be officers. Blacks are supposed to be those guys that take orders, and not necessarily those that give them. If you give orders, it means you had to kiss somebody's rear end to get into that position.

One day I wore my uniform over to Howard University in Washington to help recruit officer candidates. Howard is a black school, like the one I went to in Texas, Jarvis Christian College. I thought I would feel at home. The guys poked fun at me, calling me Uncle Sam's flunky. They would say the Marine Corps sucks. The Army sucks. They would say their brother or uncle got killed, so why was I still in. They would see the Purple Heart and ask me what was I trying to prove. The women wouldn't talk to you either.

I felt bad. I felt cold. I felt like I was completely out of it.

*   *   *

. . . You had to keep track of time on your own. And the first couple of weeks, I just couldn't put it all together. The interrogations and beatings came in cells where you couldn't see out. You would get so beat out until you might sleep a few minutes and think you'd been asleep all night. But afterwards, you could keep the days together. Being somewhat accustomed to the Western way, Sunday was not a big workday for them. And then you knew a week had rolled around.

In the first few years they wouldn't give us any reading material, and, of course, no mail. And they never let us learn their language, because they felt that we might hear too much. I only learned the words for "yes" and "no" and the words *lai mau,* meaning "come quick," which would get the camp commander in an emergency.

They didn't want us to communicate, because we could pass information and keep each other's spirits up. Communicating was one of the quickest ways that you could get tortured.

In the few first days we knocked on walls and made signals if we saw each other. Morse code was too slow. So we put the alphabet in a five by five matrix. The first series of taps located the letter vertically, the next series horizontally. We combined J and K, or we would just use six straight taps for a K. Once in a while you would try to talk very low, but that was very hazardous.

They had a public-address system in the camp that they would pipe into the cell. They would read things in their behalf about the Communist way and downgrading the United States, blah, blah, blah, all the time. They would sanitize the broadcast they pumped to the GIs in the South. Whenever you heard something about how the war was going, my general philosophy was to turn it 180 degrees around and you might get close to the truth.

When Dr. King was assassinated, they called me in for interrogation to see if I would make a statement critical of the United States. I said no, I don't know enough about it. They wanted all of us to make statements they could send abroad or make tapes they could play to the GIs. They wanted me to tell black soldiers not to fight because the United States is waging a war of genocide, using dark-skinned people against dark-skinned people. I would tell them no. This is not a black-white war. We're in Vietnam trying to help the South Vietnamese. It is a matter of helping people who are your friends.

Once they found out they couldn't get anything out of me on the racial front, they would harass me a little harder than my white comrades. They would call me a lackey and an Uncle Tom and say, "You suck your brother's liver. You drink your brother's blood."

My personal feeling is that black people have problems and still have problems in America. But I never told them that, because I had no intention of helping them to defeat us. We deal with our problems within our own country. Some people just do not live up to the great ideals our country stands for. And some blacks don't take advantage of the privileges and opportunities we have. Although black people are kind of behind the power curtain, we have just as much claim to this country as any white man. America is the black man's best hope. . . .

71

Humanity and Stress

These selections from three contributors to another oral history of the war, two of them nurses and the other a black soldier, illustrate differing human reactions to the stresses of Vietnam. Gail Smith was a hospital nurse in Vietnam, Robert Rawls a black rifleman in the airborne cavalry, Lynda Van Devanter a nurse in an evacuation hospital.

. . . It was apparently not uncommon for Vietnam vets to come back angry, and when some became upset, their method of coping was to become violent. And they all had guns in Vietnam. They used them on each other over there. Guys came into the hospital after gunfights among themselves, especially when the town was off-limits—you know, when guys couldn't get downtown to see the girls. They would start shooting up each other. Practically every night there was somebody getting shot. One night this guy went off the handle and took his gun and went into the shower. Another guy was taking a shower, and he shot and killed him and ran. The MPs and one of the officers that was in charge ran after him, and they shot him in the legs. He turned and shot one of the MPs. Shot him in the head. And the guy still kept running. One of the officers was shot in the right side of the chest.

I was working. They called me to go to the emergency room when they came in. We were trying to resuscitate all three of them at the same time—and the one that lived was the guy that had done the killing. For the first time I saw what damage a .45 could do. It was incredible—it blew an enormous hole in his chest. We put in a chest tube on one side. I saw all this blood pouring and pouring out of the tube and I said, "Wait

Source: Al Santoli, ed., *Everything We Had: An Oral History of the Vietnam War by Thirty-three American Soldiers Who Fought It* (New York: Random House, 1981), 143–46, 156, 162–63. Reprinted by permission.

a minute. Roll this guy over." The chest tube was coming out of his back. It just went right through him.

When dope would get scarce, when heroin would become scarce, there were a lot of gunfights over that. It was incredible among the enlisted men. The officers were mostly doctors and nurses, and we knew enough to stay away from stuff like that—because we knew we had to stay on the ball, because we had to take care of everybody.

There was a lot of drinking going on among doctors and nurses. But you don't want to get drunk because you know you have to perform and you don't know when you're going to be called upon. You have to be on your toes.

They busted our compound once for heroin, just heroin, not for acid or coke, not anything else, just heroin. And they said, "Anyone who doesn't turn themselves in will have to go to LBJ." That's Long Binh Jail. They put bunk beds in the hospital, there were so many of them from the enlisted people that were on our compound, and they all had to do with hospital work, working in the laundry or supply or as medics. I had a medic die right in front of me—just from taking heroin too long. Pneumonia was the end result. It was two weeks before he was to go home and he went home in a box.

These guys would come to work stoned all the time. My medics would shoot up my patients, my patients would . . . I caught them in the bathroom shooting each other up. Once I tried to stop it. Then I realized that he was a lot bigger than I was. I thought, "My medics, I can't do anything about them because they're stoned all the time—not stoned, but they're on heroin—and the administration isn't sending them away." You could report it to their CO and nothing would be done about it. I guess there were too many. I don't know.

Who knows? There was bad stuff going down. Like the food on our compound being sold to the Vietnamese and the restaurants, and I didn't have enough food for my patients. They wouldn't let us give the patients seconds. I tried to report that and nothing was done about it. I mean, you guess why . . . I'd get in more trouble with the Army and I thought, "What the hell, I might as well put in my time." I knew I was going to hate the Army. But what surprised me was nothing comes as close to organized crime. I thought organized crime was the last word in bad guys, but I swear, the Army has them beat. You just pay off the right person and that's it. That's what goes down.

I knew my patients were shooting up. They would come in and we would have to rule out gastroenteritis or appendicitis because they were sick from heroin or were withdrawing from it, so we had to be careful. And so I told them. I got to that point. I never thought I would care or not if somebody was on drugs, but it got to that point. I said to them, "I have enough to worry about with patients who have been wounded in battle or have had accidents without worrying about whether you are going to run out the back door and take heroin. You want to do it, just don't do it in this ward, because frankly I don't give a damn whether you die or not. If you do, that's your problem; if you OD, that's your problem, not my problem. I can't afford to worry about it. That costs me too much emotionally." I had too much invested in other people to divide myself with something like that. . . .

When I came home, I cried when I saw my parents, but that was the last time I cried for a very long time. The guys I was dating before didn't mean anything to me. My parents meant something, but I hadn't figured out what. And I just kind of went along. I went out with fellows and I thought, "Well, they're nice. So what?" I had no interest in sex, no interest in anybody. Then one day on the ski patrol I fell and hurt my thumb. It hurt really bad and I started to cry. It wasn't because I was crying about my thumb. It had come to a head. I was beginning to realize that the problem was I didn't feel anything about anybody anymore. I had no feelings, no feelings of love or hate or anything. Just nothing. And I didn't know why. I guess it was because I was emotionally exhausted. I had been through the highs and the lows and the fears and the hatred and the caring for a year and I had nothing left to give anymore. There was nothing that could compare with what had happened to me.

I dated somebody for that year and I began to realize that I cared about him, and as I began to care about him, I began to realize how much I hadn't cared about anything else. I was beginning to open my eyes and see what had been wrong before. . . .

*   *   *

. . . The blacks used to make a shoestring that they braided up and tied around their wrist, and everywhere a whole lot of blacks used to go, they'd give a power sign. About six or seven different handshakes. That was about the time that Huey Newton and all them was around. But for the guys in the bush, the grunts, you know, one of my best friends was a white guy. There was no racism between him and me, nothing like that. That was mostly back in the rear. Out in the bush everybody was the same. You can't find no racism in the bush. We slept together, ate together, fought together. What else can you ask for?

I knew this one guy. I could remember how many times a day he pissed, that's how well I knew the guy. We was real close, man, close. He was a Sicilian and I always used to kid him: "Hey, you think I could join the family when we get out of here?" This guy was so close that he should've been my brother, but . . . he died. . . .

*   *   *

Vietnam was the first place I delivered a baby by myself. It seemed like a Saturday afternoon. It might have been, I don't know why, but for some reason it seemed like a Saturday afternoon. It was very quiet. There were no other patients around. I was feeling very depressed and this lady came in. I got pissed off at first, because we were supposedly there for taking care of military casualties. We were only supposed to take care of civilian situations if we possibly had the time. But this particular day, I got her onto a gurney and started leading her back to the OR because I could tell she was very close to delivery and I had already put in a call to one of the surgeons to come down and deliver it. He didn't have time to get there.

She looked over at me and said, "Baby come, baby come." I looked down and there was the head. I just grabbed myself a sterile towel and held it under, and that kid just popped his little head out and turned around on his side, and popped his little shoulders out, and there was this little squalling bundle of humanness. And the life came back again. It was creation of life in the midst of all that destruction. And creation of life restored your sanity.

Those moments when we had a little baby around were very precious. I have a couple of slides of me sitting in the operating room with my foot up on the table, in my fatigues and combat boots, with a scrub shirt over the top of me, holding a little tiny bundle in my arms, feeding it. Those were the things that kept you going. That there was still life coming. There was still hope.

72

"The Bouncing Betty Is Feared Most"

Tim O'Brien writes of combat he experienced in Vietnam. The first piece presented here illustrates the feeling of compassion that in the midst of combat can awaken toward an enemy who has become specific and personified. The second essay demon-

Source: Tim O'Brien, *If I Die in a Combat Zone: Box Me Up and Ship Me Home* ([New York]: Delacorte Press/Seymour Lawrence, 1973), 109–11, 119–21. Reprinted by permission.

*strates a particular demand that Vietnam fighting placed on the
nerves of American ground troops.*

She had been shot once. The bullet tore through her green uniform
and into her buttock and went out through her groin. She lay on her
side, sprawled against a paddy dike. She never opened her eyes.

She moaned a little, not much, but she screamed when the medic
touched at her wound. Like a pair of twin geysers, blood gushed out of
the holes, front and back.

Her face lay on some dirt. Flies were all over her, feeding on her
blood, buzzing like an army of sexually aroused cannibals. There was
no shade. It was mid-afternoon of a hot day. The medic said he did not
dare squirt morphine into her, it would kill her before the wound did.
He tried to patch the holes, but she squirmed and twisted, rocked
and swayed, never opening her eyes. She flickered in and out of consciousness.

"She's a pretty woman, pretty for a gook. You don't see many pretty
gooks, that's damn sure."

"Yes. Trouble is, she's shot dead through the wrong place." A dozen
GIs hovered over her.

"Look at that blood come, Jesus. Like a fuckin' waterfall, like
fuckin' Niagara Falls. She's gonna die quick. Can't mend up them bullet
holes, no way."

"Fuckin'-aye. She's wasted."

"I wish I could help her." The man who shot her knelt down. "Didn't
know she was a woman, she just looked like any dink. God, she must
hurt. Get the damn flies off her, give her some peace."

She stretched her arms out above her head. She spread her fingers
wide and put her hands into the dirt and squeezed in a sort of rhythm.
Her forehead was wrinkled in a dozen long, flushed creases; her eyes
were closed.

The man who shot her peered into her face. He asked if she couldn't
be given shade.

"She's going to die," one soldier said.

"But can't we give her some shade?" He swatted at a cloud of flies
over her head.

"Can't carry her, she won't let us. She's NVA, green uniform and
everything. Hell, she's probably an NVA nurse, she probably knows
she's just going to die. Look at her squeeze her hands and rock. She's
just trying to hurry and press all the blood out of herself."

We called for a dustoff helicopter and the company spread out in a
wide perimeter around the shot woman. It was a long wait, partly

because she was going to die, helicopter or no helicopter, and partly because she was with the enemy.

Her hair was lustrous black. The man who shot her stroked her hair. Two other soldiers and a medic stood beside her, fanning her and waving at the flies. Her uniform was crusted an almost black color from her blood, and the wound hadn't clotted much. The man who shot her held his canteen to her lips and she drank some Kool-Aid.

Then she twisted her head from side to side. She pulled her legs up to her chest and rocked, her whole body swaying. The man who shot her poured a trickle of water onto her forehead.

Soon she stopped swaying. She lay still and seemed either dead or unconscious. The medic felt her pulse and shrugged and said she was still going, just barely. She moaned now and then, almost talking in her sleep, but she was not being shrill or hysterical. The medic said she was not feeling any more pain.

"Damn, she is pretty. It's a crime. We could have shot an ugly old man instead."

When the helicopter came, she was still. Some soldiers lifted her onto a poncho and took her to the chopper. She lay curled up on the floor of the helicopter, then the bird roared and went into the air. Soon the pilot radioed down and asked what we were doing, making him risk his neck for sake of the dead woman.

*   *   *

The Bouncing Betty is feared most. It is a common mine. It leaps out of its nest in the earth, and when it hits its apex, it explodes, reliable and deadly. If a fellow is lucky and if the mine is in an old emplacement, having been exposed to the rains, he may notice its three prongs jutting out of the clay. The prongs serve as the Bouncing Betty's firing device. Step on them, and the unlucky soldier will hear a muffled explosion; that's the initial charge sending the mine on its one-yard leap into the sky. The fellow takes another step and begins the next and his backside is bleeding and he's dead. We call it "ol' step and a half."

More destructive than the Bouncing Betty are the booby-trapped mortar and artillery rounds. They hang from trees. They nestle in shrubbery. They lie under the sand. They wait beneath the mud floors of huts. They haunted us. Chip, my black buddy from Orlando, strayed into a hedgerow and triggered a rigged 105 artillery round. He died in such a way that, for once, you could never know his color. He was wrapped in a plastic body bag, we popped smoke, and a helicopter took him away, my friend. And there was Shorty, a volatile fellow so convinced that the mines would take him that he spent a month AWOL. In July he came back to the field, joking but still unsure of it all. One day, when it was very hot, he sat on a booby-trapped 155 round.

When you are ordered to march through areas such as Pinkville— GI slang for Song My, parent village of My Lai—the Batangan Peninsula or the Athletic Field, appropriately named for its flat acreage of grass and rice paddy, when you step about these pieces of ground, you do some thinking. You hallucinate. You look ahead a few paces and wonder what your legs will resemble if there is more to the earth in that spot than silicates and nitrogen. Will the pain be unbearable? Will you scream or fall silent? Will you be afraid to look at your own body, afraid of the sight of your own red flesh and white bone? You wonder if the medic remembered his morphine. You wonder if your friends will weep.

It is not easy to fight this sort of self-defeating fear, but you try. You decide to be ultracareful—the hard-nosed, realistic approach. You try to second-guess the mine. Should you put your foot to that flat rock or the clump of weed to its rear? Paddy dike or water? You wish you were Tarzan, able to swing with the vines. You try to trace the footprints of the man to your front. You give it up when he curses you for following too closely; better one man dead than two.

The moment-to-moment, step-by-step decision-making preys on your mind. The effect sometimes is paralysis. You are slow to rise from rest breaks. You walk like a wooden man, like a toy soldier out of Victor Herbert's *Babes in Toyland*. Contrary to military and parental training, you walk with your eyes pinned to the dirt, spine arched, and you are shivering, shoulders hunched. If you are not overwhelmed by complete catatonia, you may react as Philip did on the day he was told to police up one of his friends, victim of an antipersonnel mine. Afterward, as dusk fell, Philip was swinging his entrenching tool like a madman, sweating and crying and hollering. He dug a foxhole four feet into the clay. He sat in it and sobbed. Everyone—all his friends and all the officers— were very quiet, and not a person said anything. No one comforted him until it was very dark. Then, to stop the noise, one man at a time would talk to him, each of us saying he understood and that tomorrow it would all be over. The captain said he would get Philip to the rear, find him a job driving a truck or painting fences.

Once in a great while we would talk seriously about the mines. "It's more than the fear of death that chews on your mind," one soldier, nineteen years old, eight months in the field, said. "It's an absurd combination of certainty and uncertainty: the certainty that you're walking in mine fields, walking past the things day after day; the uncertainty of your every movement, of which way to shift your weight, of where to sit down.

"There are so many ways the VC can do it. So many configurations, so many types of camouflage to hide them. I'm ready to go home."

73

Learning to Understand War

These are excerpts from a novel about marines in Vietnam by James H. Webb, a veteran of the conflict. Will Goodrich, formerly a student at Harvard, considers the horrors of war on civilians. Robert E. Lee Hodges reflects on what he has learned in the field: the ghosts he addresses are the shades of his warrior ancestors. At the end of the novel Goodrich, nicknamed Senator, now a wounded veteran, addresses an antiwar rally.

Goodrich ate his dinner, surveying the ghost town that had once bustled with villagers. Sometimes, when he could shake the permeating fear out of his mind and focus on it, the futility of what they were doing overwhelmed him. Abusing the land until it became unworkable, killing and being killed, and yet nothing changing beyond the tragedy of the immediate event.

Those tragedies had accumulated in his mind like particles of silt in a filter, until they had completely plugged up his logical processes, preventing the saner portions of his existence from registering any longer. Every day, some new horror inflicted in the name of winning Hearts and Minds. It either numbs you or it infuriates you, he lamented. No wonder the other people didn't get uptight when I shot that old mamasan on my first patrol.

He tried to count the tragedies. The villages they had assaulted on line for fear of being ambushed when they crossed open areas: "reconnaissance by fire," Hodges called it. Shot dogs and chickens and hogs. Accidental wounds and deaths of civilians. They were a routine, almost boring occurrence.

Marines denying villagers their extra food, on the premise that the food would only wind up with the enemy. Destroying unused C-rations, punching holes in the cans and tossing them into burn holes with the trash. It had become a familiar sight, from some black-humored theater of the absurd, whenever the company pulled out of an old perimeter. The last part of the company column would still be on one side of a hill, or on one edge of a village, as a horde of tattered villagers massed on the other end, like an anxious army of rats. And the column hardly clear

Source: James H. Webb, *Fields of Fire* (Englewood Cliffs, New Jersey: Prentice-Hall, 1978), 166–67, 171–72, 338–39. Reprinted by permission.

of the hill or village when the rats began to cover it, children and women and old men scampering about the trash holes, flicking out C-ration tins with long sticks. Occasionally, the company would mortar its own perimeter with White Phosphorous rounds after leaving it, to scare the scavengers away. But it never achieved more than a momentary effect.

Then denying the villagers their own food as well: not being able to distinguish between an enemy rice-collection point and a family's storage area, so taking all rice beyond a villager's immediate needs. Or, if no helicopter was available, destroying the rice by urinating on it or dropping smoke grenades in it.

The prisoners. Goodrich had come to Vietnam with a Miniver Cheevy view of war, believing that reason would rule over emotion, that once a combatant had been removed from the fray he would be accorded a certain sum of dignity. He had also thought the North Vietnamese soldiers and the fabled Viet Cong would face captivity with a sort of gallantry. It had confused and amazed him to see prisoners shit in their pants and grovel before him. And he could not get used to men being beaten and kicked, for no apparent reason.

And worse. He had watched Wild Man shoot a bottle off one prisoner's head, on a dare. The prisoner had fainted, then shit in his pants when he was awakened. He had seen Bagger try to talk a wounded soldier into killing himself, handing him a bayonet knife and placing the tip of it into the soldier's belly. He had been amazed to see Waterbull, normally a nonparticipant in the abuses, toss a prisoner into the water of a bomb crater when he had tired of carrying the enemy soldier, who had been shot through the knee. Waterbull then yelled jocularly that the prisoner was trying to drown himself. Goodrich had helped fish him out of the water, to the taunts of some of the others.

The pain of watching living corpses. The worst had been two North Vietnamese soldiers who had been either napalmed or hit by White Phosphorus, it wasn't clear which, and had walked to their perimeter to surrender. A villager had patiently guided them. They were scorched from head to foot, blinded, their hair burnt off and their skin pink and cracked, like a hot dog on a charcoal grill. Their throats were also scorched. They could not speak or cry. The villager identified them as enemy soldiers.

The insanity was not so much in the events, but that they were undirected, without aim or reason. They happened merely because they happened. The only meaning was in the thing itself. . . .

I can tell from the crack of a rifle shot the type of weapon fired and what direction the bullet is traveling. I can listen to a mortar pop and know its size, how far away it is. I know instinctively when I should prep a treeline with artillery before I move into it. I know which draws and fields should be crossed on line, which should be assaulted, and which are safe to cross in column. I know where to place my men when we stop and form a perimeter. I can shoot a rifle and throw a grenade and direct air and artillery onto any target, under any circumstances. I can dress any type of wound, I have dressed all types of wounds, watered protruding intestines with my canteen to keep them from cracking under sunbake, patched sucking chests with plastic, tied off stumps with field-expedient tourniquets. I can call in medevac helicopters, talk them, cajole them, dare them into any zone.

I do these things, experience these things, repeatedly, daily. Their terrors and miseries are so compelling, and yet so regular, that I have ascended to a high emotion that is nonetheless a crusted numbness. I am an automaton, bent on survival, agent and prisoner of my misery. How terribly exciting.

And how, to what purpose, will these skills serve me when this madness ends? What lies on the other side of all this? It frightens me. I haven't thought about it. I haven't prepared for it. I am so good, so ready for these things that were my birthright. I do not enjoy them. I know they have warped me. But it will be so hard to deal with a life empty of them.

And there are the daily sufferings. You ghosts have known them, but who else? I can sleep in the rain, wrapped inside my poncho, listening to the drops beat on the rubber like small explosions, then feeling the water pour in rivulets inside my poncho, soaking me as I lie in the mud. I can live in the dirt, sit and lie and sleep in the dirt, it is my chair and my bed, my floor and my walls, this clay. And like all of you, I have endured diarrhea as only an animal should endure it, squatting a yard off a trail and relieving myself unceremoniously, naturally, animally. Deprivations of food. Festering, open sores. Worms. Heat. Aching crotch that nags for fulfillment, any emptying hole that will relieve it.

Who appreciates my suffering? Who do I suffer for?

The mortar fired behind him, five more rounds at the high dike, and the ghosts were gone. Hodges stood slowly and dusted off his trousers, carrying the radio with him as he began to check lines. . . .

"HO! HO! HO CHI MINH!"

And a thousand corpses rotted in Arizona.

"THE N.L.F. IS GONNA WIN!"

And a hundred ghosts increased his haunted agony.

Snake, Baby Cakes, and Hodges, all the others peered down from uneasy, wasted rest and called upon the Senator to Set The Bastards

Straight. And those others, Bagger, Cannonball, and Cat Man, now wronged by a culture gap that overrode any hint of generational divide. Goodrich took the microphone and cleared his throat. Well, here goes. He thought of them again, wishing some of them were in the crowd.

"IT'S TIME THE KILLING ENDED." He was surprised at the echoes of his voice that careened across the field. The crowd cheered. It shocked and emboldened him at the same time. Kerrigan and Braverman were watching him closely. He nodded to them and they nodded back. Braverman was squinting. "I'D LIKE TO SEE THE WAR END. SOON." More cheers. He gave the two men a small smile. There. I said it. Dues are paid.

He eyed the crowd. His blood was rushing. His head pounded from the rapid pulsing of the blood through his temples. "ISN'T THAT WHY YOU CAME HERE? TO TRY AND END IT?" More cheers. Yeah. Groovy. End the war. "THEN WHY ARE YOU PLAYING THESE GODDAMN *GAMES*? LOOK AT YOURSELVES. AND THE FLAG. JESUS CHRIST. HO CHI MINH IS GONNA WIN. HOW MANY OF YOU ARE GOING TO GET HURT IN VIETNAM? I DIDN'T SEE ANY OF YOU IN VIETNAM. I SAW DUDES, MAN. DUDES. AND TRUCK DRIVERS AND COAL MINERS AND FARMERS. I DIDN'T SEE YOU. WHERE WERE YOU? FLUNK-ING YOUR DRAFT PHYSICALS? WHAT DO YOU CARE IF IT ENDS? YOU WON'T GET HURT."

He stood dumbly, staring at querulous, irritated faces, try to think of something else to say. Something patriotic, he mused feebly, trying to remember the things he had contemplated while driving to the rally. Or maybe piss them off some more. Another putdown, like some day they'll pay. Pay what? It doesn't cost them. Never will cost them. Like some goddamn party.

He gripped the mike, staring at them. "LOOK. WHAT DO ANY OF YOU EVEN KNOW ABOUT IT, FOR CHRIST SAKE? HO CHI FUCKING MINH. AND WHAT THE HELL HAS IT COST—"

Kerrigan stripped the mike from his nerve-damaged hand without effort, then peered calmly through the center of his face, not even both-ering to look him in the eye. "You fucking asshole. Get out of here."

Goodrich worked his way down the platform, engulfed by confused and hostile stares. Many in the crowd were hissing at him. He chuckled to himself. Snake would have loved it, would have grooved on the whole thing. Senator, he would have said, you finally grew some balls.

He noticed the car then. There were swastikas painted in bright red on both doors. On the hood, someone had written "FASCIST PIG." Across the narrow street a group of perhaps twenty people watched him, all grinning conspiratorially. Braverman stood at their head, holding a can of spray paint.

The paint was still wet. Goodrich smeared it around with his hand, then took his shirt off and rubbed it. The markings would not come off. Finally he stopped his futile effort and stared at the leering Braverman. He thought of flying into a rage, of jumping into his car and running over all of them, but he found that he was incapable of great emotion. It would never make any sense, and there was no use in fighting that. He swung his head from side to side, surprising everyone, including himself, by making a series of sounds that resembled a deep guffaw. Finally he raised his head.

"Fascist, huh? Hey, Braverman." He pointed a crutch. "Pow."

Then he drove away.

74

Forgotten Veterans

The recent dedication of a monument in Washington, D.C., to nurses in the Vietnam war is a small reminder that in and outside of combat areas they have had to confront the worst of its manglings and its deaths. Jacqueline Navarra Rhoads describes her tour in Vietnam and what it meant to come home.

. . . We wanted to save everyone. We had a lot of ARVNs (Army of the Republic of Vietnam), we called them "Marvin the ARVN." We tried to take care of the Americans first, but we also had to take care of whoever needed care—period, whether he was a Vietnamese, a POW, or whatever. In fact, when we tried to save Cliff, they brought in the Vietnamese who had laid the mine. He had an amputation. He was bleeding badly and had to be treated right away. And we saved him. I guess in my heart I felt angry about what happened.

We were short on anesthesia and supplies. And we were giving anesthesia to this POW, which made me angry because I thought, "What if—what happens if someone comes in like Cliff and we don't have any

Source: Dan Freedman, ed., Jacqueline Rhoads, associate ed., *Nurses in Vietnam: The Forgotten Veterans* (Austin: Texas Monthly Press, 1987), 15–16, 21–23. Reprinted by permission.

anesthesia left because we gave it all to this POW?" Again, because I was very strongly Catholic, as soon as I heard myself thinking this, I thought, "God, how can you think that? The tables could be turned, and what if it was Cliff in the POW's place, and how would I feel if he received no anesthesia simply because he was an enemy?" First of all, it shocked me and embarrassed me. It made me think, "Gosh, I'm losing my values, what's happened to me?" I had been taught in nursing school to save everybody regardless of race, creed, color, ethnic background, whatever. Life is life. But suddenly I wasn't thinking that anymore. I was thinking, "I'm American, and they're the enemy. Kill the enemy and save the American." . . .

I came back home on a Friday, on a Pan American flight that landed in Seattle. I remember how we were told not to wear our uniforms, not to go out into the streets with our uniforms on. That made us feel worthless. There was no welcome home, not even from the Army people who processed your papers to terminate your time in the service. That was something. I felt like I had just lost my best friend. I decided to fly home to upstate New York in my uniform anyway. Nobody said anything. There were no dirty looks or comments. I was kind of excited. I wanted to say to people, "I just got back from Vietnam." Nobody cared. When I got home, my parents had a big banner strung up across the garage, "Welcome Home, Jacque." But that was about it. My parents were proud of me, of course. But other civilians? "Oh, you were in Vietnam? That's right, I remember reading something in the newspaper about you going there. That's nice." And then they'd go on talking about something else.

You were hungry to talk about it. You wanted so badly to say, "Gee, don't you want to hear about what's going on there, and what we did, and how proud you should be of your soldiers and your nurses and doctors?" I expected them to be waiting there, waving the flag. I remember all those films of World War II, with the tape that flew from the buildings in New York City, the motorcades. Of course, I had my mother. My mom was always willing to listen, but of course she couldn't understand it when I started talking about "frag wounds" or "claymore mines." There was no way she could.

The first six months at home, I just wanted to go back to Vietnam. I wanted to go back to where I was needed, where I felt important. The first job I took was in San Francisco. It was awful. Nobody cared who I was. I remember the trouble I got into because I was doing more than a nurse was supposed to do. I got in trouble because I was a "minidoctor." They kept saying, "You're acting like you're a doctor! You're doing all these things a doctor is supposed to do. What's the big idea? You're a nurse, not a doctor." And I thought, how can I forget all the stuff I learned—putting in chest tubes, doing trachs. True, doctors only do that, but how do you prevent yourself from doing things that came automatically to you for 18 months? How do you stop the wheels, and become the kind of nurse you were before you left?

I was completely different. Even my parents didn't recognize me as the immature little girl who left Albion, New York, just out of nursing school. San Francisco was a bomb, and there wasn't an Army post for miles around Albion. So that's why I came back to San Antonio. All my friends were back in and around Fort Sam Houston, so I just naturally gravitated back toward my network. I came to San Antonio in 1974 to get my B.S. in nursing from Incarnate Word College. The best thing I did was to get into the reserve unit there. That's where I met my husband. It gave me a chance to share my feelings with other Vietnam veterans. It kept me in touch with Army life, the good things and the bad. It was like a family.

On weekends at North Fort Hood, we really do sit around the campfire and talk about 'Nam, about what we as reservists can do to be better prepared than we were back there. If there is another Vietnam-type war, God forbid, I just know I'd want to be part of it. I couldn't sit on the sidelines. We usually just talk about these things among ourselves. I think the reason a lot of people are hesitant to talk about it is that they don't know anyone who wants to listen. A lot of people don't want to hear those kinds of stories. A lot of people just want to forget that time altogether. I don't know why. I guess I'm just not like that.

I'm not saying you don't pay a price for your memories. Last year, I had an intense flashback while flying on a Huey (helicopter) around North Fort Hood. It was the last day of this reserve unit exercise and I was invited on this tour of the area. We were flying a dust off, a medevac helicopter, just like the ones we had back then. It was my first time up in a helicopter since. I thought "Gee, this is going to be great." One of the other nurses said to me, "Are you sure you want to do this? You're pretty tired." I brushed her aside, "No problem." We sat in back in seats strapped in next to where they held the litters. I was sitting in the seat, the helicopter was reving [sic] up . . . I don't know how to describe it. It was like a slide show, one of the old-fashioned kind where you go through this quick sequence . . . flick, flick, flick . . . now I know where they got the term flashback.

At first, it was as though I was daydreaming. What scared me to death was that I couldn't turn it off. I couldn't control my mind. The cow grazing in the field became a water buffalo. Fields marked off and cross-sectioned became cemeteries. We flew over this tent, it was the 114th (reserve hospital unit) and suddenly it became the 18th surg. I was scared. All I could do was grasp the hand of this friend of mine. We couldn't talk above the helicopter roar. I just started to cry, I couldn't control myself. I saw blood coming down onto the windshield and the wiper blades swishing over it. There was blood on the floor, all over the passenger area where we were sitting. The stretchers clicked into place had bodies on top of them. I was crying. The nurse next to me kept shouting about whether I was all right. My contacts were swimming around, I wanted the ride to end. I could see why GIs felt scared . . . I couldn't just turn around and open up to the nurse sitting next to me. How could you explain something like that?

I had had a flashback or two before, but the difference was I could control them. Even when the nurse started shaking me, I couldn't turn it off. I just looked past her toward the racks in the helicopter, with bodies on stretchers, body bags on the floor, blood everywhere. When we landed, everyone saw I was visibly upset. The pilot came over to see if I was OK. The only thing I could say was, "It brought back a lot of memories." How could I explain my feelings to these people at North Fort Hood. A lot of them were too young to remember Vietnam as anything more than some dim kind of image on the nightly news. I was scared to death, because all these feelings were brought back that I never knew I had.

I still try to think of the good memories from Vietnam, the people we were able to save. A flashback has certain negative connotations. It's a flashback when they can't think of another way of explaining it. I guess I'm lucky it took 14 years for it to hit me like that. The one positive thing I can say about it is that it felt awfully good to come back and hover down to that red cross on the top of the tent. It felt good to come home.

Part 5

MEANINGS

Vietnam entered the minds and imaginations of participants and observers, and became the occasion for much thinking about individual responsibility and about American society. Cold warriors saw Vietnam as a ground for testing American discipline and resolve. Soldiers had to make whatever accommodation to it might compound integrity to private belief and perception with loyalty to country or fighting unit. Men of draft age with scruples about the war found themselves alone confronting an issue that their consciences could not evade. Black nationalists held that the Vietnamese were a foreign colony of the United States as black American communities were an internal colony of the white race. Then, after the war had ended, Vietnam took on for politicians and policymakers a practical meaning of another sort: what had gone wrong, and how could American foreign policy avoid future Vietnams?

The war, in effect, threw people into themselves. Lacking past examples on which to draw, it required individual Americans to come to their own terms with it: to learn how, or whether, to fight in it, or how to resist it. Soldiers in the field needed to achieve the primal human act of marshaling intelligence against primitive stimuli and emotion. War resisters at home had to reconcile childhood patriotism and acquired politics, or reject the one for the other. They had to discover who they were in relation to their fellow resisters, the nation with which they were now in conflict, and their new-found antiwar creed. Defenders of the war had to explain, in the face of increasingly discouraging news, what the point of it was. Americans of all kinds, then, if they were at all reflective were under the necessity of coming to terms with their contradictory selves.

In April 1975, as the South Vietnamese army fled toward Saigon, hundreds of thousands of South Vietnamese citizens followed suit. Scenes like this one in Xuan Loc were repeated as people attempted to board American helicopters which had brought supplies to the army. Few could be accommodated in this hopeless scramble for a lift to safety. *(Courtesy, U.P.I.)*

75

"Tough Minds, Analytical Minds"

In this address of June 14, 1963, before the Conference on Cold War Education at Tampa, Florida, Roger Hilsman as Assistant Secretary of State for Far Eastern Affairs considers American policy needs in Asia and discusses Vietnam at length. In the course of his remarks, Hilsman stresses cool virtues of self-control that were much respected in the circle of President Kennedy. Vietnam, then, might be for Kennedy people an occasion for the exericse of virtues appropriate to the age. The second passage here is Hilsman's later description of the American intention to devise a counterinsurgency policy that would combine military defense with social development. By the sound of it, he was in the Kennedy liberal mode, wishing for Vietnam the kinds of reforms that liberals have wished to promote abroad, and in other ways at home. The two entries together present the combination of toughness and social reform that numbers of liberal cold warriors wished to achieve.

First, we must remain strong. Strong militarily and economically, and strong morally. Our will to sacrifice when necessary must be steadfast. We know that the Communists are led by their dogma to underestimate the strength and will of democratic peoples. As we remain strong and determined, we shall make clear to the Communists that their challenges to free men can never succeed in the long run. Equally important is the fact that the confidence of all free peoples that communism can be resisted and defeated depends to a large extent on their knowledge that our strength and will and our helping hand are equal to the task. As I stressed at the outset, steady nerves are more than ever before a vital component of this struggle.

Secondly, free-world power and diplomacy must be matched to-

Source: The Department of State Bulletin, XLIX, No. 1254, July 8, 1963, 45, 49; Hilsman is quoted in David Burner and Thomas West, The Torch Is Passed: The Kennedy Brothers and American Liberalism (New York: Atheneum, 1984), 115.

gether and used in just the proper proportions and quantities, with careful thought, skill, and precision. In the prenuclear age some errors, some bumbling, could perhaps be tolerated without disastrous consequences. But ever since man has learned the secret of nuclear fire, learned this long before there is any assurance that he can control it, a major error or misstep, a serious accident, could result in the almost instantaneous incineration of the population centers of the world and the mutilation and poisoning of large areas of the earth.

Just as our power must be applied in exceedingly precise amounts, and in full knowledge of the ability and will of the opponent to bring to bear his power, so must our policy objectives be defined with the greatest care and accuracy. If these objectives are defined unwisely, unrealistically, or unclearly, we may expose ourselves to unnecessary setbacks, even to disaster.

Precision, wisdom, realism: these require the utmost in cool and unemotional judgment and what I called earlier cool, deliberate analysis. Tough minds, analytical minds, are required to carry this nation through the dangerous era in which we live. Our minds must be keen enough to recognize that no situation is simple; that untidiness is characteristic of most problems; that there are no shortcuts to success, no neat, swift solutions anywhere. Today the critical issues we face demand of all of us the capacity to live in a complex world of untidy situations and yet do what is required of us with steady nerves and unflinching will.

Thirdly, while we are combating Communist imperialism in all its forms, we must remember that it is not enough to be against something and that in the last analysis success depends upon our ability to build, to construct, to contribute to man's spiritual and material welfare. We are cooperating with many free peoples in great efforts at nation building, while the Communists try to tear down, in order to impose their hold and their system on the world.

Fourthly, there is a larger need for tolerance in international life. Happily there is a growing understanding among us of the diverse ways by which different peoples seek to obtain happiness and security in a troubled world. In passing I also wish to observe that, remembering our own unfinished business in fulfilling the ideals of the American Constitution, we must be tolerant of the shortcomings we may see in other societies. While we are justifiably proud of our institutions and our freedoms and stand as leaders in the democratic world, our prestige and influence in the world suffer whenever we fall short of our own ideals.

Finally, we must have knowledge, deeper and wider knowledge than we have ever had before, of ourselves and of other peoples, their motives and their hopes. With knowledge we can gain the understanding and the insight on which wise policy must be based. President Kennedy expressed this idea in a speech at San Diego State College in California last week: No country can possibly move ahead, no free society can possibly be sustained, unless it has an educated citizenry whose qualities of mind and heart permit it to take part in the complicated and increasingly sophisticated decisions which are demanded not only of the President and the Congress but of all the citizens, who exercise the ultimate power. . . .

What has often occurred to me is that, if the United States is not only going to meet the Communist threat but carry off the difficult task of helping to create a new and stable world in the process, then Americans are going to need very steady nerves.

By this phrase "steady nerves," I mean not only not being timid but two additional qualities: first, the capacity for cold, deliberate analysis in order to know when to act and when to bide one's time; second, the unemotional self-discipline and self-control that enables one to act effectively as a result of that analysis. I mean the kind of self-control that enabled President Kennedy to use United States power with such coolness and skill as he did during the Cuban crisis. In negotiations, also, extraordinary qualities of mind and will are demanded, among which the element of cold calm in dealing with complex situations is increasingly important. President Kennedy was speaking of this in his inaugural address when he said: "Let us never negotiate out of fear. But let us never fear to negotiate."

The quality of "steady nerves" is needed in both of the fundamental tasks before us. For there are two separate tasks.

One is the meeting of crises; the other is the slower, but more positive, task of nation building, of helping to build a system of stable, strong, and independent states which have solved the problem of both political and economic development. . . .

*   *   *

Our three pronged policy is to protect the people; don't chase the Viet Cong, just use your troops to protect the people. Then, behind that screen, you have social and political reform, land reform—and very deep reform—education, everything. And then the sea of the people in which Mao says the guerrillas swim like fish will have dried up. And if necessary, you can arm the people, but it probably won't be necessary. Now, the point is that we were all grossly misinformed about the convolutions, the thickness, the obstacles, that Vietnamese culture represents.

76

"The Destruction of an Entire Society"

American governmental officials like Roger Hilsman had wanted to organize the rural Vietnamese population on reformist principles. Frances FitzGerald gives an assessment of what actually happened to the Vietnamese.

The physical suffering of South Vietnam is difficult to comprehend, even in statistics. The official numbers—859,641 "enemy," over 165,268 ARVN soldiers and about 380,000 civilians killed—only begin to tell the toll of death this war has taken. Proportionately, it is as though twenty million Americans died in the war instead of the forty-five thousand to date. But there are more to come. In the refugee camps and isolated villages people die of malnutrition and the children are deformed. In the cities, where there is no sanitation and rarely any running water, the adults die of cholera, typhoid, smallpox, leprosy, bubonic plague, and their children die of the common diseases of dirt, such as scabies and sores. South Vietnam knows nothing like the suffering of India or Bangladesh. Comparatively speaking, it has always been a rich country, and the American aid has provided many people with the means of survival. But its one source of wealth is agriculture, and the American war has wreaked havoc upon its forest and paddy lands. It has given great fortunes to the few while endangering the country's future and forcing the many to live in the kind of "poverty, ignorance, and disease" that South Vietnam never knew before.

Still, the physical destruction is not, perhaps, the worst of it. The destruction of an entire society—"That is, above all, what the Vietnamese blame the Americans for," said one Vietnamese scholar. "Willfully or not, they have tended to destroy what is most precious to us: family, friendship, our manner of expressing ourselves." For all these years, the columns in the Saigon newspapers denouncing Americans for destroying "Vietnamese culture" have sounded somehow fatuous and inadequate to those Americans who witnessed the U.S. bombing raids. But the Vietnamese kept their sights on what is permanent and irreparable. Physical death is everywhere, but it is the social death caused by destruction of the family that is of overriding importance.

Source: Frances FitzGerald, *Fire in the Lake: The Vietnamese and the Americans in Vietnam* (Boston: An Atlantic Monthly Press Book, Little, Brown and Company, 1972), 428–34. Reprinted by permission.

The French colonial presence and the first Indochina war swept away the Vietnamese state and the order of the village, but it left the family. And the family was the essence, the cell, as it were, that contained the design for the whole society. To the traditional Vietnamese the nation consisted of a landscape, "our mountains and our rivers," and the past of the family, "our ancestors." The land and the family were the two sources of national as well as personal identity. The Americans have destroyed these sources for many Vietnamese, not merely by killing people but by forcibly separating them, by removing the people from the land and depositing them in the vast swamp-cities.

In a camp on the Da Nang sand-flats a woman sits nursing her baby and staring apathetically at the gang of small children who run through the crowded rows of shacks, wheeling and screaming like a flock of sea gulls after a ship's refuse. "It is hard to do anything with the children," she says. Her husband is at first ashamed to talk to the visitors because of his torn and dirty clothes. He has tried, he says, to get a job at the docks, but the Vietnamese interpreter for the Americans demanded a price he could not pay for putting his name on the list. Nowadays he rarely goes out of the barbed-wire enclosure. His hands hang stiffly down, as if paralyzed by their idleness.

An American in Vietnam observes only the most superficial results of this sudden shift of population: the disease, the filth, the stealing, the air of disorientation about the people of the camps and the towns. What he cannot see are the connections within the mind and spirit that have been broken to create this human swamp. The connections between the society and its product, between one man and another, between the nation and its own history—these are lost for these refugees. Land had been the basis of the social contract—the transmission belt of life that carried the generations of the family from the past into the future. Ancestor worshipers, the Vietnamese saw themselves as more than separate egos, as a part of this continuum of life. As they took life from the earth and from the ancestors, so they would find immortality in their children, who in their turn would take their place on the earth. To leave the land and the family forever was therefore to lose their place in the universe and to suffer a permanent, collective death. In one Saigon newspaper story, a young ARVN officer described returning to his home village after many years to find his family gone and the site of his father's house a patch of thorns revealing no trace of human habitation. He felt, he said, "like someone who has lost his soul."

The soul is, of course, not a purely metaphysical concept, for it signifies a personal identity in life as well as death. For the Vietnamese to leave the land was to leave a part of the personality. When in 1962 the Diem regime forced the peasants to move behind the barbed wire of the strategic hamlets, the peasants found that they no longer trusted each other. And for an excellent reason. Once landowners or tenants, they became overnight improvidents and drifters who depended for their survival on what they could beg or take from others. Their behavior became unpredictable even to those who knew them.

The American war only completed the process the Diem regime had begun, moving peasants out of the villages and into the refugee camps and the cities, the real strategic hamlets of the war. For these farmers, as for their distant ancestors, to leave the hamlet was to step off the brink of the known world. Brought up as the sons of Mr. X or Mr. Y, the inhabitants of such a place, they suddenly found themselves nameless people in a nameless mass where no laws held. They survived, and as the war went on outside their control, they brought up their children in this anarchic crowd.

It was not, of course, the cities themselves that were at fault. To leave the village for the towns was for many Vietnamese far from a personal tragedy. In the 1940's and 1950's the enterprising young men left their villages voluntarily to join the armies or to find some employment in the towns. The balance of village life had long ago been destroyed, and, in any case, who was to say that the constant toil and small entertainment of a peasant's life was preferable even to the harshest of existences in a city? To join the army was in fact to see the world; to move to a town was to leave a life of inevitability for one of possibility. Though, or perhaps because, the hold of the family and the land was so strong, it contained also its contradiction—the desire for escape, for the death of the father and the end of all the burdensome family obligations. But it was one thing to escape into the new but ordered life of the NLF and quite another to escape to the anarchy of the American-occupied cities.

They are not like village children, these fierce, bored urchins who inhabit the shacks and alleyways of Saigon. When a Westerner visits these slums, the women look out shyly from behind their doorways, but the children run out, shoving and scratching at each other for a better view. They scream with hysterical laughter when one of their number falls off the planking and into the sewage. In a few moments they are a mob, clawing at the strangers as if they were animals to be teased and tortured. The anger comes up quickly behind the curiosity. A pebble sails out and falls gently on the stranger's back, and it is followed by a hail of stones.

There are street gangs now in every quarter of Saigon. Led by army deserters and recruited from among the mobs of smaller children, they roam like wolf packs, never sleeping in the same place twice, scavenging or stealing what they need to live on. Many of their numbers are orphans;

the rest are as good as orphans, for their parents remain helpless peasants in the city. As a result, these boys are different from other Vietnamese. In a society of strong parental authority and family dependence, they have grown up with almost no discipline at all. Like the old street gangs of Harlem and Chicago, they have special manners, special codes. It is as though they were trying to create an entire society for themselves—a project in which they cannot succeed. . . .

. . . Since 1954—indeed since 1950 with the American sponsorship of the French war in Indochina—the United States has had only one concern and that was the war to destroy the revolutionary movement. It has not won that war and it has not destroyed the revolution, but it has changed Vietnam to the point where it is unrecognizable to the Vietnamese. . . .

. . . In 1954 South Vietnam held great promise as an economic enterprise. Unlike so many countries, it could feed its population and, with some agricultural development, produce enough raw materials to create foreign exchange. Its rich farmland perfectly complemented the mineral resources and the industry of the north. Given a modicum of outside aid, the Vietnamese with their relatively skilled population might have succeeded in breaking through that cycle of poverty and underdevelopment that affects so many countries of the world. But the American war has undermined those possibilities—by the side effects of its own military presence as much as by the bombing. The phenomenon is a curious one. The United States has had no direct economic interest in Vietnam. Over the years of the war it has not taken money out of Vietnam, but has put large amounts in. And yet it has produced much the same effects as the most exploitative of colonial regimes. The reason is that the overwhelming proportion of American funds has gone not into agricultural or industrial development but into the creation of services for the Americans—the greatest service being the Saigon government's army. As a whole, American wealth has gone into creating and supporting a group of people—refugees, soldiers, prostitutes, secretaries, translators, maids, and shoeshine boys—who do not engage in any form of production. Consequently, instead of having no capital, as it had at the moment of the French conquest, South Vietnam has an immense capital debt, for a great percentage of its population depends on the continued influx of American aid. The same was true to a lesser degree in 1954, and Saigon experienced an acute depression in the months between the French withdrawal and the first direct American commitment of aid. But now the balance of the population has changed so that the agriculture of the country scarcely suffices to feed its population, much less to create foreign exchange.

77

Black Radicals Look at Vietnam

Black and white radicals would find likenesses between the American treatment of the Vietnamese and the nation's treatment of its own black community. One rendering of the argument described the American government as imposing imperialism both on Vietnam and on blacks in this country, who were perceived as an internal colony given no true connections to the rest of American society. The first selection here, dated January 6, 1966, is a statement issued by the Student Non-Violent Coordinating Committee (SNCC), a group that had previously put Americans of both races to working for the right of black Mississippians to vote. The second selection is a letter from the radical Black Panthers to the South Vietnamese insurgents. It bears the date August 29, 1970, and the name of Huey P. Newton, a Panther official.

The Student Non-Violent Coordinating Committee assumes its right to dissent with United States foreign policy on any issue, and states its opposition to United States involvement in the war in Vietnam on these grounds:

We believe the United States government has been deceptive in its claims of concern for the freedom of the Vietnamese people, just as the government has been deceptive in claiming concern for the freedom of the colored people in such other countries as the Dominican Republic, the Congo, South Africa, Rhodesia and in the United States itself.

We of the Student Non-Violent Coordinating Committee have been involved in the black people's struggle for liberation and self-determination in this country for the past five years. Our work, particularly in the South, taught us that the United States government has never guaranteed the freedom of oppressed citizens, and is not yet truly determined to end the rule of terror and oppression within its own borders.

We ourselves have often been victims of violence and con-

Source: Clyde Taylor, ed., *Vietnam and Black America: An Anthology of Protest and Resistance* (Garden City, N.Y.: Anchor Books, Anchor Press/Doubleday, 1973), 258–60, 290–93. Reprinted by permission.

finement executed by U.S. government officials. We recall the numerous persons who have been murdered in the South because of their efforts to secure their civil and human rights, and whose murderers have been allowed to escape penalty for their crimes. The murder of Samuel Younge in Tuskegee, Alabama is no different from the murder of people in Vietnam, for both Younge and the Vietnamese sought and are seeking to secure the rights guaranteed them by law. In each case, the United States government bears a great part of the responsibility for these deaths.

Samuel Younge was murdered because United States law is not being enforced. Vietnamese are being murdered because the United States is pursuing an aggressive policy in violation of international law. The United States is no respector of persons or law when such persons or laws run counter to its needs and desires. We recall the indifference, suspicion and outright hostility with which our reports of violence have been met in the past by government officials. We know for the most part that elections in this country, in the North as well as the South, are not free. We have seen that the 1965 Voting Rights Act and the 1964 Civil Rights Act have not yet been implemented with full federal power and concern. We question then the ability and even the desire of the United States government to guarantee free elections abroad. We maintain that our country's cry of "preserve freedom in the world" is a hypocritical mask behind which it squashed liberation movements which are not bound and refuse to be bound by the expediency of the United States cold war policy.

We are in sympathy with and support the men in this country who are unwilling to respond to the military draft which would compel them to contribute their lives to United States aggression in the name of the "freedom" we find so false in this country.

We recoil with horror at the inconsistency of this supposedly free society where responsibility to freedom is equated with responsibility to lend oneself to military aggression. We take note of the fact that 16% of the draftees from this country are Negro, called on to stifle the liberation of Vietnam, to preserve a "democracy" which does not exist for them at home.

We ask: Where is the draft for the Freedom fight in the United States?

We therefore encourage those Americans who prefer to use their energy in building democratic forms within the country. We believe that work in the civil rights movement and other human relations organizations is a valid alternative, knowing full well that it may cost them their lives, as painfully as in Vietnam.

*   *   *

In the spirit of international revolutionary solidarity the Black Panther Party hereby offers to the National Liberation Front and Provisional Revolutionary Government of South Vietnam an undetermined number of troops to assist you in your fight against American imperialism. It is appropriate for the Black Panther Party to take this action at this time in recognition of the fact that your struggle is also our struggle, for we recognize that our common enemy is the American imperialist who is the leader of international bourgeois domination. There is not one fascist or reactionary government in the world today that could stand without the support of United States imperialism. Therefore our problem is international, and we offer these troops in recognition of the necessity for international alliances to deal with this problem.

Such alliances will advance the struggle toward the final act of dealing with American imperialism. The Black Panther Party views the United States as the "city" of the world, while we view the nations of Africa, Asia and Latin America as the "countryside" of the world. The developing countries are like the Sierra Maestra in Cuba and the United States is like Havana. We note that in Cuba the people's army set up bases in the Sierra Maestra and choked off Havana because it was dependent upon the raw materials of the countryside. After they won all the battles in this countryside the last and final act was for the people to march upon Havana.

The Black Panther Party believes that the revolutionary process will operate in a similar fashion on an international level. A small ruling circle of seventy-six major companies controls the American economy. This elite not only exploits and oppresses Black people within the United States; they are exploiting and oppressing everyone in the world because of the overdeveloped nature of capitalism. Having expanded industry within the United States until it can grow no more, and depleting the raw materials of this nation, they have run amuck abroad in their attempts to extend their economic domination. To end this oppression we must liberate the developing nation—the countryside of the world—and then our final act will be the strike against the "city." As one nation is liberated elsewhere it gives us a better chance to be free here.

The Black Panther Party recognizes that we have certain national problems confined to the continental United States, but we are also aware that while our oppressor has domestic problems these do not stop him from oppressing people all over the world. Therefore we will keep fighting and resisting within the "city" so as to cause as much turmoil as possible and aid our brothers by dividing the troops of the ruling circle.

The Black Panther Party offers these troops because *we are the van-*

guard party of revolutionary internationalists who give up all claim to nationalism. We take this position because the United States has acted in a very chauvinistic manner and lost its claim to nationalism. *The United States is an empire which has raped the world to build its wealth here. Therefore the United States is not a nation.* It is a government of international capitalists and inasmuch as they have exploited the world to accumulate wealth this country belongs to the world. The Black Panther Party contends that the United States lost its right to claim nationhood when it used its nationalism as a chauvinistic base to become an empire.

On the other hand, the developing countries have every right to claim nationhood, because they have not exploited anyone. The nationalism of which they speak is simply their rightful claim to autonomy, self-determination and a liberated base from which to fight the international bourgeoisie.

The Black Panther Party supports the claim to nationhood of the developing countries and we embrace their struggle from our position as revolutionary internationalists. We cannot be nationalists when our country is not a nation but an empire. We contend that it is time to open the gates of this country and share the technological knowledge and wealth with the peoples of the world.

History has bestowed upon the Black Panther Party the obligation to take these steps and thereby advance Marxism-Leninism to an even higher level along the path to a socialist state, and then a non-state. This obligation springs both from the dialectical forces in operation at this time and [from] our history as an oppressed Black colony. The fact that our ancestors were kidnapped and forced to come to the United States has destroyed our feeling of nationhood. Because our long cultural heritage was broken we have come to rely less on our history for guidance, and seek our guidance from the future. Everything we do is based upon functionalism and pragmatism, and because we look to the future for salvation we are in a position to become the most progressive and dynamic people on the earth, constantly in motion and progressing, rather than becoming stagnated by the bonds of the past.

Taking these things under consideration, it is no accident that the vanguard party—without chauvinism or a sense of nationhood—should be the Black Panther Party. Our struggle for liberation is based upon justice and equality for all men. Thus we are interested in the people of any territory where the crack of the oppressor's whip may be heard. We have the historical obligation to take the concept of internationalism to its final conclusion—the destruction of statehood itself. This will lead us into the era where the withering away of the state will occur and men will extend their hand in friendship throughout the world.

This is the world view of the Black Panther Party and in the spirit of revolutionary internationalism, solidarity and friendship we offer these troops to the National Liberation Front and Provisional Government of South Vietnam, and to the people of the world.

78

War and Rape

Susan Brownmiller's work Against Our Will *is a leading feminist commentary on rape as a social phenomenon and an expression of male domination of women. Since war is about not only violence but domination, consideration of it is important to Ms. Brownmiller's study. A section of her book is given to rape in Vietnam. The incident described at the beginning of these excerpts is told in Daniel Lang's book* Casualties of War *and the film of that title. Ms. Brownmiller's remarks suggest a connection that some men may be tempted to make between rape and manhood. Rape was a feature of the atrocity at My Lai. Ms. Brownmiller's recollection of the split between feminism and the rest of the antiwar forces bears on the development of feminism as a separate movement, fixed exclusively on women's issues.*

New Yorker writer Daniel Lang detailed one specific incident of GI gang rape in Vietnam. In November, 1966, a squad of five men on reconnaissance patrol approached the tiny hamlet of Cat Tuong, in the Central Highlands. Their five-day mission was to have been a general search for VC in the area, but when they entered the village they searched instead for a young girl to take along with them for five days of "boom boom." It was understood by the men that at the end of the patrol they would have to kill her and hide her body. Lang used pseudonyms for the five soldiers and the real name of the victim, Phan Thi Mao, a name that the soldiers never learned until their court-martial proceedings.

Mao was picked out by the men because for some reason a gold

Source: Susan Brownmiller, *Against Our Will: Men, Women and Rape* (New York: Simon and Schuster, 1975), 101–03, 112–13. Reprinted by permission.

tooth in her mouth amused them. She was perhaps twenty years old. As the soldiers knew precisely the intent of their action, so, too, did the women of the village, who cowered, wept and clung to one another as Mao's hands were bound efficiently behind her back before she was marched down the road. In one of the most pathetic incidents of the entire affair, Mao's mother ran after the soldiers with her daughter's scarf, the only act of protection she could think of. One of the men took it and tied it around their captive's mouth.

Of the five men in the patrol only one, Private First Class Sven Eriksson, did not participate in Mao's rape and murder. As Lang described the ordeal, individual acts of superfluous cruelty practiced on Mao appeared to be a competition for a masculinity pecking order. Eriksson, for refusing to take his turn in Mao's gang rape, was derided by the patrol leader, Sergeant Tony Meserve, as a queer and a chicken. One of the followers, Manuel Diaz, later haltingly told the military prosecutor that fear of ridicule had made him decide to go along with the rest: "Okay, let's say you are on a patrol. These guys right here are going to start laughing you out. Pretty soon you're going to be an outcast from the platoon."

After her murder, Phan Thi Mao was reported as "one VC, killed in action." Eriksson's resolve that the crime would not go unpunished met with a curious wall of resistance from his superiors back in the base camp, and the men in his platoon who heard the story began to view him as a whistle-blowing troublemaker. He became half convinced that he narrowly escaped a fragging. "Whatever I could do depended on finding someone with both the rank and the conscience to help me," he told Daniel Lang. "Otherwise I'd stay boxed in by the chain of command."

Summarily transferred to another camp one day after the alleged fragging, Eriksson finally managed to tell his story to a sympathetic Mormon chaplain who alerted the Criminal Investigation Division. Mao's decomposing body was found on the hill where Eriksson said it would be and her sister was located and was carefully interrogated. A separate court-martial was held for each of the four men in the winter of the following year. In each of the trials Eriksson's manhood was brought into question by the defense. "It was just that he was less than average as far as being one of the guys," a sergeant in his old platoon testified, while Sergeant Tony Meserve was depicted by his superior officer as "one of the best combat soldiers I have known." With one exception the defendants went through their court-martial convinced they were guilty of no wrongdoing. The man who drew the heaviest penalty, life imprisonment, had his sentence cut on review to eight years. . . .

As a matter of historical record, by the time The Winter Soldier Investigation [an informal gathering of testimonies by Vietnam veterans]

Prostitution became a big business in wartime Saigon. *(Courtesy, U.P.I.)*

had been convened, the feminist movement and the antiwar movement had gone their separate and distinct ways, each absorbed with its own issues to the exclusion of the other, with no small amount of bitterness among movement troopers whose energies, ideologies and sense of priority pulled them in one direction or the other. As a woman totally committed to the feminist cause I received several requests during this time to march, speak and "bring out my sisters" to antiwar demonstrations "to show women's liberation solidarity with the peace movement," and my response was that if the peace movement cared to raise the issue of rape and prostitution in Vietnam, I would certainly join in. This was met with stony silence on the part of antiwar activists whose catchwords of the day were "anti-imperialism" and "American aggression," and for whom the slogan—it appeared on buttons—"Stop the Rape of Vietnam" meant the defoliation of crops, not the abuse of women. Communications between feminist groups and antiwar groups were tense as they sought to raise our consciousness and we sought to raise our own. I am sorry that the peace movement did not consider the abuse of women in Vietnam an issue important and distinctive enough to stand on its own merits, and I am sorry that we in the women's movement, struggling to find our independent voices, could not call attention to this women's side of the war by ourselves. The time was not right.

79

"I *Hate* What Vietnam Has Done to Our Country!"

Norman Schwarzkopf, later the commander of the American and coalition forces during Desert Storm, was a lieutenant colonel in Vietnam. Here, in the course of an interview about a young American soldier killed accidentally by what is called "friendly fire," Schwarzkopf reveals what the war in Vietnam or more particularly the reaction at home was capable of doing to sensitive members of the military.

Source: C. D. B. Bryan, *Friendly Fire* (New York: G. P. Putnam's Sons, 1976), 304–05. Reprinted by permission.

... "The public seems to have lost faith in the military because of the war in Vietnam," Schwarzkopf continued. "After all, we're only an arm of policy of the United States government. We're public servants. If the public no longer has confidence in us, then what good are we? I think right now in the officer corps there are an awful lot of people who feel confused about the public's attitude. I came into the Army because I wanted to serve my country. I took an oath saying that I'd protect this country from all enemies foreign and domestic—I didn't say *I'd* determine who the enemies were! I said I'd merely protect the country after somebody else made that determination. So this war comes around in Vietnam; the duly elected government officials send us, the Army, to fight the war. We go to Vietnam and fight the best way we know how— not needlessly wasting lives for the most part. We did the best we could, and it dragged on and on and on. Many of us were sent back a second time. A lot of young officers have been sent back a third time. I'm talking about the kid who went over first as a platoon leader, returned as a captain and commanded an infantry company and then, a third time, went over as a major. Three times he's gone off not knowing whether he was going to come back alive. He's got ten years in the service and in that ten years has been separated from his wife and family for three of them. He didn't go off to Vietnam because he wanted to. He was sent by his country. Now, suddenly, public opinion is violently antimilitary as though it had all been the kid's idea! So here he is, a young Army major with ten years' service and he's going to sit down and think. 'All of a sudden I'm being blamed for all this,' and he hurts. He's hurt! He doesn't understand why he's bearing the brunt of this animosity when the guys who sent him to Vietnam seven years ago are now back on college campuses writing articles about how terrible it is that he's there in Vietnam!" ...

"... My feeling now is that we should get out. What we're gaining by being over there is no longer significant, and of course, we are getting out. We're withdrawing much faster than I ever thought we could. But I think this is an important point: the government sends you off to fight its war—again, it's not *your* war, it's the government's war. You go off and fight not only once, but twice, okay? And suddenly a decision is made, 'Well, look, you guys were all wrong. You're a bunch of dirty bastards. You never should have been there!' Now this is going to make me think long and hard before I go off to war again. This is me, Norm Schwarzkopf, personally. I don't think there will ever be another major confrontation where huge armies line up on both sides. If that happens, it's inevitably going to be nuclear weapons and the whole thing. So I think all wars of the future are going to be—and again, God forbid, I hope we don't have any. War is a profanity. It really is. It's terrifying.

Nobody is more antiwar than an intelligent person who's been to war. Probably the most antiwar people I know are Army officers—but if we do have a war, I think it's going to be similar in nature to Vietnam and Korea. Limited in scope. And when they get ready to send me again, I'm going to have to stop and ask myself, 'Is it worth it?' That's a very dangerous place for the nation to be when your own army is going to stop and question." . . .

. . . "I *hate* what Vietnam has done to our country! I *hate* what Vietnam has done to our Army! . . ."

80

An Appeal to Conscience

The British philosopher Bertrand Russell was a leading critic of the war and an organizer of an International War Crimes Tribunal, an event that called together critics of the war to denounce American activities in Vietnam. The Tribunal was criticized, even within the antiwar movement, for the bias it brought to its deliberations. In this statement dated June 18, 1966, Russell appeals to Americans to turn from the war. Its claim that the war was for the sake of capitalist economic interests reflected one common antiwar conviction.

I appeal to you, citizens of America, as a person concerned with liberty and social justice. Many of you will feel that your country has served these ideals and, indeed, the United States possesses a revolutionary tradition which, in its origins, was true to the struggle for human liberty and for social equality. It is this tradition which has been traduced by the few who rule the United States today. Many of you may not be fully aware of the extent to which your country is controlled by industrialists who depend for their power partly upon great economic holdings in all parts of the world. The United States today controls over sixty per cent of the world's natural resources, although it contains only six per cent of the world's population. The minerals and produce of vast areas

Source: Bertrand Russell, "Appeal to the American Conscience," in *War Crimes in Vietnam* (New York: Monthly Review Press, 1967), 116–20.

of the planet are possessed by a handful of men. I ask you to consider the words of your own leaders, who sometimes reveal the exploitation they have practised. The *New York Times* of February 12, 1950 said:

> 'Indo-China is a prize worth a large gamble. In the North are exportable tin, tungsten, manganese, coal, lumber and rice; rubber, tea, pepper and hides. Even before World War II Indo-China yielded dividends estimated at 300 million dollars per year.'

One year later, an adviser to the United States State Department said the following:

> 'We have only partially exploited South-East Asia's resources. Nevertheless, South-East Asia supplied ninety per cent of the world's crude rubber, sixty per cent of its tin and eighty per cent of its copra and coconut oil. It has sizeable quantities of sugar, tea, coffee, tobacco, sisal, fruits, spices, natural resins and gums, petroleum, iron ore and bauxite.'

And in 1953, while the French were still in Vietnam fighting with American backing, President Eisenhower stated:

> 'Now let us assume we lost Indo-China. If Indo-China goes, the tin and tungsten we so greatly value would cease coming. We are after the cheapest way to prevent the occurrence of something terrible—the loss of our ability to get what we want from the riches of the Indo-Chinese territory and from South-East Asia.'

This makes clear that the war in Vietnam is a war like that waged by the Germans in Eastern Europe. It is a war designed to protect the continued control over the wealth of the region by American capitalists. When we consider that the fantastic sums of money spent on armament are awarded in contracts to the industries on whose boards of directors sit the generals who demand the weapons, we can see that the military and large industry have formed an interlocking alliance for their own profit.

The truth is that the Vietnamese popular resistance is just like the American revolutionary resistance to the British, who controlled the economic and political life of the American colonies in the eighteenth century. Vietnamese resistance is like the resistance of the French Maquis, the Yugoslav partisans and the guerrillas of Norway and Denmark to the Nazi occupation. That is why a small peasant people is able to hold down a vast army of the most powerful industrial nation on earth.

I appeal to you to consider what has been done to the people of Vietnam by the United States Government. Can you, in your hearts, justify the use of poison chemicals and gas, the saturation bombing of the entire country with jelly-gasoline and phosphorus? Although the American Press lies about this, the documentary evidence concerning the nature of these gases and chemicals is overwhelming. They are poisonous and they are fatal. Napalm and phosphorus burn until the victim is reduced to a bubbling mass. The United States has also used weapons like the 'lazy dog,' which is a bomb containing ten thousand slivers of razor-sharp steel. These razor darts slice to ribbons the villagers upon whom these weapons of sheer evil are constantly used. In one province of North Vietnam, the most densely populated, one hundred million slivers of razor-sharp steel have fallen in a period of thirteen months.

It is even more revealing and terrible that more Vietnamese died during the reign of Diem, from 1954 to 1960, then since 1960, when the Vietnamese partisans took up armed resistance to the American occupation in the South. What the papers have called the 'Vietcong' is, in fact, a broad alliance, like the popular fronts of Europe, including all political views ranging from Catholics to Communists. The National Liberation Front has the most ardent support of the people and only the wilfully blind will fail to see this.

Do you know that eight million Vietnamese were placed in internment camps under conditions of forced labour, with barbed wire and armed patrols? Do you know that this was done on the direction of the United States Government and that torture and brutal murder were a continuous feature of life in these camps? Are you aware that the gases and chemicals which have been used for five years in Vietnam blind, paralyse, asphixiate, cause convulsions and result in unbearable death?

Try to imagine what it would mean if an enemy were bombing the United States and occupied it for twelve years. How would you feel if a foreign power had saturated New York, Chicago, Los Angeles, St[.] Louis, San Francisco and Miami with jelly-gasoline, phosphorus and lazy dogs? What would you do if an occupying army used these toxic gases and chemicals in every town and hamlet they entered? Can you really think that the American people would welcome so savage an aggressor? The fact is that everywhere in the world people have come to see the men who control the United States Government as brutal bullies, acting in their own economic interests and exterminating any people foolhardy enough to struggle against this naked exploitation and aggression.

When the United States began its war against the Vietnamese, after having paid for nearly all of the French war against the same people, the US Defence Department owned property valued at 160 billion dollars. This value has since doubled. The US Defence Department is the world's largest organization, owning thirty-two million acres in the United States and millions more in foreign countries. By now, more than seventy-five cents out of every hundred are spent on present wars and preparation for future war. Billions of dollars are placed in the pockets of the US military, thereby giving the Pentagon economic power affecting every facet of American life. Military assets in the United States are three times as great as the combined assets of US Steel, Metropolitan Life Insurance, American Telephone and Telegraph, General Motors and Standand Oil. The Defence Department employs three times the number of people working in all these great world corporations. The billions of dollars in military contracts are provided by the Pentagon and fulfilled by large industry. By 1960, 21 billion dollars were spent on military goods. Of this colossal sum, 7½ billion were divided amongst ten corporations and five corporations received nearly one billion dollars each. I ask you to consider carefully that in the executive offices of these corporations there are more than 1,400 retired army officers, including 261 generals and officers of flag rank. General Dynamics has 187 retired officers, 27 generals and admirals and the former Secretary of the Army on its payroll. This is a ruling caste, which stays in power no matter who is elected to nominal public office, and every President finds himself obliged to serve the interests of this all-powerful group. Thus, American democracy has been emptied of life and meaning because the people cannot remove the real men who rule them.

It is this concentration of power which makes it necessary for the Pentagon and big industry to continue the arms race for its own sake. The sub-contracts they award to smaller industries and war contractors involve every American city and, thus, affect the jobs of millions of people. Four million work for the Defence Department. Its payroll is twelve billion dollars, twice that of the US automobile industry. A further four million work directly in arms industries. In many cities military production accounts for as much as eighty per cent of all manufacturing jobs. Over fifty per cent of the gross national product of the United States is devoted to military spending. This vast military system covers the world with over 3,000 military bases, for the simple purpose of protecting the same empire which was described so clearly in the statements of President Eisenhower, the State Department adviser and the *New York Times* which I mentioned earlier to you. From Vietnam to the Dominican Republic, from the Middle East to the Congo, the economic interests of a few big corporations linked to the arms industry and the military itself determine what happens to American lives. It is on their orders that the United States invades and oppresses starving and helpless people.

Yet, despite the immense wealth of the United States, despite the fact that with only six per cent of the world's people, approaching two-thirds of the world's resources are in its possession, despite the control over the world's oil, cobalt, tungsten, iron ore, rubber and other vital resources, despite the vast billions of profits that are gained by a few American corporations at the cost of mass starvation amongst the peoples of the world, despite all this, sixty-six million Americans live at poverty level. The cities of America are covered in slums. The poor carry the burden of taxation and the fighting of colonial and aggressive wars. I am asking all of you to make an intellectual connection between events which occur daily around you, to try to see clearly the system which has taken control of the United States and perverted its institutional life into a grotesque arsenal for a world empire. It is the vast military machine, the great industrial combines and their intelligence agencies which are regarded by the people of three whole continents as their main enemy in life and the source of their misery and hunger. If we examine the governments which depend for their existence upon American military force, we shall always find regimes which support the rich, the landlords and the big capitalists. This is true in Brazil, in Peru, in Venezuela, in Thailand, in South Korea, in Japan. It is true the world over. . . .

81

The Draft and Social Class

College students, both supporters and opponents of the war, had a disproportionate safety from the draft. For some time not only undergraduate but graduate deferments were available. That allowed students to stretch out their years of safety from the draft. In 1968 graduate deferments ended, which shortened the time of shelter from conscription, and under President Nixon Congress replaced the whole system with a draft lottery. Even then a possible way of legally avoiding the draft existed, as it had before: to know the clever ways of attaining medical exemptions. Fallows writes of students who managed to gain student deferment, medical disqualification, or

Source: James Fallows, "What Did You Do In the Class War, Daddy?" *The Washington Monthly,* October 1975, 5–7, 9–10, 17. Reprinted by permission.

some other legal way out of the draft. They thereby avoided more difficult alternatives: military service or principled disobedience to conscription and the acceptance of prison. The ability of affluent college youth to stay out of the draft drew attention to the divisions among social classes in this country and the privileges enjoyed by the well-to-do.

Many people think that the worst scars of the war years have healed. I don't. Vietnam has left us with a heritage rich in possibilities for class warfare, and I would like to start telling about it with this story:

In the fall of 1969, I was beginning my final year in college. As the months went by, the rock on which I had unthinkingly anchored my hopes—the certainty that the war in Vietnam would be over before I could possibly fight—began to crumble. It shattered altogether on Thanksgiving weekend when, while riding back to Boston from a visit with my relatives, I heard that the draft lottery had been held and my birthdate had come up number 45. I recognized for the first time that, inflexibly, I must either be drafted or consciously find a way to prevent it.

In the atmosphere of that time, each possible choice came equipped with barbs. To answer the call was unthinkable, not only because, in my heart, I was desperately afraid of being killed, but also because, among my friends, it was axiomatic that one should not be "complicit" in the immoral war effort. Draft resistance, the course chosen by a few noble heroes of the movement, meant going to prison or leaving the country. With much the same intensity with which I wanted to stay alive, I did not want those things either. What I wanted was to go to graduate school, to get married, and to enjoy those bright prospects I had been taught that life owed me.

I learned quickly enough that there was only one way to get what I wanted. A physical deferment would restore things to the happy state I had known during four undergraduate years. The barbed alternatives would be put off. By the impartial dictates of public policy I would be free to pursue the better side of life.

Like many of my friends whose numbers had come up wrong in the lottery, I set about securing my salvation. When I was not participating in anti-war rallies, I was poring over the Army's code of physical regulations. During the winter and early spring, seminars were held in the college common rooms. There, sympathetic medical students helped us search for disqualifying conditions that we, in our many years of good health, might have overlooked. Although, on the doctors' advice, I made a half-hearted try at fainting spells, my only real possibility was beating the height and weight regulations. My normal weight was close to the cut-off point for an "underweight" disqualification, and, with a diligence born of panic, I made sure I would have a margin. I was six-feet-one-inch tall at the time. On the morning of the draft physical I weighed 120 pounds.

Before sunrise that morning I rode the subway to the Cambridge city hall, where we had been told to gather for shipment to the examination at the Boston Navy Yard. The examinations were administered on a rotating basis, one or two days each month for each of the draft boards in the area. Virtually everyone who showed up on Cambridge day at the Navy Yard was a student from Harvard or MIT.

There was no mistaking the political temperament of our group. Many of my friends wore red arm bands and stop-the-war buttons. Most chanted the familiar words, "Ho, Ho, Ho Chi Minh/NLF is Gonna Win." One of the things we had learned from the draft counselors was that disruptive behavior at the examination was a worthwhile political goal, not only because it obstructed the smooth operation of the criminal war machine, but also because it might impress the examiners with our undesirable character traits. As we climbed into the buses and as they rolled toward the Navy Yard, about half of the young men brought the chants to a crescendo. The rest of us sat rigid and silent, clutching x-rays and letters from our doctors at home.

Inside the Navy Yard, we were first confronted by a young sergeant from Long Beach, a former surfer boy no older than the rest of us and seemingly unaware that he had an unusual situation on his hands. He started reading out instructions for the intelligence tests when he was hooted down. He went out to collect his lieutenant, who clearly had been through a Cambridge day before. "We've got all the time in the world," he said, and let the chanting go on for two or three minutes. "When we're finished with you, you can go, and not a minute before."

From that point on the disruption became more purposeful and individual, largely confined to those whose deferment strategies were based on anti-authoritarian psychiatric traits. Twice I saw students walk up to young orderlies—whose hands were extended to receive the required cup of urine—and throw the vial in the orderlies' faces. The orderlies looked up, initially more astonished than angry, and went back to towel themselves off. Most of the rest of us trod quietly through the paces, waiting for the moment of confrontation when the final examiner would give his verdict. I had stepped on the scales at the very beginning of the examination. Desperate at seeing the orderly write down 122 pounds, I hopped back on and made sure that he lowered it to 120. I walked in a trance through the rest of the examination, until the final meeting with the fatherly physician who ruled on marginal cases such as mine. I stood there in socks and underwear, arms wrapped around me in the chilly building. I knew as I looked at the doctor's face that he understood exactly what I was doing.

"Have you ever contemplated suicide?" he asked after he finished looking over my chart. My eyes darted up to his. "Oh, suicide—yes, I've been feeling very unstable and unreliable recently." He looked at me, staring until I returned my eyes to the ground. He wrote "unqualified" on my folder, turned on his heel, and left. I was overcome by a wave of relief, which for the first time revealed to me how great my terror had been, and by the beginning of the sense of shame which remains with me to this day.

It was, initially, a generalized shame at having gotten away with my deception, but it came into sharper focus later in the day. Even as the last of the Cambridge contingent was throwing its urine and deliberately failing its color-blindness tests, buses from the next board began to arrive. These bore the boys from Chelsea, thick, dark-haired young men, the white proles of Boston. Most of them were younger than us, since they had just left high school, and it had clearly never occurred to them that there might be a way around the draft. They walked through the examination lines like so many cattle off to slaughter. I tried to avoid noticing, but the results were inescapable. While perhaps four out of five of my friends from Harvard were being deferred, just the opposite was happening to the Chelsea boys.

We returned to Cambridge that afternoon, not in government buses but as free individuals, liberated and victorious. The talk was high-spirited, but there was something close to the surface that none of us wanted to mention. We knew now who would be killed.

As other memories of the war years have faded, it is that day in the Navy Yard that will not leave my mind. The answers to the other grand questions about the war have become familiar as any catechism. Q. What were America's sins? A. The Arrogance of Power, the Isolation of the Presidency, the Burden of Colonialism, and the Failure of Technological Warfare. In the abstract, at least, we have learned those lessons. For better or worse, it will be years before we again cheer a president who talks about paying any price and bearing any burden to prop up some spurious overseas version of democracy.

We have not, however, learned the lesson of the day at the Navy Yard, or the thousands of similar scenes all across the country through all the years of the war. Five years later, two questions have yet to be faced, let alone answered. The first is why, when so many of the bright young college men opposed the war, so few were willing to resist the draft, rather than simply evade it. The second is why all the well-educated presumably humane young men, whether they opposed the war or were thinking fondly of A-bombs on Hanoi, so willingly took advantage of this most brutal form of class discrimination—what it signifies that we let the boys from Chelsea be sent off to die.

The "we" that I refer to are the mainly-white, mainly-well-educated children of mainly-comfortable parents, who are now mainly embarked on promising careers in law, medicine, business, academics. What makes them a class is that they all avoided the draft by taking one of the thinking-man's routes to escape. These included the physical deferment, by far the smartest and least painful of all; the long technical appeals through the legal jungles of the Selective Service System; the more disingenuous resorts to conscientious objector status; and, one degree further down the scale of personal inconvenience, joining the Reserves or the National Guard. I am not talking about those who, on the one hand, submitted to the draft and took their chances in the trenches, nor, on the other hand, those who paid the price of formal draft resistance or exile. . . .

It may be worth emphasizing why our failure to resist induction is such an important issue. Five years after Cambodia and Kent State, it is clear how the war could have lasted so long. Johnson and Nixon both knew that the fighting could continue only so long as the vague, hypothetical benefits of holding off Asian communism outweighed the immediate, palpable domestic pain. They knew that when the screaming grew too loud and too many sons had been killed, the game would be all over. That is why Vietnamization was such a godsend for Nixon, and it is also why our reluctance to say No helped prolong the war. The more we guaranteed that we would end up neither in uniform nor behind bars, the more we made sure that *our* class of people would be spared the real cost of the war. (Not that we didn't suffer. There was, of course, the *angst,* the terrible moral malaise we liked to write about so much in the student newspapers and undergraduate novels.)

The children of the bright, good parents were spared the more immediate sort of suffering that our inferiors were undergoing. And because of that, when our parents were opposed to the war, they were opposed in a bloodless, theoretical fashion, as they might be opposed to political corruption or racism in South Africa. As long as the little gold stars kept going to homes in Chelsea and the backwoods of West Virginia, the mothers of Beverly Hills and Chevy Chase and Great Neck and Belmont were not on the telephones to their congressmen, screaming *you killed my boy,* they were not writing to the President that his crazy, wrong, evil war had put their boys in prison and ruined their careers. It is clear by now that if the men of Harvard had wanted to do the very most they could to help shorten the war, they should have been drafted or imprisoned en masse.

This was not such a difficult insight, even at the time. Lyndon Johnson clearly understood it, which was the main reason why the *graduate school* deferment, that grotesque of class discrimination, lasted through the big mobilizations of the war, until the springtime of 1968. Even when that deferment was gone, Johnson's administrators came up with the intelligence-test plan for draft deferments, an even bolder attempt to keep those voluble upper classes off the President's back. . . .

From its struggles in World War II, this country created a cushion of class toleration; our heritage from Vietnam is rich with potential for class hatred. World War II forced different classes of people to live together; Vietnam kept them rigidly apart, a process in which people like me were only too glad to cooperate. On either side of the class divide, the war has left feelings that can easily shade over into mistrust and hostility. Among those who went to war, there is a residual resentment, the natural result of a cool look at who ended up paying what price. On the part of those who were spared, there is a residual guilt, often so deeply buried that it surfaces only in unnaturally vehement denials that there is anything to feel guilty about. In a land of supposed opportunity, the comfortable hate to see the poor. Beneath all the explanations about self-help and just deserts, there remains the vein of empathy and guilt. Among the bright people of my generation, those who have made a cult of their high-mindedness, the sight of legless veterans and the memories of the Navy Yard must also touch that vein. They remind us that there was little character in the choices we made. . . .

82

"The Cost of Failure Was High"

In a speech of April 25, 1985, President Ronald Reagan's Secretary of State George Shultz gives his view of the lessons both true and false that Americans took from the Vietnam venture. Shultz speaks on behalf of the Reagan administration's support of right-wing regimes.

Source: "The Meaning of Vietnam," Current Policy No. 694, United States Department of State, Bureau of Public Affairs, Washington, D.C., April 1985, 1–4.

... Let me discuss what has happened in Southeast Asia, and the world, since 1975; what light those postwar events shed on the war itself; and what relevance all this has to our foreign policy today.

The first point—and it stands out for all to see—is that the communist subjection of Indochina has fulfilled the worst predictions of the time. The bloodshed and misery that communist rule wrought in South Vietnam, and in Cambodia and Laos, add yet another grim chapter to the catalog of agony of the 20th century. . . .

We left Indochina in 1975, but the cost of failure was high. The price was paid, in the first instance, by the more than 30 million people we left behind to fall under communist rule. But America, and the world, paid a price.

Our domestic divisions weakened us. The war consumed precious defense resources, and the assault on defense spending at home compounded the cost; years of crucial defense investment were lost, while the Soviets continued the steady military buildup they launched after the Cuban missile crisis. These wasted years are what necessitated our recent defense buildup to restore the global balance.

For a time, the United States retreated into introspection, self-doubt, and hesitancy. Some Americans tended to think that *American* power was the source of the world's problems, and that the key to peace was to limit *our* actions in the world. So we imposed all sorts of restrictions on ourselves. Vietnam—and Watergate—left a legacy of congressional restrictions on presidential flexibility, now embedded in our legislation. Not only the War Powers Resolution but a host of constraints on foreign aid, arms exports, intelligence activities, and other aspects of policy—these weakened the ability of the President to act and to conduct foreign policy, and they weakened our country. Thus we pulled back from global leadership.

Our retreat created a vacuum that was exploited by our adversaries. The Soviets concluded that the global "correlation of forces" was shifting in their favor. They took advantage of our inhibitions and projected their power to unprecedented lengths: intervening in Angola, in Ethiopia, in South Yemen, and in Afghanistan. The Iranian hostage crisis deepened our humiliation.

American weakness turned out to be the most *destabilizing* factor on the global scene. The folly of isolationism was again revealed. Once again it was demonstrated—the hard way—that American engagement, American strength, and American leadership are indispensable to peace. A strong America makes the world a safer place. . . .

A lot of rethinking is going on about the Vietnam war—a lot of healthy rethinking. Many who bitterly opposed it have a more sober assessment now of the price that was paid for failure. Many who supported it have a more sober understanding now of the responsibilities that rest on our nation's leaders when they call on Americans to make such a sacrifice. We know that we must be prudent in our commitments. We know that we must be honest with ourselves about the costs that our exertions will exact. And we should have learned that we must maintain the ability to engage with, and support, those striving for freedom, so that options *other* than American military involvement remain open. . . .

Vietnam and Central America—I want to tackle this analogy head-on.

Our goals in Central America *are* like those we had in Vietnam: democracy, economic progress, and security against aggression. In Central America, our policy of nurturing the forces of democracy with economic and military aid and social reform has been working—without American combat troops. And by virtue of simple geography, there can be no conceivable doubt that Central America is vital to our own security. . . .

The ordeal of Indochina in the past decade—as well as the oppressions endured by the people of Cuba and every other country where communists have seized power—should teach us something. The experience of Iran since the fall of the Shah is also instructive. Do we want another Cuba in this hemisphere? How many times must we learn the same lesson, and what is America's responsibility? . . .

83

An Opponent of the War Joins the Military

Albert Gore, later Vice President, like Fallows' young peers was opposed to the war. But he chose one of the two alternatives to their shunning of military service. In a segment of an interview published in February 1988 he explains why. The second set of excerpts here are from an address that Gore as Vice President delivered on June 9, 1994, at Harvard University's twenty-fifth commencement after his graduation from the

Source: U.S. News and World Report, February 15, 1988, 17; Remarks as Delivered by Vice President Al Gore, Harvard Commencement Day, Harvard University, Thursday, June 9, 1994, 2–3, 7, 13.

*institution. He describes the continuing national mood of cyni-
cism that he traces in part to the war in Vietnam.*

Q. **You debated whether to serve in Vietnam before deciding to go—**

I felt the war was wrong, but I decided to serve mainly because I
come from a small town of 2,000 people. If my draft board had been in
Washington, or in New York, or Los Angeles or Chicago, it might have
seemed more of an abstract relationship. But in Carthage, Tenn., it was
no secret who was on the draft board, what the rough quota was each
month. And if you didn't go, it was no secret that one of your friends
would have to go in your place. . . .

Now, what made it easier for me to understand the correctness of
that judgment was the irony that the most effective way for me to express
opposition [to the Vietnam War] was to go to it. At a time when my
father [then U.S. Senator Albert Gore, Sr.] was an articulate opponent
of the war about to run for re-election, I was under no illusion about the
significance of either choice that I made to his career. But to the extent
that it had any impact at all, I could strengthen his hand a bit by being
a part of the war. Now, that was not the reason I went, but it was a
factor, which made it easier to understand that I had a duty to serve.

*   *   *

. . . While we went to class and heard lectures and wrote papers and
listened to music and talked and played sports and fell in love, the war
in Vietnam was blasting that small country apart physically and ripping
America apart emotionally. A dark mood of uncertainty from that tragic
conflict clouded every single day we were here.

The year 1969 began with the inauguration of Richard Nixon, a
ceremony that seemed to confirm for many of us the finality of a change
in our national mood and ratify the results of a downward spiral that
had begun with the assassination of President Kennedy five years, two
months, and two days earlier.

Throughout our four years at Harvard the nation's spirits steadily
sank. The race riot in Watts was fresh in our minds when we registered
as freshmen. Though our hopes were briefly raised by the passage of civil
rights legislation and the promise of a war on poverty, the war in Vietnam
grew steadily more ominous and consumed the resources that were
needed to make good on the extravagant promises for dramatic progress
here at home.

The year before our graduation, our hopes were once again briefly
raised by the political insurgency we helped inspire and that we hoped
might somehow end our national nightmare. Then, months later, those

hopes were cruelly crushed by the assassinations of Martin Luther King, Jr., renewed race riots—this time nationwide—and then the assassination of Robert Kennedy, and what seeemd like the death of any hope that we might find our way back to the entrance of the dark tunnel into which our country had wandered. . . .

My personal attitudes toward the career I have chosen changed dramatically during that time. I left Harvard in 1969 disillusioned by what I saw happening in our country and certain of only one thing about my future: I would never, ever go into politics.

After returning from Vietnam and after seven years as a journalist, I rekindled my interest in public service. Yet I believe the same disillusioning forces that for a time drove me away from politics have continued for the country as a whole.

After all, the war raged on for five more years and the downward spiral in our national mood reached a new low when the Watergate scandal led to the growing belief that our government was telling lies to our people.

The resignation of President Nixon, his subsequent pardon, the Oil shocks, 21% interest rates, hostages held seemingly interminably and then swapped in return for weapons provided to terrorists who called us "the Great Satan," a quadrupling of our national debt in only a dozen years, a growing gap between rich and poor, and steadily declining real incomes—all of these continued an avalanche of negative self-images which have profoundly changed the way Americans view their government.

A recent analysis of public opinion polling data covering the years since my class came to Harvard demonstrates the cumulative change in our national mood. When my class entered as freshmen in the fall of 1965, the percentage of people who believed that government generally tries to do the right thing was over 60%. Today it is only 10%. The percentage believing that government favors the rich and the powerful was then 29%. Today it is 80%. And it is important to note that these trends hold true for Democrats and Republicans, conservatives and liberals.

In fact, this may be an apocryphal story, but someone actually claimed the other day the situation has gotten so bad that when they conducted a new poll and asked people about their current level of cynicism, 18% said they were more cynical than five years ago, 9% thought they were less cynical, and 72% suspected the question was some kind of government ploy, and refused to answer. . . .

Cynicism is deadly. It bites everything it can reach—like a dog with a foot caught in a trap. And then it devours itself. It drains us of the will to improve; it diminishes our public spirit; it saps our inventiveness; it withers our souls. Cynics often see themselves as merely being world-weary. There is no new thing under the sun, the cynics say. They have not only seen everything; they have seen *through* everything. They claim that their weariness is wisdom. But it is usually merely posturing. Their weariness seems to be most effective when they consider the aspirations of those beneath them, who have neither power nor influence nor wealth. For these unfortunates, nothing can be done, the cynics declare.

Hope for society as a whole is considered an affront to rationality; the notion that the individual has a responsibility for the community is considered a dangerous radicalism. And those who toil in quiet places and for little reward to lift up the fallen, to comfort the afflicted, and to protect the weak are regarded as fools.

Ultimately, however, the life of a cynic is lonely and self-destructive. It is our human nature to make connections with other human beings. The gift of sympathy for one another is one of the most powerful sentiments we ever feel. If we do not have it, we are not human. Indeed it is so powerful that the cynic who denies it goes to war with himself. . . .

In the end, we face a fundamental choice: cynicism or faith. Each equally capable of taking root in our souls and shaping our lives as self-fulfilling prophecies. We must open our hearts to one another and build on all the vast and creative possibilities of America. This is a task for a confident people which is what we have been throughout our history and what we still are now in our deepest character.

I believe in our future.

84

"We Are . . . Revolutionaries Without a Revolution"

Michael Ferber and Staughton Lynd write of the Resistance, a movement that counseled disobedience to the draft. Entering the armed forces was one alternative to the legal avoidance of the military that James Fallows describes; draft resistance was the other choice. Draft resisters were not motivated mainly by a

---

Source: Michael Ferber and Staughton Lynd, *The Resistance* (Boston: Beacon Press, 1971), 112–14. Reprinted by permission.

fear of conscription: some of them, in fact, deliberately rejected perfectly available legal means of avoiding conscription. In the passage here, Ferber describes a rally in Boston Common on October 16, 1967, before a service in the Arlington Street Unitarian Church, where resistance people were to turn in their draft cards. The cards would then be sent back to the selective service system, and the resisters would voluntarily face the consequences. This passage describes the potential clash between the draft resistance, which drew on individual conscience, and the demand among other radicals for collective action. Nick Egleson was a past president of Students for a Democratic Society.

When Rev. Williams gave the call for the draft cards, no one knew what would happen. Maybe fifty, or seventy-five? A trickle of men started down the aisle to the row of men or to the candle. The aisle soon filled, the line grew longer, the doors were opened to let in those from outside who wanted to join. The organ played, flash bulbs popped, and TV cameras hummed away. It must have been twenty minutes before it was over. More than sixty burned their cards at the candle, and over two hundred handed them in. The New England Resistance was born.

One of the best speeches in the rally before the service had been Nick Egleson's. He spoke of the anguish we feel in the movement, anguish that is born of powerlessness and uncertainty:

> We are . . . revolutionaries without a revolution. We have no base of power to give us an alternative to moral acts, no route on which an end to this war can be a milestone, no evidence to give us hope that there will be a role for the agents of change we feel ourselves to be.

He then spoke of the temptations that beset those who are anguished:

> The first temptation, one which now affects the draft resistance movement, is to measure actions in the movement by a code of individual conduct. Some refuse to enter the army because no moral man could engage in combat in Vietnam; some dissociate themselves from the Selective Service System because association with the machinery of slaughter is unconscionable; others assume the jeopardy of draft refusal even if they are not subject to the draft because no moral man can let others suffer injustice alone.
>
> In this country such an individual code easily becomes the pri-

mary or only standard for political conduct. This country's individ-
ualist ethic points in this direction; the religious frame of reference
into which much political dissent has been pushed by repression
and political intolerance leads in this direction; and the absence of
widespread political experience closes off the possibility of other,
political, standards. . . .

Equipped only with a standard of individual conduct and a
calculus of right and courage we lose sight not only of the many
kinds of change needed but also of the motivation for change. So
equipped, we easily confine our organizing to the campus. People
there are not immediately threatened by the draft. One and only
one main force can move them to assume a jeopardy in order to
protest it: a standard of individual conduct. We feel we must organize the campus.

But all the while the men of Charlestown and South Boston
and Riverside, of Roxbury and Dorchester and of the working-
class parts of cities all over the country are threatened by the draft
and are more gently coerced by the security of enlistment. . . .

Our solution must be to begin to organize those most threatened by the US armed forces. How many people gave out information about the October 16 rally in Boston in poor and working-
class neighborhoods? Who put up posters speaking the language
of those communities? Who tried to counter, thereby, the image
the press promotes of us as hippies, cowards, and peace finks? Who
suggested in those places that we—not the US Army—speak to
people's immediate and long-range interests?

The first temptation Nick described was a real one to the Resistance,
and I tried to bring home his point in a different way in the speech I gave
during the service, though I could not accept his tacit near-equations of
"moral" with symbolic, personal, middle-class self-sacrifice and "political" with practical, mass, working-class self-interest. I am not sure my
religious terms would have been adequate for all the parts of Nick's
argument, but they seemed to meet the problem uppermost in my mind
then, the conflict between private "virtue" and public engagement:

> We are brought to a third difference among us. Earlier today
> Nick Egleson spoke out against the kind of resistance whose pri-
> mary motivation is moralistic and personal rather than political.
> He is saying that we must make ourselves relevant to the social and
> political condition of the world and must not just take a moral
> posture for our own soul's sake, even though that too is a risk.
> To some extent this argument depends on terminology rather

than fact. Today we have heard our situation described in religious terms, moral terms, political terms, legal terms, and psychological terms. Very few of us are at home in all these different modes of speech, and each of us habitually uses only one of them to talk and think in. But what is happening today should make it clear that these different modes of speech all overlap one another and they often all say the same essential things. Albert Camus, who struggled in a more serious Resistance than ours, believed that politics is an extension of morality, that the truly moral man is engaged in politics as a natural outcome of his beliefs.

To return to Nick's concern, the real difference is not between the moral man and the political man, but between the man whose moral thinking leads him to political action and the man whose moral thinking leads him no farther than to his own "sinlessness." It is the difference between the man who is willing to go dirty himself in the outside world and the man who wishes to stay "clean" and "pure."

Now this kind of "sinlessness" and "purity" is arrogant pride, and I think we must say No to it. The martyr who offers himself meekly as a lamb to the altar is a fool unless he has fully taken into account the consequences of his sacrifice not only to himself but to the rest of the world. We cannot honor him for his stigmata or his purple hearts unless he has helped the rest of us while he got them.

Reading these speeches again after two years I see in them the germ of the antagonism between the Resistance (or part of it) and SDS, but I also see the germ of a conciliatory dialogue. That the dialogue got little further is a permanent loss to the movement.

85

"It Changed the Lives of Those Who Took Part"

This account and the others in the collection by Alice Lynd give further insight into the minds of draft resisters. This entry records comments by Martin Jezer, who tells of events at Sheep Meadow in New York City during the April 1967 Spring Mobilization to End the War in Vietnam. When Jezer speaks of the resistance as transforming the lives of its participants, he could be speaking for the rest of the contributors to Alice Lynd's collection.

Up until the night before April 15th, no one was sure how many people would burn their draft cards at the Mobilization; indeed, we were not at all sure whether the action would even take place. About 120 people had signed the pledge to burn their cards if 500 others did it at the same time, so the pledge was not binding. Moreover, the Spring Mobilization Committee had disowned the draft card burners and were pressuring them to postpone or cancel their plans. Many Mobilization leaders support civil disobedience, but they were afraid that a radical act like draft card burning would scare away many people new to the Movement.

At a meeting the night of April 14th, we decided to burn our cards in the Sheep Meadow at 11 A.M. despite the Mobilization's opposition. We also decided that 50 would be the minimum number of burners to make it an important political act. There was a tense moment when Bruce Dancis asked, "How many will burn their cards if 50 do it at the same time?" Hands shot up around the room. The count was 57. We were in business.

That night I hardly slept. I recalled how it was the night before my graduation from college. . . . That was a celebration of my ability to get good grades and to conform, intellectually, to the current catechism of uncritical Americanism. Although I was something of the campus radical, by contemporary standards I was just a good, harmless white liberal, impressed with and convinced of my own powerlessness, prepared to allow politicians, generals, and corporate managers to make decisions over my life. . . . Burning a draft card, I thought, would be a more mean-

Source: We Won't Go: Personal Accounts of War Objectors, collected by Alice Lynd (Boston: Beacon Press, 1968), 220–22, 224–25. Reprinted by permission.

ingful graduation. I had finally begun to be educated, to see through the myths of the American propaganda machine.

The next morning we gathered on the rocks in the Sheep Meadow. Friends of ours, veterans, women, and pacifists, linked arms and attempted to clear space for us. There were no uniformed police in sight. Soon the press, FBI men, and all kinds of ill-mannered people began pushing, shoving, pressing through the protective circle. Confusion reigned; an orderly demonstration seemed impossible. So we began burning our cards. Someone held up an empty tin can of Maxwell House Coffee with flaming paraffin inside. We lit our cards with matches, cigarette lighters, and from the flames of each other's cards. It was a pretty sight, draft cards—burning. Gary Rader, from Illinois, materialized from out of the crowd and set his card aflame. It was a wonderfully courageous act. He's an Army Reservist and was wearing his "green beret" uniform. Photographers trampled us to get his picture. He seemed very happy; smiling, shaking hands with those near him. Then, to bring some order to the demonstration, we all sat down.

The photographers fell back, our protective circle was restored. We began singing freedom songs and chanting, "Resist! Resist!" and "Burn Draft Cards, Not People." People in the audience were applauding us, shouting encouragement. Then some guys began to come out of the audience with draft cards in hand. They burned them. Alone, in pairs, by threes they came. Each flaming draft card brought renewed cheering and more people out of the crowd. Someone passed us daffodils. "Flower Power," we cried happily. . . . Some of the draft card burners were girls, wives or girlfriends of male card burners. . . . It lasted this way for about half an hour. About 175 people burned their cards. This was more than had signed the pledge. . . .

Burning my draft card was a recognition that I had finally learned something. But that I decided to commit what the U.S. government considers a heinous crime is due to a large degree to those responsible for my education. They instilled in me a sense of values, principle, and morality. They taught me that we were a peace-loving democracy, and I believed them. The education of Martin Jezer is the realization that if this *is* to be a peace-loving democracy, functioning on principled, moral values, it is for us, for me, to make it so. . . .

. . . The most important effect of the draft card burning was that it changed the lives of those who took part. I've been told many times that the Movement can't succeed, that you can't change people's hearts, that social change is gradual, and that we New Leftists are doomed to become frustrated, old, radicals. This is not true, for to the degree that the Movement has led its participants to change their lives, it has been successful. It has given people the insight to drop out of a brutal and dehumanized society, and it has given people the strength to devote their lives toward the creation of a community where love of one's fellow replaces the profit motive as the highest value.

Love is a word new radicals use often. I've had to overcome a lot of cynicism before I could use the word honestly, and not in the kind of rhetoric that American politicians use when they speak of democracy. Love, in all its wondrous manifestations, is the New Left's most positive contribution to political thought, and commitment to love, more than any other innovation, distinguishes it from the Old Left. The New Left is concerned with moving individuals as individuals into a better world, not in creating blind mass movements that seek only power, without an accompanying change of consciousness. For me, the burning of my draft card was, symbolically, my graduation or entrance into this world.

To destroy one's draft card, to place one's conscience before the dictates of one's government is in the highest tradition of human conduct. This country was not created by men subservient to law and government. It was created and made great by civil disobedients like Quakers who refused to compromise their religion to suit the Puritan theocracy; by Puritans who openly defied British authority; by . . . Sons of Liberty who burned stamps to protest the Stamp Act and who dumped tea in Boston harbor; by abolitionists who ignored the Fugitive Slave law, by slaves who refused to act like slaves; by workingmen who insisted, despite the law, on their right to organize; by black Americans who refused to ride in the back of the bus; and by the more than one hundred young Americans already in prison for refusing to acquiesce in the misguided actions of their government.

So when people tell me that I have no respect for law and order and that I do not love my country, I reply: "Jefferson, Tom Paine, Garrison, Thoreau, A. J. Muste, the Freedom Riders, these are my countrymen whom I love; with them I take my stand."

86

The Crime of Obedience

William Sloane Coffin, Jr., here describes a moment in which he obeyed orders. As an intelligence officer, he was a minor participant at the end of World War II in a policy of pushing back into the custody of the Soviet authorities people who had fled from Communist brutality. The refugees in the instance he recounts had fought on the side of the Germans not out of a liking for Nazism but in detestation of Communism. Guilt at the memory of what he had done in following military orders in the matter gave force to Coffin's decision during the Vietnam years to commit civil disobedience: he would not again commit the crime of submission to what he considered injustice.

I tried to talk to some of the American colonels, who I could see were finding the operation more and more distasteful. But their doubts were only increasing their desire to get the job over and done with. They had their orders and they were going to obey them. They told me the screening would soon be completed. Across the demarcation line the Soviets had been alerted. In nearby Landshut a train of boxcars was ready. The American first division was training secretly for a predawn "attack." When each deserter and traitor woke up he would find himself surrounded by enough GI's to prevent his escape or suicide. Those not to be repatriated would be herded off into a far corner of the camp to prevent their helping their comrades.

As it happened, the very night before this attack was to take place, the Russians in the camp organized an elaborate evening of entertainment—poetry reading, singing, dancing, skits. All nine colonels were invited. The evening was to be in their honor. I could understand the colonels' reluctance to attend. But I was incensed when I was told to make up some excuse for them and alone to represent them all, while they spent the evening drinking in the hotel where they were quartered.

Arriving at the door of the main hall of the camp, I was met by the commandant and escorted to a chair in the front row. There were no empty seats. Hundreds of Russians stood against the wall, while other hundreds sat on the floor, filling every aisle. A chorus started to sing a

Source: William Sloane Coffin, Jr., *Once to Every Man: A Memoir* (New York: Atheneum, 1978), 76–78. Reprinted by permission.

song I knew well, Lermontov's patriotic verses describing the battle of Borodino against Napoleon. Soon the entire audience was singing— three thousand voices. This was followed by balalaikas, dances and poetry reading, some men reading their own verses. They were all about Russia.

For a while I thought I was going to be physically ill. Several times I turned to the commandant sitting next to me. It would have been so easy to tip him off. There was still time. The camp was minimally guarded. Once outside the men could tear up their identity cards, get other clothes. It was doubtful that the Americans would try hard to round them up. Yet I couldn't bring myself to do it. It was not that I was afraid of being court-martialed; the commandant probably wouldn't give me away. But I too had my orders. It was one thing to let individual deserters escape in the woods. It was something else again to blow a Top Secret operation ordered by Washington itself with the Soviet government ready to make a terrible row if it failed. The closest I came was at the door, when the commandant said good night. In Russian it's "peaceful" night. When he said it I almost blurted out, "There's nothing peaceful about this place. Get out and quick." But I didn't. Instead I drove off cursing the commandant for being so trusting.

At 5:45 the next morning, the first division moved in as planned. Despite the fact that there were three GI's to every returning Russian, I saw several men commit suicide. Two rammed their heads through windows sawing their necks on the broken glass until they cut their jugular veins. Another took his leather bootstraps, tied a loop to the top of his triple-decker bunk, put his head through the noose and did a back flip over the edge which broke his neck. Others, less successful, were bandaged up and carried on stretchers to the boxcars into which the rest of the men had been herded. They were peering out through barred windows.

At the demarcation line, the Soviets were ready, only with passenger cars. There were nurses too, solicitous of the men's health, and officers inquiring gently where they came from and the names of relatives who should be notified of their forthcoming return. Suddenly I realized the men were being deceived all over again, deceived into believing that all was forgiven so that their families would be involved in their own punishment. As once they had trusted us, now they were trusting the Soviets.

I walked away as fast as I could. As I passed the baggage car I couldn't help noticing two Red Army sergeants looting the men's belongings. Beside myself with frustration, I jumped in and knocked them both out. But it was a futile, stupid act. If I hadn't had the courage to fight for the lives of these men, why fight for their belongings?

According to a terse announcement in *Pravda,* Vlassov and his generals were hanged on August 2, 1946. Exactly what happened to the two thousand officers and men we repatriated from Plattling, I do not know. The Soviet government has been very quiet about its many citizens who bore arms against it. From what a Soviet officer later told me, which was confirmed by American intelligence reports, everyone was at least imprisoned for some length of time.

My part in the Plattling operation left me a burden of guilt I am sure to carry the rest of my life. Certainly it influenced my decision in 1950 to spend three years in the CIA opposing Stalin's regime. And it made it easier for me in 1967 to commit civil diobedience in opposition to the war in Vietnam. The forced repatriation of those two thousand Russians showed me that in matters of life and death the responsibility of those who take orders is as great as those who give them. And finally what I did, or rather didn't do, at Plattling has made me sympathize with the Americans I consider war criminals in the Vietnam conflict. Some of them at least must now be experiencing the same bad moments I have had so often thinking of the lives I might have saved.

87

The End of the Vietnam Syndrome?

In the years following the end in 1973 of the American involvement in Vietnam and the victory of the Communists two years later, at least two opposing views of a proper American foreign policy were articulated, each having a slogan. Americans suspicious of the motives of American interventions abroad had as their principle "no more Vietnams." Other Americans, troubled at the shame and sense of impotence that came out of the American failure along with the timidity about getting into foreign entanglements, defined a "Vietnam syndrome." They meant a sick mood of national self-doubt and a fear of action abroad. The Gulf War, numbers of people believed, had ended

Source: The Los Angeles Times, March 2, 1991, 1, 14. Reprinted by permission.

the Vietnam syndrome, as this article from The Los Angeles Times *demonstrates. It is by staff writers Edwin Chen and Paul Richter.*

The war was won and, as the feelings of common soldiers came rushing to the surface, there was one common thread.

"I think this war has healed the wounds of the Vietnam War," said Maj. Baxter Ennis. "Our country really came together spiritually."

For Spec. 4 Brannon Lamar of North Augusta, S.C., it was summed up in a single event: "When we took all those POWs and didn't mistreat them or gun them down, I wanted to cry," he said. "I was so proud to be a U.S. soldier. Maybe we are the good guys this time."

And Emmet Robinson, a burly sergeant in the 82nd Airborne Division, called his men together to make sure even the youngest of them did not miss the point: "Twenty years ago, I went into a situation like this for the first time," he barked.

"Twenty years ago, I came home a loser. . . . You've done something you have a right to be proud of."

Indeed so. After a lightning victory over Iraq that exceeded all expectations, America's fighting men and women are coming home as heroes to a country that—because of them—is no longer tormented by the humiliating memory of Vietnam.

Their victory has charged America with a surge of patriotism that has made military commanders popular heroes, brought predictions of surging military enlistments, and purged the country of the "Vietnam syndrome" that made Americans reluctant to commit military force for 25 years.

"By God, we've kicked this Vietnam syndrome," President Bush declared to state legislators Friday at a Washington conference of the American Legislative Exchange Council.

Burying the ghost of Vietnam could mean Americans may now be inclined toward a more assertive foreign policy—a prospect that some view with hope and others with apprehension.

"We've been living with the Vietnam syndrome for so long, and this war brings back the imagery of World War II," said Rep. Jim Leach (R-Iowa). "There's been an underestimation of our strength for a long time."

Robert W. Hess, who was an Army sergeant in World War II and is now commander of the Garden Grove, Calif., VFW post, agreed. "Once people see how well things like this can turn out, I think people will be willing to do more of them," he said.

On the other hand, some worried that the Vietnam syndrome could be replaced with a "Kuwait syndrome," in which the country might become too cocky about its military capacities and to quick to resort to force.

"Our irrational fears that the military can't do the job may be replaced with the equally unrealistic belief that they're invincible and should be used for any and all problems," said Alan Brinkley, a professor of history at City University of New York. "There's a healthy aspect to the end of this Vietnam syndrome, and there's a dangerous one."

There were some reassuring voices on this point, though, including some from foreign leaders, who might be expected to fear a more interventionist America. "If the superpower is managed by democracy's rules, there is no danger," said Turkish President Turgut Ozal.

Yet there is more to the end of the Vietnam syndrome than a new willingness to dispatch troops to the Third World.

For many of the troops in the field today, it means rendering proper respect for the sacrifices of soldiers.

In the Gulf, "the military did its job," Capt. Clint Esarey of the 82nd Airborne said Friday. "Now it's up to the American public to do its job and welcome these guys back home."

For others, including the chairman of the Joint Chiefs of Staff, Gen. Colin L. Powell, the syndrome has meant that force should never be used unless the nation was willing to commit all its energies and powers at once.

The Reagan Administration sought to shake off the Vietnam syndrome as it invaded Grenada in 1983 and bombed Libya in 1986. But its decision-making was marked by a debilitating intramural fight that pitted a reluctant Secretary of Defense Caspar W. Weinberger against a more assertive Secretary of State George P. Shultz.

The malaise colored the debate about whether the United States should go to war in the Gulf to begin with. It was a key reason that many of the predictions about the war were so wide of the mark, some say.

"People thought we'd get bogged down, that there would be thousands of body bags coming back, that the Arab allies would turn against us and we'd lose even if we won," said Tony Coelho, a former Democratic congressman from California. "But the experts were remembering the last war, and they were all wrong."

Indeed, Coelho observed that the Vietnam syndrome is part of a skepticism about America's abilities that stems not only from the Southeast Asian experience, but from a series of frustrations in military and foreign affairs.

They include the military's troubles in building reliable high-tech weapons, the technical failures of the space effort, the logistics snarls during the invasions of Panama and Grenada—and even America's embarrassing performance in its economic competition with Japan and Germany.

"We've been in such a downer for so long," said Coelho, now an investment banker in New York. "It's looked like we couldn't get anything done in the world."

"I think there will remain a lot of caution," asserted Stanley Karnow, author of "Vietnam: A History." "Remember that even [Desert Storm commander Gen. H. Norman Schwarzkopf] warned that there was a lot of risk in a ground war. We're not returning to the days when President [John F.] Kennedy could warn in his inaugural that we would defend any friend, oppose any foe."

Even so, it doesn't diminish the pride that most Americans—and perhaps especially the troops—feel over the role they have played in the Gulf.

"I'm feeling great," said Sgt. Margaret Taylor of Charleston, S.C. "We stood up to a tyrant."

And Sgt. Robinson, the former Vietnam paratrooper now in the Gulf with the 82nd Airborne, said he's happy to have had a chance to improve his score. "I'm 50-50 now. Won one and lost one."

Vietnam Memorial. When soldiers came home from Vietnam, they received no general homecoming or welcome, no outpouring of support and respect as heroic defenders of freedom abroad. Many returning veterans simply slipped quietly back into the lives they had left behind. The dedication of the Vietnam Memorial in Washington, D.C., in 1982 marked the beginning of a process of reconciliation that is still going on.

A SELECTED BIBLIOGRAPHY

By at least one estimate, in the past twenty years more than seven thousand titles have appeared dealing with Vietnam and the Indochina wars. Added to the enormous number of books produced before 1973, the year of the Paris Peace Agreements and the formal withdrawal of United States troops from Vietnam, the amount of scholarship available about Vietnam and the American involvement in Vietnam is daunting to even the most experienced student. Among other things it assures that this bibliography will be very selective. Except whenever a history or a commentary stands out for the singularity of its contribution to understanding an issue related to Vietnam, we have chosen to concentrate on materials that have appeared since 1985 and where appropriate only the most recent of this scholarship (for pre-1985 materials consult one of the sources listed in the section below on reference works).

A reason why publishing works related to Vietnam, and especially the American engagement there, has proven a growth industry is that the American involvement there during what is sometimes called the Second Indochina War, 1954–1975, was among the most divisive events in the nation's history. The American public split along a variety of lines. They fell into the familiar categories of "hawks" who supported the war and "doves" who opposed it. Social and class differences separated white collar parents and college students from working class families having no student deferments to shelter them from the draft. Race became a factor: African Americans claimed that blacks, especially poor blacks, were disproportionately represented in the military and carried an excessive responsibility for the fighting, and dying, in Vietnam. Against left intellectuals critical of American policy, the war pitted anticommunist neo-conservatives and a populist anticommunism located in veterans' organizations and traditionalist religions, and among blue collar hardhats. There was also a generational split. Many young people flocked to various organizations within the peace movement to demonstrate against the war and to support candidates like Eugene McCarthy and Robert F. Kennedy. Some youth dropped out altogether and became part of the counterculture, consciously separating themselves from older generations. Evidence suggests a regional division over the war, much of the urban, cosmopolitan Northeast urging disengagement and the more rural and poorer South, home to a large number of military bases, more generally supportive of the war. Feminist authors have begun to trace gender oppression among American attitudes toward the war. They define a paternalistic foreign policy that reflected domestic American patriarchialism and observe the patronizing treatment of American female military personnel and the especially brutal conduct of some American soldiers toward Vietnamese women.

In addition to being among the country's most divisive wars Vietnam was also the longest conflict in which the United States had been involved. Historians continue to argue over how the nation got into Vietnam. Most are agreed, however, on the stages of escalating American participation in South Vietnam's war against the North. Military advisers were sent to South Vietnam in 1954 during the Eisenhower administration. During the Kennedy years, going from 1961 to November 1963, the number of advisers increased greatly. Direct military intervention began, of course, with Lyndon Johnson. At the end of the Johnson presidency, running from 1963 to 1969, American military personnel in Vietnam reached a peak of approximately 540,000. Richard Nixon, becoming Chief Executive in 1969, presided over the slow but steady withdrawal of American forces. By December 1972 about 24,000 U.S. troops remained in South Vietnam. Nixon resigned his office in August 1974 and by the end of that year there were only fifty American military personnel in South Vietnam. As the South Vietnamese regime collapsed in April 1975, President Gerald Ford ordered the evacuation of all American personnel from the United States embassy in Saigon. When they left, more than twenty years of American military presence in Vietnam came to an end. During that generation of war 46,163 Americans had been killed in action, another 10,298 Americans died of noncombat causes and approximately 1,800 were declared missing, and more than 300,000 were wounded. Between January 1961 and January 1973 the South Vietnamese suffered the loss of 635,357 killed, 415,000 of whom were civilians, and 1,434,026 wounded, 935,000 of them civilians. Casualty figures for the Vietcong and North Vietnamese during the same period are less certain: estimates for military killed in action range from 666,000 to 924,048; civilian losses in North Vietnam have been estimated at 65,000.

Also contributing to the ongoing interest in Vietnam and the debate over its meaning was the maturing of the Vietnam generation of Americans—the young men and women who in the 1960s and early 1970s had fought the war or campaigned against it. Hawk or dove, veteran or protester, those who grew up in the Vietnam era now head families and corporations. They fashion the institutions of education and culture. They write the nation's textbooks and novels, they make its movies, and they partake in government and determine its interests. A former antiwar activist, Bill Clinton, now holds the presidency and serving alongside him as Vice President is a Vietnam veteran, Al Gore. And the experience of Vietnam, the conflicts it engendered, continue to influence that generation's thinking and stamp its activities. The Vietnam generation, like other generations shaped in war, is obsessed with its history.

And just as the Vietnam era's young people found fascination in the wars that defined their parents lives, World War II and Korea, so too are their children, now of college age and older, absorbed by the event that did so much to fashion the lives of their own parents, the event that, good and bad, is their legacy. Enrollments in college courses dealing with Vietnam are among the highest on campus. Courses in subjects related to the war are in equally high demand.

All that surrounded the war or preceded the war or was created by the war— all that went to make up what is known as the sixties—stimulates great interest among the young: the civil rights movement, the youth movement, feminism, the rise of the New Left, and the counterculture. Students sense that everything in their own world is somehow touched by Vietnam. Although they may not share the ideological commitments and the social and intellectual enthusiasms of their parents, they seem determined to understand Vietnam. They are, however, more confused about the meaning of Vietnam, less certain of its moral content, and more curious about its ambiguities and consequences than the generation who lived through the war. But their interest is not academic: it's personal.

The American involvement in Vietnam had an immediacy and public intimacy absent from all other recent military actions, including the Persian Gulf War of 1991. Vietnam, one critic notes, was "the world's first television war." Nightly news coverage of events in Vietnam accompanied by grisly images of wounded or dead American soldiers and Vietnamese civilians stunned an American public that preferred a more sanitized and romantic view of war. Supporters of the war claimed, and continue to claim, that the media gave too much attention to the antiwar movement and contributed to the American loss in Vietnam by turning the public against the war. Critics of the war argue that the media have been made a scapegoat by military leaders and politicians who pursued poor policies: the bureaucracy was responsible for Vietnam, not the media.

Both critics and supporters of the war talk about the American defeat in Vietnam although by the usual standard of judging military success, winning battles, American troops conducted themselves effectively. Even the all-out assault on the South by the North Vietnamese and Vietcong in the 1968 Tet Offensive, which is usually viewed as the turning point in the American commitment to Vietnam, was repelled by American and South Vietnamese forces. But the winning of battles did not determine the outcome of the war. The rapid collapse of South Vietnam in face of an invasion by the North in January 1975, two years after the Paris Peace Agreement, and the mad scramble of evacuees to board American helicopters at the end of April with the fall of Saigon— reported as it occurred by journalists and captured by news cameras—have conveyed an image of the United States run to ground and defeated. Like the issue of the role of the media during the war, the conclusion that Vietnam was the nation's first wartime defeat assures that the American involvement in Southeast Asia will continue to provoke interest and argument.

The study of the Indochina wars and the United States in Vietnam might begin, then, with some of the images that had such an important place in fixing American policy in Southeast Asia and in influencing American attitudes toward the Vietnamese and the war. In the fall of 1983 the Public Broadcasting Service (PBS) aired a thirteen-part series, *Vietnam: A Television History* (Boston: WGBH Educational Foundation, 1983). The documentary rapidly became one of the most significant teaching tools on the war; colleges across the country designed courses around the series, which was a visual and oral account of the some thirty years of American engagement in Vietnam beginning soon after the expulsion of the Japanese from the country in 1945. Although acclaimed by most reviewers, the program received criticism. Many believed that the series was deeply flawed, driven by ideology: too disapproving of the United States and far too unreproachful of the Vietnamese Communists. Reed Irvine, one of the founders of the conservative media watchdog group Accuracy in Media, Inc. (AIM), was among the harshest critics. AIM produced two video programs, *Vietnam: The Real Story* (1984) and *Vietnam: The Impact of Media* (1985), purporting to expose the liberal bias in the PBS series and offering a sustained rebuttal to much within the documentary. Other criticisms of the series are R. C. Raack, "Caveat Spectator," *OAH Newsletter*, 12 (February 1984): 25–28, and Stephen J. Morris, "Vietnam, A Dual-Vision History," *The Wall Street Journal* (December 20, 1983): 30. Stephen Vlastos, "Television Wars: Representations of the Vietnam War in Television Documentaries," *Radical History Review*, 36 (1986): 115–132, analyzes the PBS program and AIM's criticisms.

Among the fine guides and reference works to the many sources, books, articles, public documents, and other materials dealing with Vietnam and the American involvement in Indochina are three volumes of bibliography produced for the Center for Armament and Disarmament at California State University, Los Angeles, under the general editorship of Richard Dean Burns. They are Milton Leitenberg and Richard Dean Burns, *The Vietnam Conflict: Its Geographical Dimensions, Political Traumas, and Military Developments* (Santa Barbara, CA: ABC-Clio, 1973); Richard Dean Burns and Milton Leitenberg, *The Wars in Vietnam, Cambodia and Laos, 1945–1982: A Bibliographic Guide* (Santa Barbara, CA: ABC-Clio, 1984); and Lester H. Brune and Richard Dean Burns, *America and the Indochina Wars, 1945–1990: A Bibliographical Guide* (Claremont, CA: Regina Books, 1992). The Burns bibliographies provide brief descriptions of the sources they list. James S. Olson in *The Vietnam War: Handbook of the Literature and Research* (Westport, CT: Greenwood Press, 1993) has assembled a collection of bibliographic essays that provide a more thorough and critical assessment of recent works on Vietnam. Marc Jason Gilbert's *The Vietnam War: Teaching Approaches and Resources* (Westport, CT: Greenwood Press, 1991) similarly offers a critical treatment of materials. Two sources organized very much alike help sort out the bewildering array of names, events, places, military acronyms, and statistics, among the other detail associated with the American involvement in Vietnam: William J. Duiker, *Historical Dictionary of Vietnam* (Metuchen, NJ: Scarecrow Press, Inc., 1989) and James S. Olson, ed., *Dictionary of the Vietnam War* (Westport, CT: Greenwood Press, 1988). Other reference guides include D. J. Sagar, *Major Political Events in Indo-China, 1945–1990* (New York: Facts on File, Inc., 1991); Louis A. Peake, *The United States in the Vietnam War, 1954–1975: A Selected, Annotated Bibliography* (New York: Garland Publishing, Inc., 1986); and Michael Cotter, *Vietnam: A Guide to Reference Sources* (Boston: G. K. Hall and Co., 1977).

One of the most extensive collections of materials on Vietnam—including items in French and Vietnamese—is housed at Cornell University's Olin Library. Many of these are listed in Christopher Sugnet, John T. Hickey, and Robert Crispino, *Vietnam War Bibliography: Selected from Cornell University's Echols Collection* (Lexington, MA: Lexington Books, D. C. Heath and Co., 1983). The World Bibliographical Series, Robert G. Neville, Executive Editor, contains two volumes relevant to the study of Indochina and its history: David

G. Marr, comp., with the assistance of Kristine Alilunas-Rodgers, *Vietnam* [Vol. 147] (Oxford, England: Clio Press, 1992) and Helen Cordell, comp., *Laos* [Vol. 133] (Oxford, England: Clio Press, 1991). Documents sources on the American engagement in Southeast Asia are abundant. One is essential: *The Pentagon Papers, The Senator Gavel Edition*, 5 vols. (Boston: Beacon Press, 1971–1972). Volumes one through four are documents and volume five contains some supplementary essays and an index. In *The Pentagon Papers: As Published by The New York Times* (New York: Quadrangle Books, 1971), Neil Sheehan and others have assembled a useful selection of documents along with commentary that serve as a good introduction to the papers. Despite its pretentious title, Gareth Porter's *Vietnam: The Definitive Documentation of Human Decisions*, 2 vols. (Stanfordville, NY: Earl M. Coleman Enterprises, Inc., 1979) is a valuable selection of documents covering the years from 1941 through 1975. The documentation in the Pentagon Papers concludes in 1968.

The war in Vietnam has inspired much fiction and nonfiction: novels—many good, most not so good—short stories, plays, and, perhaps most important and revealing, many personal narratives and wartime reminiscences of combatants and noncombatants, supporters of the war and antiwar activists. Many of these are described in Sandra M. Wittman, *Writing About Vietnam: A Bibliography of the Literature of the Vietnam Conflict* (Boston: G. K. Hall and Co., 1989). There are other guides to areas of special interest. Myron J. Smith, Jr.'s *Air War, Southeast Asia, 1961–1973: An Annotated Bibliography and 16mm Film Guide* (Metuchen, NJ: Scarecrow Press, 1979), for example, lists studies covering this critical component of the American military campaign. Interest in the special problems of the Vietnam veterans has created a growing body of literature, much of it reported in Norman M. Camp, Robert H. Stretch, and William C. Marshall, *Stress, Strain, and Vietnam: An Annotated Bibliography of Two Decades of Psychiatric and Social Sciences Literature Reflecting the Effect of the War on the American Soldier* (Westport, CT: Greenwood Press, 1988).

The American involvement in Vietnam was the longest continuous military engagement this nation has had with a foreign power in its history, spanning three decades. A number of professional historians and journalists have tried in general works to capture that story and the events that led to it. Among the most prominent of these is journalist Stanley Karnow's *Vietnam: A History*, revised and updated ed. (New York: Penguin Books, 1991), which originally appeared in 1983 as the companion volume for the controversial PBS series *Vietnam: A Television History*, Karnow serving as one of the producers and chief correspondent. Recent broad histories include George C. Herring, *America's Longest War: The United States and Vietnam, 1950–1975*, rev. ed. (New York: Knopf, 1986); William S. Turley, *The Second Indochina War: A Short Political and Military History, 1954–1975* (Boulder, CO: Westview Press, 1986); and James S. Olson and Randy Roberts, *Where the Domino Fell, America and Vietnam, 1945 to 1990* (New York: St. Martin's Press, 1991). A series of twenty-nine volumes on a variety of topics relating to Vietnam—each of the volumes contains a large selection of photographs—has been assembled in Robert Manning, editor-in-chief, *The Vietnam Experience* (Boston: Boston Publishing Company, 1981–1988). Marilyn B. Young's *The Vietnam Wars, 1945–1990* (New York:

Harper-Collins, 1991) is very critical of American policy toward Vietnam as is journalist Neil Sheehan's Pulitzer Prize-winning *The Bright and Shining Lie: John Paul Vann and America in Vietnam* (New York: Random House, 1988). Gabriel Kolko, a historian who makes his radical sympathies explicit, argues in *Anatomy of a War: Vietnam, the United States, and the Modern Historical Experience* (New York: Pantheon, 1985) that the United States intervention in Southeast Asia was part of its imperial design to establish an American hegemony in the Pacific. One of the earliest works to stress the American misunderstanding of the commitment of the Vietnamese, and especially the Communist Vietnamese, to nationalism is Frances Fitzgerald's *Fire in the Lake: The Vietnamese and the Americans in Vietnam* (Boston: An Atlantic Monthly Press Book, Little, Brown and Company, 1972). Ms. Fitzgerald has been criticized for her sympathetic portrait of the Communist National Liberation Front. Works—revisionist histories—that view the American role in Vietnam in a more positive light include Guenter Lewy, *America in Vietnam* (New York: Oxford University Press, 1978) and Timothy J. Lomperis, *The War Everyone Lost—And Won: America's Intervention in Vietnam's Twin Struggles* (Baton Rouge: Louisiana University Press, 1984). Lomperis gives special attention to the military history of the American involvement and argues that the United States could have defeated the North Vietnamese, thereby establishing a strong and stable government in South Vietnam. Revisionist histories defending the American presence in Vietnam, however, are few in number.

The Vietnamese struggle for autonomy has a history longer than that of the United States and grows out of a culture, as Frances Fitzgerald among others has observed, richly influenced by China and yet fiercely jealous of its independence. The history and culture of Vietnam are described in Keith Weller Taylor, *The Birth of Vietnam* (Berkeley: University of California Press, 1983) and Milton E. Osborne, *Southeast Asia: An Introductory History*, 5th ed. (New York: Harper-Collins, 1991). Also see Pham Kim Vinh's *The Vietnamese Culture: An Introduction* (Costa Mesa, CA: Pham Kim Vinh Research Institute, 1990). A brief overview of the history of Vietnam may be found in John K. Whitmore, "An Outline of Vietnamese History Before the French Conquest," *Vietnam Forum*, 8 (Summer/Fall 1986): 1–9. See also Whitmore's longer *Vietnam, Ho Quy, and the Ming* (New Haven, CT: Yale University Southeast Asian Studies Program, 1985). A recent study of Vietnamese culture and the Vietnamese outlook on the world is Neil L. Jamieson's *Understanding Vietnam* (Berkeley: University of California Press, 1993). A series of studies by Joseph Buttinger concentrates largely on the political life of the Vietnamese: *The Smaller Dragon: A Political History of Vietnam* (New York: Praeger, 1958); *Vietnam: A Dragon Embattled*, 2 vols. (New York: Praeger, 1967); and *Vietnam: A Political History* (New York: Praeger, 1968). A source that recounts some of the longstanding and bitter antagonisms between China and Vietnam is Henry McAleavy's *Black Flags in Vietnam: The Story of a Chinese Intervention* (New York: Macmillan, 1968). Edgar Wickberg's *Historical Interaction of China and Vietnam* (New York: Paragon Book Gallery, 1969) provides a more thorough assessment of the Chinese influence on Vietnam and the Vietnamese response. Truong B. Lam's *Resistance—Rebellion—Revolution: Popular Movements in Vietnamese History*

(New York: Gower, 1984) also examines the relations between the Chinese and the Vietnamese people. The religious and ethnic diversity of Vietnam are discussed in Pierro Gheddo's *The Cross and the Bo-Tree: Catholics and Buddhists in Vietnam*, trans. by Charles U. Quinn (New York: Sheed and Ward, 1970) and in three anthropological works by Gerald C. Hickey: *Village in Vietnam* (New Haven, CT: Yale University Press, 1967); *Sons of the Mountain: Ethnohistory of the Vietnamese Central Highlands to 1954* (New Haven, CT: Yale University Press, 1982); and *Free in the Forest: Ethnohistory of the Vietnamese Central Highlands, 1954–1976* (New Haven, CT: Yale University Press, 1982).

Before the Americans came to Vietnam there were the French. And before the United States fought the Second Indochina War (1954–1975) France battled the Vietminh forces led by Ho Chi Minh in the First Indochina War (1945–1954). The story of French colonialism and the almost hundred years of French occupation of Indochina that began in the mid-nineteenth century is told in John F. Cady, *The Roots of French Imperialism in Eastern Asia* (Ithaca, NY: Cornell University Press, 1954); Milton E. Osborne, *The French Presence in Cochinchina and Cambodia: Rule and Response, 1859–1905* (Ithaca, NY: Cornell University Press, 1969); and Martin Murray, *The Development of Capitalism in Colonial Indochina, 1870–1940* (Berkeley: University of California Press, 1980). Somewhat dated but still considered a classic is Virginia Thompson's *French Indo-China* (New York: Octagon Books, 1968, reprint; orig. published, 1937), which describes French expansion in Southeast Asia. The spread of French influence in late nineteenth-century Vietnam is considered in Gerald C. Hickey's *Kingdom in the Morning Mist: Mayrena in the Highlands of Vietnam* (Philadelphia: University of Pennsylvania Press, 1984). Life for the Vietnamese peasants under French rule is told in three books: Ngo Ving Long, *Before the Revolution: The Vietnamese Peasants Under the French* (Cambridge, MA: MIT Press, 1973); Pham Cao Duong, *Vietnamese Peasants Under French Domination, 1901–1945* (Lanham, MD: University Press of America, 1985); and Tu Binh Tran, *The Red Earth: A Vietnamese Memoir of Life On a Colonial Rubber Plantation* (Athens: Ohio University Press, 1985).

Vietnamese nationalism and the Vietnamese tradition of resistance to foreign occupation were the sources of much of the anti-French sentiment that led to the First Indochina War. Background on the Vietnamese independence movement is provided in Mark M. McLeod, *The Vietnamese Response to French Intervention, 1862–1874* (New York: Praeger, 1991); William J. Duiker, *The Rise of Nationalism in Vietnam, 1900–1941* (Ithaca, NY: Cornell University Press, 1975); Troung Buu Lam, *Patterns of Vietnamese Response to Foreign Intervention, 1858–1900* (New Haven, CT: Yale University Press, 1967); and Thomas Hodgkin, *Vietnam: The Revolutionary Path* (New York: St. Martin's Press, 1981). Also see Ralph B. Smith's "The Development of Opposition to French Rule in Southern Vietnam, 1880–1940," *Past and Present*, 54 (1972): 94–129, and two studies by David Marr, *Vietnamese Anti-Colonialism, 1885–1925* (Berkeley: University of California Press, 1971) and *Vietnamese Tradition on Trial, 1920–1945* (Berkeley: University of California Press, 1981).

When France determined to resume her control over Vietnam at the end of the Second World War many Vietnamese were prepared to resist this reassertion of French colonialism. The First Vietnam War, 1946–1954, is the subject of French historian Jacques Dalloz's *The War in Indochina, 1945–1954* (Savage, MD: Barnes and Noble, 1990) and Ellen J. Hammer's *The Struggle for Indochina, 1940–1955* (Stanford, CA: Stanford University Press, 1966). Also see Donald Lancaster, *The Emancipation of French Indochina* (New York: Octagon Books, 1974). French journalist Bernard Fall, who covered most of the major events in Vietnam until his death during the Second Vietnam War, was a harsh critic of French policies in Vietnam. (Later, he was equally severe in his treatment of the American program.) In *Street Without Joy: Insurgency in Indochina*, 4th ed. (London: Pall Mall Press, 1965), he describes French military activities during the war. The military history of the war is also covered in Edgar O'Ballance, *The Indo-China War, 1945–1954: A Study in Guerrilla Warfare* (London: Faber and Faber, 1964). Vo Nguyen Giap's *Unforgettable Days* (Hanoi: Foreign Language Publishing House, 1978) is an account of the war by the commanding general of the Vietminh forces that finally defeated the French. The decisive battle of the conflict at Dien Bien Phu, which began in early March 1954 and ended with the French surrender on May 7, is described by Bernard Fall in *Hell in a Very Small Place: The Siege of Dien Bien Phu* (Philadelphia: Lippincott, 1967) and by Jules Roy in *The Battle of Dien Bien Phu*, trans. by Robert Baldich (New York: Harper and Row, 1965). Giap gives his view of the confrontation in *Dien Bien Phu* (Hanoi: Foreign Language Publishing House, 1962). The conclusion of the war and the consequences of the fall of France in Indochina are examined in three works: Lawrence Kaplan, Denise Artaud, and Mark R. Rubin, *Dien Bien Phu and the Crisis of Franco-American Relations, 1954–1955* (Washington, DC: Scholarly Resources, 1989); Philippe Devillers and Jean Lacouture, *End of a War: Indochina, 1954* (New York: Praeger, 1969); and Robert F. Randle, *Geneva 1954: The Settlement of the Indochinese War* (Princeton, NJ: Princeton University Press, 1969). Edward Rice-Maximin's *Accommodation and Resistance: The French Left, Indochina and the Cold War, 1944–1954* (Westport, CT: Greenwood Press, 1986) offers a fresh view of the relation of western politics after World War II to activities affecting Indochina.

The French loss in Vietnam, so many westerners reasoned, signaled a triumph for the Vietnamese Communists that posed a threat to western-style democracies. Vietminh leaders, however, claimed that their attachment to Communism was of much less importance than their desire to unify their nation as an independent Vietnam. Scholars and analysts continue to debate the place of Communism and nationalism in the later history of Vietnam and the relative strength of the one to the other. Whether viewed as a nationalist, a Communist, or a combination of both, Ho Chi Minh was Vietnam's best known political figure. A number of good biographies exist. See especially Jean Lacouture's *Ho Chi Minh: A Political Biography* (New York: Random House, 1968) and journalist David Halberstam's *Ho* (New York: Random House, 1971). Ho Chi Minh's writings and speeches are available in four volumes of his *Selected Works* (Hanoi: Foreign Language Publishing House, 1962–1964) and in his *Prison Diary* (Hanoi: Foreign Language Publishing House, 1967). Edited collections of Ho's works are perhaps more readily accessible. See, for example, Bernard B. Fall, ed., *Ho Chi Minh on Revolution: Selected Writings, 1920–1964* (New York:

Praeger, 1967) and Jack Woodis, ed., *Ho Chi Minh: Selected Articles and Speeches, 1920–1967* (New York: International Publishers, 1970). On the origins and nature of the Communist movement in Vietnam, consult these histories: Khanh Huyunh Kim, *Vietnamese Communism, 1925–1945* (Ithaca, NY: Cornell University Press, 1982); William J. Duiker, *The Communist Road to Power in Vietnam* (Boulder, CO: Westview Press, 1981); Douglas Pike, *History of Vietnamese Communism, 1925–1976* (Palo Alto, CA: Hoover Institution Press, 1978); and Robert F. Turner's sharply disapproving *Vietnamese Communism: Its Origins and Development* (Stanford, CA: Hoover Institution Press, 1975).

Whatever Communism may have meant to Ho Chi Minh and his followers, the United States in its Cold War strategy of confronting what it understood to be the aggressive intentions of the Communists could not ignore the presence of Communism in Southeast Asia. The specific collection of events and reasons that led to the American involvement in Vietnam are still hotly contested issues. But few would question that American interest in Indochina began with an uneasiness about the presence of a threatening ideology in the region that escalated over time into a full-blown war against Communism. The United States then used anticommunism, and the loss of American lives, to justify and make sense of its continuing presence in Southeast Asia. Contributing to the debate over the origins of the American engagement in Vietnam are a number of studies. See, for example, these works all of which argue for a complex set of factors, domestic and international, that led to the involvement: Gary R. Hess, *The United States Emergence as a Southeast Asian Power, 1940–1950* (New York: Columbia University, 1987); Andrew J. Rotter, *The Path to Vietnam: Origins of the American Commitment to Southeast Asia* (Ithaca, NY: Cornell University Press, 1987); and Robert M. Blum, *Drawing the Line: The United States and Containment in Southeast Asia, 1945–1949* (New York: Norton, 1982). Studies more critical of American policymakers include George M. Kahin, *Intervention: How America Became Involved in Vietnam* (New York: Knopf, 1986); Richard J. Barnet, *Roots of War: The Men and Institutions Behind U.S. Foreign Policy* (New York: Atheneum, 1971); and Gabriel Kolko, *Anatomy of a War: Vietnam, the United States, and the Modern Historical Experience* (1985). Sandra C. Taylor in "Vietnam: In the Beginning," *Reviews in American History*, 17 (June 1989): 306–311, surveys the historical literature dealing with the initial phase of the American presence in Southeast Asia from 1941 to 1956. Conflicting views about the role of the United States in Southeast Asia, including the origins of the involvement and other issues surrounding the war, have been assembled in John Norton Moore, ed., *The Vietnam Debate: A Fresh Look at the Arguments* (Lanham, MD: University Press of America, 1990). Susan Jeffords's *The Remasculinization of America: Gender and the Vietnam War* (Bloomington: Indiana University Press, 1989) offers a provocative feminist perspective on the United States and the Second Indochina War.

The increasing commitment of the United States to Vietnam was closely related to American politics, especially American presidential policymaking. Essays on the leadership skills and Southeast Asia policies of Presidents from Harry S Truman through Gerald R. Ford are collected in David L. Anderson, ed., *Shadow on the White House: Presidents and the Vietnam War, 1945–1975*

(Lawrence: University Press of Kansas, 1993). It is generally believed Franklin Roosevelt hoped that World War II would bring an end to European colonialism in the region; he was not, however, prepared to prevent the French or British from reestablishing dominion there. On Roosevelt's thinking two good essays are Gary R. Hess, "Franklin Roosevelt and Indochina," *Journal of American History*, 59 (September 1972): 353–368, and Walter LaFeber, "Roosevelt, Churchill and Indochina: 1942–1945," *American Historical Review*, 80 (December 1975): 1277–1295. Edward R. Drachman's *United States Policy Toward Vietnam, 1940–1945* (Rutherford, NJ: Fairleigh Dickinson University Press, 1970) is also useful on the FDR years. An abundance of literature discusses extensively or in passing the bearing of other presidencies on Southeast Asia.

The Truman years began the Cold War era and serious American interest in Southeast Asia. In his two volume biography of Truman, *Conflict and Crisis: The Presidency of Harry S Truman, 1945–1948* (New York: Norton, 1977) and *Tumultuous Years: The Presidency of Harry S Truman, 1949–1953* (New York: Norton, 1982), Robert J. Donovan provides a good review of White House policies. David McCullough's *Truman* (New York: Simon and Schuster, 1992) is a more recent and more readable single volume history, but it is also less analytical. On Truman's attitude to the reassertion of French power in Indochina, see George C. Herring's "The Truman Administration and the Restoration of French Sovereignty in Indochina," *Diplomatic History*, 1 (Spring 1977): 97–117. Melvyn P. Leffler's *A Preponderance of Power: National Security, the Truman Administration, and the Cold War* (Stanford, CA: Stanford University Press, 1992) discusses the place of Southeast Asia in the Cold War strategies of Truman and his advisers. Also see Lloyd C. Gardner, *Approaching Vietnam: From World War II Through Dienbienphu, 1941–1954* (New York: Norton, 1988). David S. McLellan's *Dean Acheson: The State Department Years* (New York: Dodd, Mead, 1976) examines the public life of Dean Acheson, Truman's Secretary of State and one of the principal architects of the Cold War policy of containment. Acheson's memoirs, *Present at the Creation: My Years in the State Department* (New York: Norton, 1969), describe his policies and views for the years 1941 to 1953. Douglas Brinkley's *Dean Acheson: The Cold War Years, 1953–1971* (New Haven, CT: Yale University Press, 1992) assesses Acheson's thinking after 1953 and the role he played as foreign policy adviser to later Presidents.

The American involvement in Southeast Asia deepened during the Republican administration of Dwight D. Eisenhower and the American commitment to opposing Communism was further strengthened by the articulation of the "domino theory." David L. Anderson's *Trapped by Success: The Eisenhower Administration and Vietnam, 1953–1961* (New York: Columbia University Press, 1991) is an excellent treatment of Eisenhower's Indochina policies. Among other things Anderson demonstrates how the United States became tied to South Vietnam and to supporting the administration of Ngo Dinh Diem. Eisenhower in two volumes of memoirs, *The White House Years: Mandate for Change, 1953–1956* (Garden City, NY: Doubleday, 1963) and *The White House Years: Waging Peace, 1956–1961* (Garden City, NY: Doubleday, 1965), gives his own account of his policies. Some of Ike's chief strategists are discussed in H. W. Brands, Jr.,

Cold Warriors: Eisenhower's Generation and American Foreign Policy (New York: Columbia University Press, 1988). Succeeding Acheson at the State Department was John Foster Dulles, Eisenhower's chief adviser on foreign affairs. Dulles pursued an aggressive anticommunist policy. Two recent studies of Dulles are Frederick Marks III, *Power and Peace: The Diplomacy of John Foster Dulles* (Westport, CT: Praeger, 1993) and Richard H. Immerman, ed., *John Foster Dulles and the Diplomacy of the Cold War: A Reappraisal* (Princeton, NJ: Princeton University Press, 1989). On the administration's decision not to aid the French at Dien Bien Phu, see George C. Herring and Richard H. Immerman, "Eisenhower, Dulles, and Dienbienphu: 'The Day We Didn't Go to War' Revisited," *Journal of American History*, 71 (September 1984): 343–363.

John F. Kennedy inherited a "time-bomb" in Vietnam, one historian asserts. That is an arguable view, of course. It suggests that decisions made during previous administrations made inevitable the escalating American involvement in Vietnam. President Kennedy ought to be judged for his own decisions. Although it is by no means clear that Kennedy welcomed a further commitment in Vietnam, he was a tenacious cold warrior and anticommunist. It was his decision substantially to increase American aid to South Vietnam, to expand the American military presence there, and to give the military a larger combat role. Recent favorable assessments of the Kennedy presidency are Irving Bernstein, *Promises Kept: John F. Kennedy's New Frontier* (New York: Oxford University Press, 1990) and David Burner, *John F. Kennedy and a New Generation* (Glenview, IL: Scott, Foresman and Company, 1988). Thomas Reeves's *A Question of Character: John F. Kennedy in Image and Reality* (New York: Free Press, 1990) describes Kennedy's private self and his public persona. The Kennedy ideology and its influence on foreign policy are a subject of David Burner and Thomas R. West, *The Torch is Passed: The Kennedy Brothers and American Liberalism* (St. James, NY: Brandywine Press, 1991). Works that give special attention to John Kennedy and Vietnam include William J. Rust, *Kennedy in Vietnam: American Foreign Policy, 1960–1963* (New York: Da Capo Press, 1987); R. B. Smith, *An International History of the Vietnam War: The Kennedy Strategy* (New York: St. Martin's Press, 1987); and John M. Newman, *JFK and Vietnam: Deception, Intrigue, and the Struggle for Power* (New York: Warner Books, 1992). In *The Making of a Quagmire: America and Vietnam During the Kennedy Era* (New York: Knopf, 1965), David Halberstam argues that it was a mistake for Kennedy to support the corrupt Diem regime in South Vietnam for as long as he did. Kennedy administration advisers have received a good deal of attention and many have offered their own view of events. David Halberstam's *The Best and the Brightest* (New York: Random House, 1972) describes many of the principals who served during the 1960s in the Kennedy and Johnson White Houses. Works by Kennedy advisers include Roger Hilsman, *To Move a Nation: The Politics of Foreign Policy in the Administration of John F. Kennedy* (Garden City, NY: Doubleday, 1967); George W. Ball, *The Past Has Another Pattern: Memoirs* (New York: Norton, 1982); Walt W. Rostow, *The Diffusion of Power, 1957–1972* (New York: Macmillan, 1972); Frederick Nolting, *From Trust to Tragedy: The Political Memoirs of Frederick Nolting, Kennedy's Ambassador to Diem's Vietnam* (New York: Praeger, 1988); and Dean Rusk, *As I Saw It: The*

Memoirs of Dean Rusk (New York: Norton, 1990). Warren I. Cohen's *Dean Rusk* (Totowa, NJ: Cooper Square, 1980) is a more critical assessment of Kennedy's Secretary of State; and the head of JFK's Defense Department is the subject of Henry L. Trewhitt's *McNamara: His Ordeal in the Pentagon* (New York: Harper and Row, 1978). When Lyndon Johnson became president after Kennedy's assassination, Rusk stayed on at State and McNamara at Defense, and Ball and Rostow remained as advisers.

Events in South Vietnam and the evolution of the war during the years between the signing of the Geneva Accords in 1954 and President Johnson's build-up of American military forces beginning in 1965 are examined in a number of studies. Two biographies of "America's Mandarin" in South Vietnam, Ngo Dinh Diem, are Anthony T. Bouscaren, *The Last of the Mandarins: Diem of Vietnam* (Pittsburgh, PA: Duquesne University Press, 1965) and Denis Warner, *The Last Confucian* (New York: Macmillan, 1963). Ellen J. Hammer's *A Death in November: America in Vietnam, 1963* (New York: Dutton, 1987) discusses the collapse of the Diem regime and the American involvement in the coup that resulted in Diem's death. Two works that look at the function of the American military during this early period are Ronald H. Spector, *Advice and Support: The Early Years of the United States Army in Vietnam, 1941–1960* (New York: Free Press, 1985; orig. published, Washington, DC: Center for Military History, 1983) and Robert H. Whitlow, *U.S. Marines in Vietnam: The Advisory and Combat Assistance Era, 1954–1964* (History and Museums Division, U.S. Marine Corps; Washington, DC: U.S. Government Printing Office, 1977). The development and operations of the Communist insurgency movement in the South, the National Liberation Front (NLF) or Vietcong as insurgents came to be called, are described and analyzed in two books by Douglas Pike, *Viet Cong: The Organization and Techniques of the National Liberation Front of South Vietnam* (Cambridge, MA: MIT Press, 1966) and *The Viet-Cong Strategy of Terror* (Saigon: U.S. Mission, 1970). William Andrews, *The Village War: Vietnamese Communist Revolutionary Activity in Dinh Truong Province, 1960–1964* (Columbia: University of Missouri Press, 1973) and Jeffrey Race, *War Comes to Long An: Revolutionary Conflict in a Vietnamese Province* (Berkeley: University of California Press, 1972) discuss guerrilla campaigns in the villages and provinces of the South. In *Portrait of the Enemy* (New York: Random House, 1986), David Chanoff and Doan Van Toai have assembled interviews with ex-Vietcong. The American inability to build an effective counterinsurgency program, the subject of spirited debate among experts, is examined in Larry E. Cable, *Conflict of Myths: The Development of American Counterinsurgency Doctrine and the Vietnam War* (New York: New York University Press, 1986) and D. Michael Schafer, *Deadly Paradigms: The Failure of U.S. Counterinsurgency Policy* (Princeton, NJ: Princeton University Press, 1987). Also see Andrew R. Krepinevich's *The Army and Vietnam* (Baltimore, MD: Johns Hopkins University Press, 1986). Robert W. Chandler's *War of Ideas: The U.S. Propaganda Campaign in Vietnam* (Boulder, CO: Westview Press, 1981) describes the American effort to win the "hearts and minds" of the Vietnamese. And Milton E. Osborne's *Strategic Hamlets in South Vietnam: A Survey and Comparison*, Data Paper 55 (Ithaca: Cornell University, Southeast Asia Program, 1965) is the description of another program begun in February 1969 aimed at fighting Communist influence in the South by relocating peasants in protected villages.

When President Kennedy died, Lyndon Baines Johnson inherited a badly confused American policy on Vietnam. With the passage of the Gulf of Tonkin Resolution on August 7, 1964, however, Johnson turned the American involvement in Southeast Asia into a full-scale war: LBJ's war. During the course of the war he would find himself coming under increasing disapproval from a press that had grown skeptical of American intentions and operations in Vietnam and from a public puzzled about the necessity of waging a war that seemed to have no clear purpose and to serve no vital national interest. The literature on Johnson and Vietnam is large.

Johnson in *The Vantage Point: Perspectives of the Presidency, 1963–1969* (New York: Holt, Rinehart and Winston, 1971) gives his own assessment of his presidency. Among students of the Johnson presidency who give a more detached and critical appraisal, see Vaughn Davis Bornet, *The Presidency of Lyndon B. Johnson* (Lawrence: University Press of Kansas, 1984); Doris Kearns, *Lyndon Johnson and the American Dream* (New York: Harper and Row, 1976); and Paul K. Conkin, *Big Daddy from the Pedernales: Lyndon Baines Johnson* (Boston: G. K. Hall, 1986). In two volumes of biography, *The Years of Lyndon Johnson: The Path to Power* (New York: Knopf, 1982) and *The Years of Lyndon Johnson: Means of Ascent* (New York: Knopf, 1990), Robert A. Caro describes in harsh terms the development of the Johnson personality and political style. Two works by Larry Berman place special emphasis on Johnson's decision to escalate the war: *Lyndon Johnson's War: The Road to Stalemate* (New York: Norton, 1989) and *Planning a Tragedy: The Americanization of the War in Vietnam* (New York: Norton, 1982). Also see Brian VanDeMark, *Into the Quagmire: Lyndon Johnson and the Escalation of the Vietnam War* (New York: Oxford University Press, 1991). John Galloway's *The Gulf of Tonkin Resolution* (Rutherford, NJ: Fairleigh Dickinson University, 1970) describes the issues and events surrounding the incident in the Tonkin Gulf, which was the immediate occasion for the American escalation of involvement in Vietnam.

The history of policymaking in the Johnson White House is described in a number of books. See especially David M. Barrett, *Uncertain Warriors: Lyndon Johnson and His Vietnam Advisers* (Lawrence: University Press of Kansas, 1993) and Henry F. Graff, *The Tuesday Cabinet: Deliberation and Decision on Peace and War under Lyndon B. Johnson* (Englewood Cliffs, NJ: Prentice-Hall, 1970). In 1967 Johnson turned to a group of senior foreign policy experts—which included, among others, Dean Acheson, W. Averell Harriman, and George F. Kennan—to advise him on Vietnam. The work of this Senior Advisory Group, or the "Wise Men" as it was more commonly called, is told in Walter Isaacson and Evan Thomas, *The Wise Men: Six Friends and the World They Made* (New York: Simon and Schuster, 1986). By early 1968 the "Wise Men" were telling Johnson that his war was unwinnable. Also see the memoirs and studies of Kennedy officials George Ball, Walt Rostow, Dean Rusk, and Robert McNamara— cited in the section on the Kennedy era—all of whom also served Johnson. Clark Clifford, a senior Johnson policy adviser who succeeded McNamara at Defense in 1968, in *Counsel to the President: A Memoir* (New York: Random House,

1991) describes his efforts to convince LBJ not to expand the war. Allen J. Matusow's *The Unraveling of America: A History of Liberalism in the 1960s* (New York: Harper and Row, 1984) chronicles how Johnson eventually lost the support of liberals for the further prosecution of the war. And Johnson's deteriorating relationship with the media is analyzed in James Deakin, *Johnson's Credibility Gap* (Washington, DC: Public Affairs Press, 1968) and Kathleen J. Turner, *Lyndon Johnson's Dual War: Vietnam and the Press* (Chicago: University of Chicago Press, 1985). On the accuracy and fairness of the media's coverage of the war in general, see Daniel Hallin, *The "Uncensored War": The Media and Vietnam* (New York: Oxford University Press, 1986) and William M. Hammond, *Public Affairs: The Military and the Media, 1962–1968* (U.S. Army, Center for Military History; Washington, DC: U.S. Government Printing Office, 1990). How much influence a negative press had on Johnson's decision not to seek re-election in 1968 is one of the issues examined in Herbert Y. Schandler's *The Unmaking of a President: Lyndon Johnson and Vietnam* (Princeton, NJ: Princeton University Press, 1968).

The United States military strategy in Vietnam remains a source of lively debate among experts who are primarily divided over whether American forces were constrained by the politicians and the press from using the full force of their arsenal or whether the military placed too much faith in its superior firepower and used conventional tactics to fight a very unconventional guerrilla war. The belief that American forces were hindered at home finds a voice in Wilbur H. Morrison, *Vietnam: The Winnable War* (New York: Hippocrene Books, 1990); U.S. Grant Sharp, *Strategy for Defeat: Vietnam in Retrospect* (Novato, CA: Presidio Press, 1978); and Harry G. Summers, Jr., *On Strategy: A Critical Analysis of the Vietnam War* (Novato, CA: Presidio Press, 1983). Works that argue that the military should have given more emphasis to counterinsurgency and pacification include Lewis Walt, *Strange War, Strange Strategy: A General's Report on Vietnam* (New York: Funk and Wagnalls, 1970); William Colby and James McCargar, *Lost Victory: A Firsthand Account of America's Sixteen-Year Involvement in Vietnam* (Chicago: Contemporary Books, 1989); and Guenter Lewy, *America in Vietnam* (1978). Another view holds that neither more firepower nor a more effective counterinsurgency program would have secured an American victory. See, for example, Eric M. Bergerud, *The Dynamics of Defeat: The Vietnam War in Hau Nghia Province* (Boulder, CO: Westview Press, 1990).

Official works surveying American military operations in Vietnam include Shelby L. Stanton's *The Rise and Fall of An American Army: U.S. Ground Forces in Vietnam, 1965–1973* (Novato, CA: Presidio Press, 1985) and Jeffrey Clarke, *The U.S. Army in Vietnam: Advice and Support, the Final Years, 1960–1975* (Washington, DC: U.S. Government Printing Office, 1988). Also see Leroy Thomas, *The U.S. Army in Vietnam* (New York: Sterling, 1990). On the role of the Army Special Forces in Vietnam, see Stanton, *Green Berets at War: U.S. Special Forces in Asia, 1956–1975* (Novato, CA: Presidio Press, 1990). Stanton was himself a Special Forces officer. Robin Moore's *The Green Berets* (New York: Crown, 1965) is a more colorful fictionalized account. Navy operations are discussed in Frank Uhlig, Jr., *Vietnam: The Naval Story* (Annapolis, MD: Naval Institute Press, 1988) and Edward J. Matolda and Oscar P. Fitzgerald, *The United States Navy and the Vietnam Conflict*, 3 vols. (Washington, DC: U.S. Government Printing Office, 1980–1988); Marine activity is summarized in Charles R. Anderson, *Vietnam: The Other War* (New York: Warner Books, 1990).

The air war against the Vietnamese was the American military's most controversial program. Many strategists found it ineffective. Others condemned it for the devastation it wrought on the Vietnamese countryside. Raphael Littauer and Norman Uphoff, eds., *The Air War in Indochina* (Boston: Beacon Press, 1972) is a good general account of American air operations in Southeast Asia. Jack Broughton's *Going Downtown: The War Against Hanoi and Washington* (New York: Orion Books, 1988) argues that the Air Force could have waged a more effective campaign had it not been for bureaucratic interference from Washington. Critics of the air campaign point out, among other things, that although the United States by 1971 had detonated three times as many bombs in Vietnam as it had in all the theaters of war in World War II, still the enemy was unrelenting. The most important critical appraisals of the air war are James C. Thompson, *Rolling Thunder: Understanding Policy and Program Failure* (Chapel Hill: University of North Carolina Press, 1980); Mark Clodfelter, *The Limits of Air Power: The American Bombing of North Vietnam* (New York: Free Press, 1989); and Earl H. Tilford, Jr., *Crosswinds: The Air Force's Setup in Vietnam* (College Station: Texas A&M University Press, 1993). On the ecological consequences of the bombing and the American use of chemicals and defoliants, see William A. Buckingham, Jr., *Ranch Hand: The U.S. Air Force and Herbicides in Southeast Asia, 1961–1971* (Washington, DC: U.S. Government Printing Office, 1982); John Lewallen, *Ecology of Devastation: Indochina* (Baltimore, MD: Penguin, 1971); and Arthur Westing, *The Environmental Aftermath of Warfare in Vietnam* (London: Taylor and Frances, 1982). The long-term consequences of the bombing for American military personnel are the subject of the Institute of Medicine, *Veterans and Agent Orange: Health Effects of Herbicides Used in Vietnam* (Washington, DC: National Academy Press, 1994). Two stimulating works that argue that it was the very confidence in its technological superiority that led the United States to trouble in Vietnam are Loren Baritz, *Backfire: A History of How American Culture Led Us Into Vietnam and Made Us Fight the Way We Did* (New York: Morrow, 1985) and James William Gibson, *The Perfect War: Techno-War in Vietnam* (New York: Atlantic Monthly, 1987).

The history of the Vietnam war—like that of every other war—is most dramatically told, and perhaps best understood, in the remembrances, recollections, and writings of those who fought its battles or in some other way were touched by its campaigns. Oral history collections include Al Santoli, *Everything We Had: An Oral History of the Vietnam War by Thirty-three American Soldiers Who Fought It* (New York: Random House, 1981); Mark Baker, *Nam: The Vietnam War in the Words of the Men and Women Who Fought There* (New York: Morrow, 1981); Harry Maurer, *Strange Ground: Americans in Vietnam, 1945–1975, An Oral History* (New York: Henry Holt, 1989); Otto J. Lehrack, *No Shining Armor: The Marines at War in Vietnam, An Oral History* (Lawrence: University Press of Kansas, 1992); and Eric M. Bergerud, *Red Thunder, Tropic Lightning: The World of a Combat Division in Vietnam* (Boulder, CO: Westview

Press, 1993). Also see Craig Howes, *Voices of the Vietnam POWs: Witnesses to Their Fight* (New York: Oxford University Press, 1993) and Bernard Edelman, ed., *Dear America: Letters Home from Vietnam* (New York: Norton, 1985). There is a large body of full-length personal accounts by those who served in the military or worked in some other capacity in Vietnam. Three of the better known of these works are Philip Caputo's *A Rumor of War* (New York: Holt, Rhinehart and Winston, 1977); Ron Kovic's *Born on the Fourth of July* (New York: McGraw Hill, 1976); and journalist Michael Herr's extraordinary essays in *Dispatches* (New York: Knopf, 1977). The response of African Americans to the Vietnam experience is analyzed in Robert W. Mullen's *Blacks in Vietnam* (Washington, DC: University Press of America, 1981). Personal narratives of black soldiers in Vietnam are Stanley Goff and Robert Sanders's *Brothers: Black Soldiers in the Nam* (New York: Berkley Books, 1986) and Wallace Terry's outstanding *Bloods: An Oral History of the Vietnam War by Black Veterans* (New York: Random House, 1984). The voices of Hispanic troops are heard in Charley Trujillo, ed., *Soldados: Chicanos in Vietnam* (Albuquerque, NM: Chusma House, 1989). Lloyd B. Lewis's *The Tainted War: Culture and Identity in Vietnam War Narratives* (Westport, CT: Greenwood Press, 1985) is a scholar's effort to sort through the themes of this war literature. And Christian G. Appy's *Working-Class War: American Combat Soldiers and Vietnam* (Chapel Hill: University of North Carolina Press, 1993) is a recent effort to provide a social and economic portrait of those who fought in the war.

By one estimate, as many as 11,000 women served with the American military during the Vietnam war. Most worked as nurses, but some had other assignments. More than twenty years after the end of the war, American nurses have recently been honored with their own statue at the Vietnam War Memorial. The names of eight women are etched into the Memorial's wall. Among the earliest and best of the narratives of American women in Vietnam is Lynda Van Devanter's *Home Before Morning: The Story of an Army Nurse in Vietnam* (New York: Beaufort Books, 1983). Oral histories include Dan Freedman, ed., and Jacqueline Rhoads, associate ed., *Nurses in Vietnam: The Forgotten Veterans* (Austin: Texas Monthly Press, 1987); Keith Walker, *A Piece of My Heart: The Stories of 26 American Women Who Served in Vietnam* (Novato, CA: Presidio Press, 1985); and Kathryn Marshall, *In the Combat Zone: An Oral History of American Women in Vietnam* (Boston: Little, Brown, 1987). Elizabeth Norman's *Women at War: The Story of Fifty Military Nurses Who Served in Vietnam* (Philadelphia: University of Pennsylvania Press, 1990) documents the experiences of women who served in Vietnam between 1965 and 1973. In *Forever Sad Hearts* (New York: Avon Books, 1982) author Patricia L. Walsh, herself a nurse in Vietnam, has written a moving novel of an American woman working in a civilian hospital in Da Nang. Carol Lynn Mithers's essay "Missing In Action: Women Warriors in Vietnam," in John Carlos Rowe and Rick Berg, eds., *The Vietnam War and American Culture* (New York: Columbia University Press, 1991), explains why women's stories of Vietnam have been ignored for so long. And in a perceptive essay Jacqueline Lawson examines attitudes toward women during the Vietnam war: "'She's a pretty woman . . . for a gook': The Misogyny of the Vietnam War," *Journal of American Culture*, 12 (Fall 1989): 55–65. For other works dealing with gender issues see Joe P. Dunn, "Women and the Vietnam War: A Bibliographic Review," *Journal of American Culture*, 12 (Spring 1989): 79–86 and the essays in "Gender and the War: Men, Women and Vietnam," a special edition of *Vietnam Generation*, vol. 1, no. 3–4 (Summer-Fall 1989).

The Vietnamese have also told their story of the war. David Chanoff and Doan Van Toai's *Portrait of the Enemy* (1986) is a collection of interviews with North Vietnamese officials and former members of the Vietcong who give their impressions of the war and their enemy. Personal histories of Vietcong members are Truong Nhu Tang, with David Chanoff and Doan Van Toai, *A Viet Cong Memoir* (New York: Random House, 1985) and Mrs. Nguyen Thi Dinh, *No Other Road to Take, Memoir of Mrs. Nguyen Thi Dinh*, trans. by Mai Elliott (Ithaca, NY: Cornell University, 1976). Nguyen Thi Dinh was the NLF's delegate to the Paris peace negotiations. Douglas Pike's *PAVN: People's Army of Vietnam* (Novato, CA: Presidio Press, 1986) describes the North Vietnamese army. In *On the Other Side: 23 Days with the Viet Cong* (New York: Quadrangle Books, 1972), reporter Kate Webb relates what she experienced as a prisoner of the Vietcong. The perspectives of South Vietnamese officials are represented by Bui Diem and David Chanoff, *In the Jaws of History* (New York: Houghton Mifflin, 1987) and Nguyen Cao Ky, *Twenty Years and Twenty Days* (New York: Stein and Day, 1976). Both works are critical of the United States. Bui Diem was Saigon's ambassador to Washington; the flamboyant Nguyen Cao Ky had served as South Vietnam's president and then longtime vice president. Don Luce and John Sommer have gathered oral histories of the South Vietnamese people in *Vietnam: The Unheard Voices* (Ithaca, NY: Cornell University Press, 1969). A poignant story of the effects of the three Indochina wars on one South Vietnamese woman and her family is Le Ly Hayslip, with Jay Wurts, *When Heaven and Earth Changed Places: A Vietnamese Woman's Journey from War to Peace* (New York: Doubleday, 1990). Jade Ngoc Quang Huynh's *South Wind Changing* (St. Paul, MN: Graywolf Press, 1994) is a refugee's account of beatings and forced labor under the Communists after 1975, followed by escape from Vietnam. Also see the recollections gathered from various individuals—officials, veterans, wives of soldiers and others—in Al Santoli's *To Bear Any Burden: The Vietnam War and Its Aftermath in the Words of Americans and Southeast Asians* (New York: Dutton, 1985).

The principal battles of the Vietnam war took place around the Tet offensive, which began in late January 1968. Tet was the turning point in the United States involvement in Vietnam. Beginning in 1968 American officials came under increasing pressure to disengage from the war and to have the South Vietnamese bear the major burden of the fighting. On the events of Tet see Dan Oberdorfer, *Tet!* (Garden City, NY: Doubleday, 1971) and James R. Arnold, *Tet Offensive: 1968, the Final Turning Point in Vietnam* (London: Osprey, 1990). Pham Van Son's *Tet 1968: The Communist Offensive that Marked the Beginning of America's Defeat in Vietnam*, 2 vols. (Salisbury, NC: Documentary Publications, 1980) is the official South Vietnamese history of Tet by an officer in South Vietnam's army. Also see Ronald H. Spector, *After Tet: The Bloodiest Year in Vietnam* (New York: Free Press, 1992). Irwin and Debi Unger in *Turning Point: 1968*

(New York: Scribner's, 1988) place Tet within a series of critical events that were changing the temper of the American people. The fairness of the media in relating the story of Tet to the American public is questioned in Peter Braestrup, *Big Story: How the American Press and Television Reported and Interpreted the Crisis of Tet 1968 in Vietnam and Washington*, 2 vols. (Boulder, CO: Westview Press, 1977). Among the better studies of the North Vietnamese siege of the U.S. Marine and South Vietnamese encampment at Khe Sanh are John Prados and Ray W. Stubbe, *Valley of Decision: The Siege of Khe Sanh* (Boston: Houghton Mifflin Company, 1991) and Robert Pisor, *The End of the Line: The Siege of Khe Sanh* (New York: Norton, 1982). The horror of battle is told in the words of its participants in Eric Hammel's *Khe Sanh: Siege in the Clouds, An Oral History* (New York: Crown, 1989). Some of the fiercest fighting and worst destruction of the war took place around the city of Hue, which had been seized by the North Vietnamese and the Vietcong. Before the Marines recaptured the city, Communist troops slaughtered civilians. On Hue, see Keith W. Nolan, *Battle for Hue: Tet, 1968* (Novato, CA: Presidio Press, 1983) and Alje Vennema, *The Viet Cong Massacre at Hue* (New York: Vantage Press, 1976). Not long after Hue, on March 16, 1968, American soldiers in Son My, a hamlet of My Lai, executed some 300 or 400 civilians. On the incident at My Lai, see Richard Hammer's *One Morning in the War: The Tragedy at Son My* (New York: Coward-McCann, 1970) and two books by investigative journalist Seymour Hersh, *My Lai 4: A Report on the Massacre and Its Aftermath* (New York: Random House, 1970) and *Cover-up: The Army's Secret Investigation of the Massacre at My Lai 4* (New York: Random House, 1972).

Despite the success of U.S. and ARVN (Army of the Republic of [South] Vietnam) forces in turning back the enemy, the ability of the North Vietnamese army and the NLF to launch a major campaign in the South came as a devastating psychological blow to the American people, who had been repeatedly told that American firepower was wearing down the enemy. The war's end, Washington had promised, was imminent. Tet sliced a credibility gap between the administration and the public and gave support to an already active antiwar movement on the American home front. Many sources deal with the opposition to the war— part of the ever expanding body of work on the turbulent era commonly referred to as the sixties.

Surveys of antiwar activity include Thomas Powers, *The War at Home: Vietnam and the American People, 1964–1968* (New York: Grossman, 1973); Nancy Zaroulis and Gerald Sullivan, *Who Spoke Up? American Protest Against the War in Vietnam, 1963–1975* (Garden City, NY: Doubleday, 1984); and Charles DeBenedetti and Charles Chatfield, *An American Ordeal: The Antiwar Movement of the Vietnam Era* (Syracuse, NY: Syracuse University Press, 1990). More recent studies are Tom Wells, with a forward by Todd Gitlin, *The War Within: America's Battle Over Vietnam* (Berkeley: University of California Press, 1994) and Melvin Small and William D. Hoover, eds., *Give Peace a Chance: Exploring the Vietnam Antiwar Movement; Essays from the Charles DeBenedetti Memorial Conference* (Syracuse, NY: Syracuse University Press, 1992). A number of the essays in Barbara L. Tischler, ed., *Sights on the Sixties* (New Brunswick, NJ: Rutgers University Press, 1992) look at the opposition to the war. Kenneth J.

Heineman's *Campus Wars: The Peace Movement at American State Universities in the Vietnam Era* (New York: New York University Press, 1993) examines the peace movement on four campuses: Michigan State University, Kent State, Pennsylvania State, and the State University of New York at Buffalo. Political opposition to the war and the influence of antiwar activity on politics are the subject of Melvin Small's *Johnson, Nixon, and the Doves* (New Brunswick, NJ: Rutgers University Press, 1988) and William C. Berman, *J. William Fulbright and the Vietnam War: The Dissent of a Political Realist* (Kent, OH: Kent State University Press, 1988). African American criticisms of American involvement in Southeast Asia are collected in Clyde Taylor, ed., *Vietnam and Black America: An Anthology of Protest and Resistance* (Garden City, NY: Doubleday-Anchor, 1973). On resistance to the draft, see Sherry Gershon Gottlieb, *Hell No, We Won't Go: Resisting the Draft During the Vietnam War* (New York: Viking, 1991) and David Surrey, *Choice of Conscience: Vietnam Era Military and Draft Resisters in Canada* (New York: Praeger, 1982). In *Destructive Generation: Second Thoughts About the Sixties*, former New Left activists Peter Collier and David Horowitz criticize the radical politics of the 1960s and the antiwar movement. William F. Gausman's *Red Stains on Vietnam Doves* (Denver, CO: Veracity Publications, 1989) is a conservative and polemical condemnation of antiwar dissenters.

In 1968, Richard M. Nixon, the Republican candidate for the presidency, announced that he had a secret plan to end the war in Vietnam. The announcement may have provided Nixon the small margin he needed for victory in a very close election. The plan was never made public and American participation in the war dragged on for four more years, though with decreasing numbers of troops, until the signing of the Paris Peace Agreements in January 1973. The policies of the Nixon White House have yet to receive a full scholarly assessment. A number are in progress. Historian Stephen Ambrose provides commentary on the Nixon character in a three-volume biography (New York: Simon and Schuster): *Nixon: The Education of a Politician, 1913–1962* (1987); *Nixon: The Triumph of a Politician, 1962–1972* (1989); and *Nixon: Ruin and Triumph of the Presidency* (1992). Nixon's foreign policy is examined in Robert S. Litwack's *Détente and the Nixon Doctrine: American Foreign Policy and the Pursuit of Stability, 1969–1976* (New York: Cambridge University Press, 1984) and C. L. Sulzberger, *The World and Richard Nixon* (New York: Prentice-Hall, 1987). Nixon has described and defended his policies in a number of volumes of memoirs: *RN: The Memoirs of Richard Nixon* (New York: Grosset and Dunlap, 1978); *No More Vietnams* (New York: Arbor House, 1985); and *In the Arena: A Memoir of Victory, Defeat and Renewal* (New York: Simon and Schuster, 1990). Henry Kissinger began his years with the Nixon administration as a foreign policy adviser to the President. Later he served both Nixon and Ford as Secretary of State. In that office he was principal negotiator for the United States at the Paris peace conference and is sometimes credited with bringing American participation in the war to an end. His two volumes of memoirs cast much light on the processes by which the United States disengaged itself from Southeast Asia: *The White House Years* (Boston: Little, Brown, 1979) and *Years of Upheaval* (Boston: Little, Brown, 1982). Works more critical of Kissinger than these self-assessments are Robert D. Schulzinger, *Henry Kissinger: Doctor of Diplomacy* (New York: Columbia University Press, 1989); Roger Morris, *Uncertain Greatness: Henry Kissinger and American Foreign Policy* (New York: Harper and Row, 1977); and Seyom Brown, *The Crisis of Power: An Interpretation of United States Foreign Policy During the Kissinger Years* (New York: Columbia University Press, 1979).

The long road to an armistice and the withdrawal of U.S. troops from Vietnam is the subject of a number of thoughtful analyses. In *When Governments Collide: Coercion and Diplomacy in the Vietnam Conflict, 1964–1968* (Berkeley: University of California Press, 1980), Wallace J. Thies assesses Lyndon Johnson's failed efforts to bring Hanoi to a peace settlement. Gareth Porter's *A Peace Denied: The United States, Vietnam, and the Paris Agreement* (Bloomington: Indiana University Press, 1975) provides valuable documentation of the negotiations that led finally to the Paris treaty. Allen E. Goodman's *Lost Peace: America's Search for a Negotiated Settlement of the Vietnam War* (Stanford, CA: Hoover Institution Press, 1978) argues that irreconcilable differences between the United States and the North Vietnamese were the reason the peace settlement failed. Tad Szulc's *The Illusion of Peace: Foreign Policy in the Nixon Years* (New York: Viking Press, 1978) gives most of its attention to the Paris negotiations and is critical of the Nixon peace. Also critical of the settlement are Stuart A. Herrington, *A Peace with Honor? An American Reports on Vietnam, 1973–1975* (Novato, CA: Presidio Press, 1983) and Arnold Isaacs, *Without Honor: Defeat in Vietnam and Cambodia* (Baltimore, MD: Johns Hopkins University Press, 1983). On the military events immediately preceding the settlement, see Gerald H. Turley, *The Easter Offensive: The Last American Advisors, Vietnam, 1972* (Novato, CA: Presidio Press, 1985), which describes the North Vietnamese assault on the South as U.S. troops prepared to withdraw. The American response to the offensive was to renew the bombing of the North—known as the Linebacker operation—and to mine major North Vietnamese harbors, including Haiphong. See A. J. C. LaValle, ed., *Airpower and the 1972 Spring Invasion* (Office of Air Force History; Washington, DC: U.S. Government Printing Office, 1976, reprint 1985), which describes the air operations. Martin F. Herz and Leslie Rider's *The Prestige Press and the Christmas Bombing, 1972: Images and Reality in Vietnam* (Washington, DC: Ethics and Public Policy Center, 1980) argues that the press badly misrepresented the American air campaign and suggests that the bombing was instrumental in achieving the 1973 cease-fire.

In the aftermath of the American withdrawal from Vietnam, South Vietnam's ability to resist the North unraveled. When the North Vietnamese launched a spring offensive in 1975, the South collapsed. Vietnam was then united under a Communist government as the Socialist Republic of Vietnam and Saigon was renamed Ho Chi Minh City. A number of works deal with the collapse of South Vietnam: William E. Le Gro, *Vietnam From Cease-Fire to Capitulation* (U.S. Army, Center for Military History; Washington, DC: U.S. Government Printing Office, 1981); David Butler, *The Fall of Saigon* (New York: Simon and Schuster, 1985); and Alan Dawson, *55 Days: The Fall of South Vietnam* (Englewood Cliffs, NJ: Prentice-Hall, 1977). Eyewitness reports of the chaos in the South in its final days in April 1975 are collected in Larry Englemann, *Tears Before the Rain: An Oral History of the Fall of South Vietnam* (New York: Oxford University Press, 1990). A. J. C. LaValle's *Last Flight from Saigon* (Office of Air Force History; Washington, DC: U.S. Government Printing Office, 1978, reprint 1985) describes Saigon's final hours. Cao Van Vien, a South Vietnamese, relates events in *The Final Collapse* (U.S. Army, Center for Military History; Washington, DC: U.S. Government Printing Office, 1983); Van Tien Dung's *Our Great Spring Victory* (New York: Monthly Review Press, 1977) gives a North Vietnamese view.

Vietnam under Communist rule has not been a peaceful or prosperous nation. The new regime has been repressive, but apparently there was not the bloodbath of reprisals some had feared. In *Vietnam Under Communism, 1975–1982* (Stanford, CA: Hoover Institution, 1983), Nguyen Van Canh describes a harsh Communist government that established reeducation camps to assure political purity and to eliminate the influences of American culture. On life in Vietnam after 1975, see William J. Duiker, *Vietnam Since the Fall of Saigon* (Columbus: Ohio University Press, 1989) and Melanie Beresford, *Vietnam: Politics, Economics, and Society* (New York: Pinter, 1988). The declining economic fortunes of Vietnam are further assessed in Joel Charney and John Spragens, Jr., *Obstacles to Recovery in Vietnam and Kampuchea* (Boston: Oxfam America, 1984) and Robert E. Long, ed., *Vietnam Ten Years After* (New York: Wilson, 1985). Less than three years after the fall of Saigon, Vietnam was embroiled in another war, striking against the Khmer Rouge Communists across the border in Cambodia and occupying the country. In February 1979 China invaded Vietnam and after bitter fighting lasting a little more than two weeks withdrew; hostilities remained. The Third Indochina War, involving Vietnam, China, and Cambodia, lasted from 1978 to 1989. See King C. Chen, *China's War with Vietnam, 1979: Issues, Decisions, and Implications* (Stanford, CA: Hoover Institution Press, 1987) and David W. P. Elliott, ed., *The Third Indochina Conflict* (Boulder, CO: Westview Press, 1981).

The United States involvement in Southeast Asia included operations beyond the borders of Vietnam, in Laos and Cambodia. Starting in the 1950s, various American administrations covertly initiated or supplied anticommunist movements throughout Indochina. As the war in Vietnam intensified these activities often expanded into major military campaigns conducted by American troops or supported by the American military. The contest for superiority among the various regional factions involved in these wars was bitter. As the American people learned of the involvement of United States forces, America's "other wars" in Laos and Cambodia became a source of public controversy and political divisiveness.

The strategic importance of Laos to the United States during the Vietnam war was a consequence of North Vietnam's use of the Ho Chi Minh Trail—which wound through northeastern Laos—to move supplies and troops into the South. The American government had been funding a secret war in Laos since 1954, led by the Central Intelligence Agency, against the Pathet Lao, the Laotian Communist organization assisted by the North Vietnamese. An overview of relations between Laos and the United States is supplied in Charles A. Stevenson's *The End of Nowhere: American Policy Toward Laos Since 1954* (Boston: Beacon Press, 1972) and Norman B. Hannah's *The Key to Failure: Laos and the Vietnam War* (Lanham, MD: Madison Books, 1987). On the origins and development of the Communist Pathet Lao, see MacAlister Brown and Joseph J. Zasloff, *Apprentice Revolutionaries: The Communist Movement in Laos, 1930–1945* (Stanford, CA: Hoover Institution Press, 1986). The CIA's secret war in Laos is the subject of two books by Christopher Robbins, *Air America: The Story of the CIA's Secret Airlines* (New York: Putnam, 1979) and *The Ravens: The Men Who Flew in America's Secret War in Laos* (New York: Crown, 1987), and John Prados's *President's Secret Wars: CIA and Pentagon Covert Operations Since World War II* (New York: Morrow, 1986). Jane Hamilton-Merritt's recent *Tragic Mountains: The Hmong, the Americans, and the Secret Wars for Laos, 1942–1992* (Bloomington: Indiana University Press, 1993) is very critical of the American treatment of its Laotian allies, the Hmong people. Also see Timothy N. Castle, *At War in the Shadow of Vietnam: U.S. Military Aid to the Royal Lao Government, 1955–1975* (New York: Columbia University Press, 1993). Fred Branfman, ed., *Voices from the Plain of Jars* (New York: Harper and Row, 1972) is a collection of stories of Laotians responding to the U.S. bombings of their country. The 1971 American invasion of Laos is described in Keith W. Nolan, *Into Laos: The Story of Dewey Canyon II / Lam Son 719, Vietnam 1971* (Novato, CA: Presidio Press, 1986).

Nowhere were the effects of the Second Indochina War more devastating and brutal than in Cambodia. A survey of Cambodia's history to 1953, when it acquired independence, is David P. Chandler, *A History of Cambodia* (Boulder, CO: Westview Press, 1983). Marie Alexandrine Martin in *Cambodia: A Shattered Society*, trans. by Mark W. McLeod (Berkeley: University of California Press, 1994), tells the story of Cambodia since the end of World War II. Michael Vickery's *Cambodia, 1975–1982* (Boston: South End Press, 1984) describes the modern political history of Cambodia. Ben Kiernan's *How Pol Pot Came to Power* (London: Verso, 1985; also New York: Routledge, 1987) assesses the development of Cambodian Communism from the 1930s until 1975 when the Khmer Rouge seized power. Under the directions of President Richard Nixon, the United States between March 18, 1969, and August 15, 1973, conducted a secret bombing campaign—known as Operation Menu—against Cambodia. In late April 1970 the American military supplied troops and air cover to support a South Vietnamese incursion into Cambodia; the operation lasted about three months. The details and implications of America's other war in Cambodia are described in William Shawcross's excellent critical study *Sideshow: Kissinger, Nixon, and the Destruction of Cambodia* (New York: Simon and Schuster, 1979). Also see Keith William Nolan's *Into Cambodia: Spring Campaign, Summer Offensive, 1970* (Novato, CA: Presidio Press, 1970). The murderous activities of the fanatical Khmer Rouge, a faction of Cambodian Communists, are witnessed in several sources. Among the best is William Shawcross's *The Quality of Mercy: Cambodia, Holocaust, and Modern Conscience* (New York: Simon and Schuster, 1984). Descriptions of the horrors of the Khmer genocide are given in a number of personal stories: James Fenton, *Cambodian Witness: An Autobiography of Someth May* (New York: Random House, 1987); Joan D. Criddle and Teeda Butt Mam, *To Destroy You Is No Loss: The Odyssey of a Cambodian Family* (New York: Atlantic Monthly Press, 1989); and Molyda Szymusiak, *The Stones Cry Out: A Cambodian Childhood, 1975–1980* (New York: Hill and Wang, 1986). Journalist Sydney H. Schanberg tells of the terrifying ordeal he suffered as a captive of the Khmer government in *The Death and Life of Dith Pran* (New York: Penguin, 1980), which became the basis for the 1984 film *The Killing Fields*.

"The Vietnam War remains today," historian Marilyn Young writes, "and is likely to remain for the foreseeable future a zone of contested meaning; and the struggle over its interpretation is central to contemporary American politics, foreign and domestic, and of American culture as well." Vietnam, whatever meanings are attached to it, has exercised a powerful influence on American thought and institutions. An industry of works deals with the meaning and legacy of Vietnam, only a sampling of which can be included here.

A recent collection of essays by some of the best authorities on Vietnam is William Head and Lawrence E. Grinter, eds., *Looking Back on the Vietnam War: A 1990s Perspective on the Decisions, Combat, and Legacies* (Westport, CT: Praeger, 1993). Also see the essays in James F. Veninga and Harry A. Wilmer, eds., *Vietnam in Remission* (College Station: Texas A&M University Press, 1985) and those in Alf Louvre and Jeffrey Walsh, eds., *Tell Me Lies About Vietnam: Cultural Battles for the Meaning of the War* (Philadelphia: Open University Press, 1988). A good survey that measures the impact of the war on American life is Kim McQuaid's *The Anxious Years: America in the Vietnam-Watergate Era* (New York: Basic Books, 1988). John Hart Ely's *War and Responsibility: Constitutional Lessons of Vietnam and Its Aftermath* (Princeton, NJ: Princeton University Press, 1993) looks at the implications of the war for American legal thought. The issue of whether American POWs and those missing in action (MIA) are still in Indochina continues to haunt the country and has surfaced often as a subject of national political debate. H. Bruce Franklin's provocative *M. I. A. or Mythmaking In America* (New Brunswick, NJ: Rutgers University Press, 1993; expanded and updated edition) explains how and why Americans have created a powerful myth of surviving servicemen in Southeast Asia. Over two and one half million soldiers served in Vietnam at one time or another—approximately a million in combat—and adjustment back into American life after Vietnam for these veterans has had its special problems. The difficulties encountered by returning veterans are discussed in Herbert Hendin and Ann Pollinger Haas, *Wounds of War: The Psychological Aftermath of Combat in Vietnam* (New York: Basic Books, 1984) and Murray Polner, *No Victory Parades: The Return of the Vietnam Veterans* (New York: Holt, Rinehart and Winston, 1971). In *Legacy of a War: The American Soldier in Vietnam* (Armonk, NY: M. E. Sharpe, 1986), Ellen Frey-Wonters and Robert S. Laufer argue that most vets made the adjustment without incident. The plight of Indochinese refugees, many of whom have migrated to the United States, is documented in some recent studies. See, for example, Paul James Rutledge's *The Vietnamese Experi-*

ence in America (Bloomington: Indiana University Press, 1992) and Al Santoli's interviews with Vietnamese refugees in *New Americans: An Oral History* (New York: Viking Press, 1988).

The implications of Vietnam for American foreign policy have been enormous. Although no good history has yet to document these influences, it is clear that every American President since the war ended, including President Clinton, has shaped his foreign policy in the shadow of Vietnam. Even a cursory survey of the rhetoric that accompanied the Gulf War of 1991 suggests that for the politicians, for the military, for the press, and for the public, the issues of national identity and purpose that surrounded the Vietnam war were once again stirred to life. There was much talk by President Bush and among his policymakers, as there had been in the Reagan White House, about overcoming the "Vietnam syndrome." On the influence of Vietnam on the nature of American foreign policy, see as illustrations Ole R. Holsti and James N. Rosenau, *American Leadership in World Affairs: Vietnam and the Breakdown of Consensus* (Winchester, MA: Allen and Unwin, 1984) and John Taft, *American Power: The Rise and Decline of U.S. Globalism, 1918–1968* (New York: Harper and Row, 1989). Taft argues that Vietnam caused many American liberals to become isolationists.

Writers have detected cultural consequences of the war. In *The Vietnam War and American Culture* (New York: Columbia University Press, 1991), John Carlos Rowe and Rick Berg have gathered a fine sampling of essays. Also see the essays in D. Michael Schafer's *The Legacy: The Vietnam War in the American Imagination* (Boston: Beacon Press, 1990). In *Out of the Sixties: Storytelling and the Vietnam Generation* (New York: Cambridge University Press, 1993), David Wyatt describes the influence of the war on some prominent cultural figures, among them filmmaker George Lucas and rock music artist Bruce Springsteen, who came of age during the Vietnam era. Andrew Martin's *Receptions of War: Vietnam in American Culture* (Norman: University of Oklahoma Press, 1993) examines the ways in which literature and film have depicted the Vietnam war. The literary influence of the war is also examined and on display in these studies: Timothy J. Lomperis, *Reading the Wind: The Literature of the Vietnam War— An Interpretive Critique* (Durham, NC: Duke University Press, 1987); Philip D. Beidler, *Re-Writing America: Vietnam Authors in Their Generation* (Athens: University of Georgia Press, 1991); W. D. Ehrhart, ed., *Carrying the Darkness: American Indochina, The Poetry of the Vietnam War* (New York: Avon, 1985). On the use of art as a response to the war, see Lucy R. Lippard, ed., *A Different War: Vietnam in Art* (Seattle, WA: Real Comet Press, 1990). On the lively subject of Vietnam, the arts, and popular culture there is a growing body of works. Jeffrey Walsh and James Aulick's *Vietnam Images: War and Representation* (New York: St. Martin's Press, 1987) is a useful introduction. Works on film and Vietnam include Michael Anderegg, *Inventing Vietnam: The War in Film and Television* (Philadelphia: Temple University Press, 1991); Albert Auster and Leonard Quart, *How the War Was Remembered: Hollywood and Vietnam* (Westport, CT: Greenwood/Praeger, 1988); and Linda Dittmar and Gene Michaud, eds., *From Hanoi to Hollywood: The Vietnam War in American Film* (New Brunswick, NJ: Rutgers University Press, 1990). And on the relation between the war and American values, on how Americans define themselves as a consequence of the war, see Walter H. Capps, *The Unfinished War: Vietnam and the American Conscience* (Boston: Beacon, 1982); Lloyd Lewis, *The Tainted War: Culture and Identity in Vietnam War Narratives* (1985); and Myra MacPherson, *Long Time Passing: Vietnam and the Haunted Generation* (Garden City, NY: Doubleday, 1984).

The editors wish to acknowledge with gratitude the assistance of the reference staff of Bender Library, The American University, and especially Ms. Mary M. Mintz and Ms. Krista Box for their tenacity in pursuing sources for this volume and their graciousness in answering our numerous inquiries.